OXFORD IB DIPLOMA PROGRAMME

2ND EDITION

ENGLISH B

COURSE COMPANION

Kawther Saa'd AlDin
Kevin Morley

OXFORD
UNIVERSITY PRESS

OXFORD
UNIVERSITY PRESS

Great Clarendon Street, Oxford, OX2 6DP, United Kingdom

Oxford University Press is a department of the University of Oxford. It furthers the University's objective of excellence in research, scholarship, and education by publishing worldwide. Oxford is a registered trade mark of Oxford University Press in the UK and in certain other countries

First published in 2018

British Library Cataloguing in Publication Data
Data available

978-0-19-842236-5

10

Paper used in the production of this book is a natural, recyclable product made from wood grown in sustainable forests. The manufacturing process conforms to the environmental regulations of the country of origin.

Printed in China by Golden Cup

Acknowledgements
The publisher and authors would like to thank the following for permission to use photographs and other copyright material:

Cover: Arcaid Images/Alamy Stock Photo; **p2:** Darren Baker/Picfair; **p3, 4, 9:** Shutterstock; **p12(r):** apomares/iStockphoto; **p13:** Courtesy of the National Palace Museum, Taiwan; **p16:** Shutterstock/OUP; **p18:** Shutterstock; **p19:** olandesina/iStockphoto; **p23, 25, 35:** Shutterstock; **p26:** The House on Mango Street, Sandra Cisneros, 1991/Reproduced by permission of Penguin Random House; **p28:** PhotoMediaGroup/Shutterstock, Sergey Lavrentev/Shutterstock; **p31:** Laikwunfai/iStockphoto; **p41:** Faizal fahmi/Picfair; **p42:** Shutterstock; **p44:** © Getty Images; **p45:** Shutterstock; **p48:** noonland/Westend61/Superstock; **p49:** Bettmann/Getty Images; **p56:** Pixabay; **p64:** Ariadne Van Zandbergen/Alamy Stock Photo; **p68:** Shutterstock; **p78:** Westend61/Superstock; **p90:** Fox Photos/ Getty Images; **p91:** Illustration Works/Alamy Stock Photo; **p92:** Shutterstock; **p97:** Tim Platt/Getty Images; **p99:** Beacon Communications/20th Century Fox/Kobal/REX/Shutterstock; **p102:** 123rf; **p107:** David Corio/Getty Images; **p109:** Pigeon English, Stephen Kelman, 2011/Reproduced by permission of Bloomsbury Publishing; **p110:** Shutterstock/OUP; **p114:** Shutterstock; **p115(l):** Bill Cheyrou/Alamy Stock Photo; **p115(r):** NBC/Getty Images; **p118:** © Getty Images; **p120(t):** Hulton Archive/Getty Images; **p120(b):** Shutterstock; **p123:** AF archive/ Alamy Stock Photo; **p124:** Graham Denholm/Getty Images; **p127, 128(l):** Shutterstock; **p128(r):** WENN Ltd/Alamy Stock Photo; **p134:** Jim West/ Alamy Stock Photo; **p135(t):** Steve Skjold/Alamy Stock Photo; **p135(b):** Shutterstock; **p136(tl, tr, br):** Shutterstock; **p136(bl):** iStockphoto; **p140:** ZUMA Press Inc/Alamy Stock Photo; **p141:** Shutterstock; **p144:** Jim West/Alamy Stock Photo; **p147:** Getty Images; **p152(t):** OUP; **p154(t):** Mike Goldwater/Alamy Stock Photo; **p154(b):** Gareth Boden/OUP; **p155, 157:** Shutterstock; **p159(l):** David Cole/Alamy Stock Photo; **p159(r):** Caroline Penn/Panos; **p160:** CBW/ Alamy Stock Photo; **p163:** Shutterstock; **p164:** Shutterstock/OUP; **p166(bm):** Picfair; **p166(ml):** DeepGreen/iStockphoto; **p166(bl):** Professor25/iStockphoto; **p166(tl, tr, mr, br):** Picfair; **p170(l):** Christopher Scott/Alamy Stock Photo; **p170(r):** Alamy Stock Photo; **p174:** Q2A Media Services Inc.; **p177:** Hans Blossey/ Alamy Stock Photo; **p178:** Shutterstock; **p184:** GEORGE STEINMETZ/ National Geographic Creative; **p191:** United Nations/UN Photo/Evan Schneider; **p195(l):** Mario Tama/Getty Images; **p195(r):** Alison Wright; **p198:** Shutterstock; **p206:** RAVEENDRAN/Getty Images; **p41:** Corbis; **p213:** Picfair; **p214(tl):** Image Source/Getty Images; **p214(tr):** LeoPatrizi/Getty Images; **p214(bl):** Pixabay/jcarloshep0/CC0 1.0; **p214(br):** Shutterstock; **p220:** Pixabay/johnhain/CC0 1.0; **p234, 249, 256:** Shutterstock; **p258(tl):** AFP/Getty Images; **p258(tr):** Topical Press Agency/Getty Images; **p258(bl):** Rue des Archives/Granger, NYC – All Rights Reserved , New York; **p258(br):** Photofusion/REX/Shutterstock; **p259, 269:** UniversalImagesGroup/Getty Images; **p262:** Don Cravens/Getty Images; **p263:** Michael Ochs Archives/Getty Images; **p270:** Getty/Photolibrary/Shutterstock/OUP; **p271:** Gallo Images/Getty Images; **p273:** CHARLES TASNADI/AP/ REX/Shutterstock; **p275:** Shutterstock; **p280:** Wesley Allen/SWNS.com; **p285:** Afro Newspaper/Gado/Getty Images; **p287:** Shutterstock; **p289(l):** Getty/Brand X Pictures/OUP; **p289(r):** C05H19; **p290:** PjrStudio/Alamy Stock Photo; **p293:** Shutterstock; **p295:** Science & Society Picture Library/Getty Images; **p296:** Bloomberg/Getty Images; **p299:** © Alamy Ltd/OUP; **p300:** Shutterstock; **p302:** TwilightShow/iStockphoto/OUP; **p307:** FatCamera/iStockphoto/OUP; **p308:** Peopleimages/iStockphoto/OUP; **p309:** Africa Media Online/Alamy Stock Photo; **p312(t):** Shutterstock; **p312(l):** Kevin Frayer/Getty Images; **p312(r), 313, 317:** Shutterstock; **p318:** sjbooks/Alamy Stock Photo; **p321:** Daria Voskoboeva/ iStockphoto; **p322:** Shutterstock/OUP; **p323:** OJO Images/Getty Images; **p326:** Stefanocapra /Dreamstime; **p328:** agsandrew/iStockphoto; **p329, 331(l):** Shutterstock; **p331(r):** Sellingpix/Dreamstime; **p332:** UA_IFTN_NEU/Alamy Stock Photo; **p338:** Robin Heighway-Bury/ Alamy Stock Photo; **p340, 345:** Shutterstock; **p346:** Rod Collins/Alamy Stock Photo; **p348:** Shutterstock; **p353:** 123rf/ Shutterstock/OUP; **p355:** Pixsooz/iStockphoto; **p357:** Shutterstock; **p358(l):** Cathy Yeulet/123rf; **p358(r):** vgajic/iStockphoto; **p360:** This Full House, Virginia Euwer Wolff, 2009/HarperCollins; **p363, 371:** Shutterstock; **p375(l):** National Geographic Creative/Alamy Stock Photo; **p375(r):** Shutterstock; **p376:** David Cooper/Getty Images; **p377:** Shutterstock; **p381:** Vitalij Cerepok/EyeEm/ Getty Images; **p382(tl):** Library of Congree/Public Domain; **p382(tr, bl, br):** Pixabay; **p387:** Thinkstock; **p401:** Shutterstock; **p409:** Imagens Evangélicas/ Flickr/CC BY 2.0; **p416:** Shutterstock;

Artwork by Aptara Inc.

Every effort has been made to contact copyright holders of material reproduced in this book. Any omissions will be rectified in subsequent printings if notice is given to the publisher.

Course Companion definition

The IB Diploma Programme Course Companions are resource materials designed to support students throughout their two-year Diploma Programme course of study in a particular subject. They will help students gain an understanding of what is expected from the study of an IB Diploma Programme subject while presenting content in a way that illustrates the purpose and aims of the IB. They reflect the philosophy and approach of the IB and encourage a deep understanding of each subject by making connections to wider issues and providing opportunities for critical thinking.

The books mirror the IB philosophy of viewing the curriculum in terms of a whole-course approach; the use of a wide range of resources, international mindedness, the IB learner profile and the IB Diploma Programme core requirements, theory of knowledge, the extended essay, and creativity, activity, service (CAS).

Each book can be used in conjunction with other materials and indeed, students of the IB are required and encouraged to draw conclusions from a variety of resources. Suggestions for additional and further reading are given in each book and suggestions for how to extend research are provided.

In addition, the Course Companions provide advice and guidance on the specific course assessment requirements and on academic honesty protocol. They are distinctive and authoritative without being prescriptive.

IB mission statement

The International Baccalaureate aims to develop inquiring, knowledgable and caring young people who help to create a better and more peaceful world through intercultural understanding and respect.

To this end the IB works with schools, governments and international organizations to develop challenging programmes of international education and rigorous assessment.

These programmes encourage students across the world to become active, compassionate, and lifelong learners who understand that other people, with their differences, can also be right.

The IB learner Profile

The aim of all IB programmes is to develop internationally minded people who, recognizing their common humanity and shared guardianship of the planet, help to create a better and more peaceful world. IB learners strive to be:

Inquirers They develop their natural curiosity. They acquire the skills necessary to conduct inquiry and research and show independence in learning. They actively enjoy learning and this love of learning will be sustained throughout their lives.

Knowledgable They explore concepts, ideas, and issues that have local and global significance. In so doing, they acquire in-depth knowledge and develop understanding across a broad and balanced range of disciplines.

Thinkers They exercise initiative in applying thinking skills critically and creatively to recognize and approach complex problems, and make reasoned, ethical decisions.

Communicators They understand and express ideas and information confidently and creatively in more than one language and in a variety of modes of communication. They work effectively and willingly in collaboration with others.

Principled They act with integrity and honesty, with a strong sense of fairness, justice, and respect for the dignity of the individual, groups, and communities. They take responsibility for their own actions and the consequences that accompany them.

Open-minded They understand and appreciate their own cultures and personal histories, and are open to the perspectives, values, and traditions of other individuals and communities. They are accustomed to seeking and evaluating a range of points of view, and are willing to grow from the experience.

Caring They show empathy, compassion, and respect towards the needs and feelings of others. They have a personal commitment to service, and act to make a positive difference to the lives of others and to the environment.

Risk-takers They approach unfamiliar situations and uncertainty with courage and forethought, and have the independence of spirit to explore new roles, ideas, and strategies. They are brave and articulate in defending their beliefs.

Balanced They understand the importance of intellectual, physical, and emotional balance to achieve personal well-being for themselves and others.

Reflective They give thoughtful consideration to their own learning and experience. They are able to assess and understand their strengths and limitations in order to support their learning and personal development.

A note on academic honesty

It is of vital importance to acknowledge and appropriately credit the owners of information when that information is used in your work. After all, owners of ideas (intellectual property) have property rights. To have an authentic piece of work, it must be based on your individual and original ideas with the work of others fully acknowledged. Therefore, all assignments, written or oral, completed for assessment must use your own language and expression. Where sources are used or referred to, whether in the form of direct quotation or paraphrase, such sources must be appropriately acknowledged.

How do I acknowledge the work of others?

The way that you acknowledge that you have used the ideas of other people is through the use of footnotes and bibliographies.

Footnotes (placed at the bottom of a page) or endnotes (placed at the end of a document) are to be provided when you quote or paraphrase from another document, or closely summarize the information provided in another document. You do not need to provide a footnote for information that is part of a 'body of knowledge'. That is, definitions do not need to be footnoted as they are part of the assumed knowledge.

Bibliographies should include a formal list of the resources that you used in your work. The listing should include all resources, including books, magazines, newspaper articles, Internet-based resources, CDs and works of art. 'Formal' means that you should use one of the several accepted forms of presentation. You must provide full information as to how a reader or viewer of your work can find the same information. A bibliography is compulsory in the extended essay.

What constitutes misconduct?

Misconduct is behaviour that results in, or may result in, you or any student gaining an unfair advantage in one or more assessment component. Misconduct includes plagiarism and collusion.

Plagiarism is defined as the representation of the ideas or work of another person as your own. The following are some of the ways to avoid plagiarism:

- Words and ideas of another person used to support one's arguments must be acknowledged.
- Passages that are quoted verbatim must be enclosed within quotation marks and acknowledged.
- CD-ROMs, email messages, web sites on the Internet, and any other electronic media must be treated in the same way as books and journals.
- The sources of all photographs, maps, illustrations, computer programs, data, graphs, audio-visual, and similar material must be acknowledged if they are not your own work.
- Works of art, whether music, film, dance, theatre arts, or visual arts, and where the creative use of a part of a work takes place, must be acknowledged.

Collusion is defined as supporting misconduct by another student. This includes:

- allowing your work to be copied or submitted for assessment by another student
- duplicating work for different assessment components and/or diploma requirements.

Other forms of misconduct include any action that gives you an unfair advantage or affects the results of another student. Examples include, taking unauthorized material into an examination room, misconduct during an examination, and falsifying a CAS record.

CONTENTS

How to use your enhanced online course book

This *English B enhanced online course book* is designed to prepare you for your DP assessments by giving you a wide range of practice. In addition to the activities you will find in this book, further practice and support are available on the online course book.

Throughout the book you will find the following icons. By clicking on these you can access the associated interactive activity or document.

Digital contents

Click here for a list of pages on which all additional practice activities and support materials can be found within your online course book.

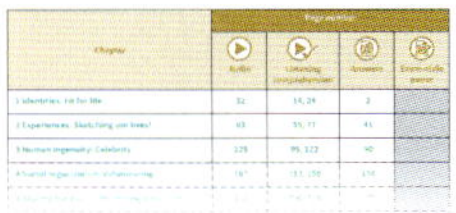

Listening comprehension

In order for you to practice the listening component of Paper 2, you will find a wide range of embedded audio exercises throughout the book. There are three listening comprehension activities per chapter, each indicated by an icon in the margin, as shown below.

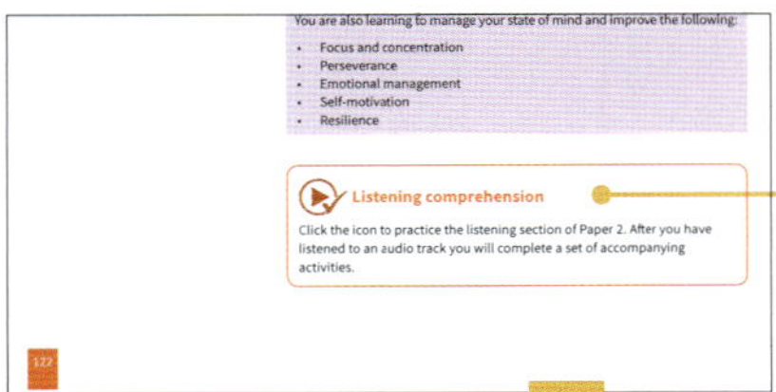

Audio clip with accompanying interactive, auto-marked, comprehension activity, as follows.

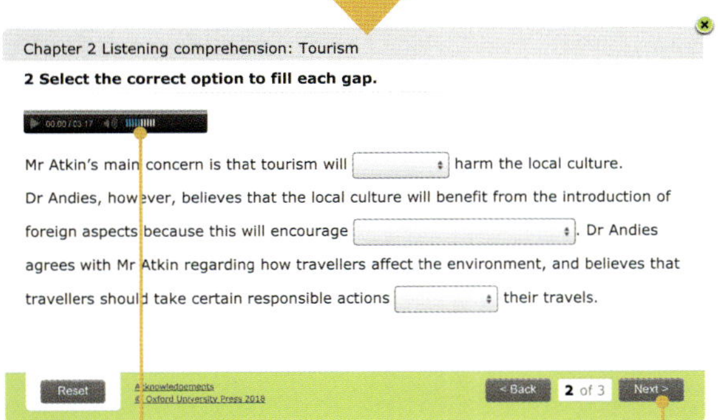

Listen to the audio track here.

Click here to move between screens. The final screen will show your results upon pressing the "submit" button.

Audio clip

Click this icon to listen to the audio clip that accompanies each printed listening comprehension.

Exam-style papers

Two exam-style papers, with accompanying audio tracks, are available on page vi, one for Standard Level and one for Higher Level.

On these screens you will find links to the SL and HL exam papers, along with accompanying audio tracks.

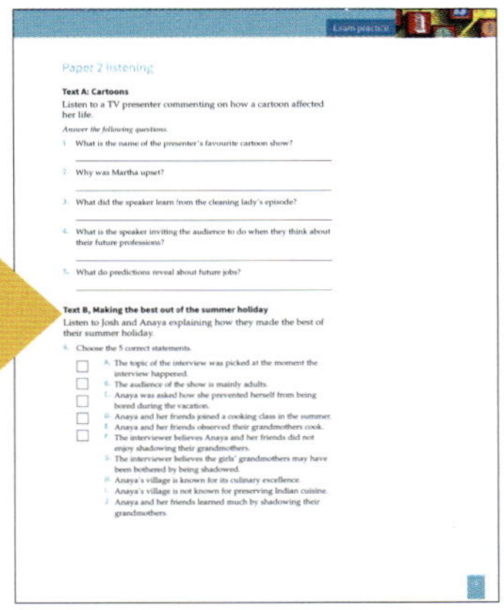

Answers and transcripts

Answers to all activities throughout the chapter (both printed and interactive), as well as transcripts for the listening activities, may be found on the opening page of each chapter.

Click the icon on the opening page of each chapter.

INTRODUCTION

IB values and the needs of 21st-century language learners

As teachers we are engaged with 21st-century learners of English. The new edition of the *English B* course book has been designed to meet the needs of this new generation of learners. It is in complete alignment with the IB vision to create a collaborative, global community united by a mission to make a better world through education.

To this end the *English B* course book has made full use of the four core values of an IB education and adapted them to the needs of learners of English.

Global contexts

The new *English B* course book focuses on learning from a global perspective so that students can increase their understanding of language and culture, which, in turn, can help them to become more globally engaged.

The content and activities of the ten chapters in the course guide allow students of English B to develop insights into these global issues:

- The concepts of culture and diversity
- Intercultural understanding
- Global engagement
- International-mindedness and global citizenship
- Interdependence and globalization
- Identity and cultural diversity
- Social justice and human rights
- Peace building and conflict resolution
- Sustainable futures

Significant content

The new edition of the *English B* course book has been designed to provide students with a highly relevant exploration the five prescribed themes of the Language B guide for first examinations in 2020.

Each chapter is concept-driven and based on one of the key themes of the new Language B guide:

- Identities
- Experiences

- Human ingenuity
- Social organization
- Sharing the planet

Every chapter provides a wealth of opportunities for linguistic and conceptual development. For example, chapter 3 "Celebrity" explores the theme of *Human Ingenuity*. The chapter asks students to inquire into three related topics: *Artistic expression, Media and communication,* and *Entertainment*.

These themes also provide a framework to study broad and powerful organizing concepts related to language acquisition. Each chapter focuses on one of the five conceptual understandings given in the Language B guide: Audience, Context, Meaning, Purpose, and Variation.

Each chapter also contains exercises in conceptual understanding to help students understand and manipulate a designated concept in a meaningful manner. Students reinforce conceptual learning by undertaking specific listening, reading, speaking and writing assessment tasks related to their understanding of these concepts.

For instance, chapter 3 focuses on *Purpose*. In Chapter 3 students analyse and produce reviews and interviews. To reinforce conceptual understanding, students are required to think about the purpose of the input reviews or interviews they read and listen to, and later create.

Each chapter also contains "TOK moments" giving students opportunities to relate the ideas and concepts explored within a chapter to language as one of the TOK ways of knowing.

Student-centred, inquiry-based learning

The *English B* course book is holistic in approach and explores themes that promote personal and intellectual growth. The 10 content chapters are organized around a clear and consistent inquiry-based structure that will help students to develop cognitive and linguistic abilities. All tasks are designed to encourage group work and cooperative learning

Each chapter begins with an overarching research question and an opportunity for initial discussion and reflection. Students can then investigate the specific research question for each section of the chapter.

Each section combines elements of language development with a structured inquiry.

Input: Reading/Listening

- Before reading/listening activities to ascertain prior knowledge
- A listening or reading text related to the specific topic and research question of each section

- Listening or reading comprehension exercises with extensions for Higher Level
- Exercises modelled on Paper 1 assessment rubrics and designed to help students understand the content of the text and concepts related to it

Processing: Interaction

Follow-up interactive tasks reinforce students' understanding of content, concepts and the language contained in the input text.

In this section students have ample opportunities to develop interactive skills while furthering the investigation.

Output: Speaking

Here students can practice:

- Internal assessment (Standard Level) – guided analysis of a visual stimulus
- Internal assessment (Higher Level) – guided exploration of a literary extract

During these activities students can use topic-specific language to consolidate and discuss concepts related to inquiry.

Output: Writing

Here students will find guidelines and scaffolds to help them analyse and practice specific text types. They will also find practice Paper 1 writing activities in which they can demonstrate conceptual understanding.

Both speaking and writing activities contain rubrics using the new IA and Paper 1 assessment criteria for reflective peer and self-assessment.

Conclusions and student reflections

Each section gives students the opportunity to reconsider each research question, and thereby arrive at enduring understandings relating to each topic. As a concluding exercise students can discuss their conclusions regarding the overarching theme and research question of the chapter.

Approaches to learning

In addition to the communicative activities generated by inquiry, the revised *English B* course book develops a range of Approaches to Learning (ATL) skills.

Each chapter contains 'ATLs' sidebars providing specific topic-related activities to promote the five core Approaches to Learning: Communication skills, Social skills, Research skills, Thinking Skills, and Self-management Skills.

By undertaking these ATL activities, learners of English will become aware of their relevance to other areas of the curriculum, which will help them to develop skills for a lifetime of learning.

Beyond the classroom

At the end of each chapter students will also find a concluding activity page, "Beyond the classroom". Here they can explore opportunities of using the skills and understandings they have developed in the chapter in practical, everyday contexts such as CAS, local community involvement, and online communications.

Assessment practice

Each chapter provides ample opportunities for exam practice. Students will find opportunities for practicing all the skills necessary in preparation for:

- Paper 1 (Writing)
- Paper 2 (Listening and Reading)
- The Internal assessment SL (a visual stimulus) and HL (a literary extract).

Chapter 11 provides advice on the Extended Essay, and examination practice for the new internal and external assessments may be found on the digital book.

1 IDENTITIES: FIT FOR LIFE

Chapter summary

Theme
Identities

Topics
Lifestyles, health, wellbeing

Research question for the chapter
What ideas and images do we associate with a healthy lifestyle?

Additional research questions for each text

- **A** How can physical exercise contribute to our wellbeing?
- **B** How do young adults deal with the stress in their lives?
- **C** How do we become healthy adults?

TOK questions

- As readers, how do we know how to identify the audience of a text?
- As writers, how do we know how to address our audience?

Communication skills

Listening skills

- Receptive
- Productive

Oral and interactive skills
Presentations

Written text types
Personal letters and emails

Research question for the chapter:

What ideas and images do we associate with a healthy lifestyle?

1. In class, discuss the research question for the chapter: What ideas and images do we associate with a healthy lifestyle?
2. Study the diagram below. What does it communicate about a healthy lifestyle? What are your thoughts and reactions to the diagram, the poster and the question?
3. In your opinion what role does the media play in promoting healthy (and unhealthy) lifestyles?

What justifications would you give for your answers?

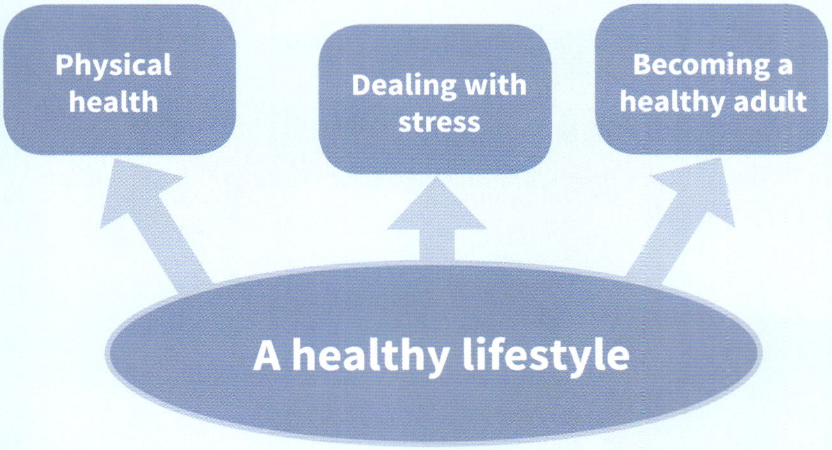

Using the research questions for the chapter

At the start of each chapter you will find a research question to consider and discuss in class. At the end of your discussions, make a note of your initial conclusions . You are encouraged to make a list of any points which might need further research.

At the end of each chapter you will be asked to reflect on your answers to the research question. Think about the question and re-examine your notes.

- To what extent have your views changed?
- To what extent have your views remained the same?
- What new understandings about the topic have you achieved?
- What new questions about the topic do you have?

Section A: Lifestyles

Using the research questions for each section

Each chapter is divided into three sections. Each section starts with its own research question for you to consider and discuss in class. At the end of your discussions, make a note of your initial conclusions. You will be asked to re-examine each research question at the end of each section.

Research question A:

How can physical exercise contribute to our wellbeing?

1. What are your first thoughts and reactions to the question above? Make a list of points.
2. What reasons would you give for your answers?
3. What more would you need to know and what would you need to do before you could come to a definitive conclusion about the question?

Before you read

- Before you start, as a class brainstorm the meaning of the phrase "a healthy teenage lifestyle".
- What ideas and images does the phrase suggest?
- Look at the pictures below. How might they relate to the idea of an unhealthy lifestyle?

Think about the photographs and their meaning.

a) Describe what is happening in each picture. How does it relate to the research question for this section?

b) What is the message of each photograph?

Justify your answers.

The article you are going to read lists eight benefits of exercise for teenagers.

In groups, predict the eight most relevant benefits of exercise for teenagers from the list A–P below.

Transfer and social skills ATLs

Working in groups can be difficult, especially when there is disagreement. In this exercise make sure you:

- work collaboratively
- listen to other people's points of view
- manage and resolve conflict
- build consensus
- make fair and equitable decisions.

A. A better social life

B. A greater sense of wellbeing

C. A lower heart rate

D. An improved complexion

E. Avoiding injury

F. Better mood control

G. Better sleep patterns

H. Decreased risk of medical problems

I. Greater confidence

J. Greater enjoyment of leisure activities

K. Improved powers of concentration

L. Longer life

M. Lower stress levels

N. Muscle strengthening

O. Potential weight loss

P. Stronger bones

The 8 biggest benefits of exercise for teenagers

Exercise guidelines for teenagers

The NHS recommends that teenagers need an hour of physical activity every day to help stay healthy. The 60 minutes of exercise should combine moderate-intensity aerobic activity, like walking fast, to vigorous-intensity aerobic activity, including running. On 3 days a week, there should also be muscle- strengthening moves, like push-ups and bone-strengthening exercise, including running. Many sports and activities help towards these targets, including playing football, gymnastics and martial arts training.

1. Weight control

Because exercise helps use oxygen, it causes your body to burn stored fat and helps you maintain a normal weight. For instance, if you walk seven kilometers a day, four times a week, you can burn about 1,600 calories. If you don't change your diet at all and keep walking the same distance over six months, you'll lose 5 kilos.

2. Stronger muscles

Most people know that exercise keeps muscles strong. But did you know that strong muscles also burn more calories? Muscle mass is a metabolically active tissue. In other words, the more muscle mass you have, the more calories you burn even when you're not working out. However, men have more muscle mass, so they burn calories faster and lose weight more easily than girls.

3. Stronger bones

Studies show that regular, moderate resistance and strengthening activities like walking, running, jogging, and dancing also burn weight. Such exercises also boost bone mass and keep muscles strong.

4. Better skin

As exercise boosts oxygen to the skin, it also helps increase the natural production of collagen, the connective tissue that plumps your skin. Your skin colour is also improved after exercise because of the increase in blood flow. Exercise also boosts circulation and the delivery of other nutrients to your skin that remove toxins or poisons.

5. Less stress

Regular exercise reduces the amount of stress hormones in the body, resulting in relaxed blood vessels and lower blood pressure. A slower heart rate after exercise also reduces muscle tension on your face.

6. Improved mood

Research shows that regular exercise reduces symptoms of mild to moderate depression and enhances psychological fitness. Exercise can even produce changes in endorphin levels in the body. Endorphins are hormones in the brain associated with happy, positive feelings.

7. Fewer illnesses

Regular exercise appears to help boost the immune system, thus helping to reduce the number of colds, flu, and other infections.

8. More brainpower

Exercise boosts blood flow to the brain and helps it receive oxygen and nutrients. The better shape you're in, the faster you activate brain waves that are responsible for quick thinking. So, for example, if you have a problem, you may find answers during your daily exercises.

But when do I find time to exercise?

The great thing about exercise is you don't have to do it all at one time. After all, not many teenagers have time to walk 7 kilometers after school! But you can do the distance in short bursts throughout your day. Here are two ideas of how to slot some exercise into your day:

- Walk around the school playground during lunchtime instead of sitting or standing around – you can still chat with your friends!
- Take a one-mile walk after school with friends or the family dog.

If you stick to the walking programme, you'll soon see the benefits.

http://www.webmd.boots.com/fitness-exercise/guide/benefits-of-exercise-teenagers

Reading comprehension

Read the text carefully and identify whether the statements below are true or false.

Tick [✓] the correct response then justify it with a relevant brief quotation from the text.

		True	False
Example:	Teenagers should exercise about 60 minutes a day.	✓	
Justification	"teenagers need an hour of physical activity every day to help stay healthy."		

		True	False
1.	You can lose five kilos a month by walking.		
Justification:			
2.	If you are more muscular, you can lose more weight.		
Justification:			
3.	Dancing is classed as a bone-strengthening exercise.		
Justification:			
4.	Increased collagen will help to remove poisons from the skin.		
Justification:			
5.	Exercise cannot decrease the outward signs of stress.		
Justification:			
6.	Physically active people are just as likely to be as unhappy as non-active people.		
Justification:			
7.	Exercise can help you fight off illnesses.		
Justification:			
8.	Thinking is a recognized form of exercise.		
Justification:			

Transfer and communication skills ATLs

When tackling the reading comprehension exercises in this book, remember to use techniques to improve your reading-for-meaning skills to gather specific information.

- Read each question critically and make sure you understand the task exactly.
- Preview and skim read texts to build understanding.
- Make sure you can summarize the main points and conclusions of the text.
- Locate exact phrases in the text to show understanding of specific questions.

You can also use the reading comprehension techniques you are developing here in your other subjects!

Answer the following questions

9. According to the article, what is the biggest single problem facing teenagers who want to walk the recommended daily distance for a healthy lifestyle?

10. What promise do the writers make to readers in their closing remarks?

Multiple-choice questions – conventions

11. What type of text is *The 8 biggest benefits of exercise for teenagers?*

A. A speech
B. A news report
C. A set of guidelines
D. A medical report

12. The main purpose of the text is to:

A. narrate a story
B. describe a situation
C. explain a problem
D. give advice.

13. The opinions in the text seem:

A. very balanced
B. emotional
C. biased
D. logical.

14. The text is addressed to:

A. parents
B. teachers
C. teenagers
D. everyone.

Critical thinking skills ATLs

Look at your answers for questions 11 to 14. How do you know your answers are correct?

For each of your responses find a quote in the text to support your answers. Use these thinking skills:

- Recognize unstated ideas and bias.
- Interpret information.
- Gather and organize relevant information to formulate an argument.

Transfer and thinking skills ATLs

In this Course Companion you will find numerous ATLs boxes such as this one. "ATLs" stands for "Approaches To Learning". They are designed to help you become a better learner both in English and in your other subjects.

For example, on this page you are learning presentation skills. You can use these skills in multiple contexts in all your other subjects. Moreover, you are learning for life. You will be able apply these skills in situations beyond the classroom, at college and in the world of work.

HL extension HL

Now look again at the predictions about the contents of the article you made before reading the text. How many of your predictions were correct? How many were incorrect? Go through the list of other potential benefits of physical exercise again. Choose three additional benefits of exercise for teenagers that are not mentioned in the text, and then write three additional paragraphs for the article. Write between 100 and 150 words.

Presentation skills

The process of presenting a topic to an audience is an important communication skill. Its purpose is to inform the listeners or persuade them of a point of view. During the English B course you may wish to give an oral presentation on a topic you have studied. When you present, it is very important to:

A. select appropriate material for the presentation

B. organize your ideas and material into a clear structure.

Brainstorming

Think about why you are making your presentation.

- What do you want to achieve?
- What do you want your audience to learn?
- What action do you want your audience to take following your presentation?
- How can you best design your presentation?

To help answer these questions, you can use a chart like this to brainstorm your initial thoughts.

Topic:	Examples and explanations
Introduction: Context and thesis statement	
Supporting idea one	
Supporting idea two	
Supporting idea three	
Conclusion, including a summary and a final thought	

As you fill in the table, ask yourself these questions:

- What are the main points you wish to make?
- Are these points structured in a logical, coherent way?

Oral activity: Presentation

Read the following news report.

Research shows 25% of teenagers think playing computer games is exercise

Nearly a quarter of young people believe that playing a computer game is a form of exercise, according to a government study released today.

The research, published by the Youth Sport Council, raises serious questions about the physical fitness of today's young people. It says that youngsters are at a critical point in terms of ensuring their mental and physical wellness

The report warns that many young people are not taking part in any physical activity.

However, the study found that 70 per cent of respondents wanted to do more exercise and 75 per cent said they enjoyed sport.

Transfer and self-management skills ATLs

You can also use the organizational and communication skills you are using in this exercise to create presentations in your other subjects.

Organization skills

- Set goals that are challenging and realistic
- Plan strategies and take action to achieve personal and academic goals
- Use appropriate strategies for organizing complex information

Communicating through language activities

- Preview and skim texts to build understanding
- Read critically and for comprehension
- Read a variety of sources for information
- Make inferences and draw conclusions
- Paraphrase accurately and concisely
- Take effective notes in class
- Make effective summary notes
- Use organizers for an academic writing task
- Write for different purposes
- Organize information logically
- Structure information into a presentation

Using the news report as a starting point, create a presentation for middle-school students explaining both the benefits of physical exercise and the dangers of a lack of exercise.

The presentation should last for four minutes.

Use the chart and the advice above to brainstorm your initial ideas.

Topic:	Examples and explanations
Introduction: Context and thesis statement	
Supporting idea one	
Supporting idea two	
Supporting idea three	
Conclusion, including a summary and a final thought	

Planning and drafting

Once you have created a first draft of your presentation you can then reflect on how you can improve what you have produced.

Do you think you have done a good job of introducing the topic?

- Have you explained the context of the presentation clearly?
- Is your thesis statement clear and effective?
- Suggest any improvements or rephrasing.

Is your argument effective?

- Will each of the supporting points you make be clear to your audience?
- Is there a clear topic sentence in each of the supporting arguments?
- Does each supporting point relate clearly to your thesis statement?
- Suggest any improvements or rephrasing.

Are there reasons, examples, or different explanations to support the topic sentence?

Is there a clear conclusion?

- Does the conclusion relate to the thesis statement?
- Does the conclusion relate to the supporting points?
- Have you made a final point which relates the conclusion of your presentation to the wider world?
- Suggest any improvements or rephrasing.

Connecting ideas

The final stage is to develop the flow of your presentation. This can be achieved by using linking statements to show clearly how your main points fit together. Common linking statements include:

- *"The next point to consider is ..."*
- *"Another important issue is ..."*
- *"We can now see that ..."*

Addressing the audience

- Who is the audience for the presentation?
- Have you made sure that your language and examples are suitable for your audience?

Communication skills ATLs

In this exercise you will have to:

- take effective notes
- make an effective summary
- organize and structure information logically.

Practicing and rehearsing

It is also very useful to practice your presentation at least once before you deliver it to the class. When practicing your presentation, you can use this chart to help each other in your group to improve their performances.

Oral communication skills

	Good	Improvement possible	Needs some improvement	Needs a lot of improvement
Eye contact	Has good eye contact with audience.	Has eye contact with the audience most of the time.	Sometimes has eye contact with the audience.	Does not have eye contact with the audience.
Enthusiasm	Shows great enthusiasm for the topic.	Shows enthusiasm for the topic.	Shows some enthusiasm for the topic.	Shows little enthusiasm for the topic.
Preparation and organization	Very prepared and well organized.	Mostly prepared and well organized.	Somewhat prepared and organized.	Not very prepared or organized.
Clear speech	Speaks very clearly and is very easy to understand.	Speaks clearly most of the time and is fairly easy to understand.	Sometimes speaks clearly and is sometimes easy to understand.	Does not speak clearly and is quite difficult to understand.
Knowledge of topic	Shows excellent understanding of the topic.	Shows good understanding of the topic.	Shows some understanding of the topic.	Shows little understanding of the topic.

Once you are ready, deliver your presentation. Your listeners may use the table above to give you feedback.

Internal assessment (SL)

Look at the visual stimulus below. The image relates to the theme of "identities".

Brainstorming

- What is the main idea in the photograph? How does it relate to the title of this section, "Lifestyles"?
- What do you see in the background of the photograph? What does this tell you about the location and context of the photograph?
- Look at the foreground of the photograph. Describe the person or people you can see.
- What is happening in the picture? How does the action relate to the title of this chapter, "Fit for Life"?

Preparation and presentation

Based on your answers to the questions above, prepare a four-minute presentation on the photograph.

Remember that the presentation should not only include a description of the photograph, but should also connect it to the topics of *Identities, health and lifestyles*. It should also highlight the connection between the photograph and an Anglophone culture. Present your photograph and topic to your classmates. Remember that in the actual examination you will have 15 minutes to prepare your presentation.

Research and self-management skills ATLs

You will find detailed information about all the SL and HL assessments for this course in *The Language B guide for first examinations 2020* (IBO).

Make sure you are familiar with the assessment criteria for all the assessment components.

If you understand the marking criteria, it is much easier to see the areas in which you need to improve in order to achieve the next level of proficiency in each of the assessment activities.

Peer assessment

Assess the presentations given by your classmates. Use the following criteria to guide your assessment:

	Internal assessment (SL and HL)
Criterion A	Language
Criterion B	1. Message: visual stimulus (SL) 1. Message: literary extract (HL) 2. Message: Conversation
Criterion C	**Interactive skills—communication**

Suggest ways in which your classmates can improve their presentation techniques.

Internal assessment (HL)

Read the following passage. Then answer the questions that follow.

The training of Mu Lan –the woman warrior

"White Tigers" is Maxine Hong Kingston's childhood fantasy of living the life of Fa Mu Lan, the woman warrior. This section is written in the first person– that is, from the young Mu Lan's point of view. In the fantasy, having been attracted by a distant bird she follows it up into the mountains until she comes to the magical hut of a mysterious old couple. The old man and the old woman receive Mu Lan and say they want to train her to become a great warrior and help her family take revenge on the local baron who has been exploiting and oppressing them.

'What do you want to do?' the old man asked. 'You can go back right now if you like. You can go pull sweet potatoes, or you can stay with us and learn how to fight barbarians and bandits.'

'You can avenge your village,' said the old woman. 'You can recapture the harvests the thieves have taken. You can be remembered by the Han people for your dutifulness.'

'I will stay with you', I said.

...

'The first thing you have to learn,' the old woman told me, 'is how to be quiet.' They left me by streams to watch for animals. 'If you are noisy, you'll make the deer go without water.'

When I could kneel all day without my legs cramping and my breathing became even, the squirrels would bury their hoardings at the hem of my shirt and then bend their heads in a celebration dance. At night, the mice and toads looked at me, their eyes quick stars and slow stars. Not once did I see a three-legged toad, though; you need strings of cash to bait them.

The two old people led me in exercises that began at dawn and ended at sunset so that I could watch our shadows grow and shrink and grow again, rooted in the earth. I learned to move my fingers, hands, feet, head, and entire body in circles. I walked putting heel down first, toes pointing outward thirty to forty degrees, making the ideograph 'eight,' making the ideograph 'human.' Knees bent, I would swing into the slow, measured 'square step', the powerful walk into battle.

After five years my body became so strong that I could control even the directions of the pupils inside my irises. I could copy owls and bats, the words for 'bat' and 'blessing' homonyms. After six years the deer let me run beside them. I could jump twenty feet into the air from a standstill, leaping like a monkey over the hut. Every creature has a hiding skill and a fighting skill a warrior can use. When the birds alighted on my palm, I could yield my muscles under their feet and give them no base from which to fly away.

But I could not fly like a bird that led me here, except in large, free dreams.

An extract from the chapter "White Tigers" from *The Woman Warrior*, by Maxine Hong Kingston

Note

In your internal assessment, the literary extract will not exceed 300 words. You will be shown two, one from each of the works of literature studied in class.

Brainstorming

In small groups, discuss the following questions then summarize your discussion in point form.

- What motivates the old man and woman to train Fa Mu Lan to become the Woman Warrior?
- Describe and explain the different stages of Mu Lan's training.
- How does the old couple use nature to teach Mu Lan about fighting?
- On the evidence of the text, how does the physical training contribute to Mu Lan's wellbeing and sense of purpose?
- How would you react if you had to undergo such a rigorous training programme? Explain and justify your answer.

Classmates listening to the presentation should prepare individual questions about the text. They can put these questions to you at the end of your presentation.

Peer assessment

Assess the presentations given by your classmates. Use the following criteria to guide your assessment:

	Internal assessment (HL)
Criterion A	Language
Criterion B	1. Message: literary extract 2. Message: Conversation
Criterion C	Interactive skills: communication

Suggest ways in which your classmates can improve their presentation techniques.

Listening comprehension

Click the icon to practice the listening section of Paper 2. After you have listened to an audio track you will complete an accompanying activity. This activity will help you to practice multiple choice questions. Answering multiple choice questions is not as easy as it seems. The three options are always close in meaning.

Paper 1: Personal letter writing

We write personal letters to people we know well, such as friends or members of our family. These days we still tend to write letters on special occasions: to invite, to thank someone, to express sympathy or congratulations. Other personal letters are written to maintain a friendship or personal relationship. Writing a letter shows that you care about your reader, and that you are willing to spend time writing to them. We should also remember that people tend to keep personal letters and will re-read them, sometimes long after they have been received.

The writers of personal letters will want to make sure that their words express their exact thoughts and their feelings towards their audience, the reader. You do not want your reader to misunderstand your meaning, so the personal letter has to hit the right note, and have the exact effect intended. This means that the language must be chosen carefully.

This is a very difficult task. The choice of a single wrong word or bad grammar can change the meaning or tone of a letter, so you will have to be selective and proofread extremely carefully.

In *English B* Paper 1, you may wish to write a personal letter in response to a set prompt. Such a personal letter may require you undertake several things within one letter:

- narrate an event
- describe a person or object
- describe your feelings or reactions
- explain your thoughts and ideas
- give advice or instructions
- explain a situation you find yourself in.

You should adopt an informal, personal tone and register suitable to the subject matter and audience. You can use moderate amounts of slang, abbreviations and colloquial expressions in informal letters. When in doubt, remember this task is an assessment of how well, not how badly, you can write English.

Structure

You may wish to start with your address and a date. Keep in mind that you will also need to be able to open and close the letter correctly with an informal salutation and ending. The most frequent salutation is 'Dear', followed by the reader's first name. In personal letters, you could use 'Love', 'Best wishes', 'Cheers', to close the letter. Your signature (i.e., your first name) goes below the close.

Writing activity: Personal letters

Here are three opportunities to practice writing personal letters.

Exam tip

At **Standard Level** you should write between 250 and 400 words.

At **Higher Level** you should write between 450 and 600 words.

Plan, draft, revise and redraft:

1. Re-read: *The 8 biggest benefits of exercise for teenagers*. Do you agree or disagree with the content and message of the guidelines? Write a letter to a friend describing your reactions to the text.
2. Imagine you are Mu Lan in the literary extract you read earlier. Write a personal letter to your family describing your life on the mountain with the old couple and your training programme.
3. You are worried about an older relative who has gone through some serious life changes recently and seems to have become very inactive. Read this poster and use some of the information to write to a friend or another family member describing the relative and suggesting a plan of action.

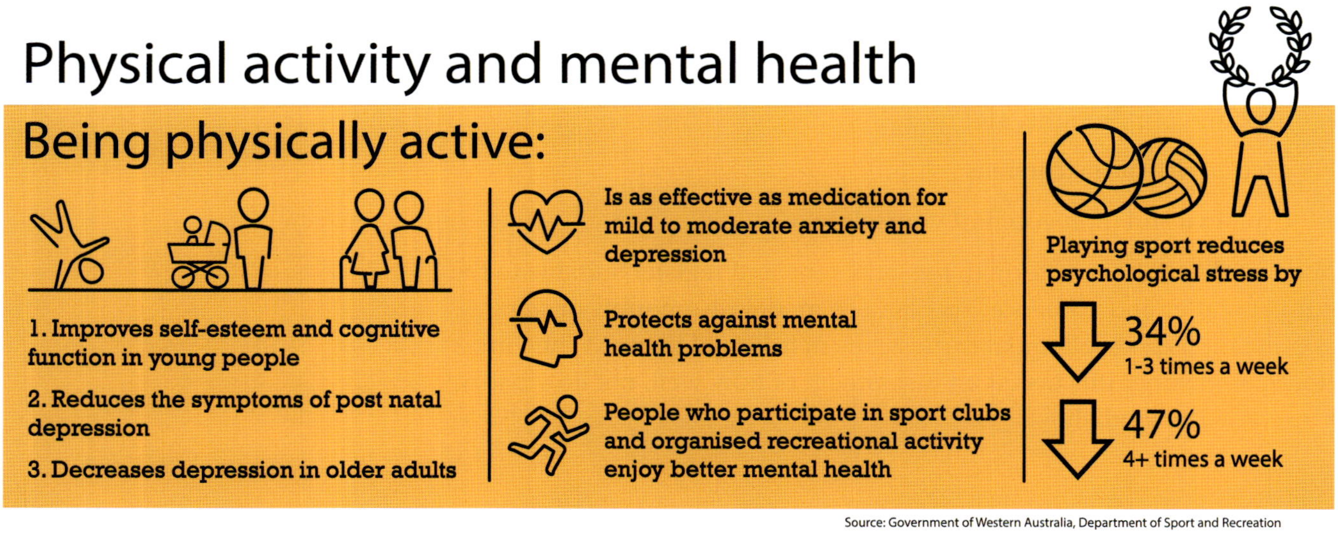

Brainstorming

During the first stage write down as many ideas as you can about the content of your letter.

1. Reflect

- Reflect on everything you have learned in this section.
- Choose your focal point and your point of view. What information would you like to emphasize?

2. Generate

- Generate ideas to be used in your letter.
- Research additional material or relevant facts to support your opinion.

Planning

Use the chart below to help you decide what content to include. Give specific details as much as possible.

Choosing possible content	
Explain a situation you find yourself in	
Narrate an event	
Describe a person or object	
Describe your feelings or reactions	
Explain your thoughts and ideas	
Give advice or instructions	

Writing to a specific audience

- Having written down the content of your letter, always visualize the person you are writing to.
- While you are writing, keep in mind how you normally talk to the person you are writing to.
- Use a tone of voice and vocabulary in your letter as though you were talking to your correspondent in person.

Re-read the completed draft of your written text and revise where necessary.

Remember you will be assessed on three criteria: Criterion A: Language, Criterion B: Message, Criterion C: Conceptual understanding (including audience, context and purpose).

Conceptual understanding: Audience

Audience is a very important concept in the study of language. Authors create texts for a person or a group of people who will read, listen or view it.

Defining an audience

When an author plans a text, one of the most important questions to consider is "Who is the audience I am trying to reach?" Authors need to consider a number of factors to define their audience. These include:

- social status
- income
- age group
- gender
- cultural background
- physical location
- special interests.

For example, using the list above, can you define the audience for the textbook you are holding?

A TOK moment: As readers, how do we know how to identify the audience of a text? TOK

The Theory of Knowledge recognises the following ways of knowing: sense perception, reason, emotion, faith, imagination, intuition, memory, and language.

Which of these ways of knowing are most helpful when you want to identify the audience for a text?

Re-examine the text in this section: *The 8 biggest benefits of exercise for teenagers.*

Using the following criteria, identify the specific audience for the text.

- social status
- income
- age group
- gender
- cultural background
- physical location
- special interests

What ways of knowing did you use to reach your answers?

Further research

Find a variety of texts that promote a healthy lifestyle. Using the criteria above and appropriate ways of knowing, identify the audience for each text. Look carefully for clues in the text.

Conclusion to research question A

Now that you have completed the section, consider research question A,

"How can physical exercise contribute to our wellbeing?"

Look at the notes you took at the beginning of this section. To what extent have your opinions on the subject changed since the beginning of the chapter? To what extent have your opinions remained the same?

What ideas have you learned in this section?

Section B: Mental health

Research question B:

How do young adults deal with the stress in their lives?

1. What are your first thoughts and reactions to the question above? Make a list of points.
2. What reasons would you give for your answers?
3. What more would you need to know and what would you need to do before you could come to a definitive conclusion about the statement?

Before you read

Discussion

In groups put the following causes of stress into levels from 1 to 5. You could also use the information here to conduct a questionnaire about stress in your class or year group.

What are the biggest causes of stress in young adults?

- A relationship break-up
- Alcohol or drug use
- Arrival of a new family member
- Change in responsibilities at home
- Change of residence
- Changes due to puberty
- Changing a course of study
- Changing school
- Chronic allergies
- Confusion of sexual identity
- Dating someone new
- Death of a loved one
- Divorce of parents
- Excessive studying
- Financial worries
- Getting pregnant or causing pregnancy
- Having an argument
- Health problems in the family
- Outstanding personal achievement
- Parents' unemployment
- Personal injury or illness
- Sleeping less than eight hours per night
- Trouble with grades
- Visitors in the home
- Working while attending school

The dangers of long-term stress

The following text is taken from a manual for teenagers, Fighting Invisible Tigers. *The book's author, Earl Hipp. uses the metaphor of the 'tiger' to stand for the stress that we can feel in our day-to-day lives.*

What happens when you live with stress constantly? When your life is full of tigers that never go away? You gradually adapt to higher and higher stress levels, and you may never find the time to calm down, rest, and recuperate. Soon you're living with an *unhealthy* amount of stress and calling it normal. Long-term stress can be dangerous because you may not be aware of the physical and emotional toll it is taking on you.

Why is long-term stress such a problem for so many people? We aren't taught about stress, so we don't recognize it even when we are up to our eyeballs in it. We all have stress factors in our lives that we're powerless to do anything about (parental decisions, school rules, homework, problems with friends, feeling unsafe). We face so many challenges that it isn't practical or possible to rest after each one.

We're the products of a driven culture. We're taught from an early age that it's good to compete, win, stay busy, and always be productive. Most of us don't know how to relax. Relaxation skills aren't valued by our culture. It's more common (and accepted) to hurry and always do too much than it is to relax and be quiet for a period of time.

Even our attempts at play can be filled with competition and pressures to be great at everything we do. Recreation is supposed to be re-creation – a chance to renew ourselves. Instead, it turns into *wreckreation*. We end up feeling more strung out and wrung out than when we started. We all do our best to live in our world full of tigers. We try to be responsible and handle everything that comes our way.

Here are some of the things young people do in an effort to keep it all together: skipping meals, sleeping less, spending excessive time with friends and family, never talking about feelings and toughing it out by pretending to cope independently. When you try harder to keep up as the stress in your life increases, you may forget to take time for rest and recuperation. Without realizing it, you gradually lose your energy, positive attitude, and performance edge.

Here are some of the symptoms young people have reported: more trouble with teachers, needing a lot of sleep or not sleeping well, wanting to eat all the time or never eating, headaches, stomach aches, colds, infections, sore muscles, escapist behaviour -- overdoing one thing (TV, music, studying, sleeping) and ignoring other things, withdrawing from friends and family ("Just leave me alone!"), crying for no apparent reason, feeling like an idiot, restlessness, anxiety, worrying all the time, feeling like everything is out of control ("like I'm out of control"), depression, sadness, and irritability.

You may be too busy adapting and coping with your stress factors to notice how you are changing. Unconsciously, you keep modifying your definition of what constitutes an acceptable level of stress. Suddenly the symptoms of overload seem to come out of nowhere. One minute you think you're fine, and the next you find yourself doubling over with cramps, tossing and turning at night, yelling at your mom, having two-day headaches, biting your nails, or gobbling whole crates of chips.

From *Invisible Tigers*

Reading comprehension

Choose the correct answer from A, B, C, or D.

1. The text is:
   - **A.** an article about dealing with stress
   - **B.** an extract from a self-help book
   - **C.** a blog on teenage mental health
   - **D.** a news story about teenagers.

2. The target audience for the text is probably:
   - **A.** social workers and administrators
   - **B.** young people and their parents
   - **C.** mental health professionals
   - **D.** the general public.

3. The writer seems to be:
   - **A.** a concerned parent
   - **B.** a newspaper journalist
   - **C.** a guidance counselor
   - **D.** a humanities teacher.

4. According to the text, living with high stress levels means:
   - **A.** we learn to relax despite high stress levels
   - **B.** we can forget how much stress we have
   - **C.** we become dangerous to others
   - **D.** we can make very bad decisions.

5. According to the text, why is long-term stress such a problem?
   - **A.** We do not know it exists.
   - **B.** We are not educated enough about it.
   - **C.** We lack the strength to deal with it.
   - **D.** We forget how to relax.

6. The writer defines the term "a driven culture" (line 11) as a society that:
   - **A.** is demanding and full of tension
   - **B.** leaves no room for individual expression
   - **C.** is very progressive and positive
   - **D.** values self-reflection and relaxation.

7. The writer creates the term "*wreckreation*" to define leisure activities that:
   - **A.** are frequently violent and destructive
   - **B.** lack any sort of purpose or direction
   - **C.** have no creative or artistic element
   - **D.** create even more stress and tension.

Social skills ATLs

In the English Language Acquisition Course Companion you are encouraged to use your collaborative skills to tackle some of the reading comprehension exercises as pairwork.

You might try to answer questions in pairs, or small groups, and discuss the various possible alternative responses.

8. When the writer says young people are trying "to keep it all together", he means they are trying to:

A. understand what they are doing
B. work towards achieving excellence
C. cope with the pressure they are under
D. be positive and creative in their outlook.

9. The writer concludes by saying:

A. stress can cause bad habits such as overeating
B. stress might cause irrational behaviour
C. we find it hard to measure the stress in our lives
D. we fail to notice the effect stress has on us.

Vocabulary in context

Define the following phrases in your own words.

10. "up to our eyeballs" (line 6) Answer:

11. "strung out and wrung out" (line 15) Answer:

12. "performance edge" (line 21) Answer:

Transfer and research skills ATLs

Use these information literacy skills to complete your HL extension task:

- Collect and classify data
- Access information to be informed and inform others
- Create new information
- Present information in a new format
- Collect and analyse data to identify solutions

HL extension HL

Throughout the text the writer gives examples of the effects of long-term stress on teenagers.

Identify the effects and then categorize them in the following chart. One example of each has been done for you.

Physical symptoms of stress	Mental symptoms of stress	Behavioral symptoms of stress
Headaches	Forgetting to rest	Skipping meals

When you have completed the extension task, write a paragraph of approximately 100 words to explain to other IB students the dangers of stress, and the benefits of relaxation.

Oral activity: Presentation

Here are some random tips created for university students dealing with general exam stress. First put the sentences in a more logical sequence so that they make better sense. Once you have sequenced the sentences, you are going to use the information and apply it to a different audience.

In groups assess and then choose the most important points to create a five-minute presentation for your fellow IB students. The purpose of the task is to create a presentation to your fellow students giving tips about how to handle their English B or another DP examination.

15 stress tips for the day of an exam

1. After the exam do not spend endless time criticising yourself about where you think you went wrong. Often our own self-assessment is far too harsh.
2. Always write a plan for essays and other written tasks. Brainstorm ideas then put them in order.
3. Congratulate yourself for the things you did right and learn from the questions in which you know you could have done better, and then move on.
4. Don't bottle things up. If you are worried about how you did, talk it through with someone, such as a friend, a parent or a teacher.
5. Get up in good time so you're not rushing and you have time to eat breakfast.
6. If you are making notes for an essay, plan the conclusion first and work backwards from there.
7. If you still can't remember the information then move on to another question and return to the problem question later.
8. If your essay plan is not adequate, add more points before writing again.
9. If your mind goes blank, don't panic! Help the thinking part of your brain by taking slow, deep breaths for about one minute.
10. Look at all the questions before you decide which questions to answer. Pick questions you are confident writing about.
11. Remember to bring everything you need, like extra pens and pencils.
12. Stay calm. Getting excessively anxious is counter-productive, as you will not be able to think as clearly.
13. Take a deep breath before you start to read the paper. Breathing in this way calms your whole nervous system.
14. The quickest and most effective way of eliminating feelings of stress and panic is to close your eyes and take several long, slow deep breaths.
15. Work out the time allowance for each question, and stick to it.

Thinking skills ATLs

In this exercise, and others in this book, you will need to use critical thinking skills. In these tasks there is no "right answer". As you conduct the task you will have to come to your own conclusions about what is the right answer by using reasoned arguments.

Use these critical thinking skills to help you to find answers.

- Analyse and evaluate the issues and ideas.
- Gather and organize relevant information to formulate a sensible argument.
- Interpret the data available.
- Evaluate evidence.
- Draw reasonable conclusions and generalizations.
- Test your generalizations and conclusions.
- Revise your understanding based on any new information.

Brainstorming

Select the ideas you wish to use and adapt. Choose the most important points to create a five-minute presentation for your fellow DP students. If necessary, alter your points so they are relevant to English B students. You may wish to add specific information of your own to help your audience handle specific exam papers.

Use this table again to plan and redraft your presentation.

Topic:	Examples and explanations
Introduction: Context and thesis statement	
Supporting idea 1	
Supporting idea 2	
Supporting idea 3	
Conclusion, including a summary and a final thought	

Use the advice you received to help you to structure your presentation.

Have you made sure that your language and examples are suitable for your audience?

Always rehearse and practice before giving your final presentation.

Note: You may wish to record the discussion and/or the presentation. You may want to use the recording as a prompt for one of the practice writing exercises later in the chapter.

Peer assessment

In small groups, assess the discussion or the presentation given by your classmates. You may use the oral communication skills on page 11 as a basis for your comments.

Listening comprehension

Click the icon to practice the listening section of Paper 2. This activity will help you practice short-answer questions. You should be able to answer each question by quoting a few words from the audio text. Remember you may lose the mark if your answer is too long because your quote will not answer the question exactly.

Internal assessment (SL)

Take a look at the visual stimulus below. The image relates to the theme of "Identities".

Brainstorming

In pairs, choose one of the photographs, then discuss and answer the following questions.

- What do you see in background of your chosen picture? What does the background tell you about the location and context of the picture?
- Look at the foreground of the picture. Describe the object(s) you can see.
- What is the main idea in the picture? How does it relate to the theme of the chapter: "Fit for Life"?

Presenting

Based on your answers to the questions above, prepare a four-minute presentation on the photograph.

Remember that the presentation should not only include a description of the visual stimulus, but should also connect it to the topic of celebrity and an Anglophone culture. Present your photograph and topic to your classmates. Remember that in the actual examination you will have 15 minutes to prepare your presentation.

Peer assessment

In small groups, assess the presentations given by your classmates. You may use the IA assessment criteria in the Language B guide as a basis for your comments.

Exam tip

Internal assessment (SL)

You will have a choice of two photographs both related to one of the five syllabus themes.

- Identities
- Experiences
- Human ingenuity
- Social organization
- Sharing the planet

You will have 15 minutes to prepare.

The recorded internal assessment (SL) will consist of three parts:

Part 1: Presentation

You will begin by making a presentation for up to four minutes about the content and ideas communicated in your image. You should relate your ideas to the theme chosen by your teacher.

Part 2: Follow-up questions and discussion of the photograph related to the theme of the photograph.

Part 3: General discussion

The last section is a general conversation with your teacher about another of the five syllabus themes.

Internal assessment (HL)

Read the short episode "The First Job", taken from* The House on Mango Street *by Sandra Ciscernos, and then answer the questions that follow.

The first job

The narrator, Esperanza, is a young Mexican-American teenager whose name means 'hope' in Spanish. The book, The House on Mango Street, *follows her life in a poor Latino neighbourhood of Chicago as she makes a difficult and at times traumatic transition from childhood to adulthood. The book is told in a series of short episodes. In this one,* 'The First Job', *Esperanza and her family are under pressure for her to find a job, as her school is expensive and they need money.*

It wasn't as if I didn't want to work. I did. I had even gone to the social security office the month before to get my social security number. I needed money. The Catholic high school cost a lot, and Papa said nobody went to public school unless you wanted to turn out bad.

I thought I'd find an easy job, the kind other kids had, working in the dime store or maybe a hotdog stand. And though I hadn't started looking yet, I thought I might the week after next. But when I came home that afternoon, all wet because Tito had pushed me into the open water hydrant–only I had sort of let him–Mama called me in the kitchen before I could even go and change, and Aunt Lala was sitting there drinking her coffee with a spoon. Aunt Lala said she had found a job for me at the Peter Pan Photo Finishers on North Broadway where she worked, and how old was I, and to show up tomorrow saying I was one year older, and that was that.

So the next morning I put on the navy blue dress that made me look older and borrowed money for lunch and bus fare because Aunt Lala said I wouldn't get paid 'til the next Friday, and I went in and saw the boss of the Peter Pan Photo Finishers on North Broadway where Aunt Lala worked and lied about my age like she told me to and sure enough, I started that same day.

In my job I had to wear white gloves. I was supposed to match negatives with their prints, just look at the picture and look for the same one on the negative strip, put it in the envelope, and do the next one. That's all. I didn't know where these envelopes were coming from or where they were going. I just did what I was told.

It was real easy, and I guess I wouldn't have minded it except that you got tired after a while and I didn't know if I could sit down or not, and then I started sitting down only when the two ladies next to me did. After a while they started to laugh and came up to me and said I could sit down when I wanted, and I said I knew.

When lunchtime came, I was scared to eat alone in the company lunchroom with all those men and ladies looking, so I ate real fast standing in one of the washroom stalls and had lots of time left over, so I went back to work early. But then break time came, and not knowing where else to go, I went to the coatroom because there was a bench there.

I guess it was the time for the night shift or middle shift to arrive because a few people came in and punched the time clock, and an older Oriental man said hello and we talked for a while about my just starting, and he said that we could be friends and next time to go in the lunch room and sit with him, and I felt better. He has nice eyes and I didn't feel so nervous anymore. Then he asked if I knew what day it was, and when I said I didn't, he said it was his birthday and would I please give him a birthday kiss. I thought I would because he was so old and just as I was about to put my lips on his cheek, he grabs my face with both hands and kisses me a hard on the mouth and doesn't let go.

Brainstorming

In small groups, discuss the following questions then summarize your discussion in point form.

1. Describe in detail the circumstances surrounding the job the narrator gets at Peter Pan Photo Finishers.
2. How do we know that the narrator lacks self-confidence and is shy?
3. Identify the different sources of stress the narrator is dealing with throughout the passage.
4. How does the narrator deal with the stress she is under?
5. What do you imagine might have happened after the final scene in the story?

Note

In your internal assessment, the literary extract will not exceed 300 words. You will be shown two, one from each of the works of literature studied in class.

Exam tip

In your internal assessment at Higher Level you will be given a choice of two extracts chosen by your teacher, one from each of the literary works you have studied in class. You will have 20 minutes to prepare your thoughts on the extract.

The internal assessment will consist of three parts:

Part 1: Presentation

You will begin by making a presentation for up to four minutes about what you understand from the extract, discussing the events, ideas and messages in the extract itself.

Part 2: Follow-up questions

A discussion of the literary extract follows in which your teacher will ask you to expand on your observations of the extract.

Part 3: General discussion

The last section is a general conversation with your teacher using one of the syllabus' five general themes as a starting point.

These themes are:

- Identities
- Experiences
- Human ingenuity
- Social organization
- Sharing the planet

Presenting

Based on your answers to the questions above, prepare a four-minute presentation on the contents of the extract.

Remember that the presentation should include answers to the questions above and focus, as much as possible, on the extract alone. Make your presentation to your classmates. Remember that in the actual examination you will have 20 minutes to prepare your presentation.

Students listening to the presentation should prepare individual questions about the presentation. They can put these questions to you at the end of your presentation.

Communication skills ATLs

In this Course Guide you will find lots of practical advice about how to become a better speaker, reader and writer of English. However, you will learn better if you take a proactive interest in your own learning. Here are some tips:

- Preview and skim read texts to build understanding.
- Read critically and for comprehension.
- Highlight new information and clarify what you do not understand.
- Take your own notes to remember key points.
- Make effective summary notes for studying.
- Organize your notes in a logical manner.

Exam tip

At Standard Level you should write between 250 and 400 words.

At Higher Level you should write between 450 and 600 words.

Paper 1: Emails

Some would argue that email is replacing letter writing. Certainly more and more personal correspondence is done via the Internet. We have also seen the rising use of texting and emoticons.

Some basic rules

- When sending messages to people who you know put their addresses in the **To:** field.
- When sending messages to many people who don't know each other, put their addresses in the **Bcc:** field.
  ('Bcc' stands for 'Blind carbon copy', and using this field means that you're not sharing the addresses with everyone on the email list.)
- Think before you send. Once you send an email message, you cannot take it back or make it disappear.
- Be calm. Don't send angry messages (known as 'flaming').
- Use upper and lowercase letters properly. Using all uppercase letters gives the sense that I AM SHOUTING AT YOU! See?
- You can use emoji, but do so sparingly.

Writing activity: Emails

Here are three opportunities to practice writing personal emails.

Plan, draft, revise and redraft one of these stimuli.

1. Your best friend abroad is suffering from stress in the face of their upcoming IB written exams. Use the information from your presentation, and elsewhere in this section, to write an email to your friend offering understanding and practical advice.
2. Imagine you are Esperanza from 'A first job'. Write an email to a very close friend recounting what happened to you, and your reactions.
3. Examine the poster. Write an email to a friend expressing your reactions to the ideas contained in the poster. Give examples from your own personal experience to support your point of view.

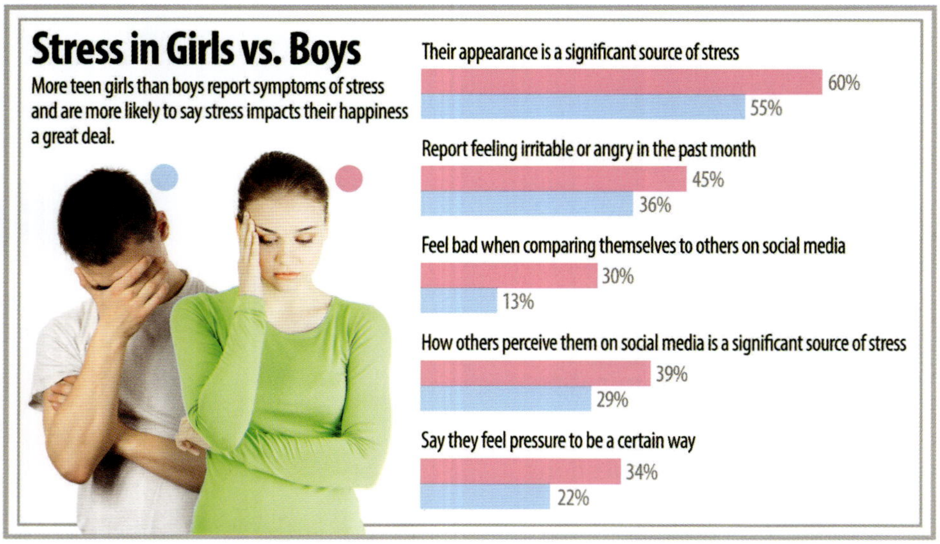

Brainstorming

1. Reflect

- Reflect on everything you have learned in this section.
- Choose your focal point and your point of view. What information would you like to emphasize?

2. Generate

- Generate ideas to be used in your text.
- Research additional material or relevant facts to support your opinion.

Planning

- You may wish to use the chart here to help you plan your email. Decide what the **purpose** of the email is.
- Think about what measures you will take to make sure your text is well written and effective.
- Use the chart below to help you decide what content you wish to include. It helps to give specific details.

Choosing possible content	To be used? Yes/ No	Your notes on possible content
Explain a situation you find yourself in		
Narrate an event		
Describe a person or object		
Describe your feelings or reactions		
Explain your thoughts and ideas		
Give advice or instructions		

Writing to a specific audience

- Having written down all that you want to talk about in your email, always visualize the person you are writing to.
- While you are writing, keep in mind how you normally talk to that person.
- Use a similar tone of voice and vocabulary in your email, as if you were talking to your correspondent in person.

Drafting

Write a draft of the body of your text.

Make sure to use all the conventions and formatting associated with an email.

Re-read the completed draft of your review and revise where necessary.

Remember you will be assessed on three criteria: Criterion A: Language, Criterion B: Message, Criterion C: Conceptual understanding (including audience, context and purpose).

Conceptual understanding: Audience

As you may have seen in the writing exercise above, finding the right level of language for your **audience** is really important. One secret of successful communicators is that they always write and speak in the style that suits their purpose and their audience. For instance, your friends on the Internet may expect you to write informally or to use slang in your email. If you were writing an article for a school magazine, you would probably use a more formal register. When you send an email to a college of higher education enquiring about entry to a particular course would you write in a very informal manner? Why not? What register would you use?

Conclusion to research question B

How do young adults deal with the stress in their lives?

1. Now that you have completed this section, what are your thoughts and reactions to the question above?
2. What justifications would you give for your answers?
3. What big ideas have you learned about the nature of stress and how to deal with it?

A TOK moment: As writers, how do we know how to address our audience?

TOK

In the English B syllabus the text types are organized into three categories: Personal, Mass media and Professional texts.

Written text types

	Personal Communication	Mass Communication	Professional Communication
Author	The author of text writes as "self".	Writer has a specific social or professional role (journalist advertiser) and a persona (expert/advisor/blogger)	Writer has a specific relationship to the audience; customer, job applicant, college applicant
Audience	Specific. Sometimes reader is addressed directly or text is directed to implied audience e.g. beloved	Community of strangers united by a common interest	A specific individual or small group with specific organizational or professional role
Relationship between Writer & Audience	The reader is specific. Diaries, letters, some poems. May be addressed to an implied audience.	Will depend on the purpose of the text. For example advertisements and flyers will target very different audiences according to their content and purpose.	Formal relationship
Register	Depends on text type & purpose and suggested relationship in the text between writer and audience (informal, formal, personal etc.)	Depends on text type & purpose and suggested relationship in the text between writer and audience (informal, formal, personal etc.)	Unemotional, formal language using reasoned arguments

Study the text type chart above and then identify the potential audience in each of these scenarios.

1. You are a blogger writing on teenage lifestyle issues.
2. You are a journalist writing for a local newspaper article about a factory fire.
3. You are a storyteller writing a fable with a moral featuring farmyard animals.
4. You are a student journalist for the school magazine writing up an interview with a doctor on eating disorders among secondary school students.
5. You are a student writing an essay on an issue of human rights for an international competition.
6. You are selling unwanted sports equipment over the Internet.

Analyse each text.

A. Define the audience of each text.

B. Identify the register (level of formality) you would use for each text.

C. Explain your choices.

What ways of knowing have you used to guide you in finding answers to the questions above: sense perception, reason, emotion, faith, imagination, intuition, memory, language?

Which ways of knowing were the most important in this instance?

Section C: A healthy life

Research question C:

How do we become healthy adults?

1. What are your first thoughts and reactions to the question?
2. What justifications would you give for your answers?
3. How do the the title chapter, "Fit for life", and the contents you have examined so far relate to this research question?

Before you listen

Young adults (aged approximately 16–26) are at a pivotal time of life. During this time they may go into higher education, launch their working career, and develop serious personal relationships. However, the transition to adulthood can also be a time of increased vulnerability and risk.

At this time many will be moving out of the homes, schools and communities that have supported them as children and adolescents.

As a result some young adults lose their way; they become unemployed or homeless or engage in antisocial activities. Globally, many young people lack access to health care, or develop mental health conditions. Some young people engage in excesses including alcohol abuse, illicit drug use, or other reckless behaviour.

So how do you find the correct balance between the desires for independence and experimentation and the need for security and good health?

Debate this point in class before undertaking the listening activity that follows.

Exam tip

Paper 2

Remember that listening is part of Paper 2
This paper assesses receptive skills (reading and listening)

At Standard Level this paper is 1 hour 45 minutes in total.

The listening comprehension is 45 minutes and is worth 25 marks.
There will be comprehension exercises on three audio passages.
The reading comprehension is 1 hour and is worth 40 marks.
There will be comprehension exercises on three reading texts.
Both the listening recordings and the reading texts are drawn from the five themes given in the Language B guide.

At Higher Level this paper is 2 hours in total.

The listening comprehension is 1 hour and is worth 25 marks.
There will be comprehension exercises on three audio passages.
The reading comprehension is 1 hour and is worth 40 marks.
There will be comprehension exercises on three reading texts.
Both the listening recordings and reading texts are drawn from the five themes given in the Language B guide. One of the HL reading text is literary.

Listening comprehension

Life balance – advice for young adults

Listen to a lifestyle counselor talking about how to get the best out of life and then answer the questions that follow.

Answer the following questions.

1. According to the speaker what is the main benefit of finding life balance?
2. According to the speaker how would you ensure that a social event contributes to your life balance?
3. Which two activities may cause young people to avoid thinking about any difficulties they might have?
4. What does the speaker suggest young people create in order to be more productive?
5. ***Choose the five statements made by the speaker in the broadcast.***

A. The speaker believes some people try to take on too many responsibilities.
B. At work it is important to focus on the tasks you really enjoy.
C. Physical exercise can be a way of avoiding problems.
D. Laughter can be a great medicine.
E. We should avoid making mistakes if we want to avoid stress.
F. A 10-minute break can be a great stress buster.
G. The speaker believes we should prioritise.
H. Taking a short break can help us to find new solutions to a difficulty.
I. Being bored is a sign of an unbalanced lifestyle.
J. The speaker is a great believer in multitasking.

Complete the sentences below with phrases from the recording.

6. If things become too much for you …
7. If you are a student you can always …
8. You can find a life balance and happiness if …
9. All individuals have different needs so …
10. The speaker thinks the advice will help young people…

HL extension HL

Listen to the recording again. This time find 6 individual guidelines or pieces of advice given by the speaker. Write your answers in column A. Then listen to the recording and find any examples mentioned by the speaker. Note: Not all the guidelines have examples.

	(A) Guidelines/ advice	(B) Examples		(A) Guidelines/ advice	(B) Examples
1			4		
2			5		
3			6		

Oral activity: Presentation

You have been asked to deliver a presentation to the graduating year group of your school. The title is "Five lessons for life after high school".

Here are 16 lifestyle tips from an article written for Elite magazine. Choose the five most important points to create a five-minute presentation for your fellow IB students. Once you have selected the most relevant ideas to use, apply them to this new context and audience: how to handle their lives as adults

How To Live The Good Life

Living the good life can mean something different for everyone. However, there is still a general understanding as what this idea entails to most human beings living in the modern world. The good life, in its most simple form, is a series of never ending satisfaction that only grows more powerful as time goes on.

Here are several simple ways to live the good life.

1. Slow Down

Urgency and haste instantly diminish accuracy, awareness and happiness. There is a big difference between getting things done and getting things done effectively.

2. Appreciate Life's Simple Pleasures

The best things in life truly are free. From a quiet ocean sunset to sleeping in on a rainy day, life's greatest simple pleasures can only be appreciated if you notice them.

3. Foster and Nurture Relationships

Appreciate relationships and treat your friends as you would like to be treated.

4. Learn About Different Things

Every day is a chance to learn something new about the life you wish to attain or the person you wish to become. Keep inquiring and exploring.

5. Concentrate on Your Passions

Your passion is what you love to do every day because it gives you a sense of worth and fulfilment. Use your passion in the most productive and universal way possible.

6. Travel to Distant Places

Humanity has been blessed with a beautiful place to live. Experience all the natural and cultural wonders it has to offer.

7. Talk to Strangers

Meet new people who are like you and different from you in every way you could have imagined. Understanding these people will increase your knowledge of how the world works and the people in it.

8. Assist Others

What goes around comes around. You have no idea what type of fulfilment and security you will attain for yourself after you help other people more and more.

9. Be Clear on Your Goals

You will never get where you want to go if you don't know what you want and don't think you have what it takes to get it.

10. Practice General Time Management

Trying to achieve your goals without doing a little time planning is like sailing the open ocean without a compass and map. Sure it's fun but at the end of the day you need to remember why you are out there in the first place.

11. Be Spontaneous

Be spontaneous and step outside of your comfort zone at any chance you get. Experience new things that you may have been afraid of but always wanted to try for your own personal satisfaction.

12. Keep Your Promises

Stay true to your word as that is what your character is based off of and how you will always be remembered.

13. Work Hard

Being lazy and doing the bare minimum only guarantees dissatisfaction. Work hard to get closer and closer towards your goal every day.

14. Sleep Well

A tired mind is inefficient and unhappy. No one can perform to the best of their ability without rest.

15. Laugh

Stop taking life so seriously and realize that everything that makes you nervous or uncomfortable may really just be there to make you laugh.

16. Be Here Now

Right now is the time that you can use however you want to. Right now is life. Don't miss it. It is an entire world waiting to be shaped by your own desires.

Preston Waters | Elite.
http://elitedaily.com/life/motivation/live-good-life/

Brainstorming

Select the five ideas you wish to use and adapt. Choose the most important points to create a five-minute presentation for your fellow IB students. If necessary, alter the points so they are relevant to graduating high school students. Expand each point with examples and explanations relevant to your audience. It may be useful to think of role models past and present who exemplify the points you are making.

Social skills ATLs

In group-work exercises like this you can learn to work effectively with others.

- Delegate and share responsibility for decision-making.
- Manage and resolve conflict, and work collaboratively in teams.
- Listen actively to other perspectives and ideas.
- Negotiate effectively.
- Build consensus and come to agreed conclusions.

Planning

Use this table again to plan and redraft your presentation.

Topic:	Examples and explanations
Introduction: Context and thesis statement	
Supporting idea 1	
Supporting idea 2	
Supporting idea 3	
Supporting idea 4	
Supporting idea 5	
Conclusion including a summary and a final thought	

Always rehearse and practice before giving your final presentation.

Internal assessment (SL)

Take a look at the visual stimulus below. The image relates to the theme of "Identities".

Brainstorming

In pairs, discuss and answer the following questions.

- What is the main idea in the photograph? How does it relate to the title of this section of the chapter: Lifestyles?
- What do you see in the photograph? What does this tell you about the location and context of the photograph?
- Look at the foreground of the photograph. Describe the person or people you can see.
- What is happening in the picture? How does the action relate to the title of this chapter: Fit for life?

Presenting

Based on your answers to the questions above, prepare a four-minute presentation on the photograph.

Remember that the presentation should not only include a description of the photograph, but should also connect it to the topic of celebrity and an Anglophone culture. Present your photograph and topic to your classmates. Remember that in the actual examination you will have 15 minutes to prepare your presentation.

Exam tip: Internal assessment (SL)

In these examples you have been given these bullet points to help you structure your ideas. In the actual Internal assessment you will only receive a visual stimulus with a heading. The heading will be one of the five themes of the Language B course:

- Identities
- Experiences
- Human ingenuity
- Social organization
- Sharing the planet

Peer assessment

Assess the presentations given by your classmates. Use the following criteria (available in the Language B guide) to guide your assessment:

	Internal assessment (SL)
Criterion A	Language
Criterion B	1. Message: visual stimulus 2. Message: Conversation
Criterion C	Interactive skills: communication

Suggest ways in which your classmates can improve their presentation techniques.

Internal assessment (HL)

Wear Sunscreen

Mary Theresa Schmich is an American journalist and columnist for the Chicago Tribune. She won the Pulitzer Prize in 2012. Her column, "Advice, like youth, probably just wasted on the young", was published in the Chicago Tribune on June 1, 1997. In the column's introduction, Schmich presented the essay as the graduation speech she would have given if she had been asked to give one. In the speech she recommends the wearing of sunscreen, and gives other information to help young people avoid the common pitfalls of adulthood. Baz Luhrmann later popularized the monologue by setting it to music.

Ladies and gentlemen of the class of '97: Wear sunscreen:

If I could offer you only one tip for the future, sunscreen would be it. The long-term benefits of sunscreen have been proved by scientists, whereas the rest of my advice has no basis more reliable than my own meandering experience. I will dispense this advice now.

Enjoy the power and beauty of your youth. Oh, never mind. You will not understand the power and beauty of your youth until they've faded. But trust me, in 20 years, you'll look back at photos of yourself and recall in a way you can't grasp now how much possibility lay before you and how fabulous you really looked.

You are not as fat as you imagine.

Don't worry about the future. Or worry, but know that worrying is as effective as trying to solve an algebra equation by chewing bubble gum.

The real troubles in your life are apt to be things that never crossed your worried mind, the kind that blind side you at 4 pm on some idle Tuesday.

Do one thing every day that scares you.

Sing.

Don't be reckless with other people's hearts. Don't put up with people who are reckless with yours.

Floss.

Don't waste your time on jealousy. Sometimes you're ahead, sometimes you're behind. The race is long and, in the end, it's only with yourself.

Remember compliments you receive. Forget the insults. If you succeed in doing this, tell me how.

Keep your old love letters. Throw away your old bank statements.

Stretch.

Don't feel guilty if you don't know what you want to do with your life. The most interesting people I know didn't know at 22 what they wanted to do with their lives. Some of the most interesting 40 year olds I know still don't know.

Get plenty of calcium. Be kind to your knees. You'll miss them when they're gone.

Maybe you'll marry, maybe you won't. Maybe you'll have children, maybe you won't. Maybe you'll divorce at 40, maybe you'll dance the funky chicken on your 75th anniversary. Whatever you do, don't congratulate yourself too much, or berate yourself either. Your choices are half chance. So are everybody else's.

Enjoy your body. Use it every way you can. Don't be afraid of it or of what other people think of it. It's the greatest instrument you'll ever own.

Dance, even if you have nowhere to do it but your living room.

Read the directions, even if you don't follow them.

Do not read beauty magazines. They will only make you feel ugly.

Get to know your parents. You never know when they'll be gone for good.

Be nice to your siblings. They're your best link to your past and the people most likely to stick with you in the future.

Understand that friends come and go, but with a precious few you should hold on.

Work hard to bridge the gaps in geography and lifestyle, because the older you get, the more you need the people who knew you when you were young.

Live in New York City once, but leave before it makes you hard.

Live in Northern California once, but leave before it makes you soft.

Travel.

Accept certain inalienable truths: Prices will rise. Politicians will philander. You, too, will get old.

And when you do, you'll fantasize that when you were young, prices were reasonable, politicians were noble, and children respected their elders. Respect your elders. Don't expect anyone else to support you. Maybe you have a trust fund. Maybe you'll have a wealthy spouse. But you never know when either one might run out.

Don't mess too much with your hair or by the time you're 40 it will look 85.

Be careful whose advice you buy, but be patient with those who supply it. Advice is a form of nostalgia. Dispensing it is a way of fishing the past from the disposal, wiping it off, painting over the ugly parts and recycling it for more than it's worth.

But trust me on the sunscreen.

Mary Theresa Schmich

Note

In your internal assessment, the literary extract will not exceed 300 words. You will be shown two, one from each of the works of literature studied in class.

Brainstorming

In small groups, discuss the following questions then summarize your discussion in point form.

- What is the context, and audience for the speech?
- What is the speaker's purpose in giving the speech?
- What aspects of adulthood does the speaker discuss? Give examples.
- Is this speech effective? Identify two of the ideas used by the speaker to convince you. Use quotes to support your ideas.
- Which of the speaker's pieces of advice can you most learn from? Justify and explain your answers.

Presenting

Based on your answers to the questions above, prepare a four-minute presentation on the extract.

Remember that the presentation should not only include answers to questions, but should also focus, as much as possible, only on the extract lifestyle. Make your presentation to your classmates. Remember that in the actual examination you will have 20 minutes to prepare your presentation.

Students listening to the presentation should prepare individual questions about the text. They can put these questions to you at the end of your presentation.

Peer assessment

Assess the presentations given by your classmates. Use the following criteria from the Language B guide to guide your assessment:

	Internal assessment (HL)
Criterion A	Language
Criterion B	1. Message: literary extract 2. Message: Conversation
Criterion C	Interactive skills: communication

Suggest ways in which your classmates can improve their presentation techniques.

Paper 1 (HL/SL) practice

Choose one of the tasks below and write between 250 and 400 words (SL)/ 450 and 600 words (HL).

Here are three opportunities to practice writing for Paper 1.

Once you have planned your text, write a first draft.

1. You are worried about the lifestyle and wellbeing of a friend from another school. The friend seems to spend far too much time on the Internet and does not seem to be getting any exercise. Choose one of the text types below to show your concern and offer some practical advice.

   a) Email   b) A set of instructions   c) A personal letter

2. It is exam time at your school and you are feeling suitably nervous about the upcoming tests. You decide that you need to speak to a good friend about the anxiety that you are feeling. This friend is known for being both sensible and empathetic. Choose one of these three text types to communicate your thoughts and feelings.

   a) A personal letter   b) Email   c) Blog

3. In your English class you recently had a debate whose theme was "In the adult world money is the only true measure of happiness and fulfillment". The debate came to some interesting conclusions. Write to a friend describing the debate, its conclusions and your reactions to them. Choose one of these three text types to express your point of view on this matter.

   a) Interview   b) A personal letter   c) Email

Conclusion to research question C

How do we become healthy and fulfilled adults?

1. Now that you have completed the section, what do you now think is the answer?
2. To what extent have your opinions on the subject changed since the beginning of this chapter? To what extent have your opinions remained the same?
3. What conclusions have you come to in this section?

Note

The practice tasks on the left represent what you should expect in Paper 1. As you can see, you have to choose a text type from a list of three given for each task. To choose your text type:

1. determine the purpose of the task
2. identify your audience
3. understand the context of the task.

Then choose a text type that helps you address those three: purpose, audience, and context. Failing to do so may result in losing marks in Criterion C: Conceptual understanding.

Self-management skills ATLs

Remember your written work will be assessed against three criteria:

- Criterion A:language
- Criterion B: message
- Criterion C: conceptual understanding

(including audience, context and purpose).

How well do you understand these criteria?

Make sure you have a copy of the relevant assessment criteria for either SL or HL writing (Paper 1).

Assess your writing against these criteria. In this way you can see what you have achieved and what you need to do next to move to the next band of achievement

For example, you score a "6" in criterion B: message. Examine the criterion and ask yourself, "What must I do to reach band 7/8?" .

Conclusion to the chapter

What ideas and images do we associate with a healthy lifestyle?

When we began the chapter, you debated this research question. Look back at your notes. Now that you have completed the chapter, answer the following questions.

1. Now that you have completed the chapter, what are your conclusions about the research question?
2. To what extent have your opinions on the subject changed since the beginning of this chapter?

Justify your answers.

Beyond the classroom

CAS

Experience 1 Creativity and activity: Using text types: informal letters, emails and presentations

In your everyday lives you will have plenty of chances for practising writing informal emails and, maybe, letters. You can, however, use the information in this chapter to help you to create personal correspondence that is both fun to read and accurate.

That chapter has also given you advice on creating presentations. In the course of your DP studies you will probably have to make presentations in many of your other DP subjects. Use the techniques you have learned here and transfer them to your other subjects. You may also need to do presentations as part of your involvement in social service curricular subjects. This way the skills that you have learnt in English B will help you to succeed in other areas of your life.

Experience 2 Ideas for service

Conduct a survey in your class to see which problems are the most common among young people.

Common teenage problems		
A relationship break-up	Having an argument	Working while attending school
Alcohol or drug use	Health problems in the family	Chronic allergies
Arrival of a new family member	Outstanding personal achievement	Confusion of sexual identity
Change in responsibilities at home	Parents' unemployment	Dating someone new
Change of residence	Personal injury or illness	Death of a loved one
Changes due to puberty	Sleeping less than eight hours per night	Divorce of parents
Changing a course of study	Trouble with grades	Excessive studying
Changing school	Visitors in the home	Financial worries
		Getting pregnant or causing pregnancy

Present your findings do your class. Think about measures that might help students to deal with these issues. You might like to discuss your findings and conclusions with your student counselors and see if there are any additional measures the school can take to help students facing some of the most common problems.

Suggested reading

The Woman Warrior by Maxine Hong Kingston

The Catcher in the Rye by J D Salinger

Wintergirls by Laurie Halse Anderson

It's a funny kind of story by Ned Vizzini

The Curious Incident of the Dog in the Nighttime by Mark Haddon

The Fault in Our Stars by John Green

The Running Dream by Wendelin Van Draanen

2 EXPERIENCES
SKETCHING OUR LIVES!

Chapter summary

Theme

Experiences

Topics

- Migration
- Leisure activities
- Holidays and travel

Research question for the chapter

How would travelling to or living in another culture affect my worldview?

Additional research questions

A How is migration different from immigration? And what is the difference between migration, immigration and asylum seeking?

B To what extent does travelling improve our cultural tolerance?

C Are leisure activities similar across Anglophone cultures?

TOK question

To what extent does human activity affect language?

Communication skills

Listening skills

- Receptive
- Interactive

Oral and interactive skills

- Receptive: listening to a report/listening to presentations
- Productive: presenting to classmates
- Interactive: debate

Written text types

- Travel blogs
- Personal blogs
- Diary entries

Research question for this chapter:

How would travelling to or living in another culture affect my worldview?

1. What are your first thoughts and reactions to the question above?
2. What justifications would you give for your answer?
3. What more would you need to know before you can come to a definitive conclusion about the question?

What, in your opinion, do these images represent? Which human experiences do they highlight?

Get into four groups. Each group should choose one of the images above. Summarize what you see in your chosen image and relate it to human experience. Compile a list of words and expressions.

Thinking and communication skills ATLs

This activity involves reflection, higher-order thinking in the form of creation and the ability to express yourself in a coherent and persuasive manner.

Section A: Migration

How is migration different from immigration? And what is the difference between migration, immigration, and asylum seeking?

1. What are your first thoughts and reactions to the question above?
2. What justifications would you give for your answers?
3. What more would you need to know before you can come to a definitive conclusion about the statement?

Before you read

In groups, list some ideas and/or activities that fall under "experiences".

Brainstorm a list of at least five questions about how and why your listed ideas or activities are considered experiences.

Write a definition of what you think experiences are.

Mingle with members of other groups before you get back into your own group and report what the other groups think experiences mean.

Reflect on your definition based on what you have learned from other groups before you produce a final definition for "experiences".

Share your final definition with the class. How similar or different are different groups' definitions?

i: The Benefits and Challenges of Urbanization

By A. Renee Hutcherson

Urbanization is inevitable due to technological advances and an increasing population. Industrialization allows people to make a living in methods other than farming; this has led to many people abandoning the rural lifestyle. Urbanization is a process that is occurring in nearly every part of the world inhabited by humans. It has led to a greater quality of life for many, but it also has its challenges.

Definition

Urbanization is the process of increasing population growth in cities and suburbs; it also includes the increase of industrialization. There is more involvement in government, industry and trade in urban areas. The word urbanization derives from "urb," which is the Latin word for city. The United States and Europe had the majority of urbanization occur during the Industrial Revolution in the 19th century. There is no universal standard of how urbanized areas are classified. In America, an urbanized area has a population of at least 50,000.

Causes

Living in a rural area provides less job opportunities. Farming is one of the major forms of income in rural areas. The unpredictable nature of environmental factors, such as rain and drought, leads to a fluctuating income. The standard of living is difficult to improve; therefore, families opt to move to urban areas. There is a greater variety of jobs in cities. Lack of space in rural areas due to a growing population also leads to urbanization.

Benefits

The convenience of goods and services is one of the benefits of urbanization. There is access to more educational and medical services, which allows increased literacy and better health. There is also less use of personal vehicles and more availability of public transportation. There is more social integration in urbanized areas. People of different religions, ethnic backgrounds, social classes and races reside in the same area. This leads to more understanding and acceptance of differences. Another benefit of urbanization is the possibility of greater earning potential because of the availability of more jobs.

Challenges

The rapidity of growth in urbanized areas is a challenge. Although there are more opportunities, the constantly increasing population leads to more competition. This leads to large numbers of people that are out of work and extremely poor. Pollution is an issue that plagues many urbanized areas. Factories and vehicles emit fumes into the air, which may lead to respiratory issues. The development of more areas to build houses and businesses negatively affects the environment. The destruction of habitats displaces many animals. It may also be difficult to finance the increase of an urbanized area due to its rapid growth.

http://classroom.synonym.com/advantages-disadvantages-of-rural-urban-migration-12084349.html

ii: Advantages and Disadvantages of Rural-Urban Migration

by Ocean Malandra

A hundred years ago, only 20 percent of the world's population lived in urban areas, but the 20th century saw a dramatic shift that marks a turning point in history. Today, more people live in cities than in rural areas, and urbanization continues to grow around the world. According to the World Bank, city living is much more efficient in a variety of ways. It's easier to provide services when people live closer together. However, cities also change the way that humans interact with each other and the environment, often causing multiple problems.

[11] When families move into urban areas, they automatically place themselves in closer proximity to basic services such as hospitals and schools — urbanization often brings health care and educational opportunities to those who might not have had access to them in rural areas. Cities also offer public transportation, government run sanitation services and social programs such as libraries, health clinics and children's programs. For many people, especially in developing countries, access to these services offers many advantages in terms of creating opportunities.

[12] As large-scale agriculture displaces many traditional farmers from the rural lifestyle, the tremendous growth of modern industry in large urban areas attracts people with the promise of employment. In general, urban wages are significantly higher, so moving to the city is an opportunity to earn that was impossible in rural areas. However, the wage difference is often offset by the higher cost of living and absence of self-produced goods, including subsistence farming.

[13] Those who move from rural areas to urban ones sometimes find themselves living in shanty towns or slum areas. These new city residents are faced with problems that do not exist in the countryside: street crime, including gangs, as well as social inequality and discrimination. The urban poor struggle to make a living, even if they do earn more than they did in rural areas, because the cost of city life is significantly higher and the opportunities to produce their own food and other basic necessities are greatly reduced.

[14] Traffic congestion and industrial manufacturing, prominent features of the urban landscape, also take their toll on the natural environment and those who depend on it. A lack of clean water is a major problem among the urban poor in major cities around the world, as is air pollution from both cars and factory emissions. In fact, according to an article in the "British Medical Journal," almost 10 percent of the world's disease burden is now caused by pollution and contamination, and the number is significantly higher among the poor in developing countries. For many, and especially those who moved to urban areas for opportunity, city living proves deadly in ways not known in the countryside.

Conceptual understanding: Context

As stated in the *Language B guide*, students should understand that language should be appropriate to the situation in which one is communicating.

- How does the situation or setting influence the production or reception of a text?
- How is the relationship between the producer and the recipient(s) of a text (or the relationship of interlocutors in a conversation) reflected in language use?

1. In groups discuss the following in relation to the texts on pages 43 to 45.
   - What is the purpose of each text?
   - Who are the writers of these texts? Whose perspective do they represent: an organization (private, not-for-profit, governmental) or a personal perspective? Visit the website "People of our everyday life" to get a better understanding of the context of production.
   - Who do you think is the audience of each text? How does the writer address this audience? What language is used: formal, semi-formal or informal? How do you know?

2. Write a brief statement that summarizes your discussion. In your statement, define "context" in your own words and mention how purpose, writer and audience affect and are affected by the context of a written piece.

Reading comprehension

Read the texts on pages 43–45 and underline all the words that you do not know.

In groups of four:

- Group those words in four categories: noun, adjective, adverb and other.
- Re-examine how those words are used in the texts. Can you guess what they mean?
- From your list, identify the 10 most challenging words. Use those words to design a vocabulary matching exercise similar to the one on page 61.
- Swap your exercise with another group. How many words in the other group's list did you get right?
- Reflect on the experience. What advice would you give your fellow students on how to approach understanding the use of vocabulary in a text?

Text i

1. To what does "this" (line 2) refer?
2. What agencies are felt more noticeably in cities?
3. What is the main reason why people choose to leave their rural lifestyle?
4. The text lists several advantages and disadvantages to urbanization. Create a table with one column for advantages and another for disadvantages.

Choose the correct phrases from the text to complete the following sentences.

5. A growing populace means that …
6. Urbanization in the Western world was noticeable …
7. Categorizing urbanized areas is subject to …
8. The income of families in rural areas is not stable as a result of …
9. An increasing population in rural areas results in …
10. Urbanized areas have better education and health because …

Text ii

Match the headings below with the paragraphs in the text.

11. ☐ 12. ☐ 13. ☐ 14. ☐

A. A better economy
B. A better education
C. An early death
D. Health and human services
E. Inequality, crime and poverty
F. Job opportunities
G. Pollution and contamination
H. Social discrimination among the poor

To whom or to what do the following words or phrases refer?

15. themselves (line 7)
16. them (line 9)
17. ones (line 18)
18. these new city residents (line 19)
19. they (line 21)
20. their (line 25)

Texts i and ii

Which words go in the gaps? Choose the words from the box below.

21. ___________ texts outline the advantages and disadvantages of urbanization in relation to economic, security and social factors. Text i, **22.** ___________ puts some emphasis on the reasons for urbanization, which is lacking in text ii. Both texts emphasize the challenges of moving from a rural area into an urban one, **23.** ___________ text ii presents those challenges in a gloomier manner. **24.** ___________, one may get a better sense of the negative effects of urbanization **25.** ___________ reading that text.

alternatively	both	consequently	in contrast	prior to
and	but	however	individual	when

Internal assessment (SL)

Split into two groups.

One group focuses on the benefits of urbanization while the other considers the disadvantages of urbanization.

Research more about your assigned topic. You might consider splitting your big group into smaller groups, with each researching one advantage or disadvantage.

Prepare a role-play scenario that explains your assigned topic and present it to the whole class.

Take a look at the visual stimulus here. The image relates to the chapter theme of "Experiences".

Notes

Stuart Hall, co-founder of British Cultural Studies, developed a theory of encoding and decoding media texts. In Professor Hall's theory, audiences can have three different reactions to a media text, whether it be a film, an image or a newspaper article:

- Dominant or preferred reading: how the director/creator wants the audience to view the media text
- Opposition reading: when the audience rejects the preferred reading, and creates their own meaning of the text
- Negotiated reading: a compromise between the dominant and opposition readings, where the audience accepts parts of the director's views, but has their own views on parts as well.

Which of those approaches have you adopted? Why?

Brainstorming

In pairs, discuss the following questions.

1. What, in your opinion, is the purpose of the photograph? Justify your answer.
2. How does the photograph make you feel? Connect your feelings to the perceived benefits and disadvantages of urbanization that you researched earlier.
   - Which direction of thought is the image inviting you to take? Do you agree with the direction?

Presenting

Based on your answers to the questions above, prepare a four-minute presentation on the photograph.

Remember that the presentation should not only include a description of the photograph, but should also connect it to the theme "experiences" and the topic of "migration".

Peer assessment

In groups of four, give feedback to your classmates on their presentations. Use the Project Zero "Ladder of feedback" to structure your comments.

Clarify: Were there aspects of the presentation that you don't believe you have understood?

Value: What did you see in the presentation that you find to be particularly impressive, innovative, strong?

Offer concerns or issues: Did you detect some potential problems or challenges within the presentation? Do you disagree with some part of the presentation?

Suggest: Do you have suggestions on how to address the concerns you identified above?

Internal assessment (HL)

Read the following extract from an immigrant's journal.

http://teacher.scholastic.com/activities/asian-american/angel_island/chapter7.htm

Growing Up in Oakland

Li Keng Wong

We lived in Oakland's Chinatown from 1933 to 1948. Chinatown was a small enclave of four square blocks. Like us, most of the Chinese living here spoke the Toishan dialect because they came from the Pearl River Delta of Guangdong Province in southern China.

We attended American school and concentrated on learning English.

All the children in our neighborhood attended Lincoln Grammar School, a school within walking distance from Chinatown. The student body was made up of mostly Chinese, some Caucasians and a few Japanese. The students spoke Chinese and English. The new immigrants were put in limited-English proficiency classes and received extra help. Sister Li Hong and I were assigned to these classes. Slowly we started to learn English.

We attended Chinese school after American school each day. We had very little time to play or to get into mischief. There was very little money during the Depression years. Even though life was hard, we loved being Americans.

Although we were now Americans, we did not know many Caucasian Americans except for the teachers at school. We socialized with the other Chinese Americans in Chinatown. Chinese Americans were not allowed to buy property in certain areas of Oakland because of racial prejudice. We were also not allowed to do certain jobs like law enforcement, government work, and many professions. Because of these restrictions, many Chinese opened restaurants, grocery stores, and laundries.

Asian children wait at Angel Island

My father was one of those people. During World War II, my father opened a restaurant in Oakland's Chinatown. We children all worked in that restaurant — from waiting on tables to mopping the floor. We never got paid because, as a family business, we worked to make the restaurant succeed. The entire family worked seven days a week. Our hard work paid off when in 1948 we were able to purchase a home outside of Chinatown.

Thinking skills ATLs

This type of assessment is directly connected to metacognition as it helps you to reflect on the benchmarks used in the internal assessment, develop your understanding of the assessment criteria, reflect on performance and aim to improve it.

Brainstorming

In groups answer the following questions.

- What is the difference between migration and immigration?
- What does this difference mean in relation to the benefits and disadvantages outlined in the texts on pages 44–45?
- Define immigration in your own words, taking into consideration your responses to the two questions above.
- Find images that best represent your definition of immigration and explain them to your classmates.

In groups of four, discuss the following questions then summarize your discussion in point form.

- What is the purpose of the literary text?
- Who, do you think, is its intended audience?
- What is the context?
- How does the author illustrate his experience as an immigrant?
- What variety of English is used in the text? How appropriate is its use?

Presenting

Prepare a four-minute presentation about the excerpt in which you focus on the content of the text and connect it to the questions you discussed earlier.

Self-management skills ATLs

This is an effective formative assessment tool that will help you to reflect on your performance in order to improve it. The purpose of peer assessment is to help you to reflect on the feedback given from your peers and use it to improve your presentation skills.

Peer assessment

In groups of four, give feedback to your classmates on their presentations. Use the Project Zero "Ladder of feedback" to structure your comments.

Clarify: Are there aspects of this work that you don't believe you have understood?

Value: What do you see in this work that you find to be particularly impressive, innovative, strong?

Offer concerns or issues: Do you detect some potential problems or challenges within the work? Do you disagree with some part of the work?

Suggest: Do you have suggestions on how to address the concerns you identified above?

Paper 1: Personal blog

The *Language B Guide* defines personal, professional and mass media texts as follows.

Personal texts

Personal texts are shared by the person creating the message and an audience who may be family members, friends or groups with a common interest; a personal text may also be directed to oneself. Personal texts tend to be characterized by attention to the everyday interests or the affective needs of individuals rather than the analysis of information. Personal texts have a variety of functions, including but not limited to: describing, narrating, entertaining, recommending, persuading. The level of formality in the register of these texts will vary according to linguistic and socio-cultural norms of the target language.

Professional texts

Professional texts are created for an intended audience in contexts where no personal relationship is assumed between the producer of the text and the recipient(s); however, the producer of the text can assume that the recipient(s) will have an interest in receiving and understanding the message. Professional texts tend to be characterized by attention to the cognitive needs of individuals, the transfer of knowledge and the logical presentation of information; thus, these texts employ clear, factual language and a formal register. Professional texts have a variety of functions, including but not limited to: informing, instructing, explaining, analysing, convincing, interpreting, evaluating.

Mass media texts

Mass media texts are created for distribution to a large audience that is targeted because of an interest that, at least initially, lies primarily with the producer of the text, since the person or entity responsible for a mass media text has no way of knowing exactly who will take the time and interest to understand the message or possibly ignore it. Mass media texts tend to be characterized by the need of the producer of the text to project authority, desirability or exclusivity, and the conscious choice of a particular medium or technology that is appropriate to reach the targeted audience. The level of formality in the register of these texts will vary according to linguistic and socio-cultural norms of the target language.

– *English B Guide*, International Baccalaureate Organization, 2017, p.19

A blog entry, depending on its purpose and audience, falls under all three categories. A blog can be a sort of online diary. The main difference is that while a diary is essentially private, you write a blog so that your readers can read it.

Structure

A blog could be a narrative-driven blog, a straightforward account of what you have done. This kind of blog focuses on narrating clearly a set of events such as an excursion or an important event in the life of the blogger. Alternatively, your blog may focus on something that you have experienced, for example, a sporting event, a wedding or concert.

However, bloggers often write because they have a particular point of view that they wish to get across to the public. In that respect, a blog can be like an essay. Therefore, this kind of blog may use the same conventions such as a thesis, structured as paragraphs with topic sentences related to the thesis and a final thought or conclusion. Such a thesis-driven blog can be much more informative or opinionated.

Both blog types share one important aspect: **reflection**. You write a blog because you want to communicate something to your readers, therefore, you should make your voice heard even if you are writing a thesis-driven blog. Your opinions, reflections and feelings should be conveyed to the reader.

	Narrative-driven blog	Thesis-driven blog
Focus	Events	Ideas and opinions
Organization	Chronological account of events	A reasoned argument
Opening	Beginning of the events	Thesis/main idea
Main paragraphs	Different parts of the story with description, explanation and thoughts (reflections)	Ideas to support your main idea: point, examples and explanations with reflections
Ending	Final thought and reflections	Final thought, conclusion and reflections

Writing to an audience

Your target audience will be those people who share your interests or ideas. When you write your blog, you should address your audience directly and ask your readers to respond to your ideas. The blog will appear on the Internet and is therefore public. You will have to use more formal language than you would use in a diary, but keep it personal nonetheless. Your voice should be dominant.

Tone and style

Normally you would write a narrative-driven blog using the past tense. It is also a good idea to join your sentences using time connectives. You can be quite chatty and informal in your use of language. It is useful to include descriptive detail of events and write some thoughts and reflections. To achieve this, you need to use imaginative language. When writing about conversations, you can use reported speech.

A thesis-driven blog is still likely more subjective and contains more descriptive detail than an essay; it is a more personal form of writing in which you can offer your reflections and describe your reactions in a fairly informal manner.

How is a blog entry structured? Look at the following example.

Being a teenager in Singapore: 19-year-old Kiwi Jake on what it's really like

6 August, 2014

So you're about to move to Singapore?

Here's my perspective on being a teenager in Singapore.

> Addressing the audience–can you guess who the audience of this blog is?

I lived in Singapore from the age of 0 to the age of 14, spending time at a local kindergarten, then onto Chatsworth International School and the Australian International School. I desperately wanted to leave Singapore to go to Christ's College in Christchurch, a boarding school in New Zealand, where I spent my last four years of school. However, my experience of being a teenage in Singapore luckily didn't end there, as throughout my last years of high school, I was lucky enough to come back here every school holiday. I was living the best of both worlds.

> Ensuring the blog is personal

> Providing background information to set the scene. Which type of blog is this?

Okay, so you may think that because I didn't technically live here for the majority of my teen years that I may not have the best judgement of this city. You're wrong (I hope). I may not know about spending high-school here, or know anything about school programs such as the International Baccalaureate (yes I did have to Google how to spell it), or IGCSSCSCSSE (I think that's the correct acronym?), but what knowledge I lack in schooling in Singapore, I make up for in the social side of the nation. And that's the most important part (sorry parents).

> Reflection that is applied

> Maintaining awareness of the audience through the use of the second-person pronoun, maintaining the personal aspect through the use of "I".

First of all, we'll get the negatives about being a teenager in Singapore out of the way.

It has happened to me too many times to count: you make a good friend, then the next thing you know, their parents get another job back home or in another country. It sucks. However, it's easy to keep in contact with friends these days, and no doubt they, or you, will be visiting each other in no time. Plus, there are always new people arriving in Singapore all the time, so there's no shortage of potential besties to choose from... The weather can get quite intense. It's either hot and humid, or raining cats and dogs. Then again, you do get some great days where you feel like you're in Thailand, so don't plan to do anything weather-related a week in advance. Your plans could be ruined in a matter of minutes.

> Is the type of blog clearer?

And now to the good stuff about being a teenager in Singapore:

It is safe to be out at night. According to the Straits Times, Singapore's crime rate is at a 29-year low. Considering Singapore has an already low crime rate, you can be assured that you would be very unlucky something crime-worthy

> Explaining the disadvantages. Without the use of personal language and a somewhat informal register, the blog is structured like an essay. To make a thesis-driven blog read like one, always ensure that you use the first person singular "I" and that your register is not too formal.

happening to you. This means you can safely get the bus or train home late at night (before 12:30, or whatever your curfew might be), without really worrying about anything...

Another positive is the people you meet. Yes they come and go, but with Facebook and Skype, it's pretty easy to keep in contact with people you meet. These people aren't just any people; they're friends who you connect with that share the bond of moving away from their home country...

Explaining the advantages. Without the use of personal language and a somewhat informal register, the blog is structured like an essay. To make a thesis-driven blog read like one, always ensure that you use the first person singular "I" and that your register is not too formal.

A huge positive to Singapore is the small size. You can get anywhere in the country in a relatively quick time (depending on traffic), and there is cheap public transport everywhere. It costs you a maximum $2.80 to get from one side of the country to the other. This means you don't have an excuse to go meet up with your new mates; so get off the computer and socialize!

Emphasising point of view in the conclusion

As you can see, the positives completely outweigh the negatives. Living in Singapore as a teenager is great. It may get frustrating at times, but I can guarantee that when you leave this place, you will miss it a whole lot. You'll be back here on holiday in no time!

Writing activity

Context: Your family moved from a rural area to the city when you were a child. You recently sat with your grandfather who explained to you how the move has affected the whole family. Your task is to explain this migration to the general public.

How to approach the task

Your first step is to determine the following:

- What is the purpose of the written piece?
- Who is your audience?
- Which type of text best helps you achieve the purpose?

In the following exercise, you will write a blog entry. Refer to the texts on pages 4 and 16 to help you formulate ideas in relation to the context above.

Brainstorming

In pairs:

1. Choose a focal point that you want to explore in your blog. Will you write a narrative-driven or a thesis-driven blog?
2. Generate ideas to be used in your blog.
3. Organize your ideas by theme or topic.
4. Choose a stance and approach to take in your blog.

Planning

In pairs:

- **Decide how you will grab your audience's attention.** What should appear in your introduction? What is your conclusion? Connect your introduction and conclusion to the stance and approach you have chosen.
- **Decide the tone and style of your blog.** Do you know who your audience is? What is the best way to address this audience?
- **Decide how you are going to order your subtopics.** Which should go first? Which should appear last? What should appear in the middle? Does your chosen order ensure that your ideas will be coherent and your writing will flow smoothly?

Drafting

Individually write a draft of the body of your blog.

When you are done, revise this draft – does it make sense?

Add your introduction and your conclusion to the body. Re-read what you have written. Do the transitions make sense? Are your paragraphs well connected? How interesting is your blog? Did you maintain a connection with your audience? Is your blog personal?

Write an eye-catching title to invite people to read your blog entry.

Re-read the complete draft of your blog entry for the last time. Make any necessary changes.

Listening comprehension

Click the icon to practice the listening section of Paper 2. After you have listened to an audio track you will complete an accompanying activity. In this activity you will practice identifying true statements. Before you listen, read the statements very carefully to make sure you understand what each statement means.

Paper 1 practice

Choose one of the tasks below and write between 250 and 400 words (SL) or 450 and 600 words (HL).

Task 1: You have witnessed an act of cruelty against animals. Use a public platform to express your outrage.

Letter | Speech | Blog

Task 2: You believe human experiences are shaped by diversity, and would like to explain this belief to friends and followers.

Text message | Blog | Diary

Task 3: This picture has gone viral on social networks and it disturbed you greatly. You would like to share the reasons for your concern with other social network subscribers.

Blog | Talk | Journal

Self-management skills ATLs

One of the main tenets of self-management is affective skills. By reflecting on what you have learned and what you still need to learn, you will develop mindfulness by being aware of the issue at hand and focusing intently and solely on that issue.

Conclusion to research question A

How is migration different from immigration? And what is the difference between migration, immigration and asylum seeking?

- Now that you have completed this section what are your thoughts and reactions to the question above?
- What justifications would you give for your answers?
- What more would you need to know before you can come to a definitive conclusion about the statement?

A TOK moment TOK

Migration and Language Contact

Migration is not a new phenomenon and it isn't always motivated by war. Some migration is motivated by natural disaster, as things like tsunamis, volcanic eruptions, earthquakes, or floods destroy homes and livelihoods requiring people to flee to safer locations, sometimes permanently. In other cases, people may be required to move by a government or through the acquisition of their lands by private businesses (legitimately or illegitimately). It may be the case that "development" - the building of dams or the creation of new towns and cities - may displace a population. Migrations of peoples from long ago have largely shaped our understanding of what the "native" languages of a region are. If you go back far enough, almost everybody came from somewhere else. The movement of English, Spanish, and French speakers across the Atlantic from Europe to the Americas, for example, has drastically changed the language ecologies of the Western hemisphere. More recent and smaller migrations have further shaped the linguistic environments in which we live as well.

Whatever the cause, the movement of people also means the movement of languages from their original geographic locations to new locations and to new language ecologies. Where once users of the language may have been in contact with speakers of a specific set of other languages, in the new context, they are interacting with a very different configuration of speakers and their languages.

These changes in the linguistic environment, studied by linguists as "contact linguistics" and by sociolinguists as "language ecology", result in changes in the languages themselves. Look at the influence that Spanish is having on English in contact zones in North America, for example, and perhaps even more obviously, that English is having on Spanish in both border areas and urban centers.

As we think about the influx of refugees and safety-seekers in Europe, we can expect to see some significant modifications in the language repertoires of the migrants as Arabic speakers learn German and French and English, as their children may become more proficient in those second languages than they are in their mother-tongue (and certainly more proficient than their parents and grandparents), and as the vocabulary and structure of both the Arabic and the German that the migrants speak is altered by the new kinds and increased level of contact between a variety of different languages.

These contact phenomena touch on the well-known and oft-studied feature of linguistic variation and the implications of that variation for language identification. When is a contact variety so altered by the influence of a second language that it might no longer be considered to be the same language as the more standard variety spoken in the homeland? We often see references in the press to contact varieties that are the result of longer-term contact between different languages, varieties such as Spanglish, Franglish, Singlish (Singaporean English), Manglish (Malay-English), and other hybridized "dialects" which may at some point be judged to be so different from "standard" English as to be identified as separate languages (much like Spanish, French, and Italian split off from Vulgar Latin centuries ago).

https://www.ethnologue.com/ethnoblog/m-paul-lewis/migration-and-language-contact

Read the article on how migration affects the evolution of language.

Think of examples that support the article's argument(s) in your own language. Think of examples that refute it.

In groups of four, discuss the following questions.

1. How has immigration affected English? Give specific examples to support your answer.
2. Do you think any language has escaped the effects of migration mentioned in the article? Do some basic research to support your answer.
3. How do the arguments in the article affect our understanding of the role language, as a way of knowing?

Section B: Holidays and travel

Research question B:

To what extent does travelling improve our cultural tolerance?

1. What are your first thoughts and reactions to the question above?
2. What justifications would you give for your answers?
3. What more would you need to know before you can come to a definitive conclusion about the statement?

Before you read

Individually, what ideas do you associate with the phrase "meaningful travel"?

In pairs, discuss any questions or elements of this topic that puzzle you.

In groups, decide the best way to explore this topic to answer your questions.

Now read the following text on meaningful travel then decide if it answers any of your questions or just provides more puzzles.

How to Make Your Travel Meaningful

by Dave and Deb

Today we are appearing on our favourite daytime talk show, The Social. We're joining the ladies at their Toronto studios to talk to them about meaningful travel. Many people feel that meaningful travel is strictly about going on a volunteering vacation, but there are many ways to make your travel meaningful and we're going to talk to them about it today. Dave and I have always added meaning into our travels. Be it traveling responsibly, raising money for a cause, stopping at sanctuaries or projects, and interacting with the locals, there are many ways to enrich your travels while making your life and other people's lives better.

What is "meaningful" travel?

To us, meaningful travel is when travel enriches your life in some way. That could be done by focusing on making your own life better by discovering and learning new things about the world and yourself. It can also be making the lives richer for the people you meet, the communities you visit and the environments you explore. Meaningful travel is about being aware of your footprint, and doing what you can to help the places that you visit.

When we started ThePlanetD we originally focused on changing our lives by cycling through Africa, but it evolved to helping others. We decided to ride for Plan Canada and raise funds and

awareness for the “Because I am a girl campaign.” We stopped at projects along the way to see the work they did and share it with our readers. The trip may have started with us wanting to do something epic in our travels, but it evolved to become a trip about discovery, education and helping others.

We’ve found that the more we learn about the world and the cultures we visit the more it enriches our lives. The more you give back, the more you feel fulfilled. When volunteering or helping others you expect nothing in return, but it ends up giving you so much. It is the greatest feeling to know that you are making the world a better place in your own little way.

How travel can be meaningful?

There are so many ways to make travel meaningful. While the first thought that comes to mind is to volunteer or to give money, thinking responsibly can make your travels more meaningful too. When we travel, we try to support the local economy by hiring local guides. When we land in a destination, we search for people who run their own companies and have their own small business. Just as we like to shop small and support small business in Canada, the same can be said for our travels. Small business makes the world go round and by shopping at local markets, hiring local guides and eating at small family run restaurants, you will be helping the economy of the place you visit and create a more meaningful travel experience for yourself. We have remained friends with many of our guides and had a more authentic local experience by keeping our travels local and away from the resorts and packaged tours.

Why meaningful travel is beneficial

Not only does it help the communities that you visit, it also helps you. We’ve always said that travel is the best education anyone could have. It breaks down barriers, and strips away prejudice. It opens people’s minds and when you come home, you pass on your thoughts, observations and feelings about the places you visit.

As Mark Twain said *“Travel is fatal to prejudice, bigotry, and narrow-mindedness, and many of our people need it sorely on these accounts. Broad, wholesome, charitable views of men and things cannot be acquired by vegetating in one little corner of the earth all one’s lifetime.”*

So much of meaningful travel helps with sustainability too. When you volunteer or help with conservation, it keeps communities or wildlife reserves from being exploited. So much of meaningful travel is simply about being aware of your environment and respecting customs and culture.

Things to remember when considering “meaningful” travel…

- Think about your impact. How are you affecting the community you visit?
- Will you traveling there enrich their lives?
- Will you have the opportunity to experience the culture, nature, environment? Or will you be isolated and cut off from truly experiencing the destination?

Meaningful travel is not as daunting as people think

When it comes to adventure travel, we always say, start with baby steps. The same can be said when it comes to making your travels meaningful. It may be as easy as asking a local person at your destination where you can volunteer for a day, or where you can visit children or donate money to a school or organization.

Once you take that first step, you’ll learn and discover more opportunities.

Our first foray into more meaningful travel happened in 2003 in Cambodia. We were sitting on a beach and a man asked us if we could come to his class to speak English to his students for an afternoon. He said that while he can speak English, it helps to have the students hear a proper accent. It was one of the most fulfilling things we had ever done and it kick-started our desire to do something wherever we went.

Ways to Make your Travels Meaningful

Travel for a cause

When we did the Mongol Rally, we drove across 2 continents for the Christina Nobel Foundation, a foundation based in Mongolia that houses and educates orphaned and abandoned children. When cycling the continent of Africa we raised funds and awareness for **Plan Canada**. By being in the destinations, we could stop at projects and see where our money was going and how funds were being used. It gave our cause more of a purpose to put a human face to the charity. When we saw that they were benefitting directly from the money raised, we felt motivated to help more.

Visit a Charity

It's easy to find a project to help or visit when you are traveling. Talk to the local people and ask them for advice. In Sri Lanka, we met a tuk tuk driver named Ajith who became our friend. As we got to know him, we visited a charity that he started on his own to donate shoes to local school children. They'd otherwise be going to school bare foot in the jungle, but he raised funds to get them shoes and keeps working tirelessly to help the local economy.

Our guide Makau, in Kenya started a project to empower his own village. We visited his family and friends and he is working to bring water to his village, empower women and give them the means to go to school and he got them a cement maker to build a new school.

Going Local

Hire Local Guides and [-25-]. When we climbed to Mount Everest Base Camp, Mount Kilimanjaro, Gunung Batur, and Mount Kinabalu, we hired local guides after we arrived in the country. It's a great way to contribute to the local economy and to support small business and we made good friends doing it. We still [-26-] from Everest and Kili. Plus because we travelled with people from the area, they [-27-], were respectful of culture, and filled with information for us to learn about the destination.

Shop Local – Local artisans make their money through tourism. [-28-] at duty free or at your resort, go to the market and buy local. It's cheaper and it's handmade and authentic. Plus you get to meet the people.

Other Ideas

Cooking Courses – Food is the best way to experience culture and a cooking course is [-29-] to meet locals and learn about their way of eating. We've done cooking courses in China, Morocco, Thailand, Italy, Spain and Jordan and nearly every one of them takes you to the market to buy your fresh ingredients. This helps you support the local economy and mingle with the locals. We then [-30-] to a private home or kitchen to learn how to prepare. It's then a feast to enjoy!

Yoga Retreats – Yoga is not only amazing for wellbeing and fitness, it's popular around the world! Our best retreats have been when finding ones [-31-] our destination. We spent a month in India with a Swami we met on a beach for $2 a class! While others booked their retreats in North America paying thousands of dollars to take a course from a Western instructor, we had [-32-] and learned a lot about spirituality and culture in India while supporting a local business.

Wildlife Conservation

Elephant Sanctuaries, conservation areas and national parks are a way to add meaning to your travels. When local people see that animals bring tourist dollars, they'll stop over hunting and start conservation. In India, the tiger is nearly extinct, but now they're working hard to bring it back and National Parks are being set aside to keep them safe. In Sri Lanka and Thailand there are elephant organizations that are helping elephants live in peace. We visited an elephant orphanage in Kenya where orphans are reintegrated back into the wild.

Festivals

An amazing way to get to know local culture and meet people is to attend a festival. We've had some of our most memorable travel experiences when attending a celebration. From the annual

pilgrimage up Adams Peak in Sri Lanka, to Thaipusam in Malaysia and Holi in India, it has added new meaning to our travels. Festivals help us to understand the beliefs and religions of countries we visit and help us make new friends and meet new people.

There are countless ways to make your travels more meaningful. All you have to do is take the first step. Think about what you love and how you want to help and you too will be having a more fulfilling travel experience.

What way do you make your travels more meaningful?

Reading comprehension

Look at lines 1–72 and answer the following questions.

1. Why are Dave and Deb taking part in a talk show?
2. To whom does "them" (line 3) refer?
3. List four ways in which Dave and Deb have engaged in meaningful travel.
4. How, according to the text, can individuals enrich their lives when traveling?
5. Which word between lines 26 and 35 is closest in meaning to "impressive"?
6. Explain the following statement in your own words: "The more you give back, the more you feel fulfilled" (lines 38 and 39)
7. What, apart from fundraising, can make traveling meaningful?
8. List the ways in which Dave and Deb travel responsibly and provide their justification for those actions.
9. How, according to Dave and Deb, does meaningful travel affect the traveler?

Look at lines 73–96. Find the words below that could meaningfully replace the words in questions 10 to 15.

10. bigotry (line 74)
11. wholesome (line 76)
12. vegetating (line 77)
13. exploited (line 82)
14. impact (line 88)
15. daunting (line 95)

A. abused
B. comforting
C. consequence
D. healthy
E. ignorance
F. influence
G. intimidating
H. intolerance
I. molested
J. nourishing
K. sitting around
L. stagnating

Identify whether the sentences below are true or false and justify your answer with a relevant brief quotation from the text (lines 79–128).

		True	False
16.	Meaningful traveling generally revolves around eco-friendly tourism and appreciation of other cultures.		
Justification:			
17.	Exciting journeys should begin big.		
Justification:			
18.	Dave and Deb's meaningful traveling started in Cambodia.		
Justification:			
19.	Helping Cambodian children ignited Dave and Deb's aspiration to do more.		
Justification:			
20.	Dave and Deb wanted to do less when they witnessed where their money was being spent.		
Justification:			

Match the first part of the sentence with the appropriate ending on the right (lines 116–145).

21. When traveling for a cause, Dave and Deb …

22. Dave and Deb think that traveling people …

23. Ajith, the Sri Lankan tuk tuk Driver, …

24. Makau, the Kenyan guide …

A. cycled to raise funds for Africa.

B. started a charity with children in mind.

C. visited two continents.

D. can pair up with local people to find charities.

E. focused on helping his people in many ways.

F. focused mainly on boosting the local economy.

G. can easily locate international charities.

H. fought tirelessly to empower the underprivileged.

HL extension (lines 146–211) HL

Which phrase from the list below goes in each gap numbered from 25 to 32 in the text?

A. a somewhat fake experience
B. an amazing way
C. an authentic experience
D. before we arrive at
E. culturally enough
F. generally avoid going
G. help our guides
H. cared about their footprint
I. in addition to buying
J. instead of buying
K. normally go back
L. once we arrive in
M. shop and stay locally
N. talk to our guides
O. work locally

To whom or to what do the following words refer?

33. they (line 188)

34. they (line 190)

35. them (line 191)

36. orphans (line 195)

37. it (line 202)

Using your own words, summarize the main ideas in the text in no more than 100 words.

Listening comprehension

The impact of tourism

Listen to the excerpt from a debate that focuses on the effects of tourism on communities and identify the correct answer from the options provided.

1. Mr Atkin believes that tourism can …
   - A. deplete a country's resources.
   - B. boost a country's economy.
   - C. protect a country's resources.
   - D. damage a country's economy.
2. Mr Atkin explains that without proper management tourism will …
   - A. negatively affect people's hygiene habits.
   - B. hardly affect soil erosion.
   - C. add to the environmental issues.
   - D. boost food consumption.

Fill the numbered gaps with words from the options provided below.

Mr Atkin's main concern is that tourism will [-3-] harm the local culture. Dr Andies, however, believes that the local culture will benefit from the introduction of foreign aspects because this will encourage [-4-]. Dr Andies agrees with Mr Atkin regarding how travelers affect the environment, and believes that travelers should take certain responsible actions [-5-] their travels.

3. A. eventually
   B. mildly
   C. badly
4. A. responsible action
   B. intercultural understanding
   C. historical awareness.
5. A. throughout
   B. during
   C. before

HL extension

HL

Listen to the excerpt again and answer the following questions.

6. Which word does James Atkin use to describe how tourism affects resources?
7. How do tourists harm natural resources when they travel to a country in which water is scarce?
8. What kind of tourism is Mr Atkin targeting?
9. Dr Andies' main viewpoint is …
   - A. communities should benefit from responsible traveling.
   - B. communities should ban any form of unchecked tourism.
   - C. economies should reap the benefits of any kind of tourism.
   - D. tourists should act responsibly when they travel.
10. The debate about the impact of tourism highlighted:
    - A. Opposing but slightly similar views
    - B. Opposing but somewhat related views
    - C. The negative impact of tourism on local communities
    - D. The importance of tourism for local communities.

Oral activity: Discussion

Responsible travelling, as mentioned in the text, includes eco-tourism.

In groups do the following.

- List travelling practices that affect the ecology of touristic places negatively.
- Examine these actions and come up with ideas for ways to make them eco-friendly.
- List these modified actions in order of importance.
- Pick one action from the list that you think has the most merit and explain it to the other groups.

Research skills ATLs

This activity promotes good research practices such as comparing, contrasting and validating information, which in turn improve higher-order thinking.

Internal assessment (SL)

Take a look at the visual stimulus below. The image relates to the theme "experiences".

Brainstorming

In groups of three, discuss the picture:

- What is the picture communicating to you? What evidence from the picture supports your answer?
- How does the picture relate to the text "How to make your travel meaningful" that you read earlier?
- Which direction of thought is the image inviting you to take? Do you agree with that direction?

Presenting

Based on your answers to the questions above, prepare a four-minute group presentation.

The following points will help you.

- Address the focus of the picture.
- Describe the picture in no more than 30 seconds.
- Link the picture to the given theme.
- Connect the picture to the topic and mention the stance it invites you to take.
- Address the topic: define it, mention how it is affecting Anglophone cultures, highlight its issues, and/or suggest ways in which it can be addressed. Make sure your presentation is precise and concise; you have only four minutes.
- Decide on who will say what: this is a group presentation and all participants should get the chance to speak.

Remember that the presentation should not only include a description of the picture, but should also connect it to the theme of experiences and the topic of meaningful travel in an anglophone country/culture.

Present to your classmates.

Peer assessment

In groups of three, assess the presentations given by your classmates. Think about the following points:

- clarity of presentation and wording
- clarity of description of the image: were you able to understand the focus of the photograph?
- connection between the image and the theme/topic (experiences/meaningful travel)
- relevance of examples to anglophone culture(s).
- flow of ideas: is the flow of ideas smooth? Do presenters use appropriate cohesive devices and linking words?
- complexity of ideas: are ideas exemplified, justified and/or explained?

Suggest ways in which your classmates can improve their presentation techniques.

Peer assessment

When you and your classmates engage in assessing each other, you are developing your understanding of the course requirements and the assessment criteria. Peer assessment empowers you to determine your own learning and develop life-long learning skills.

Internal assessment (HL)

Before you read the short story below, examine the following:

What feelings do you usually associate with travelling? Is freedom while travelling a given concept, or is it contextual? Does tourism change over time? What brings about this change?

STRANGERS

Philip Spires

We arrived more than two hours later than planned, but the west of England summer light had not yet faded even to dusk. A soft golden glow was just growing across the sunset, which had just tinged a flat-calm sea beyond this tumbling village. We were tourists here, strangers in this small, tightly-knit place.

For us it was just part of a tour, a long weekend snatched in common from the clutches of our combined, ever demanding careers. I felt utterly liberated, that beautiful evening, as we walked the quarter mile or so down the steep dry cobbles from the obligatory car park into the car-less village, the deadlines and demands of advertising for once confined outside the limits of this small place. And I could tell from the spring in Jenny's step that her battles with bottom sets in Lewisham were now further distant than our three days on the road.

There was a small gift shop, a tourist-trap trinket place, just a hundred yards along the lane. I bought the newspaper our early departure from St. Ives had denied me, my daily fix of political gossip now long established as an essential feature of my adoption into London life. I explained that we were strangers here, had driven down the side road in the hope of finding something interesting and had nothing booked.

The shopkeeper said we had just three options — the Old Hotel just down the lane, a bed and breakfast at the bottom by the harbour or the farm near the junction with the main road, back where we had turned off.

"It was different years ago," he said, "when lots of people used to stay over, but now it's all day trippers and holiday homes. Ten years ago we had half a dozen guest houses, but they've all closed down."

The Old Hotel was just two hundred yards from the shop, at the head of the steep cove that housed the tangled triangle of the village. It was a bit beyond the price we usually paid and had AA stars framed over its reception desk, but we fell for the place and checked in, just for one night. It was the kind of mock Jacobean black and white inn, whose lack of a straight line just might have suggested it was original. But the beams were hollow and the plaque above the entrance said, "Refurbished 1958."

"Do you have any luggage to bring from the car park?" the receptionist asked. The name tag pinned to her blouse said, 'Hilary, Manageress'. "We have a man with a donkey and sledge who will bring it down for you." She wasn't joking.

I lifted our two hold-alls and said it was all we had. She smiled, offering politeness but communicating knowledge tinged with judgment. It was in an era when it was still unusual for a couple to sign in without obviously trying to appear married.

We took the key for room number six. There were only eight and the other seven keys were still hanging on their hooks when we took the lift — yes, the lift! — to the upper floor. Number six was at the back, of course, right above the kitchen extractor fan and overlooked an enclosed yard with a yellowed corrugated plastic roof. It hid an array of lidless dustbins, from which a hint of an aroma sweetened the still air when we opened the windows to encourage the previous occupant's cigarette smoke to leave. We dropped the bags and walked down to the sea to absorb the last of the late springtime sun at its setting.

The beach was shingle and small, hard-packed against a harbour wall that extended a good fifty yards into the shallow sea. A couple of clapperboard buildings, largely rotten, clung to its prominence, their profit long past, but their structures all but remaining. There were doors missing and one structure had no interior, the uncovered entrance revealing merely sky beyond. At one time, clearly, the locals had something of a living from this place, fishing perhaps, maybe small trade, smuggling in poor times, salvage by design, who knows. And then came the tourists, the stranger trade of nineteenth century invention that evaporated when the trunk road widened and rendered the place no more than a day trip from anywhere this side of Birmingham or London.

As we walked back up the deceptively steep single track that bisected the village, we passed several open doorways seeking air on this unseasonably balmy evening at the end of May. After London everything here felt so cosy, so small, warm and unthreatening, as if the place itself were welcoming us into its embracing fold.

We saw just two other people, both descending the path, and independently both offered greeting. "Isn't it pretty," said Jenny. "Don't you wish you lived here?" I declined to answer.

We ate at the Old Hotel. There was nowhere else. We ordered the grilled sole with parsley butter. Potatoes and broccoli were the 'legumes de saison'. It took over half an hour for the food to appear. We finished the bottle of house white we had ordered to go with the fish long before even the smell of cooking wafted through from the kitchen. We got significant giggles speculating on how far out into the Bristol Channel the boat had to go to catch our order. We ate. It wasn't bad, and then we moved across to the bar, the four steps needed to change location effectively redefining us from guests to locals. A concertina glass partition separated the areas in theory, but tonight it had been opened wide for ventilation. The rest of the evening became a tale of three women, Hilary, Sue and Sandra, all of whom have dreamt.

The hotel bar is the only place to drink, so it's a pub, complete with its regulars. A half a dozen men are collectively and determinedly engaged in preventing the oak top from rising, their planted elbows firmly ensuring its continued sojourn on earth. They are passing the time of night with what seems to be a predictable set of platitudes. "I bought the D-reg because I thought it would work out cheaper in the long run, what with the smaller servicing bills and the like... ...But you ought to do more of that sort of thing yourself and then you wouldn't have to pay anything at all... ... Yes, I know, but I just don't have the time. Have you, these days?... ...Give us another, Sandra... ...You go just beyond the first turning... ...Down past the egg farm where my brother used to work... ...They are really cheap if you buy them by the sack... ...bloody heavy, mind you..."

She is forty going on sixty, utterly contemptuous of what she sees before her, yet utterly resigned - or condemned - to servicing its every need. She is rather large and quite square, both in face and body. She's been like that ever since she can remember. Black hair, cut quite, but not very short and swept to a wave at the front showing that she has spent not a little time tonight cleansing and preening herself before starting work behind the bar at the Old Hotel. On the other side of the argument is a series of slobs, one of whom we only ever seem to see from the back. His head is triangular with apex at the base. A pair of key-in-keyhole ears protrude. He was probably called 'wing-nut' by his classmates at school. I resist the temptation to grab an ear-key and twist it to see what it might unlock. From the bar talk we can clearly hear, the answer surely is not much.

Note

In your internal assessment, the literary extract will not exceed 300 words. You will be shown two, one from each of the works of literature studied in class.

Divide into three groups.

Each group should examine one of the following:

London	The town	The inhabitants
• Based on your reading of the short story, how do you perceive London? Support your answer with evidence from the text. • To what extent does living in the city affect our enjoyment of travelling to the countryside?	• Describe the town in your own words. • How do you imagine this town looked in the past when it was a flourishing tourist attraction? Support your description with evidence from the text.	• To what extent are the inhabitants of the town a reflection of the town itself? Support your answer with evidence from the text. • How do people who live in previously flourishing tourist attractions suffer when such attractions fade out?

In your groups, prepare a four-minute presentation addressing the guiding questions in your group's column.

Present to your classmates.

Peer assessment

After each presentation, hold a short, whole-class discussion session in which you address the following:

1. How clear was group's perspective of the chosen aspect?
2. How has the presentation improved your understanding of tourism and the issues related to it?
3. Suggest ways in which your classmates can improve their presentation techniques. Use your observations and refer to the HL Internal assessment criteria in the *Language B guide*.

Conceptual understanding

"Context is all."

– Margaret Atwood

The use of register and language in general is largely dependent on context and perspective. When the context changes, the kind of language used changes and so does the register. For example, had the narrator in the short story felt that London was not stress inducing, the language used would not have made us feel that it was. Try changing the story to describe a London that is free from stress: Which words and/or phrases will you change? Why?

Paper 1: Travel blog (mass media)

Travel blogs are essentially a mixture of a narrative and an opinion article: the travel blogger is writing a travelogue, complete with his/her opinions, feelings and pictures taken while travelling to a certain spot.

Here are a few rules that should be taken into consideration when writing a travel blog.

1. Be personal. Interact with your readers. The main purpose of travel blogs is not to share any experience; it is to share your experience. Be careful: it is about **your** experience in the place you visited, not only what you did there! Think in terms of what made that place different, how similar to or different from your culture the traditional practices in that place are, what advice you would give to visitors who plan on visiting that place. Does your blog contain many "I"s or is there a balance between "I" and "you"?
2. Focus on your writing skills. Your language needs to be both descriptive and emotive. You are, after all, writing to entertain and sometimes to persuade.

Mass media texts

Mass media texts are created for distribution to a large audience that is targeted because of an interest that, at least initially, lies primarily with the producer of the text, since the person or entity responsible for a mass media text has no way of knowing exactly who will take the time and interest to understand the message or possibly ignore it. Mass media texts tend to be characterized by the need of the producer of the text to project authority, desirability or exclusivity, and the conscious choice of a particular medium or technology that is appropriate to reach the targeted audience. The level of formality in the register of these texts will vary according to linguistic and socio-cultural norms of the target language.

– *English B Guide*, International Baccalaureate Organization, 2017, p.19

3. Choose your content wisely. Be interesting but also be honest.
4. Be aware of your audience and context.

How is a travel blog structured? Look at the following example.

Visit the mysteriously magical land of Cornwall

By Elsi H, Photo: Maharepa

January 17, 2012

Focusing on the location

Cornwall is a land of mysteries, legends and suggestions. According to ancient stories, these places are inhabited by fairies, goblins and magical creatures plus it's said that the great King Arthur was born right here in the castle of Tintagel. This myth most likely has its roots in history and many scholars argue that Arthur was a warrior who led the resistance against the invasion of the Celtic people of the Saxons. During your tour around Cornwall you will see a lot of evidence about this ancient culture, proving that this is indeed one of the six Celtic nations. Certainly, the south-western tip of Great Britain is a world apart from the rest of the island, especially nice to visit for its beautiful landscapes and mild climate.

Commenting on the history and culture of the location

Fantastic landscape of Cornwall

Description of location

Cornwall has romantic and dramatic cliffs overlooking the sea, alternating with miles of beaches, much frequented by surfers for kite surfing. On the coast, you'll encounter numerous coastal villages with the typical fishermen's houses, which are worth a stop in order to take quite a few photos. Afterwards, you should walk through the alleys and along the harbour of the small villages of Polperro, Fawey, Charlestown, on the southeast coast, and without forgetting to visit St Mawes, with its sixteenth-century castle built by Henry VIII, and Falmouth, where we find the fortitude Pendennis Castle, the largest in the region.

Giving advice

The landscapes that meet across Lizard Peninsula are the most beautiful that you will see during your tour of Cornwall. Here is the southernmost point of England, Lizard Point with stunning sea cliffs that contrast with the green meadows. Not far from the coast is the small island of St Michael's Mount. As her French namesake, it is separated from the mainland only by a strip of land that is submerged during high tide. A tour of Cornwall, however, cannot fail to reveal the inner zones, formed by attractive moorland, beautiful gardens, as well as numerous historic and prehistoric sites.

Note the use of adjectives: the blogger's viewpoint is clearly expressed

Do not miss a visit to the largest botanical centre, the Eden Project, located near St Austell, which is home to two of the world's largest biospheres.

Giving advice

Writing activity

You recently travelled to an Anglophone country whose culture was completely different from yours and found the experience both enjoyable and educating. You would like to share this experience with your classmates.

Your first step is to determine the following.

- What is the purpose of the written piece?
- Who is your audience?
- Which type of text best helps you achieve the purpose of the task? Why?

For the following exercise, you will write a travel blog. Refer to the text on page 58 to help you formulate ideas in relation to the context above.

Brainstorming

In pairs:

1. Reflect on everything you have learned in this section
Choose a country: what would you like to emphasize about this country in your travel blog?

2. Generate
a list of ideas to be used in your travel blog.

3. Sort
those ideas depending on the their main topic. Decide on examples to use. Research some facts about the country to support your blog.

Planning

Still working in pairs, decide how you will grab your audience's attention. What should appear in your introduction? What is your conclusion? Connect those to the elements you selected earlier.

Agree on the tone and style of your travel blog. Concentrate on your audience: What is the best way to address this audience? What emotive and persuasive words and phrases will help you to support your opinion?

Think about how you are going to order your subtopics: Which should go first? Which should appear last? What should appear in the middle? Does your chosen order ensure that your ideas will be coherent and your writing will flow smoothly?

Decide how you will incorporate facts into your narrative section.

Drafting

Individually, write a draft of the body of your travel blog. When you are done, revise this draft. Does it make sense?

Add your introduction and your conclusion to the body. Re-read what you have written. Do the transitions make sense? Are your paragraphs well connected? How interesting is your travel blog?

Write an eye-catching title.

Re-read the complete draft of your travel blog for the last time. Make any necessary changes.

Paper 1 practice

Read the task below then write below and write between 250 and 400 words (SL) or 450 and 600 words (HL).

While travelling in a foreign country, you enjoyed their food more than anything: it was a reflection of their customs and traditions. You decided to share your experience with fellow teenagers in your town.

Email | **Editorial** | **Blog**

Thinking skills ATLs

Reflection in this exercise will help you to develop your critical thinking abilities by assessing how what you learned has led to more questions and areas that need to be answered and explored.

Conclusion to research question B

To what extent does travelling improve our cultural tolerance?

1. Now that you have completed this section what are your thoughts and reactions to the question above?
2. What justifications would you give for your answers?
3. What more would you need to know before you can come to a definitive conclusion about the statement?

A TOK moment

TOK

Lost and Gained in Translation

The cover of my *Chinglish* playbill is decorated with a series of imperfect translations crowding the page. This is particularly appropriate for a play that takes a humorous yet profound look at the many issues involved in communication across different languages. As I laughed at the words and supertitles in David Henry Hwang's insightful play, I began to think about the tricky nature of translation. We spend a great deal of time around texts that are the product of translation, the Bible being the most obvious example, but what is changed when we exchange one word for another, one language for another, one cultural setting for another?

Chinglish is certainly not the first play to tackle such a subject. Irish playwright Brian Friel's play *Translations* deals with language and love in a similar fashion, though without comic relief. It centers on a British soldier who falls in love with an Irish girl; he has come to rename the roads and cities, to put them in English, and he does not speak Irish. We hear both characters in English, yet we know they are speaking two different languages. This play has a more utopian position, in that it suggests that two people speaking different languages can say and feel exactly the same things.

This romantic concept finds its opposite in Julia Cho's *The Language Archive*, produced by Roundabout last year. Here, language is totally separate from communication, as the character who spends his time studying and preserving dead languages cannot express himself or connect to anyone. Esperanto, "the universal language," makes an appearance here, but it becomes another overarching symbol of the difference between language and communication. The universal language doesn't help much if no one else speaks it.

Why are these plays, and so many others, so interested in this idea of translation as a metaphor for communication? In our increasingly global world, translation can be as simple as running some words through Google Translate, yet that never provides a "perfect" answer. Translation is complex because language can have so many different intentions. This is why translating is as much an art as it is a science, and also why we sometimes have to take these translations with a grain of salt.

This is often a discussion in the theatre, a point proven recently through the discussions about the Classic Stage Company's very modern translations of *Three Sisters*. There is, of course, no one translation that will ever satisfy everyone. But does this mean we should quit trying to translate such material altogether? Of course not! We are not really seeing the same play as the Russian audience Chekhov was writing for, but are we ever really seeing the same play as any other person? We are all individuals, with our own backgrounds, biases, and tastes, which means that we are all always translating, no matter what language is being spoken.

This is what I thought as I watched the action and the supertitles in *Chinglish*. I really enjoy hearing the intonations of different foreign languages when spoken by trained voices, and I quickly became accustomed to the supertitles, which are a very useful device. They are also a source of ironic comedy throughout the piece. The irony stems from the fact that we are often laughing at translations of incorrect translations, a series of removals that returns us to the question of communication versus language. Just like the characters in *Chinglish*, we all try to communicate with each other, even when it is "sleepy" (one character's substitution for "tiring"), and just like them we achieve something even when we fail. Just like Daniel Cavanaugh in *Chinglish*, I like the missteps, mistranslations, and miscommunications, because there is some other form of truth in them too. It is this kind of unintentional genius that this play, and others like it, work to illuminate.

Yet, what role does translation play when travelling? Are the problems the same? Read the following excerpt and download a translation application that can be used when travelling to determine what is gained and what is lost in translation.

Reflect on the literary works in translation that you are studying in your Language A course. Are there aspects of the works that you find difficult to understand? What is the source of this difficulty?

In groups, read the first text and decide to what extent the following statements taken from the text are true or false in your opinion. Support your answers with examples taken from other ways of knowing or areas of knowledge.

1. "two people speaking different languages can say and feel exactly the same things"
2. "translating is as much an art as it is a science"
3. "We are not really seeing the same play as the Russian audience Chekhov was writing for, but are we ever really seeing the same play as any other person? We are all individuals, with our own backgrounds, biases, and tastes, which means that we are all always translating, no matter what language is being spoken."

Reflect on your answers, then discuss the following:

What role does language play in understanding others while travelling? And are translations "metaphors for communication"?

The five best translation apps for travelers

Machine translation is hard. Fluent speakers sometimes spot howlers, and there are subtleties and nuances that even powerful computers cannot fathom— yet. But online and app-based translation is also getting better. Last December, Skype demonstrated a tool to enable live, instant English to Spanish translation on a video call. Windows Phone owners can sign up for the Translator Preview programme at skype.com. And there are several apps out there already that will stop you getting flummoxed on your next trip.

Google Translate: translate.google.com

iTranslate: itranslateapp.com

WayGo: waygoapp.com

Section C: Leisure activities

Research question C:

Are leisure activities similar across Anglophone cultures?

1. What are your first thoughts and reactions to the question above?
2. What justifications would you give for your answers?
3. What more would you need to know before you can come to a definitive conclusion about the statement?

Before you read

In groups of four, reflect on the variety of leisure time and recreational activities adolescents enjoy in your community and then answer the following questions:

- What are those activities? List as many as you can.
- How have those activities evolved over time: are they the same activities your grandparents, for example, took part in?

Reflect on the activities you have identified and their development, then come up with more ideas for adolescent activities you think will be popular in the future.

Sort your ideas into categories: activities that have roots in the past, present-day activities that evolved because of our changing world, and ones you believe will appear in the future.

Pick one idea from your list, one that featured in all three categories, expand on it and present it to your classmates. Mention your reasons for choosing it, and explain what impact you think it will have on the future.

What is leisure?

Definition

To understand the full power and potential of leisure, it is important to separate it from another closely related word, recreation. Simply stated, recreation can be understood as the activity or experience, while leisure is seen as the outcome of the experience (definition of terms, 1999). Leisure is used in professional and academic circles and is relevant when addressing the need to develop within youth with disabilities a complete and balanced lifestyle. It is also a term that, when used, denotes a specific area of educational concern for youth with disabilities, particularly when designing an educational program that will eventually enable these students to transition from school to work, post-secondary education, community, and *leisure* settings.

Leisure has several distinct, yet related meanings. True leisure is a process involving freedom, self-discovery, and growth.

Godbey, a leading scholar in the field of leisure education, defines leisure as (1985):

Living in relative freedom from the external compulsive forces of one's culture and physical environment so as to be able to act from internally compelling love in ways which are personally pleasing, intuitively worthwhile, and provide a basis for faith. (p. 9)

While this definition of leisure may sound a little on the philosophical side, it hits on some major points that are crucial in understanding the necessity of leisure experiences, and how leisure serves as a catalyst for improving quality of life. Let's take a closer look.

Freedom

The first part of Godbey's definition is living in relative freedom. Godbey goes on to explain that there are two types of freedom, "freedom to" and "freedom from." "Freedom from" refers to freedom from physical constraints such as obligations, work, or activities of daily living such as self-care and cultural constraints such as stigmas and stereotypes. "Freedom to" refers to an individual's freedom to choose what he or she wants to do. Therefore, leisure participation is a two-fold experience requiring not only being free from constraints, but also for an individual to have the freedom of choice.

Self-discovery

As established, leisure is one's ability to choose to participate in worthwhile activities. You may wonder, however, what makes a particular activity worthwhile. One is able to determine what is worthwhile through internally compelling love. Love is not limited to a feeling about other people. For example, you may think of a child's love for a doll, the doll cannot leave the child's sight, or perhaps you think of an athlete's love for his game, he practices his sport daily. Internally compelling love simply means that when we love something, it becomes a priority in our lives without effort. It is something we make time for, and something we cannot imagine our lives without. Experiencing leisure is about discovering what one loves, and as we discover what we love we can choose to do things that are personally pleasing, intuitively worthwhile, and provide a basis for faith.

Leisure is never dehumanizing or harmful. Things that are intuitively worthwhile normally reside within the morals and values of society. It may take trial and error to discover what is and what is not worth doing, especially for individuals in their teenage years. This can be the most difficult aspect of leisure. While some individuals can identify what is worth doing, others cannot, and even the individuals that can identify what is worth doing, may choose not to do it. Therefore, leisure is a process that involves exploration and understanding of who we are as individuals.

Growth

Participation in leisure allows your child to develop skills not only for a particular activity, but that are useful in other aspects of life. Developing these skills may take multiple attempts. Once your child has developed these skills, however, leisure provides a basis for faith in their abilities, the activity, and others. The confidence your child will gain through leisure experience can then carry over into other settings such as school or work, thus enabling your child to be successful in all areas of life.

You may be thinking that this idea of leisure sounds great, but are wondering how to cultivate it into your own personal life as well as how to facilitate it in your child's life. First of all, remember that experiencing leisure is all about learning who we are as individuals, and that takes time, exploration, and discovery. It may take several attempts to determine which activities bring your child most enjoyment, and this is okay. It is also important to allow your child to have as much freedom as possible, even if that is selecting a particular toy to play with. The goal of leisure for children with disabilities is to teach them that a disability does not limit their ability to have enjoyable life experiences.

Patterns of Leisure

Children's leisure experiences, particularly in their early years, are often a direct reflection of the values and preferences of their parents and other family members, as well as teachers and friends. We all know or at least can reasonably guess at the amount of peer pressure that will be exerted on your child when he or she becomes a teenager! If you are concerned about your child's leisure future, you are not alone. The expression "it takes a community to raise a child" is especially true when talking about the leisure future of children - all children.

Technology's Impact

Consider, for example, the high-tech reality of today's play options versus the low-tech varieties you had as a child.

Technology has a huge impact on the type of recreation pursued by children today. Now, information about anything in the world can be accessed over the internet instantly. Telephones smaller than a child's fist, which are wireless, take pictures and videos, play games, and allow instant communication any time of the day. Video games, so realistic that you can almost touch the figures on the TV monitor, replace board games, comic books, and Saturday morning cartoons.

Shift to Indoors

Today, children seem to be more keenly interested in the indoor activities such as watching television, playing video games and surfing the Internet. According to a recent article in USA Today, "the shift to an **[-23-]** in the past decade with a huge decline in spontaneous outdoor activities" (Cacuchon, 2005). Games of pick-up basketball, tree climbing, and kick the can have nearly vanished, and the negative **[-24-]** bodies and in their minds (Cacuchon, 2005). France Kuo, director of the Human Environment Research Laboratory, reports that studies show children who spend lots of time outdoors have longer attention spans than children who engage in indoor pursuits (as cited in Cacuchon, 2005). Additionally, childhood obesity has skyrocketed from 4% of children in the 1960s to 16% of children today according to the Center for Disease Control.

Decline in Recreation Activities

Decline in activity of 7 to 11 year olds from 1995 to 2004:

- Bicycling: 68% to 47%
- Swimming: 60% to 42%
- Baseball: 29% to 22%
- Fishing: 25% to 18%
- Touch Football: 16% to 10%

(Source: USA Today: analysis of National Sporting Goods Associations Annual survey)

Healthy Alternatives

It is more than technology that keeps children indoors. Heavy traffic and reports of crime appearing daily in the media can deter parents from allowing their children **[-25-]**. There is hope, however, as families can instill values of leisure in their children **[-26-]** wholesome activities which are not only stimulating for the child, but also enable them to learn, gain, and demonstrate skills that will benefit the child throughout his or her lifetime.

Parents want their children **[-27-]**, and through community center sports, drop-in opportunities, and related programs sponsored by churches, Scouts, 4-H, and Boys and Girls Clubs, safe opportunities for children to get away from the influence of video games and television and find activities that will promote self-discovery and growth are available.

Reading comprehension

1. How is leisure different from recreation?
2. Which phrase between lines 1 and 8 shows that the life of children with disabilities changes for the better when they take part in leisure activities?
3. What three things should proper leisure activities involve?
4. Which word between lines 11 and 17 is closest in meaning to "essential"?
5. To what does "two-fold experience" (line 24) refer?
6. From statements A to H, identify the five that are true according to the text (lines 26–54).

   A. Leisure involves participating in any activity.
   B. It is difficult to categorize meaningful activities.
   C. A meaningful activity is closely related to what we like to do.
   D. We learn what we like when we take part in activities.
   E. It is acceptable for leisure activities to be unethical.
   F. Taking part in leisure activities should help people understand themselves.
   G. Lifetime skills are developed when taking part in leisure activities.
   H. Taking part in leisure activities helps children achieve more at school.
   I. It is relatively easy to figure out what activities allow children with disabilities freedom and enjoyment.
   J. The purpose of leisure activities is to help some children overcome their disabilities.

Find the words or phrases in the text which mean the following (lines 55–84).

7. anxious
8. practiced
9. promptly
10. lifelike
11. acutely
12. impulsive
13. disappeared
14. risen steeply
15. discourage
16. introduce
17. motivating
18. foster

To whom or to what do the following words or phrases refer?

19. their (line 57)
20. which (line 67)
21. their (line 92)

HL extension

22. Define "freedom to" (line 21) and "freedom from" (line 21) in your own words.

Which phrases go in the gaps numbered from 23 to 27 in the text? Choose the phrases from the list below.

A indoor childhood has accelerated

B indoor childhood has declined

C reasons can be seen in their

D results can be seen in children's

E to aid them in choosing

F to be safe indoors

G to engage in unsupervised activities

H to help them in side-stepping

I to pursue healthful alternatives

J to take part in supervised activities

Oral activity: Discussion

Is there a true difference between leisure and recreation?

- In groups, come up with a list of different definitions and then use the following prompts to explore each one:

  "I am thinking of leisure versus recreation from the angle of [the angle you've chosen, for example, effect, reasons, types]"

  Search online for information that supports your angle.

  "I think ..."

  Describe the topic from your chosen angle in your own words.

  "A question I have regarding this angle is ..."

  Ask a question from this angle.

- What new ideas do you have about the topic that you didn't have before? What new questions do you have?

Research and thinking skills ATLs

In our modern world, research involves more than comparing and contrasting data. A huge importance is placed on validating data, especially in a world in which information is available at the click of a button. This skill also helps you improve your metacognition, higher-order thinking and problem solving through the use of synthesis and evaluation.

Listening comprehension

Click the icon to practice the listening section of Paper 2. This is a gap-filling activity. Before you listen, read the statements carefully and decide what kind of word fits the gap e.g. noun, verb, adjective. This will help you when you listen for the answers.

Internal assessment (SL)

You have been given this visual stimulus and asked to prepare a four-minute presentation on the topic the stimulus highlights, which is connected to the theme "experiences". In groups of four, prepare your presentation and present it to your classmates. The mind map below should remind you of the ground rules that you have to observe when preparing a presentation.

Divide into three groups. Each group should read the story from one perspective, that of the husband, the wife or the reader.

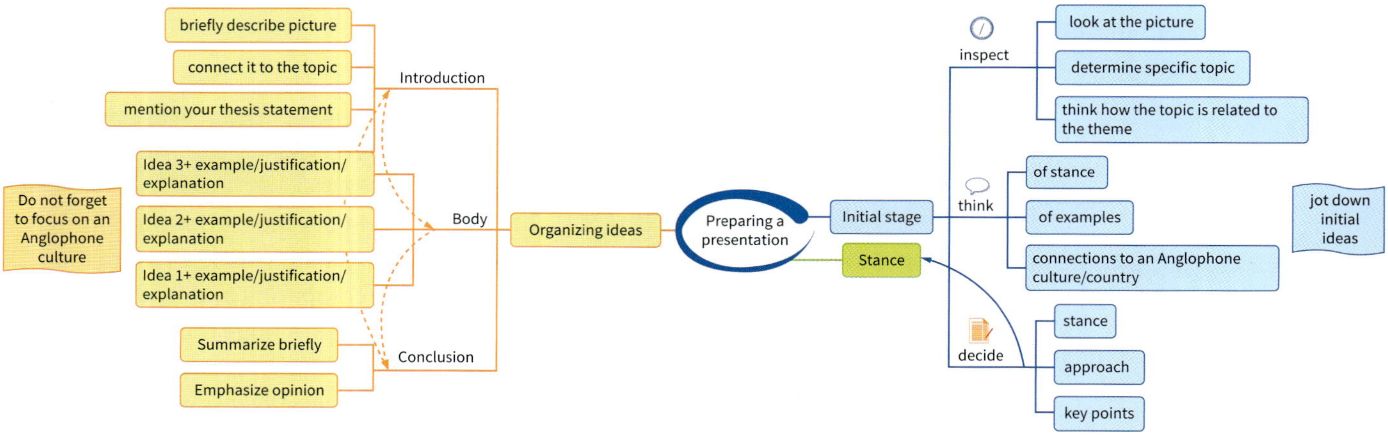

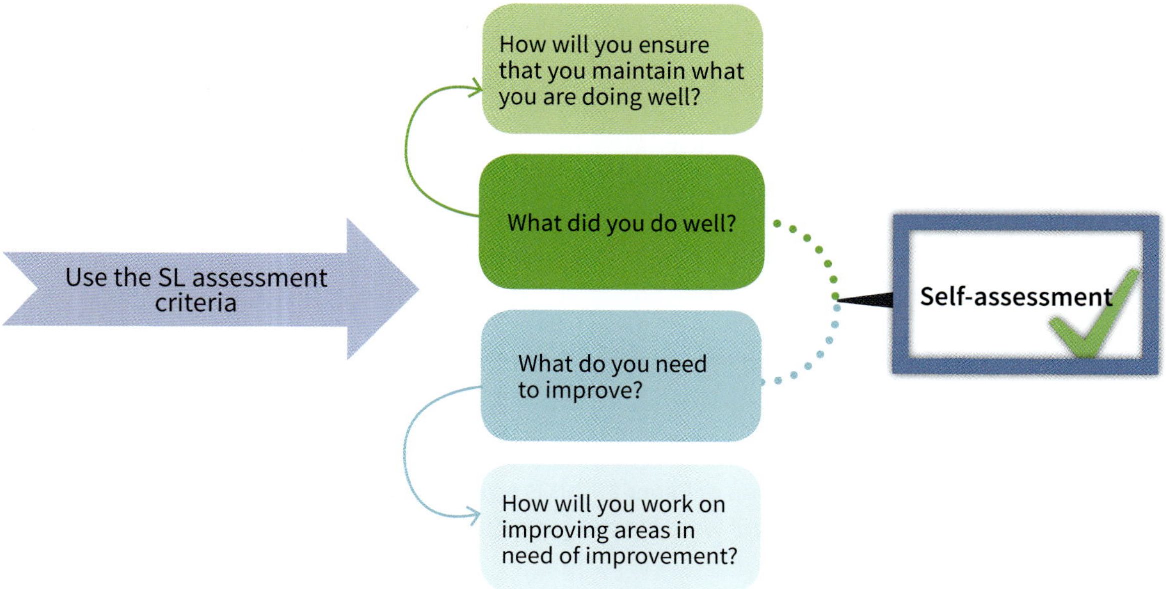

Internal assessment (HL)

The Case of The Lower Case Letter

by Jack Delany

She breezed into my office one cold September morning. I'd been enjoying a hot cup of Starbuck's finest and surfing the web for local news. The famous lexical semanticist Professor Edgar Nettleston had been found dead, a gunshot wound to the head. The police verdict was suicide.

She held out an elegant hand as she floated towards me and I glimpsed a wedding band with a stone the size of a peanut M&M.

"I'm Edith Nettleston."

"Sorry about the old man."

"I'm not. He loved me, but he loved words more. I'll be brief. My husband was working on a paper that will rock the very foundation of lexical semantics. It's worth a fortune in lecture tours, but nobody can find it. I believe his suicide note is a clue to its whereabouts."

She removed a scrap of paper from her blouse.

"edith. i'm not going to whine, i've had a good life. i've found wealth and happiness as a teacher, a seller of knowledge. but i find myself depressed beyond hope ... and so i'm choosing the hour and manner of my own demise. i have treated you badly. i demanded you dyed your brown curls blonde. i thought i could buy you when i should have won your love. i called you a witch. i'd complain: where's the woman i married? i said you ate too much. if i wanted change, i could have used a carrot rather than a stick. you probably wanted to wring my neck. forgive me. farewell."

"It's all written in lower case. My husband was a stickler for correct grammar. I refuse to believe it doesn't mean something."

"Mrs. Nettleston, I think I can help you. There's a couple of odd things about this letter. Firstly, as you say, it's written entirely in lower case. Mr. Nettleston was a world-renowned lexical semanticist, not a teenager texting his BFFs."

"Secondly, it has a more than usual number of homophones, words where there is another word with the same sound but different spelling and meaning. When dealing with a lexical semanticist, that's surely no accident."

"If we read those homophones in order, we have: whine, seller, hour, manner. And translating to their homophones: Wine cellar our manor."

Several hours later, we arrived at the Nettlestons' country house and immediately headed for the basement. A flip of a light switch revealed tunnels filled with rows of dark bottles.

"Where is it? It would take years to search this place."

"Not so fast, Mrs. Nettleston. First I have to ask you something: your wedding ring diamond, how large is it?

"It's eight carats. Edgar wouldn't stop talking about it."

"That's what I feared." I pulled out my trusty revolver. "How you must have hated him and his lexical semantics! You figured you'd kill him and keep the money from the paper yourself. You forced him to write that suicide note, thinking you knew where it was. But he was suspicious and he'd already hidden it. And he had another surprise for you: the rest of the note, it doesn't reveal where the paper is, it reveals his killer. The final homophones: dyed buy won witch where's ate carrot wring. That is: died by one which wears eight carat ring."

As the cops left with Mrs. Nettleston I took a quick trip round the maze of tunnels. It didn't take me long to find it. Most of the wine lay unpacked on racks but in one corner two cases sat stacked, one on top of each other. Carefully, I opened the lower one.

Note

In your internal assessment, the literary extract will not exceed 300 words. You will be shown two, one from each of the works of literature studied in class.

Divide into three groups. Each group should read the story from one perspective, that of the husband, the wife or the reader.

In your groups, prepare a four-minute presentation based on your reading. What evidence from the text supports your ideas?

Use the following table to help you map out your presentation:

Generating ideas	
What is the main idea of the short story?	
What are the main events that support this main idea?	
What is the husband's/wife's/narrator's point of view?	
How is the husband's/wife's/narrator's point of view presented in the story?	
Organizing your presentation	
Introduction: introduce the main idea	20 seconds
Introduce the main events in relation to the main idea	40 seconds
Explain the husband's/wife's/narrator's point of view in relation to the main idea and events	120–150 seconds
Conclusion: summarize the main ideas in your presentation and mention your opinion (optional) Present to your classmates.	30 seconds

Self-assessment

Think about your presentation. What went well? What do you need to improve? Refer to the HL Internal assessment criteria in the *Language B guide* to help you.

Paper 1: Diary entry

A diary entry is a personal account that describes what you did, saw and felt on a particular occasion. These entries could be straightforward events outlining what you did in the course of the day. However, at HL, a daily routine does not make for interesting writing. A good diary entry is likely to contain your thoughts, feelings and comments about the events of the day.

Personal texts

Personal texts are shared by the person creating the message and an audience who may be family members, friends or groups with a common interest; a personal text may also be directed to oneself. Personal texts tend to be characterized by attention to the everyday interests or the affective needs of individuals rather than the analysis of information. Personal texts have a variety of functions, including but not limited to: describing, narrating, entertaining, recommending, persuading. The level of formality in the register of these texts will vary according to linguistic and socio-cultural norms of the target language.

– Language B Guide, IBO

Diaries

Structure

- ☐ Usually spontaneous
- ☐ may be chronologial

Audience

- ☐ Written to self
- ☐ Private, not public

Style

- ☐ also reflective
- ☐ generally narrative

Writing to an audience

Unlike most text types we discuss in Language B, in real life, diaries are private rather than public. Some diary writers like to write to the diary as if it were a good friend. This technique is called direct address and allows you to talk to your diary as "you". Because you are writing to yourself, a diary can be a place where you can write down your thoughts and feelings in secret and in confidence.

Structure

Your diary entries could be a straightforward account of a day's events; however, some people keep diaries as a method of examining their lives. Therefore, a good diary entry is likely to emphasize your reflections, and comments about the events of the day. So, in terms of structure, such diary entries do not have to have a chronological structure.

Frequently the writer's opinions give structure to the writing rather than the events themselves. You might start with a phrase to focus the reader on the main event you wish to relate. You could use an exclamation, "What a day this has been!" Or you could start with an opinion, "I have never felt so insulted." Alternatively, you might like to start with a rhetorical question that you go on to answer, "How could I have imagined they could be so cruel?"

Diary writing is spontaneous and therefore the language and the ideas should sound fresh. Nevertheless, you should still use the basic rules of paragraphing with each paragraph having a topic sentence and a clear focus. This will help you and your reader to understand your thoughts.

You should finish with a final thought. This might be a concluding statement about the events in the diary entry or a question on the lines of "I wonder what will happen next."

Style

The most difficult aspect of producing an imaginative diary entry is writing in character. Diaries are written from a first-person perspective and refer to possibly fictitious events that have recently happened, but you have to remember you are writing in character to an implied audience (in this case your imaginary self). Your writing should, therefore, try to reflect the personality and mood of the diary writer.

On that point it is worth noting the tenses used for diaries. If you are writing about events that took place the day before, "yesterday", then you need to write in the simple past, "I came, I saw, I conquered." However, you may also be writing about events that have taken place earlier in the same day, "today." In this case, you may need to use present perfect tenses to describe events whose consequences can still be

felt, "Today has been wonderful. I've finally discovered the true nature of the universe."

You can be relatively informal with your use of language; however, you are advised not to use too much slang. If you do feel it is necessary, it is wise to put the word in italics to show you understand that the word is non-standard English.

1. ***In groups of four read the sample of a diary entry below and answer the questions that follow.***

A note on grammar

Diary writers are not always certain about their ideas, so it is useful to begin some sentences with phrases like: I wonder, I suppose, I think, I reckon, I imagine, I hope, I doubt.

You may also want to use verbs in the conditional tenses:

- I wonder what will happen if I were to go … (future).
- I wonder what would happen if I went … (theoretical situation in the present)
- I wonder what would have happened if I had gone … (theoretical situation in the past)

Dear Diary…

Do you know what's strange? The fact that sometimes I don't like blogging. Yes, I said it. Most bloggers wouldn't but I did because this is a diary and diaries have no filter. It's not because I can't write or I have no motivation, it is literally because I don't like thinking. Thinking too much makes my head hurt because there is too much inside my head like it's all jumbled up floating around and it makes no sense. It's hard to make sentences that make sense and go together because my head is all over the place and it just doesn't stay still. I think I just put off thinking because when I think too hard, I think about things I don't want to think about like pain, suicide, people that aren't happy etc. I don't like knowing that I can't help. I can't help my boyfriend or my grandma or my step-sister or my friends with their problems, I just have to sit there and wait. Wait for something to happen to make them okay. Do you know the pain of waiting? Do you know the feeling of knowing you're helpless? This is why I don't like blogging sometimes because it leaves me stripped and vulnerable.

Thinking is hard for me... Like really really thinking. Artificial thinking is easy like exams and solving problems but real thinking that's a challenge because real thinking has no absolute answer... Real thinking means thinking about yourself and who you are and why we're here and how things are possible. Real thinking is something that drives people mad. Is there a point in real thinking if it drives you mad? Yes. Real thinking is the gateway to the future, the gateway to happiness and the gateway to finding yourself. I may find it hard but all worthwhile things are hard at first.

Do you know what really hurts my head? The future. What uni do I want to go to? What grades will I get? Will I get a job? Will I be okay? I don't know the answer to any of these questions but one day I will. Maybe that gives me hope to carry on my normal day to day life. Maybe it just makes me fear the day that I know because the answer could be very disappointing. Questions are always a gamble because we ask them without contemplating if we want to know the answer. But we're humans and humans are curious organisms. Without curiosity we may be happier but we'd be extremely underdeveloped. Curiosity causes the growth of knowledge and knowledge, according to some guy in a book, is power. What I'm really putting off is my personal statement because I'm not smart or interesting or academic on a piece of paper. I like writing fiction or thoughts but I do not like writing how incredible I am. I believe everyone is equal and so making myself seem superior feels so wrong to me. How I'm going to write it I really don't know! I plan to do it over the summer but we will see I guess.

Sometimes I feel like I'm alive but I'm not really living. I'm just plodding along doing my thing every day but I feel tired and deflated all the time. I don't feel excited or elated I just feel average. I'm also an emotional wreck, I feel like I'm on the brink of tears every time someone says something nice or someone talks about being different or happy or sad or just most things make me want to cry. But I don't because it's normally when an advert is on or at a time when people would look at me like I'm crazy for crying. I try to hold it in. My mum said to me earlier that there was girl like me that she counselled.... Everyone perceived her as strong-willed and emotionless but really she was so sensitive deep down. She couldn't handle her emotions... If she said something she may just breakdown so she didn't. Everyone got her wrong, she was a different person on the inside. But no one ever gets to see that do they? When she said that I wanted to cry and breakdown and tell her she's right but I don't want this all stuck inside of me waiting to explode one day. But instead I smiled and nodded. It's hard to understand why I'm like this, maybe I'll feel better tomorrow.

Goodnight

- Who is the audience of the text?
- What is the purpose of the text?
- How does the writer start the diary entry?
- How does the writer finish the diary entry?
- How important is the narrative to your understanding of the diary entry?
- What descriptive details has the writer included in the diary entry?
- What are the writer's main ideas in the text?
- What are the approximate proportions of:
    - the narrative content?
    - the descriptive details?
    - the reflections of the writer?
- How does the text show the personality of the writer?

2. Write a set of guidelines on how to write a diary entry. Share your guidelines with your classmates.

Writing activity

You experienced an event that has had a great impact on your understanding of the importance of taking part in leisure activities. Reflect on the experience.

Brainstorming

Think about the following and jot your ideas down on a piece of paper.

- Context: What is the event? When and where did it take place?
- Purpose: Why are you writing this diary entry?
- Main ideas
    - Description of the event: What was the focus of the event? How was it organized? What did you like or not like?
    - Reflection: How has the event changed your understanding of the importance of taking part in leisure activities?

Planning

Decide how you will start your diary entry: What should appear in your introduction? What is your conclusion? Connect these to the conceptual understandings you have identified.

How are you going to order your ideas? Will you present them chronologically? Will you adopt the spontaneous approach? Does your chosen order ensure that your ideas will be coherent and your writing will flow smoothly?

What language you will use in your diary? Will it be descriptive? Descriptive, emotive and reflective? Connect choice of language and register to the conceptual understandings you have identified.

Drafting

Write a draft of the body of your diary.

When you are done, review this draft. Does it make sense?

Add your introduction and your conclusion to the body. Re-read what you have written. Do the transitions make sense? Are your paragraphs well connected? Are your bullet points or ideas repetitive? How interesting and personal is your diary entry?

Re-read the complete draft of your diary entry for the last time. Make any final changes.

Paper 1 practice

Choose one of the tasks below and write between 250 and 400 words for SL, and between 450 and 600 words for HL.

Task 1: The behaviour of a football coach in a recent match taught you a lesson about the importance of the acceptance of others. Reflect on what you learned.

Email | Diary entry | Opinion column

Task 2: Reflect on a recent trip. Choose your audience. Choose your context. Choose a text type that will help you to achieve the aim. Write a rationale explaining what you are going to do and why. Carry out the task, then submit both the rationale and the task to your teacher for feedback.

Conclusion to research question C

Are leisure activities similar across Anglophone cultures?

1. Now that you have completed this section what are your thoughts and reactions to the question above?
2. What justifications would you give for your answers?
3. What more would you need to know before you can come to a definitive conclusion about the statement?

Beyond the text

In this chapter, we examined some topics related to our understanding of human experiences and how they shape or affect us. However, this chapter is just the tip of the iceberg; you may also want to consider the following:

1. Does leisure have the same definition in all cultures? Consider the Chinese definition of leisure: "a man leaning against a tree to take a rest" (Huidi and Er, 2009).
2. Who should decide on the extent to which immigrants have assimilated into a society? Consider the following quote by Amy Tan: "There is this myth, that America is a melting pot, but what happens in assimilation is that we end up deliberately choosing the American things – hot dogs and apple pie – and ignoring the Chinese offerings".
3. To what extent do you agree with Marcel Proust: "The real voyage of discovery consists not in seeking new landscapes, but in having new eyes"?

A TOK moment

TOK

Key language ideas

These key language ideas will help you to understand theory of knowledge, and produce a powerful TOK essay and presentation.

Connotation

The connotation of a word is the meaning that has been acquired by a word over time, via individual and shared use. It is different, therefore, from the 'denotation' of a word, which its more formal meaning, that may be defined in a dictionary.

The connotation of a word is often more powerful than its denotation, meaning that when we use a word with one intention, we end up actually expressing a different idea. It also means that two words with a similar denotation can mean totally different things because of their connotations.

For example, the two words 'house' and 'home' have similar denotations – dwellings in which people live. However, because of the way we have used the word 'home', it has a lot more connotations, involving family, warmth, safety, and comfort.

Constructed languages

A constructed language is a language that has been deliberately designed and constructed, rather than one that has evolved over time. Examples include the language 'Esperanto' which was created in order to facilitate communication between different language-speaking cultures, and the code used to create websites (such as this one!).

Denotation

The denotation of a word is its literal meaning, and the one you will find defined in a dictionary. See our discussion above for the difference between 'denotation' and 'connotation'.

Euphemism

A euphemism is a word or phrase used in an attempt to lessen the negative aspects of an event, phenomenon, or state of being. Euphemisms are used skilfully by many people who are good at persuading others, such as those who work in the advertising industry, sales, or politics. Examples abound – we no longer buy 'second-hand' goods, we buy 'pre-loved' items (note the use of the connotation of 'loved'); military leaders do not talk about civilian (ie innocent) deaths caused by their bombing campaigns, they talk about 'collateral damage'; rather than say a person has died, we might say that person 'passed away', or is 'no longer with us'.

Linguistic relativity (or the Sapir-Whorf hypothesis)

Linguistic relativity is the concept that our ideas, beliefs, and perspectives are shaped by the language that we speak. This was based on studies made of different cultures by (amongst others) Edward Sapir and Benjamin Whorf, that linked different thought processes and world views with different languages. Although the idea influenced many works of literature (such as Orwell's 1984), it was largely replaced by the Universal Grammar theory of Chomsky.

Metaphor

Metaphors are used widely in language, and are responsible for conveying a huge proportion of language's meaning. A metaphor uses a recognisable and approachable word or phrase to compare to a real situation or condition in order to give it a different meaning. One of the most commonly quoted examples is the way William Shakespeare compares human existence to a stage and set of actors, in his play *As You Like It*:

All the world's a stage,
And all the men and women
merely players;

They have their exits and their entrances

By comparing life in this way, Shakespeare gives us the impression that life is temporary, beyond our control, and possibly absurd or tragic (or both), thus providing us with a different insight into its true nature.

Natural language

A natural language is one that has been allowed to develop independently of any design or intention, as most of the languages that we speak have done. It is the opposite of a 'constructed' language, as mentioned above.

Onomatopoeia

Onomatopoeia is an interesting language phenomenon, and illustrate how diverse the way in which language develops can be. Onomatopoeic words are formed from the sounds associated with what the word denotes, for example, the bleat of a sheep, the honk of a car horn, the sizzle of a saucepan, or the clap of a hand. These words may even end up as the name of that which makes the noise, such as a 'Cuckoo'.

Onomatopoeia also indicates that different cultures seem to hear things differently – just look at the words for the noises made by different farm animals (particularly the cockerel!) across different cultures.

Universal grammar theory

The Universal grammar (UG) theory is a theory proposed by Noam Chomsky, who argued that the human brain is 'hardwired' in order to understand grammar, and that we have an instinctive ability to learn the rules of different languages without having to be taught them explicitly. Although Chomsky's theory has been accepted for many years, it is beginning to be questioned by cognitive scientists and linguists, who point to increasing evidence that children learning to speak languages do not do so via grammatical thinking.

Read the text above and reflect on the definitions of key language ideas the writer provides in the text.

In groups of four:

- Think of examples that fall under each of the language ideas presented in the text.
- Choose the clearest examples to share with your classmates.
- Choose any text in this chapter and find examples of those language ideas in that text.
- Present your findings to your classmates.

Reflect on how the use of these key language ideas affects our understanding of a written text.

Conclusion to the chapter

Having completed the chapter, reflect on its key research question:

How would travelling to or living in another culture affect my worldview?

In groups of four, discuss the following two questions:

1. What have you learned so far?
2. What do you still want to know?

Beyond the classroom

CAS

Here are some suggestions for experiences that could form part of your CAS programme.

Experience 1

- Think of ways in which you can ensure that local tourism activities protect the environment. As part of this project, you could address your mayor or town council president to convince him/her to support the project. Write your letter.
- Reflect on the letter you have written. Which of the CAS outcomes has writing the letter helped you achieve? How?

Experience 2

- Design a project that focuses on getting to know your own county through internal tourism. This project is to be presented to the minister of tourism in your country.
- Reflect on the process of designing your project. Which of the CAS outcomes has designing the project helped you achieve? How?

Experience 3

- As part of your CAS programme, you want to raise funds to support the inclusion of meaningful leisure activities for teenagers in your town. Design a couple of greeting cards focusing on this topic that can be sold to the public to raise those funds.
- Reflect on the process of designing the greeting cards. Which of the CAS outcomes has designing the greeting cards helped you achieve? How?

Suggested reading list

The Joy Luck Club by Amy Tan

Neither Here, Nor There: Travels in Europe by Bill Bryson

Eat, Pray, Love by Elizabeth Gilbert

Seven Years in Tibet by Heinrich Harrer

Around the World in 80 Days by Jules Verne

Brick Lane by Monica Ali

Suggested films list

Seven Years in Tibet

The Immigrant

Brick Lane

Eat, Pray, Love

3 HUMAN INGENUITY: CELEBRITY

Chapter summary

Theme
- Human ingenuity

Topics
- Artistic expression
- Media and communication
- Entertainment

Conceptual understanding
Purpose

Research question for the chapter
What can we learn about a culture through its artistic expression?

Additional research questions
A What qualities do you need to become a successful musician?
B How are celebrities affected by fame?
C Why do some fans hero worship celebrities?

TOK questions
- Does the function of a text affect our understanding of it?
- To what extent is the function of a text dependent on purpose and context?

Communication skills

Listening skills
- Receptive
- Productive

Interactive skills
Interviews

Written text types
- Interviews
- Reviews

Research question for the chapter:

What can we learn about a culture through its artistic expression?

1. What are your first thoughts and reactions to the question above?
2. What justifications would you give for your answer?
3. What more would you need to know before you can come to a definitive conclusion about the question?

Critical thinking skills ATLs

Before we begin the chapter, study the poster on the left.

1. What seems to be the subject of this image? How well does the poster help us to answer the question: "What can we learn about a culture through its artistic expression?"
2. How well does the image communicate culture in an Anglophone society?
3. What improvements would you suggest to clarify and improve the message?

Section A: Artistic expression

Research question A:

What qualities do you need to become a successful musician?

1. What are your first thoughts and reactions to the question above?
2. What justifications would you give for your answers?
3. What more would you need to know before you can come to a definitive conclusion about the statement?

Before you read

Two artists were discussing the meaning of success. They decided there were four ways of defining artistic success:

A. Being able to earn money as an artist
B. Believing in what you do
C. Being famous
D. The pleasure of creating

Two of their definitions are idealistic, while two are more material. Which are which?

Now categorize the 12 statements below according to the four definitions of success A to D.

1. "Having pride in what I create."
2. "Having the power to create whatever I want as an artist."
3. "Above all I want is to enjoy the experience of creating art."
4. "l need to make money from what I create."
5. "Success equals financial security."
6. "You can sell a lot, even if some people think you are no good."
7. "The freedom to work how I want is the most important thing to me."
8. "Expressing yourself clearly in your work is a form of success."
9. "The work should express what you believe in."
10. "People knowing your name."
11. "People recognising you in public."
12. "Receiving the praise of critics."

If you were an artist or musician, would you pay more attention to your ideals or to material success? What would be your personal definition of success?

Pick at least four statements from the lists above. You may add ideas of your own to your list. Discuss your choices with the rest of your class. What definition of artistic success can you all agree on?

Movie review: 'Sing Street' is another charmer from director of 'Once'

In "Sing Street" Conor (Ferdia Walsh-Peelo) lies about having a band to impress a girl, then gathers together a group of classmates to form one to cover his tracks.

Irish director John Carney's Oscar-winning debut hit "Once" gave us a pair of songwriting collaborators on the Emerald Isle making sweet music together, having some good laughs and falling sort of in love.

His follow-up "Begin Again" repeated that winning formula with a Manhattan background and bigger budget. "Sing Street" is an entertaining take on his favorite topics, a lightweight coming of age delight stuffed with irresistible '80s pop hits and some fine original tunes, too.

Conor (authentically played by Ferdia Walsh-Peelo) is a teenager growing up in Dublin around 1985. It's a period when new bands like Spandau Ballet, The Cure, Duran Duran and A-ha are rising up the charts and the economy is in deep trouble. His parents' income (like their marriage) is shrinking, so they shift him to the least expensive private school they can find. The tough headmaster (Don Wycherley) runs it like a reformatory, and the feisty playground bully threatens to thump the daylights out of the new boy.

The only benefit to attending is that it's next to the home of a reserved young lovely named Raphina (Lucy Boynton). With her skintight denims and teased hair, she's a wannabe fashion model who doesn't have much interest in schoolboys a year below her. But when Conor tries to impress by pretending to have a band, she gives him a brief second look.

Having to turn his boast into reality, Conor recruits whatever classmates he can find into a music group. It's a nothing-to-lose gesture that miraculously lifts his horizon further than he (or the audience) could have expected.

The story plays like a charming junior version of that other Irish band movie "The Commitments," following the group they actually become a good, unknown band.

Carney peppers every scene with music. "Riddle of the Model" is Conor's first swing at a new wave love ballad, and it's wonderfully catchy. The kids are so cheerfully committed to their endeavor that they don't care who laughs at them. Carney makes it much easier to laugh with them.

Adapted from http://www.newsobserver.com/entertainment/movies-news-reviews/article76552107.html

Communication skills

ATLs

Use this exercise to practice communicating through language activities.

- Preview and skim the text to build understanding
- Read for comprehension
- Make inferences and draw conclusions
- Take effective notes
- Make effective summary notes for studying
- Use organizers for your summary notes
- Organize and depict information logically
- Structure information into a summary or report

Social skills ATLs

Use your collaborative skills to tackle some of the reading comprehension exercises as group work.

You can try to answer questions in pairs or small groups and discuss the various possible alternative responses.

At the same time practice these skills.

- Listen actively to other perspectives and ideas
- Share responsibility for decision-making
- Help others to succeed
- Manage and resolve conflict, and work collaboratively in teams
- Build consensus
- Negotiate effectively
- Give and receive meaningful feedback

Reading comprehension

Choose the correct answer from A, B, C or D.

1. Which film does the reviewer refer to as a "charmer"?

   A. Once
   B. Emerald Isle
   C. Sing Street
   D. Begin Again

2. The main character starts a band to:

   A. influence a girl
   B. become famous
   C. play music
   D. make new friends

3. The film is set in:

   A. Manhattan
   B. the Emerald Isle
   C. the UK
   D. Dublin

4. According to the text, the director's main themes are:

   A. growing up and having laughs
   B. falling in love and Eighties music
   C. growing up and making music
   D. falling in love and growing up

Choose the correct phrase from the text to complete the following sentences.

5. During the 1980s bands like Duran Duran were …
6. Conor's family are in financial trouble so they send him …
7. Conor immediately has problems at his new school with …
8. Conor is soon attracted to Raphina who has ambitions to become …
9. At first Raphina seems uninterested in …
10. However, Conor's boastful lie means that …

Choose the correct answer from A, B, C or D.

11. According to the storyline, Conor's band is:

    A. a total disaster
    B. an unexpected success
    C. a useless gesture
    D. a copy of another band

12. In the film the music is:

    A. at the centre of every scene
    B. always in the background
    C. featured in most scenes
    D. occasionally featured

13. Overall the reviewer thinks the film is:

    A. catchy
    B. humorous
    C. laughable
    D. committed

HL extension

HL

The text is a film review. A good film review will achieve a variety of purposes. It will describe, explain and criticize.

Read statements 14 to 24. Complete the chart by giving your opinion about the content of the review above. The first statement has been done for you.

The review of Sing Street	Your opinion: Agree/disagree/ not sure	Evidence in the review of *Sing Street*
Example: Informs the reader of the subject matter	Agree	It mentions the title of the film
14. Summarizes the plot of the film		
15. Describes the main characters of the film		
16. Analyses the film in terms of its artistic merit and technical skill		
17. Comments on the acting, direction, cinematography and script		
18. Gives the price of tickets to the show		
19. Analyses the film in terms of its messages and values		
20. Compares the film to similar films that came before it		
21. Entertains the readers with its comments		
22. Helps people to decide which film is most worth their time and money		
23. Alerts parents about whether or not the film is appropriate viewing for children		
24. Comments on the special effects and music soundtrack		

Research skills

ATLs

What do you know already about the content of a review?

What is the purpose of a review?

What different kinds of review are there?

Ask yourself: "What else do I need to know about defining and writing a review?"

Use your skills to find out the additional information you need to answer these questions well.

Listening comprehension

Click the icon to practice the listening section of Paper 2. After you have listened to an audio track you will complete an accompanying activity. In this activity you will read ten statements. Only five are true.

> **Communication and social skills** ATLs
>
> While you are deciding how to categorize the questions for the interview with this new band, here is an opportunity to show two further skill sets.
>
> **Communication skills**
>
> - Exchange thoughts, messages and information effectively through interaction
> - Use language to gather and communicate information
> - Preview and skim texts to build understanding
> - Read critically and for comprehension
> - Make inferences and draw conclusions
>
> **Social skills**
>
> - Work effectively with others
> - Listen actively to other perspectives and ideas
> - Encourage others to contribute
> - Delegate and share responsibility for decision-making
> - Help others to succeed
> - Manage and resolve conflict, and work collaboratively in teams
> - Build consensus

Oral activity: Interviews

One very useful interaction for language development is an interview. An interview allows you to conduct a person-to-person discussion through the carefully structured use of questions and answers. In an interview an interviewer asks questions about a specific topic. A well-constructed interview can reveal the interviewee's thoughts and feelings on important issues. Some interviews, such as a job or college interview can be very formal. Other interviews, such as an interview with an artist, are much more relaxed and personal.

Interview with a brand new band

At school some of your friends announce they have started a band. You want to interview them, either for your school newspaper or your own personal blog. You have the following 20 questions, but now you need to categorize them. With a partner read the questions and put them into these six categories:

Musical style	Performing live	Becoming better known
Starting out	Future plans	Creating music

Twenty questions for a new band:

1. Are you seeking fame and fortune?
2. As musicians, who are your major influences?
3. Can you tell us about any upcoming shows?
4. Could you briefly describe the music-making process?
5. Do you ever play any covers?
6. Do you have a recording contract?
7. Do you have a set playlist?
8. How can fans-to-be gain access to your music?
9. How did you meet?
10. How has your music evolved since you first began playing together?
11. What are the main themes of your songs?
12. What are your favourite and least favourite venues?
13. What are your rehearsals generally like?
14. What has been your biggest challenge as a band?
15. What inspired you to make music together?
16. What's the origin of your band's name?
17. What's the ultimate direction for your band?
18. Where have you performed?
19. Which songs do you perform most frequently?
20. Who writes your songs?

Note: Some questions may fit more than one category.

Put the six areas of interest for a band interview in the best, most logical order for the interview.

When you have completed the exercise, you may wish to add further questions of your own.

In pairs conduct an interview.

One person plays the interviewer and the other plays a member of the band who is their spokesperson. The interviewer must decide which specific questions from each category to ask. Use a chart like the one below to organize your interview. Create a list of "areas of interest", such as, musical style, starting out, performing future plans, becoming better known, creating music, and so on. Decide what specific questions you would like to ask.

Areas of interest	1	2
Specific questions		
Answers		

The band's spokesperson can create a cue card like the one below to create a backstory for the band. You can improvise additional information.

Musical style	
Starting out	Name, Origins of the band
Performing live	Where, When
Future plans	
Becoming better known	Website, Recordings
Creating music	Rehearsals, Song writing

Now conduct and record the interview. You may want to use the recording as a prompt for one of the writing exercises later in the chapter.

Creative thinking skills ATLs

When making choices, make sure you have completely understood the task. Always discuss the options with the rest of your group. As a group examine systematically the pros and cons of each option.

- Use brainstorming and visual diagrams to generate new ideas.
- Consider multiple alternatives, including those that might be unlikely or impossible.
- Make unexpected or unusual connections between ideas.
- Make guesses, ask "what if" questions and generate testable hypotheses.

Peer assessment

In small groups, assess the interviews given by your classmates. You can use the rubrics below as a basis for your comments.

	Good	Improvement possible	Needs some improvement	Needs a lot of improvement
Eye contact	Makes good eye contact with audience.	Makes eye contact with the audience most of the time.	Sometimes makes eye contact with the audience.	Does not make eye contact with the audience.
Enthusiasm	Shows great enthusiasm for the topic.	Shows enthusiasm for the topic.	Shows some enthusiasm for the topic.	Shows little enthusiasm for the topic.
Preparation and organization	Very prepared and well organized.	Mostly prepared and well organized.	Somewhat prepared and organized.	Not very prepared or organized.
Clear speech	Speaks very clearly and is very easy to understand.	Speaks clearly most of the time and is fairly easy to understand.	Sometimes speaks clearly and is sometimes easy to understand.	Does not speak clearly and is quite difficult to understand.
Knowledge of topic	Shows excellent understanding of the topic.	Shows good understanding of the topic.	Shows some understanding of the topic.	Shows little understanding of the topic.

Research and communication skills

ATLs

The activity on the right is an opportunity to use your research skills.

- Find, interpret, judge and create information
- Collect, record and verify information
- Make connections between various sources of information
- Revise understanding based on new information and evidence
- Recognize unstated assumptions and bias
- Evaluate evidence and arguments
- Recognize and evaluate propositions
- Draw reasonable conclusions and generalizations

You can also use communication skills to show your findings.

- Create and communicate messages effectively
- Use effectively modes of non-verbal communication
- Use a variety of visual techniques to communicate ideas
- Use appropriate forms of visual for a specific purposes and audience

The verbs "do", "make" and "create" are used frequently when discussing art.

Look at the photograph below. What is the meaning of the phrase "Make it happen"? The three verbs can confuse learners of English. What are the differences between them in meaning and usage? Create a poster to show your understanding of the three verbs and present it to your class.

Note: While interactive oral activities are no longer included in assessment, they are still an excellent way of preparing you to use English orally and develop your speaking skills.

Internal assessment (SL)

Take a look at the visual stimulus on the right. The image relates to the theme "Human ingenuity".

Brainstorming

In pairs, discuss and answer the following questions:

- What is the main idea in the visual stimulus? How does it relate to the theme of the section, "Artistic expression"?
- What do you see in background of the visual stimulus? What does the background tell you about the location and context of the photograph?
- Look at the foreground of the visual stimulus. Describe the people you can see. What is happening?
- Do you think rock music and Anglophone culture are related?
- How does the action relate to the theme of the chapter "Human ingenuity"?

Self-management skills ATLs

What are the three parts of the Internal Assessment (SL)?

How could you use the stimulus to practice for all three parts of the assessment?

Presenting

Based on your answers to the questions above, prepare a four-minute presentation on the visual stimulus.

Remember that the presentation should not only include a description of the photograph, but should also connect it to the topic of celebrity and Anglophone culture. Present the photograph and topic to your classmates.

Peer assessment

Assess the presentations given by your classmates. Use the Language B IA assessment criteria to guide your evaluation.

Criterion	SL
A	Language
B	1. Message—visual stimulus 2. Message: Conversation
C	Interactive skills—communication

Suggest ways in which your classmates can improve their presentation techniques.

Internal assessment (HL)

The *Commitments*

by Roddy Doyle

The action takes place in Dublin in the 1980s. Two friends, Derek Scully and "Outspan" Foster, get together to form a band with a third teenager, Ray. However, they soon realize that they know nothing about the music business. To solve this problem, they want to recruit a friend from school, Jimmy Rabbitte, to be their manager.

We'll ask Jimmy, said Outspan.

Jimmy'll know.

Jimmy Rabbitte knew his music. He knew his stuff all right. You'd never see Jimmy coming home from town without a new album or a 12 inch or at least a 7 inch single. Jimmy ate Melody Maker and the NME every week and Hot Press every two weeks. He listened to Dave Fanning and John Peel[1]. He even read his sister's Jackie when there was no one looking. So Jimmy knew his stuff.

The last time Outspan had flicked through Jimmy's records he'd seen names like Microdisney, Eddie and the Hot Rods, Otis Redding and The Screaming Blue Messiahs: groups Outspan had never heard of, never mind heard. Jimmy even had albums by Frank Sinatra and The Monkees.

So when Outspan and Derek decided, while Ray was out in the jacks[2], that their group needed a new direction they both thought of Jimmy. Jimmy knew what was what. Jimmy knew what was new, what was new but wouldn't be for long and what was going to be new. Jimmy had *Relax* before anyone had heard of Frankie Goes to Hollywood and he'd started slagging them months before anyone realized that they were no good. Jimmy knew his music.

Outspan, Derek and Ray's group, And And And, was three days old; Ray on the Casio and his little sister's glockenspiel, Outspan on his brother's acoustic guitar, Derek on nothing yet but the bass guitar as soon as he'd the money saved.

- Will we tell Ray? Derek asked.
- About Jimmy? Outspan asked back.
- Yeah.
- Better not.

Outspan was trying to work his thumb in under a sticker, "This Guitar Kills Fascists", his brother, an awful hippy, had put on it.

- There's the flush, he said.
- He's comin' back. We'll see Jimmy later.

They were in Derek's bedroom. Ray came back in.

- I was thinkin' there, he said.
- I think maybe we should have an exclamation mark, yeh know, after the second And in the name.
- What?
- It'd be And And exclamation mark, right, And. It'd look deadly on posters.

Outspan said nothing while he imagined it.

- What's an exclamation mark? said Derek.
- Yeh know, said Ray. He drew a big one in the air.
- Oh, yeah, said Derek.
- An' where d'yeh want to put it again?
- And And, He drew a big one in the air.
- And.
- Is it not supposed to go at the end?
- It should go up his ****, said Outspan, picking away at the sticker.

Glossary

1 radio disc jockeys
2 toilets

Note

In your internal assessment, the literary extract will not exceed 300 words. You will be shown two, one from each of the works of literature studied in class.

Brainstorming

In small groups, discuss the following questions then summarize your discussion in point form.

1. Why are Outspan and Derek so keen to recruit Jimmy as manager?
2. What attitudes do the two friends show towards Ray, the third member of the band?
3. What do Derek and Outspan think about the name of the group: And And! And?
4. On the evidence in the text, how successful do you think this band will become?
5. Comment on the language used by the three boys in the passage.
6. How does the passage relate to the theme of human ingenuity?

Note

In your IA presentations, you are expected to:

- summarize the extract
- briefly relate the extract to the literary work as a whole
- express your opinions on the characters, events, ideas and themes presented in the extract.

Presenting

Based on your answers to the questions above, prepare a four-minute presentation on the content of the text.

Remember that the presentation should include answers to the questions above. Present to your classmates. Your classmates should prepare individual questions about the text which they can ask you at the end of your presentation.

Peer assessment

In small groups, assess the presentations given by your classmates. You may use the HL IA assessment criteria available in the Language B guide to help with your comments.

Paper 1: Review

A review is a form of journalistic mass media in which you observe and evaluate a cultural artefact such as a film, a book, a play, a performance or a TV programme. You then give an overview or summary and offer your opinions and recommendations. Reviews can be found in magazines, newspapers and in blogs. Look at a second review of the film *Sing Street* and then complete the analysis that follows.

Sing Street review

Genre: Drama

Plot: A boy growing up in Dublin during the 1980s escapes his strained family life by starting a band to impress the mysterious girl he likes.

Rating: M – Contains offensive language

Duration: 105 minutes

Starring: Ferdia Walsh-Peelo, Lucy Boynton, Jack Reynor, Aidan Gillen, Mark McKenna

Director: John Carney *(Once)*

The Review

John Carney's film **Sing Street** is a joy to watch. It's intelligent as it is warming, a pubescent love story with moments of comedic heaven and its 80s soundtrack. The time-warped music features a lot in this film, taking me back to my misspent Selwyn College school days. So it was sure to be a winner.

Sing Street is a cross between Carney's earlier 2007 hit musical romantic outing **Once** mixed with the band sensibility of 90's film **The Commitments**. Also set in Ireland, the film focuses on the exploits of young student Conor Lalor, his love interest and his band with school mates called **Sing Street**, which is kind of a naff band name but appropriate given it's the 80s.

Set against a stark inner-city Dublin in 1985, Sing Street's young protagonist Conor broodily played by Ferdia Walsh-Peelo is moved to a free state-school, this in turn leads to a chance meeting after school with local beauty Raphina played by the spirited Lucy Boynton. Of course, he tells her that he's in a band (when he isn't) and invites her to be in his music video – thus begins Sing Street the band and for Conor the 'game of love'.

The film banks a lot on its success on the eighties culture and music (the family watching a Duran Duran music video on TV is a hoot). However there are also some great acting performances. Conor's elder brother Brendan superbly played by Jack Reynor, his unkempt looks and comedic delivery were spot on.

Ferdia as Conor I found was overall convincing and perfectly casted as the angst-ridden songwriter who pulls together a band with school mates, their originals aren't bad either. Dad Robert, played by Aiden Gillen, is a coup, his acting is credible as the dismissive dad, funny too.

Sure it has the cheesy ending, but the film gets away with it, almost unnoticed, due to its strong cast. It's **The Commitments** for the 21st century, a love story that seemingly works, and you have to applaud this smaller budgeted film that has been pitted against some big blockbusters and has stood its own.

The Verdict

Go see Sing Street. It will have you toe tapping and punching the air as you relive the horror that was the eighties.

Analysing a review

A review can consist of three basic features.

1. A summary – the details of the film, but without mentioning the ending!
2. A body consisting of an introduction, sometimes with a thesis, and supporting paragraphs about different aspects of the film. As you read identify the different aspects of the film reviewed.
3. A verdict – a recommendation

Use a chart like the one below to analyse the second review of Sing Street.

	Your response	**Evidence from the text**
Introduction Thesis (big idea) =		
Aspect 1 Topic =		
Aspect 2 Topic =		
Aspect 3 Topic =		
Aspect 4 Topic =		
Aspect 5 Topic =		
Verdict Final thought =		

Language and style

We know that English has different registers. These registers or levels of familiarity go from the very formal, "A most enjoyable musical experience", to the informal and familiar, "A totally cool show – a total blast!!"

You need to think about the audience and the type of publication you are writing for. If you are blogging for an audience of your peers, you could use more familiar language. If you are writing for a school magazine, but writing for your peer group, then you will want to sound chatty and still show that you have expert insightful ideas.

On the other hand if your task involves writing for a magazine where you do not know the audience, or want a less personal relationship with the readership, then you are going to have to be more formal in your use of register. A review of a film or book is an analysis so it is usually written in the present tense, as in the example on the left. However, you should write a review of an event that has already taken place, such as a concert or performance, in the past tense.

Audience

In the review above what do you think the relationship between the reviewer and the audience is? In what kind of magazine might the review have appeared?

Conceptual understanding

A review can have several purposes. In other words, the language in the text does a variety of jobs, such as instruct, describe, or explain. Complete the chart below by finding out whether the second review fulfils the same purposes as the first. Justify your answers with evidence (if any) from the text.

Does the second review of *Sing Street* …	Yes/No/ Maybe	Evidence in the text
summarize the plot of the film in a way that does not reveal the ending?		
describe the main characters of the film?		
analyse the film in terms of its artistic merit and technical skill?		
comment on the acting, direction, cinematography and script?		
analyse the film in terms of its messages and values?		
compare the film to similar films that came before it?		
entertain the readers with its comments?		
recommend which film is most worth their time and money?		
alert parents about whether or not the film is appropriate viewing for children?		

Thinking skills

ATLs

Analyse and evaluate issues and ideas	Your responses
• This is the second review of the same film that you have read. If you had to choose, which one would you say is better? How will you decide? The information and analyses you conducted earlier should help you. • How does it compare to the first review you read? Which do you prefer? Why? • Does the second review communicate a variety of ideas effectively? • Does the review use features that distinguish it clearly from other text types? • Is the review well structured? • Does the review use language appropriate to its audience? • Justify your answers.	

Paper 1 practice

Choose one of the tasks below and write between 250 and 400 words (SL) or 450 and 600 words (HL).

1. Imagine that the school band you interviewed earlier in this section performed at a festival in your local park. You attended the performance and want to recommend the band to your schoolmates via the school newspaper. Write a review of the band's performance that you saw in the park.
2. Write an enthusiastic review of a film you have recently seen. The review will be published as a post on your personal blog. Think about the different aspects of the film you want to review.
3. A café offering your favourite food has recently opened in your area. Unfortunately, when you visited the restaurant you had a poor dining experience. Write a review of the restaurant for an Internet travel guide.

Brainstorming

Follow the steps below.

1. Reflect on everything you have learned in this section. Choose your focal point and your point of view. What information do you want to emphasize?
2. Generate ideas to be used in your text. Think about the purpose of your review. Who will read your review? What will be your message to your readers?
3. Think about the language and register you will use to communicate your message and to clarify the purpose of your review.
4. Sort your ideas into a logical order. Choose good examples to support your ideas.

Thinking skills ATLs

- Analyse and evaluate issues and ideas
- Gather and organize relevant information to formulate an argument
- Interpret data
- Evaluate evidence and arguments
- Draw reasonable conclusions and generalizations

1. Why is the review the best text type to use for these written tasks?
2. How will a review help you achieve the purpose of the task?
3. Which register and style will you use? Why?
4. How does the context of the task inform the choice of content, register and style?

Planning

You could use a chart like the one below to help you plan your review. Think about what measures you will take to make sure your piece is well written and effective.

	Topic :	
Introduction Thesis (big idea) =		
Aspect 1 Topic =		Example =
Aspect 2 Topic =		Example =
Aspect 3 Topic =		Example =
Aspect 4 Topic =		Example =
Aspect 5 Topic =		Example =
Verdict Final thought =		

Self-management skills ATLs

A good writer will produce several drafts of a piece of writing in order to improve it. Always re-read critically the completed draft of any text you write and make further revisions where you can.

- Plan strategies and take action to achieve personal and academic goals
- Use appropriate strategies for organizing complex information

Drafting

Once you have completed the chart, write a first draft of your review.

- Write an eye-catching title.
- Make sure to use all the conventions and formatting associated with a review.
- Consider the context in which you are writing.
  - What is the publication?
  - Who is the audience?

What level of formality will you use to address your audience?

Re-read the completed first draft of your review and revise where necessary.

Remember you will be assessed on three criteria: criterion A, language; criterion B, message; criterion C, conceptual understanding (including audience, context and purpose).

Thinking and communication skills ATLs

This is one of the earliest photos of another Irish band, U2, just as they were starting out as teenagers. Today they are arguably one of the most successful bands on the planet. The four members of the group met at school, formed their band in 1976 and are still together, composing, recording and performing today.

Think about the rock bands you know of. Think of examples of successful bands that have experienced the positives and negatives of stardom.

What might be the reasons why most groups fail while very few succeed?

What are the most important characteristics of successful bands that stay together for long periods? In groups discuss these questions and draw up a list of your findings.

Imagine that you and the people in your discussion group were in a band. What measures would you take to make sure of your band's long-term musical and financial success in an Anglophone culture?

Conclusion to research question A

What qualities do you need to become a successful musician?

1. Now that you have completed this section what are your conclusions and reactions to the question above? What have you learned about the topic?
2. What justifications would you give for your answers?
3. What more would you need to know before you can come to a definitive conclusion about the statement?

Conceptual understanding

Remember that language can have numerous purposes. A purpose can be defined as "the use to which language is put". For example in speech we greet people, ask questions, congratulate someone on a success, ask advice, express affection and compliment each other. All of these spoken acts are considered to be different purposes.

What other purposes can you think of? Make a list.

Written language too has specific purposes. These include:

- giving instructions, guidelines or advice
- narrating stories or events
- describing people places or things
- explaining events, mechanisms and systems
- persuading an audience of a point of view.

A TOK moment

TOK

A good book review must be more than a simple summary of the story.

The chart below lists some of the purposes of a book review.

Now use the chart to find evidence of these purposes in the book review on the right.

A review can have these different purposes	Yes/No/ Maybe	Evidence in the text
It can inform the reader of the title of the book and the name of the author.		
It can explain what the book is about.		
It can describe the setting.		
It can narrate the plot.		
It can describe the central characters.		
It can explain the central character's problems.		
It can describe the supporting characters.		
It can describe a special moment in the book.		
It can describe the style of the book.		
It can persuade the reader of the quality of the book.		

Imagine that the text had a different purpose, for example, to advertise and market the book, rather than review it. How would that change the content and language of the text?

List the changes you would have to make in order to repurpose the text from a review to an advertisement.

A Review: Pigeon English by Stephen Kelman

Stephen Kelman achieves something wonderful in his debut novel, *Pigeon English*, which was shortlisted for the 2011 Man Booker prize.

Using Harri's efforts to acclimatise to English life and to accept (and investigate) the murder of another young boy—the novel's jumping off scene—Kelman creates a novel that is both about language and youth.

Kelman describes the problem of Harri's two lives, two countries; half of his family remains in Ghana, waiting. Harri consistently translates English words and idioms for the reader. He explains that AKA "stands for also known as" and that superheroes are "special people who protect you." Harri wants so much to understand his new world and to be a part of it that he cannot stop voicing his discoveries.

Harri narrates most of the story in a simple but open manner, as an eleven-year-old might and peppers the pages with Ghanian dialect. By putting together "donkey" and "hours," we have a new way to say "a long time." Common phrases are elided, "go away, you" becomes "gowayou."

Harri asks, "Who'd chook a boy just to get his Chicken Joe's?" He knows this is a serious crime. But Harri is still adjusting to life in London. He has already made some bad friends, the type of friends who vandalise churches, harass the elderly, and may very well have murdered "the dead boy," as Harri calls him throughout.

Harri and his best friend resolve to find out the truth about "the dead boy"—simply because it must be done. Harri's use of English neatly reflects both his naïveté and his confidence.

Kelman has created a fine first novel, worthy of its Man Booker prize nomination.

Section B: Media and communication

Research question B:

How are celebrities affected by fame?

1. What are your first thoughts and reactions to the question above?
2. What justifications would you give for your answers?
3. What more would you need to know before you can come to a definitive conclusion about the question?

Before you read

Fame has an incredibly powerful effect on a person. The research question for this section is, "How are celebrities affected by fame?" Examine the visual above and study the chart below listing some of positive and negative effects of being a celebrity. Discuss the matter with a partner and add your own ideas to the two lists. Share your conclusions with the rest of your class.

Positive effects of fame	Negative effects of fame
Feel adored by fans	Be a hostage to changing tastes and fashions
Feel totally in control of career	Suffer from insecurity
Have freedom to create	Suffer burn out
Have the power to influence society	Have no privacy
Feel hugely successful and fulfilled	Be mentally unstable

Research skills (ATLs)

Research the issue of the effects of fame. You might want to start by examining your ideas from the previous section, that is, why some rock bands are able to achieve long-term success, and yet others fail.

Find examples of stars who have been able to handle fame. Find examples of those who have crashed and burned. What separates the successful ones from the tragedies?

In doing so use your **media literacy skills** to:

- interact with media to use and create ideas and information
- locate, organize, analyse, and evaluate information from a variety of sources and media.

How to Interview a Celebrity

by Ken Levine

As a public service to any journalist assigned to do an inane starlet profile, here is the style sheet YOU MUST FOLLOW!!!

Whether it's for the *L.A. Times*, *Entertainment Weekly*, *Parade*, or *Mercenary Life*, there is a specific protocol you are advised to follow to the letter. So please take note:

The interview must be a lunch date at a chic café, clearly identified.

The celebrity will arrive late. You must report how late and what her excuse was. And you must forgive her. Even if the excuse is, "I forgot" or "I had to liquor up to do this because I find you repulsive," you must be charmed.

It's important to describe her outfit. Is she wearing jeans? Lead with that. She has new sunglasses? Hold page one! And, whatever you do, describe the celebrity's hair. Was it pulled back? Tousled? No one cares what she thinks but they need to know whether her hair was red, blonde, or strawberry blonde? You spent five years in journalism school. Use your skills.

Painstakingly note whether she picks at an egg white omelet or a Waldorf salad. Celebrities don't eat, they "pick at."

Note that she eats healthy and it's paying off. You must compliment a celebrity's appearance. She is "glowing" and "radiant." If she shows up looking like the dog's breakfast, she is dressed "casual" and "fun funky."

Once the budding young diva starts yammering, learn what is print-worthy and what is brain-dead nonsense. Listen carefully because often you won't be able to distinguish one from the other.

She will tell you that she is now in "a good place." Report that. She's learned some real "life lessons" on her last movie. At this point she'll start talking real fast and you might have a tough time getting it all down. So make it easy on yourself. Write her answers out before the interview.

She'll tell you what she thinks of the world situation. She'll have suggestions for how to fix it. Ignore!!! All of it. Complete balloon juice. This is where you can pick at your food.

She'll gush about her latest movie. That's the only reason she's there. It's certainly not to spend time with you. Should you excuse yourself after lunch and go to the bathroom for three minutes, by the time you get back she'll have no idea who you are.

The thing about this film was that the director (just fill in the blank here) who is a "genius" allowed her to tap into an inner place she didn't know even existed. He unleashed the "little girl" in her and maybe two or three past lives.

Do not bring up anything negative. Yes, she killed that pedestrian but it was only one and it was before she was in her "good place" and besides, she's all about Africa now, so that's what you need to focus on.

Never EVER talk about yourself or bring up any topic other than her. She will stare at you in disbelief like you just killed her puppy.

By now she's sipping her cappuccino (which must be duly reported as well as whether she stirs it lazily, holds the cup with two hands, etc. — this is vital information). Very gingerly, bring up boyfriends. She may volunteer that her relationship is "in a good place" and then you're home free.

Again, no negatives. Do not mention that she ruined a marriage or broke up a home. Listen for these words: "(blank) has given me a real sense of self and opened my eyes to so many things.' It means she's wrapping it up.

Thank her for taking the time. She will shake your hand and thank you. She's amazed you got so much information out of her. She usually never is that revealing. You'll look away for a second, a gesture of modesty. Poof! By the time you look back she'll be gone.

Write that up, see it three weeks later as a cover story in *People*, and request a transfer overseas.

https://www.huffingtonpost.com/ken-levine/how-to-interview-a-celebr_b_60360.html

Reading comprehension

Choose the correct answer from A, B, C or D.

1 The journalist says the main purpose of text is to:

- **A.** describe a celebrity
- **B.** provide guidelines to other journalists
- **C.** provide a public service
- **D.** profile a starlet.

Identify whether the journalist believes these ideas are true or false and justify your answer with a relevant brief quotation from the text.

		True	False
2.	The interview must take place in a very anonymous place.		
Justification:			
3.	Never mention whether the celebrity arrives late or why.		
Justification:			
4.	Always describe the star's sense of fashion.		
Justification:			
5.	Never discuss the star's eating habits.		
Justification:			
6.	Always have something positive to say about the celebrity's looks.		
Justification:			
7.	When she speaks, separate what is nonsense from what is important.		
Justification:			
8.	It is impossible to predict what a celebrity might say in an interview.		
Justification:			

Thinking skills ATLs

Do you think a journalist would profile a young male actor or singer in the same way?

Is the writer's language justified, or is the article sexist in any way?

To answer these questions:

- use a set of criteria to define "sexist"
- evaluate evidence and arguments about the existence of sexism in the article
- draw reasonable conclusions and generalizations.

9. Always listen carefully for her views on international politics.

Justification:

10. At all costs avoid all embarrassing topics.

Justification:

Choose the correct phrase from the text to complete the following sentences. Base your answers on information as it appears between lines 21 and 32.

11. The celebrity's reason for attending the interview is to …

12. Making her latest film has allowed the celebrity to identify with …

13. If you talk about yourself, she will react as if …

14. You should describe how the celebrity drinks her coffee; …

Choose the correct answer from A, B, C or D.

15. The word "gingerly" suggests that when discussing boyfriends the journalist must be:

A. convincing
B. careful
C. persuasive
D. forceful

Answer the following questions.

16. Which phrase suggests that the celebrity is concluding the interview?

17. Name the two final facts that should not be mentioned in the interview.

18. What does the actress say to compliment the journalist on his/her interview techniques?

Choose the correct answer from A, B, C or D and justify your answer.

19. The writer's approach to the topic of interviewing the famous is:

A. satirical
B. factual
C. persuasive
D. balanced.

20. What phrase tells us that the actress speaks to journalists no longer than absolutely necessary?

HL extension HL

What effects does fame appear to have had on the imaginary young actress that the journalist has interviewed?

Choose 10 adjectives to describe the young woman from the list below and justify your choices with evidence from the text.

adventurous	egotistical	inconsiderate	passionate	sincere
ambitious	fabulous	inspiring	petulant	sophisticated
callous	flashy	naïve	plain-speaking	soulful
cantankerous	generous	nasty	proud	subtle
charming	hot-headed	natural	quick-tempered	touchy
chic	imaginative	obnoxious	reclusive	unbalanced
cruel	immature	ostentatious	sassy	warmhearted
cynical	impulsive	outspoken	selfish	zealous

What do you think will happen to the actress interviewed in the text? Imagine where she will be and what she will be doing 10 years from now. Justify your answers.

Oral activity: Interview with a young star (role play)

Look at the picture here. Imagine the interviewer is talking to a young actress who has just made her first successful appearance in a film. As a journalist you want to conduct a fruitful interview and discover as much detail about the young actress as you can for the article which will appear on your blog.

Brainstorming

Make a list of which topics you might want to ask about and questions you might want to ask.

Closed questions usually begin with a question word such as, "when'?", "where?" or "who?" They are usually easy to answer. They can be effectively used at the beginning of an interview to encourage participation and can be very useful in fact-finding.

In an interview use **open questions**, such as, "could you tell our readers about ...?" or "could you explain/describe/tell ....". An open question starting with "why" or "how" cannot be answered with a simple "yes" or "no". Such open-ended questions encourage people to talk, explain their ideas and can produce a large amount of information.

Closed questions	Open questions
Do/did/will you ...? When/where/what/ ...? Can/have/might/should you ...? Which is better/worse/right/wrong A or B?	Why ...? How ...? Tell me about ...? What do you think about ...?
Useful for obtaining facts, basic information, quick reactions Produce short answers Lead to "yes"/"no" response	Useful for obtaining thoughts, opinions, feelings Produce longer answers Allow for thoughtful responses

Planning

Decide which closed and which open questions you might you want to ask.

When you have finished, choose your 10 strongest questions and put them in the most logical order.

Presenting

In pairs improvise an interview in which one person is the interviewer and the other person is the actress (or actor). At the end of the interview, swap roles. Record the interviews, as you may want to use the information in the section on writing practice later in this chapter.

Internal assessment (SL)

Take a look at the visual stimuli below. The images relate to the theme of the chapter: "Human ingenuity". Choose one of the two pictures and prepare a presentation.

Brainstorming

- What is the main idea in your chosen photograph? How does it relate to the title of the section: "Media and communication"?
- Look at the foreground of the photograph. Describe the people you can see.
- What is happening in the picture? How does the action relate to the title of the chapter "Celebrity"?
- Is the concept of "celebrity" unique to Anglophone culture?

Presenting

Based on your answers to the questions above, prepare a four-minute presentation on the photograph.

Remember that the presentation should not only include a description of the photograph, but should also connect it to the theme of human ingenuity and an Anglophone culture. Present your photograph and topic to your classmates.

Peer assessment

Assess the presentations given by your classmates. Consider the Language B SL IA criteria as a guide in your assessment.

	IA (SL)
Criterion A	Language
Criterion B	1. Message: visual stimulus 2. Message: conversation
Criterion C	Interactive skills: communication

Suggest ways in which your classmates can improve their presentation techniques.

Self-management skills ATLs

Prepare for your assessment

Work with a partner and take turns to practice part 2 of the Internal assessment (SL), in which a teacher asks you additional questions about the content of the photograph and the related topic.

In this way you can learn to "think like an examiner" and anticipate the kinds of questions you might be asked in the examination.

Internal assessment (HL)

"When She is Old and I am Famous"

by Julie Orringer

The narrator, 20-year-old Mira, is studying art in Florence, Italy when her younger teenage cousin, Aïda, arrives for a visit. The girls have grown up together. However, Mira has always felt inferior because of her cousin's beauty. Now that they are both older, Aïda has become an extremely successful fashion model who appears on the cover of Vogue *and who charms every man she meets. Mira is potentially a very talented painter but has little confidence in herself.*

There are great leaves, like a crown, on her head. Grapes hang in her hair, and in her hands she holds the green vines. She dances with both arms in the air. On her smallest toe she wears a ring of pink shell. Can someone tell her, please, to go home? This is my Italy and my story. We are in a vineyard near Florence. I have just turned twenty. She is a girl, a gangly teen, and she is a model. She is famous for almost getting killed. Last year, when she was fifteen, a photographer asked her to dance on the rail of a bridge and she fell. A metal rod beneath the water pierced her chest. Water came into the wound, close to her heart, and for three weeks she was in the hospital with an infection so furious it made her chant nonsense. All the while she got thinner and more pale, until, when she emerged, they thought she might be the best model there ever was. Her hair is wavy and long and buckeye brown, and her blue eyes have a stunned sad look to them. She is 5'11" tall and she weighs one hundred and thirteen pounds. She has told me so.

This week she is visiting from Paris, where she lives with her father, my uncle Claude.

(...)

Aïda. That is her terrible name. Ai-ee-duh: two cries of pain and one of stupidity. The vines tighten around her body as she spins, and Joseph snaps photographs. She knows he will like it, the way that leaves cling, the way the grapes stain her white dress. We are trespassing here in a vintner's vines, spilling the juice of his expensive grapes, and if he sees us he will surely shoot us. What an end to my tall little cousin. Between the purple stains on her chest, a darker stain spreads. Have I mentioned yet that I am fat?

(...)

Aïda rolls her shoulders and let her hair fall forward, hiding her face in shadow. They can't take their eyes off her. Uncle Claude would have scolded her for removing her sun hat. I have picked it up and am wearing it now. It is gold straw and fits perfectly. What else of hers could I put on? Not even her gloves.

"Now stand perfectly still," Joseph says, extending his thumb and index finger as if to frame Aïda. He snaps a few pictures, then lets the camera drop. He looks as if he would like to throw a net over. He will show these pictures to his friends back home, telling them how he slept with her between the grapevines. This will be a lie, I hope. "Dance again," he says," this time slower."

She rotates her hips like a Balinese dancer." Like this?"

Note

In your internal assessment, the literary extract will not exceed 300 words. You will be shown two, one from each of the works of literature studied in class.

Brainstorming

In small groups, discuss the following questions then summarize your discussion in point form.

- What are the main topics of the extract?
- What attitudes does Mira, the narrator, show towards her cousin Aïda?
- How does being so famous at a young age affect Aïda?
- Based on the evidence in the text, what advice would you give to Mira about her negative attitude towards Aïda?
- What advice would you give to Aïda to help her to cope with her fame?

Presenting

Based on your answers to the questions above, prepare a four-minute presentation on the text.

Make your presentation to your classmates. Your classmates should prepare individual questions about the extract which they can ask you at the end of your presentation.

Peer assessment

Assess the presentations given by your classmates. Use the Language B HL IA assessment criteria to guide your assessment.

	Internal assessment (HL)
Criterion A	Language
Criterion B	1. Message: literary extract 2. Message: conversation
Criterion C	Interactive skills: communication

Suggest ways in which your classmates can improve their presentation techniques.

Self-management skills ATLs

Prepare for your assessment

Work with a partner and take it in turns to practice part 2 of the Internal assessment (HL), in which a teacher asks you additional questions about the content of the extract.

Make a list of literature topics the examiner might ask you about. Here are some terms you might want to consider: plot/ theme/ conflict/ character/ characterization/ setting/ symbol/ point of view/ purpose/ narrator.

In this way you can learn to "think like an examiner" and anticipate the kinds of questions you might be asked in the examination.

Paper 1: The written interview

Another specific mass media text type is the interview. An interview is a form of magazine article that allows the interviewer to conduct and then publish a person-to-person discussion.

Reporter: "Have you got a few words for all your fans here tonight?'

Structure

An interview will have a question-and-answer structure. The interview itself may be preceded by a short introduction in which you explain who your interviewee is and where you are meeting.

Introduction

Sometimes, you will want to establish a good relationship with the interviewee, "Bernadette O'Sullivan met me at Café X to talk about her latest project." Alternatively, you can introduce the interviewee and the topic at the same time, "Bernadette, did you know how special your latest film was going to be when you first read the script?"

The main body

Whatever the situation a good interview is carefully structured. Before the interview, decide which questions you would like to ask and in what order you want to ask them. Often it makes sense to start with general questions and move on to more specific and personal ones.

Conclusion or "wrap-up"

The last question could allow the respondent to provide information about future plans,"So what do you see as the next stage?"

Format

The interview will appear in a specific way:

- A title
- An introductory paragraph about the interviewee
- A context paragraph detailing why, when and where the interview took place
- A question-and-answer format
- Speakers are introduced by names or initials, usually in bold followed by a colon
- The journalist's questions are often printed in bold.

For example:

RR: What songs did you perform when you were going through the audition process?

FW: I sang "Blackbird".

Analyzing a written interview

Ferdia Walsh-Peelo and Mark McKenna say 'Sing Street' the band is still a possibility

The stars of John Carney's coming-of-age musical comedy "Sing Street" have been on U.S. soil for just about 24 hours and they're already envisioning the American dream: Going viral.

They chat over Cokes at the Eliot Hotel in Back Bay about the film, keeping the "Sing Street" band together and a John Carney-'80s education.

What songs did you perform when you were going through the audition process?

FW: I sang "Blackbird" and I think it really helped a lot that I didn't go in and sing "Falling Slowly." John said so many people thought it was such a good idea but he's heard that song like a million times.

MM: I did an acoustic version of "Chocolate" by the 1975. It was pretty funny.

The film takes place in Dublin in the '80s, years before either of you were born, what did you have to research and learn before diving in?

FW: He sent me over loads of music videos from the '80s because that's a really good place to learn from; they have the fashion and the vibe and the sound and the movements. Just watching Talking Heads and the Cure, a lot of that is hugely influential in the performances that we're doing. It was a huge learning curve for all of us, especially me because I hadn't discovered '80s music yet. Except Mark, he was already the master.

MM: I was already really into the '80s already, so when John would be like, "Mark, you should look up this band," I'd be like, "John I already know that band." [Laughs] Or "Mark, you should watch this John Hughes film," I'd be like, "John, that's my *favorite* John Hughes film."

Even though it is decades ago, are there any major differences in growing up as a teenager in Ireland versus America that still ring true?

FW: What you see in "Sing Street" is pretty similar [to growing up in Ireland today], but not as violent.

MM: There are areas in Ireland that can still be quite rough, but the school wouldn't be like that now.

FW: I went to a rough area in school but I somehow won bullies over and became great friends with them. I know I don't seem like the type, but like in this day and age, if you play music, people just like you.

Are there any plans to keep the band going?

FW: Mark and I play good songs and we've thought about it, but we don't want to push it. John (Carney) is not coming to us saying, "If you want to do this band thing, we'll get you a record deal and we'll pay for everything." Instead he's like, "If it happens it happens." We don't want to be some kind of boy band, reminding people we're from the movie "Sing Street."

MM: We don't want to be like 10 years down the line, with long beards, still singing "Drive It Like You Stole It"...

FW: While crying. [*Laughs*]

"Sing Street" opens April 15 in New York, nationwide April 29.

by Rachel Raczka

https://www.metro.us/entertainment/ferdia-walsh-peelo-and-mark-mckenna-say-sing-street-the-band-is-still-a-possibility/zsJpdl---YZ14bEc9eMCPs

Thinking and self-management skills ATLs

Albert Einstein, when interviewed about dealing with fame said, “It is strange to be known so universally and yet to be so lonely.”

Fame can put a huge amount of stress on individuals, and involuntarily they become role models to millions. The suddenly famous are constantly in the public eye so they do not have time to analyse the ups and downs of success, or fully consider other negative aspects of fame, such as the media pressure.

Imagine you became a celebrity. What would you be? A singer? A film star? A writer? Would you be able to handle fame? What skills would you need to be able to make a success of being a success? Would fame impact your life negatively or positively? How would you use your fame and celebrity? In this exercise practice creative thinking.

- Make guesses, ask “what if” questions and generate testable hypotheses.
- Apply existing knowledge to generate new ideas.
- Create original ideas; use existing ideas in new ways.

Make notes or record your interview. When you have finished look back on what you have said.
What do you learn about yourself from the exercise?
What do you learn about the nature of fame and celebrity?

Read the interview with two of the young actors from the film Sing Street and answer the following questions.

- How successful is the interview? Give reasons for your answers.
- How does the journalist get so much information out of just four questions?
- The journalist seems to have only written up the main part of the whole interview. Why?
- How do you think the interview began in real life?
- How do you think the interview ended in real life?

Practising interview techniques

Imagine interviewing a celebrity of your choice. What questions would you like to ask?

Here are 12 interview questions you might like to use.

1. How do you cope with stress?
2. What is your next project?
3. What great event do you wish you had witnessed?
4. What has been your greatest adventure so far?
5. What has been you biggest regret?
6. What is your greatest hope for the future?
7. What is your greatest strength?
8. What is your idea of happiness?
9. What was you first big break?
10. How did you start out in the business?
11. What has been your worst moment?
12. Which thing about yourself would you like to improve most?

Choose the five or six questions you would most like to ask your chosen interviewee.

In what order would you put your questions? Remember that you may wish to change your closed questions into open ones.

With a partner conduct the interview and record it. You may want to use this as a prompt for one of the writing exercises later in this section.

Writing activity: The written interview

Here are three opportunities to practice writing up interviews.

Plan, draft, revise and redraft one of these stimuli.

Exam tip

At standard level you should write between 250 and 400 words.

At higher level you should write between 450 and 600 words.

1. Re-read the text on page 111, "How to interview a celebrity". Imagine you have actually conducted the interview with the starlet satirized in the text. Write the interview as if it was to be published in a popular gossip magazine. You may wish to use the questions and interview structure suggested by the writer in the text. Alternatively, use some of the questions suggested on page 120. Remember to use the structure, conventions and formatting appropriate to a written interview.
2. Choose a music video that you really like. Imagine you could interview one of the musicians. What questions would you ask? Use the questions to write an interview to be published in your personal blog. Remember to use the structure, conventions and formatting appropriate to a written interview.
3. In this chapter you have already conducted an interview with your imaginary future self as a celebrity. Use this interview as the basis for writing an interview to appear in a magazine, newspaper or blog of your choice. Remember to use the structure, conventions and formatting appropriate to a written interview.

Brainstorming

Follow the steps below.

1. Reflect on everything you have learned in this section. Choose your focal point and your point of view. What information do you want to emphasize?
2. Generate ideas to be used in your text. Research additional material to support your opinion.
3. What else do you need to think about? Language and register? Audience? Context and text type?
4. Sort your ideas into a logical order. Choose examples to support your ideas.

Communication skills ATLs

When you write an assignment for any subject, including English B, it is best to have a fairly clear idea of the structure of the text before you do too much drafting. You will find that the words will come more easily to you if you know in advance how the different parts of the text will join together.

In this book you will find charts and models to help you structure different text types. Consult them and use them to help you to plan what it is that you want to say.

Then you will find that it is much easier to communicate your ideas in written English fluently and accurately.

Planning

You might want to use some of the questions suggested on page 120 to help you plan your interview. Think about what measures you will take to make sure your interview is well written and effective.

Choose five or six questions to ask. For Task 3 you might want to add more specific questions about the actress's IB experiences. What order will ask them in? Remember that you may wish to change your closed questions into open ones.

Write a draft of the body of your interview. Write an eye-catching title. Make sure to use all the conventions and formatting associated with a written interview.

Consider the context in which you are writing. What is the publication? Who is the audience? What level of formality will you use to address your audience?

Re-read the completed draft of your written interview and revise where necessary.

Remember you will be assessed on three criteria: Criterion A: Language, Criterion B: Message, Criterion C: Conceptual understanding (including audience, context and purpose).

Self-management skills ATLs

Planning, drafting and then redrafting your written work can at times seem boring, pointless and a waste of time. However, in the world outside school, universities and employers prize individuals who can produce texts in clear, accurate and well constructed English.

Remember this: as you improve your texts you are also improving yourself!

You are also learning to manage your state of mind and improve the following:

- Focus and concentration
- Perseverance
- Emotional management
- Self-motivation
- Resilience

Listening comprehension

Click the icon to practice the listening section of Paper 2. This is another multiple choice activity. As you listen, mentally cross out any options that are wrong or only half true. This will help you select the best answer.

Conceptual understanding: Purpose

As we have seen in the last section, all texts have specific communicative purposes. This can be defined as "the use to which language is put".

Conduct an Internet search to find the lyrics to the song "So You Want To Be a Rock 'N' Roll Star" by The Byrds. The song was written over 50 years ago. The group, The Byrds, had enjoyed huge worldwide success for two years. However, singer Gene Clark had already left; guitarist and singer David Crosby and drummer Michael Clarke would also be gone before their next album was completed. The two remaining members of the band, Chris Hillman and Jim McGuin, wrote this song and, whether or not they knew it, this last hit signaled the end of their brief stardom.

Look at the list below and see which of these purposes the song lyrics have.

- Giving instructions, guidelines or advice to anyone thinking of becoming a rock star
- Narrating the story of the band's rise to fame
- Describing people, places or things
- Describing what it is like to be a rock star
- Persuading the audience that the lifestyle of a rock star is unhealthy and should be avoided

Does the song lyric "So You Wanna Be A Rock 'N' Roll Star?" have only one purpose? Does it have multiple purposes? Think about the title of the song "So Your Want To be a Rock 'N' Roll Star". Think of an alternative purpose of the song, for example, to persuade someone to actually become a star. How would you change the lyrics of the song to reflect this new purpose? Discuss these questions with your classmates.

A TOK moment

TOK

Now that you have looked at the concept of "purpose" in language, answer this question.

In what ways can language be used to influence, persuade or manipulate an audience?

In particular you might want to think about the role of the media and the ways in which they portray celebrities. Find an article about a celebrity from an English language magazine.

You might then ask this question: In what ways can language be used to influence, persuade or manipulate people?

At this point you might like to re-read the text "How to interview a celebrity".

In class you can debate this TOK question: What techniques are used in the media to make us believe that celebrities are extraordinary people?

Conclusion to research question B

How are artists affected by fame?

1. Now that you have completed the section, what do you now think is the answer?
2. To what extent have your opinions on the subject changed since the beginning of this chapter? To what extent have your opinions remained the same?
3. Justify your answers.

Section C: Entertainment

Research question C:

Why do some fans hero worship celebrities such as actors and singers?

1. What are your first thoughts and reactions to the question above?
2. What justifications would you give for your answers?
3. What more would you need to know before you can come to a definitive conclusion about the question?

Before you listen

In a recent questionnaire, members of the public were asked this question: "Why do fans worship celebrities, such as actors and singers?" Here are the top 10 responses.

It is easy to identify with celebrities. It is much harder to identify with people that have really made a huge contribution to the human condition.

Hero worship is a learned behaviour from the media which dominate the world around us.

There are successful actors and musicians that definitely deserve respect because of their achievements.

Celebrities command the power and influence to dictate fashions and ideas.

Fans want to recognize themselves in famous people. They can create idealized versions of themselves as pop stars, actors or actresses.

Fans are full of envy and desire. They want to be as attractive, desirable, rich and famous as their heroes.

Fans can experience drama second-hand or through the personal lives of certain celebrities.

Celebrities put a face on the values of a society people can relate to. They represent success in a very visible manner.

Excellent actors and actresses and singers communicate to us. They make us feel certain emotions and understand certain ideas. We feel close to them.

It's purely due to biology and hormones. Most people who go crazy over celebrities are in their teenage years or early twenties and are still immature.

Are you a fan? Pick at least three celebrities from different areas of the arts in different Anglophone societies and cultures. Using the list above, explain each one's popularity. You may include reasons of your own.

Of the celebrities you have picked, which one most deserves to be famous? Which one is the least deserving? What reasons and justifications do you have for your choices?

Listening comprehension

Teen idol Serena Castaneda talking about her fans

Listen to the audio clip provided of the singer and fashion designer Serena Castaneda talking about her fans in an interview with a radio DJ.

Answer the following questions.

1. What is the name of the radio show?
2. How long has it been since Serena's last appearance on the show?
3. How many live shows has Serena done so far?
4. For Serena, what is the most confusing part of touring?
5. Which group of people has contributed questions to the interview?
6. From statements A to F, select the three that are true according to the interview.
   - **A.** According to Serena, connecting with her fans is as important as performing.
   - **B.** According to the singer, she does not have the time to feel homesick.
   - **C.** The dance performances are the only new element of the show.
   - **D.** Journalists from the press take a lot of interest in her private life.
   - **E.** Serena's fans can be very critical of people making very negative comments about their idol.
   - **F.** The interviewer is not concerned by the fans' possible reactions to the interview.

Choose the correct answer from A, B, C or D. Write the letter in the box provided.

7. According to Serena, the best part of being in London is…
   - **A.** looking at the shops
   - **B.** meeting fans
   - **C.** discovering its history
   - **D.** looking at the architecture.
8. Serena enjoys the rain because it…
   - **A.** is something unusual for her
   - **B.** is a change from being on stage
   - **C.** reminds her of home
   - **D.** is a weird thing to do.
9. Serena's response to the question about British food is …
   - **A.** very unfavourable
   - **B.** polite and diplomatic
   - **C.** wildly enthusiastic
   - **D.** very indifferent.
10. Serena says she will take a holiday after her tour because …
   - **A.** she will be exhausted
   - **B.** she wants to holiday with friends
   - **C.** she has a break in her busy schedule
   - **D.** she has always wanted to visit Mexico.

HL extension HL

Here is a missing question and answer from the interview. Read it and find the missing words in the text. Write your answers in the boxes below.

Interviewer: Alpona from Rochdale wants to know: "What inspired you to launch your fashion label, Atlantica?" That's a fabulous name is by the way.

SG: Honestly, I think the first time that I (__(1)__) realized I wanted to do a clothing line was (__(2)__) a little girl came up to me and she had a picture of me. I guess it was a paparazzi shot of me and she (__(3)__) printed it out and she went to the store and she bought (__(4)__) exact replica of the outfit I had been wearing in the picture. She said that she really loved the outfit and it looked (__(5)__) sweet on her! Her mom was saying: Thank you so much (__(6)__) being a good role model. And (__(7)__) just made me feel really good. So I started thinking about that and I decided (__(8)__) create my own fashion line. The basic concept was that at all my shows I could model the outfits (__(9)__) stage and also in the media, and then my fans would be able to buy (__(10)__) same clothes and wear them on the weekend. We scouted around – (__(11)__) two years actually – to find the right design team (__(12)__) the best way to launch the concept.

Oral activity: Interview

Imagine you had to interview the greatest fan of a celebrity. What would you like to know about their motives and passion? If you could interview that person, what would you ask?

Brainstorming

First choose a celebrity then invent a backstory for the fan. Give five reasons for the celebrity's success and five reasons for the fan's hero worship of the celebrity. You could use a table like the one below.

Name of celebrity	Details about the fan
1 Name:	1 Name:
2 Age:	2 Age:
3 Nationality:	3 Nationality:
4 Personal life:	4 Occupation:
	5 Personal life:
Reasons for the celebrity's fame and success	**Reasons for the fan's hero worship**
1	1
2	2
3	3
4	4
5	5

Creative thinking skills ATLs

While you are brainstorming, be aware that you are using valuable creative thinking skills. You are:

- applying existing knowledge to generate new ideas, products or processes
- considering multiple alternatives
- creating novel solutions to authentic problems
- making unexpected or unusual connections
- generating testable hypotheses
- creating original works and ideas.

Planning

Here are some closed questions based on the list of reasons for hero worship given at the beginning of this section. You will see that the closed questions below require a simple short answer and are of limited use in finding out what the interviewee really thinks.

To develop your journalistic skills further, convert these 12 closed questions into open ones. The first one has been done as an example.

Closed questions	Open questions
1 Do you identify with your hero?	**To what extent** do you identify with your hero?
2 Do you recognize yourself in your hero?	
3 Are you influenced by what the media says about your hero?	
4 Do you envy your hero?	
5 Are you in love with him/her?	
6 Do you respect the person because of their achievements?	
7 Does this celebrity influence your way of thinking?	
8 Does this celebrity influence your fashion sense?	
9 Do you believe in the same values as your hero?	
10 Do you like to experience second-hand the drama of life through the personal life of this celebrity?	
11. Does your hero's art make you feel certain emotions and understand certain ideas?	
12. Do you think your hero worship is just a matter of biology and hormones?	

Organize your questions into the most logical order and conduct the interview. As the interviewer you may want to add one or two additional closed questions just to get the interview started. Use the information you have gathered and the questions you have chosen to create cue cards for the role play.

Presenting

In pairs conduct the interview with the fan. At the end of the first interview you can reverse the roles. Practice and record your interviews. You may wish to use the information later in the chapter for one of the Paper 2 practice writing exercises.

Research and communication skills ATLs

You might like to debate this question in class: Is celebrity worship healthy or not?

In a debate you are going to use language for the purpose of persuading an audience.

Before you debate the issue, research and make a list of a variety of useful persuasive language techniques.

See how many you can use in your debate.

Internal assessment (SL)

Take a look at the visual stimuli below. The images relate to the theme "Human ingenuity".

Choose one of the two photographs for your Internal Assessment (SL).

When you have chosen ask yourself this question: Why is one photograph more suitable than the other to use to prepare a five minute presentation?

Make a list of these reasons for preferring one photograph of two. Would they be valid for all photographs for your Internal Assessment?

Brainstorming

In pairs, choose one of the photographs, then discuss and answer the following questions.

- What is the main idea in the photograph? How does it relate to the title of the chapter, "Celebrity"?
- What do you see in background of the photograph? What does the background tell you about the location and context of the photograph?
- Look at the foreground of the photograph. Describe the person or people you can see.
- What is happening in the picture? How does the action relate to the theme of this section of the chapter, "entertainment"
- Do you think this kind of behaviour is limited to Anglophone culture, or is it a global phenomenon?

Peer assessment

Assess the presentations given by your classmates. Use the SL IA criteria to guide your assessment.

	IA (SL)
Criterion A	Language
Criterion B	1. Message: visual stimulus 2. Message: conversation
Criterion C	Interactive skills: communication

Suggest ways in which your classmates can improve their presentation techniques.

Presenting

Based on your answers to the questions above, prepare a four-minute presentation on the photograph.

Remember that the presentation should not only include a description of the photograph, but should also connect it to the topic of celebrity and an Anglophone culture. Present your photograph and topic to your classmates.

Internal assessment (HL)

Espedair Street

by Iain Banks

Iain Banks wrote the novel Espedair Street about a fictional 1970s rock band, Frozen Gold. The story is set mainly in Scotland and is narrated by the band's bass player and songwriter, Danny. In this extract Danny has not yet joined the band and is a still a painfully shy and awkward teenager with a stutter. In the passage you are about to read, Danny has just seen Frozen Gold perform for the first time. He is impressed by the group's musicianship, but he is critical of their choice of songs and their musical arrangements. After the band's performance he attempts to speak to the band's two lead singers.

'Aye,'[1] the guy said, nodding at me, giving me a little smile.

'You're v-v-very good,' I said.

'Ta.'[2] He started winding up some cable, then accepted an open guitar case from one of the roadies and put the Les Paul into it. He turned away.

I cleared my throat and said, 'Erm...'

'Yeah?' He looked back, just as the girl came over and hugged him round the neck, kissed him on the cheek, then stood beside him, arm round his waist, looking frowning down at me.

'I was w-w-w-wondering...'

'What?' he said. I watched as the girl's hand stroked his waist slowly through the silk shirt; an absent, unthinking gesture.

My nerve failed. They looked so good, they looked so together and happy and beautiful and talented, so clean and well groomed, even after that energetic set; I could smell some expensive scnet off one or other of them and I just knew I couldn't say any of the things I wanted to say. It was hopeless. I was me; big ugly stupid Danny Weir, the mutant of the household, the big lanky dingbat with the acne and the lank hair and the bad breath... I was some cheap pulp magazine, yellow and dog-eared, and these people were parchment and leather covers; I was some cheap warped EP made from recycled vinyl and these people were gold discs... they lived in another world, and they were heading for the big time; I knew it. I was doomed to Paisley and grey walls and chip suppers. I tried to speak but couldn't even stutter.

Suddenly the girl's frown deepened and she said, nodding at me, 'You're weird, aren't you?'

The guy looked at her then, a little shocked, certainly surprised; his brows and mouth trembled somewhere between a frown and a smile; he looked quickly from her to me while I stumbled out 'Y-yes, yes, that's m-m-me.'

'What?' the guy said, to me. I held out my hand but he'd turned to her again. 'What?'

'Weird,' the girl told him, 'Danny Weir; D. Weir... Weir, comma, D, in the school registration book, so, "Weird". It's his nickname.'

The guy nodded, understanding.

'That's me,' I grinned, suddenly jubilant. I gave a sort of stupid half-assed wave with one hand and then fumbled for my cigarettes.

'Remember me?' she said. I shook my head, offered them both a fag[3]; she took one. 'Christine Brice. I was in the year above you.'

'Ohh,' I said, 'yeah; of course. Yeah; Christine. Aw yeah, of course; Christine. Yeah. Yeah; how are you then, emm... how's things?' I couldn't remember her at all; I was ransacking my brains for the vaguest recollection of this blonde angel.

'All right,' she said. 'This is Dave Balfour,' she added, indicating the guy she had her arm around. We nodded to each other. 'Hi.' 'Hello.' There was a pause, then Christine Brice shrugged at me. 'What'd you think?'

'Of the b-band? The gig?' I said. She nodded. 'Aww... great... aye; great.'

'Goo...'

'B-but you need your own m-m-material, and the second half stuff needs more practice, and you could be a lot t-tighter, and the organ could make more of a c-c-c-c-contribbb...ution, and the drums need to be a lot more disciplined... and of course the name just w-w-won't... umm...' The expressions on their faces told me this wasn't going down too well.

---

[1]Aye = yes (Scotland)
[2]Ta = thanks (slang)
[3]Fag = cigarette (slang, UK)

Exam tip

In your internal assessment, the literary extract will not exceed 300 words. You will be shown two, one from each of the works of literature studied in class.

In order to prepare better for your Internal Assessment (HL), ask yourself these questions: How do teachers and examiners choose certain passages for an oral test? Why is one passage better than another?

Make a list of the passages from the two books you are reading for English B (HL) that your teacher might possibly use. Can you say what makes these passages particularly suitable?

Brainstorming

In small groups, discuss the following questions then summarize your discussion in point form.

- How much self-esteem and self-confidence does Danny possess?
- What attitudes does the narrator, Danny, show towards the members of the band?
- What attitudes do the musicians show towards Danny?
- Why is Danny so nervous about sharing his opinions about the performance with the band?
- What is the purpose of the extract? What ideas does it communicate?
- What does the passage tell us about the relationship between celebrities and their fans?
- Do you think this kind of relationship between fans and rock stars is limited to Anglophone culture, or is it a global phenomenon?

Presenting

Based on your answers to the questions above, prepare a four-minute presentation on the text.

Make your presentation to your classmates. Classmates listening to the presentation should prepare individual questions about the text which they can ask you at the end of your presentation.

Peer assessment

Assess the presentations given by your classmates. Use the HL IA criteria to guide your assessment.

Paper 1 practice

Choose one of the tasks below and write between 250 and 400 words (SL) or 450 and 600 words (HL).

Task 1: A popular singer who was a former student at your school returns to deliver a speech at graduation. You have been invited to meet this famous alumnus. You have been asked to write up the details of the meeting for the benefit of the wider school community. Choose one of these three text types to express your point of view on this matter.

Review | Interview | Email

Task 2: One of your friends is a huge fan of a certain star. The friend not only has a collection of material but also likes to attend fan conventions dressed up as their idol. You would like to tell the public about your friend's devotion. Choose one of these three text types to express your point of view on this matter.

News report | Review | Interview

Task 3: You have been appointed film critic of your student magazine. Last week you watched a film which you really enjoyed, and you feel it is worth recommending it to your fellow students. Choose one of these three text types to express your opinion about the film.

Advertisement | Review | Interview

Brainstorming

Follow the steps below.

1. Reflect on everything you have learned in this section. Choose your focal point and your point of view. What information do you want to emphasize?
2. Generate ideas to be used in your text. Research additional material to support your opinion.
3. What else do you need to think about? Language and register? Audience? Purpose? Context and text type?
4. Sort your ideas into a logical order. Choose examples to support your ideas.

Planning

You should think about the concepts below to help you plan your written text. Think about what measures you will take to make sure your text communicates its message clearly and effectively:

- context
- audience
- purpose.

Individually, write a draft of your text. Write an eye-catching title. Remember to include any special features of the text type, such as headlines, by-lines or layout.

Re-read the completed draft of your text. Remember you will be assessed on three criteria: criterion A, language; criterion B, message; criterion C, conceptual understanding (including audience, context and purpose).

Make any necessary changes.

Conclusion to research question C

Why do some fans hero worship celebrities such as actors and singers?

1. Now that you have completed the section, what conclusions have you come to? What have you learned about the relationship between celebrities and their fans?
2. To what extent have your opinions on the subject changed since the beginning of this chapter? To what extent have your opinions remained the same?
3. What about this topic would you like to find out more?

Conclusion to the chapter

Having completed the chapter, reflect on its key research question:

What can we learn about a culture through its artistic expression?

Consider the following questions:

- Now that you have completed the chapter, what are your conclusions about the research question?
- In particular, you may want to consider this issue: What seems to be the role of celebrity in Anglophone society?
- To what extent have your opinions on the subject changed since the beginning of this chapter? Justify your answers.
- What more would you like to know about the subject?

Beyond the classroom

You can use the information you have learned and the communication skills you have developed in this chapter for practical purposes beyond the classroom.

CAS

Using text types

Interviews

There are many people you can interview at home or at school: friends, family members or teachers and administrative staff. In the context of this chapter you may like to interview fellow students who are taking a group 6 arts subject such as music, art, drama or dance. If you know artists outside school, you could interview them. Such exercises are not only good English practice but will help you develop social skills too. Once again you can offer to publish material in the school magazine or on your own blog.

Reviews

There should be lots of opportunities to write reviews at school. There will be dramatic and musical performances, as well as other school-wide celebrations, such as International Mother Tongue Day or graduation ceremonies. Use these opportunities to write material for one or more of your school publications. You might want to analyse particular songs. If so, use the skills you have developed in the TOK section to examine the purpose of the lyrics. Write a review of the material. You can also develop your own blog in which you can showcase your critical writing.

Suggested reading

The Commitments by Roddy Doyle

How to Breathe Underwater (Short Stories) by Julie Orringer

Fables For Our Time by James Thurber

Fat Kid Rules The World by KL Going

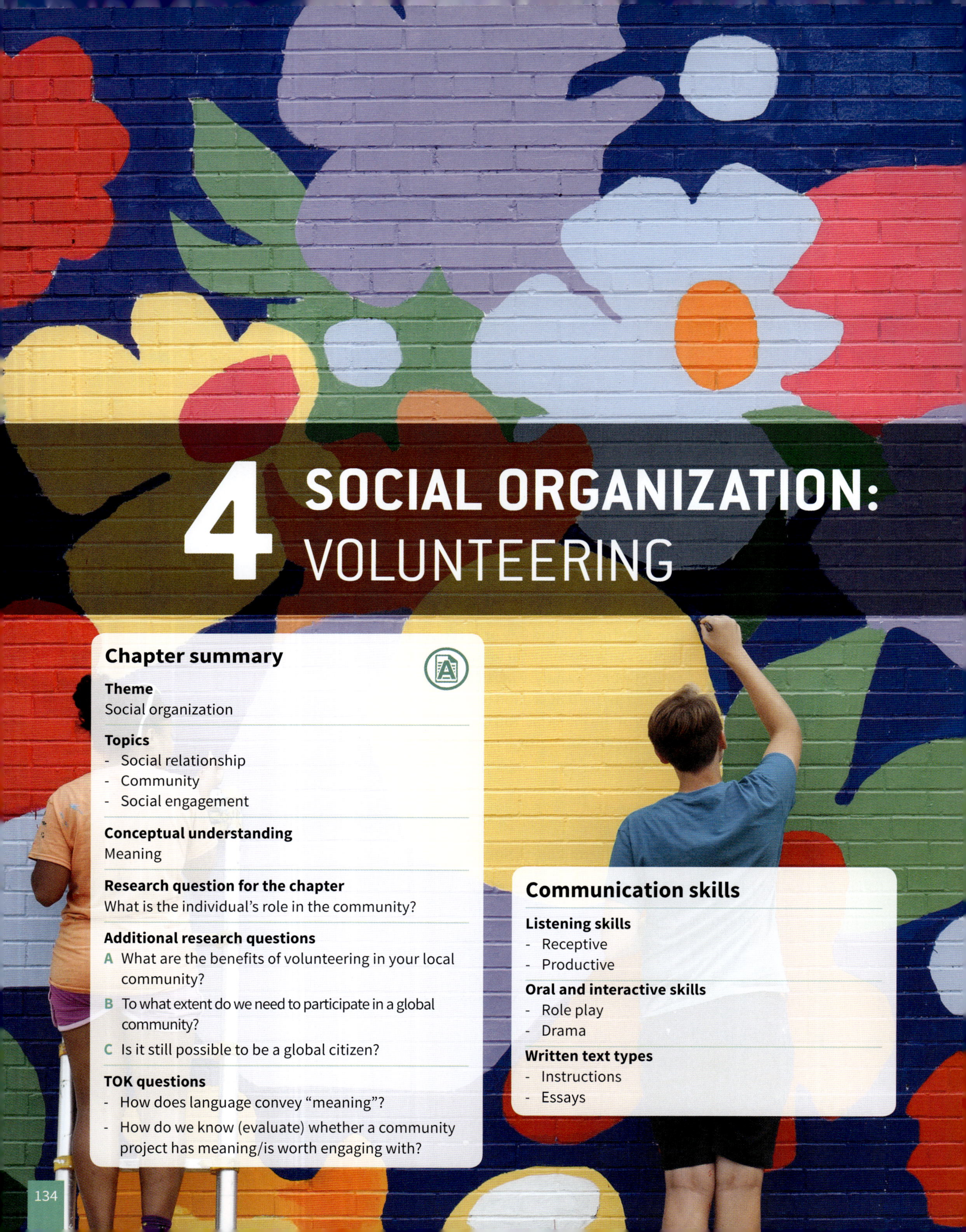

4 SOCIAL ORGANIZATION: VOLUNTEERING

Chapter summary

Theme
Social organization

Topics
- Social relationship
- Community
- Social engagement

Conceptual understanding
Meaning

Research question for the chapter
What is the individual's role in the community?

Additional research questions
A What are the benefits of volunteering in your local community?
B To what extent do we need to participate in a global community?
C Is it still possible to be a global citizen?

TOK questions
- How does language convey "meaning"?
- How do we know (evaluate) whether a community project has meaning/is worth engaging with?

Communication skills

Listening skills
- Receptive
- Productive

Oral and interactive skills
- Role play
- Drama

Written text types
- Instructions
- Essays

Research question for the chapter:

What is the individual's role in the community?

1. What are your first thoughts and reactions to the question above?
2. What justifications would you give for your answer?
3. What more would you need to know before you can come to a definitive conclusion about the question?

Community is a very broad term used to define groups of people – whether they are householders, interest groups, citizen groups, and so on. A "community of place" refers to people from a single location: a village, a district or a town. A "community of practice" is a group with shared or similar interests, such as a closed group on the internet or followers of a particular type of music. Some communities, such as a political group, are based on identity and a sense of belonging.

Think about these questions.

- What does the word "community" mean to you?
- What communities do you belong to?
- What kind of community is a school?
- In what ways does your school participate in your local community? For example, does your school have a service programme? In what ways do students participate in it?

Do you think you have a responsibility to help within the communities in which you live? Make a list of ways in which you can participate and help. You might also wish to debate this question in class.

Section A: Community

Social skills ATLs

The exercises on this page are best carried out as group or pair work.

This also gives you a chance to practice your social skills.

In order to reach a consensus agreement, make sure you have certain procedures in place that will improve the quality of your work and allow your interpersonal skills to develop.

Here are some questions to ask yourselves before you begin.

How are you going to organize the discussion?

Are you going to choose someone to "chair" the discussion?

How will you make sure that everyone gets a chance to speak?

What will you do to prevent one person from dominating the discussion?

How will you begin and wrap up the discussion?

How will you agree on your answers?

How are you going to record and communicate your findings?

Research question A:

What are the benefits of volunteering in your local community?

1. What are your first thoughts and reactions to the question above?
2. What justifications would you give for your answers?
3. What more would you need to know before you can come to a definitive conclusion about the statement?

Before you read

Examine the poster above and discuss these questions.

- Who is the poster aimed at?
- According to the poster, how can volunteering benefit the people who volunteer?
- Summarize the overall message of the poster.
- Look more closely at the four images within the poster. What are they saying about the kind of people who volunteer in the community? What qualities are needed to be an effective volunteer?

Advantages of Youth Volunteering

Volunteer work can be fulfilling for individuals of any age, but young people, especially, can benefit from volunteering at a number of organizations: nursing homes, museums, historical societies or with community groups. Teens who choose to participate in volunteer work usually acquire skills that otherwise might never have been developed. Whatever your situation is, it's worth volunteering.

1 One of the most rewarding aspects of volunteering is the ability to get to know people from all walks of life. The types of people you can hope to meet through your volunteer work will depend on the organization you are looking to volunteer with. You will certainly get to know the people you're helping but you may also meet other (---9---) that have similar interests to your own. So meeting others and expanding your (---10---) might also give you a different outlook on life. Whatever you do, volunteering allows you to (---11---) your social life, become more knowledgeable and will also teach you to be more (---12---) towards those possibly different from you.

2 If you already know what you want to do when you (---13---), it's worth volunteering with an organization that matches your interests. Even though you're not going to be paid, you are going to learn and take away life (---14---) from your experience that can help determine your (---15--) as an adult. For example, learning a new language, taking care of our environment, or being part of a service industry are all skills that are in (---16---) demand in our modern world. If you're ready to become an adult, what better way to set your path than by gathering experience?

3 If you're going to be looking at volunteering as a way to secure your future, remember that volunteer work can look really good on your college application. In fact, you may even become eligible for certain scholarships as a result of the work you have done in the past. Colleges are not just looking at your exam results. By doing volunteer work it says that you're willing to donate your own time for others, and you are passionate about something. It suggests that you truly care about your community and the environment.

4 Oftentimes, the organizations that ask for volunteers are ones that are often overlooked by the government or simply cannot afford to pay their employees. However, many of these organizations, such as conservation groups, make a big difference to society and deserve to be supported. If you're looking to make a difference in your community and later on, in our world, there is no better time to start than when you're a teenager. Participating in volunteer work can give you a real sense of achievement while helping to make a mark on society too.

5 Some teens only spend time with a close circle of friends but this can also lead to peer pressure and having very narrow views on life. So volunteering is a great way to make a difference and broaden your horizons. Volunteer work can make you a more mature, well-rounded person. There's nothing quite as beautiful as dedicating yourself to a good cause. Many adults who have volunteered as teens feel that it benefitted them greatly in later life.

Exam tip

In the reading comprehension paper you will encounter a variety of different assessment types.

Here is a list of some of the most common activities you may be asked to complete.

- Choosing a number of true sentences
- Gap-filling exercises
- Identifying precise references of key phrases or structures
- Identifying related ideas that are in different parts of the text
- Identifying specific content items
- True/false exercises with justification
- Identifying who says what
- Matching summary sentences with different paragraphs of the text
- Matching words or phrases from the text with definitions
- Multiple-choice questions

Make sure you are familiar with each of these assessment activities and know how to tackle them.

Reading comprehension

In the text the paragraph headings 1 to 5 are missing. Choose the correct heading from the list below for each paragraph.

A. A variety of choices	B. Gain wider perspectives
C. Make a practical difference	D. Get to know people from different backgrounds
E. Learn life skills	F. Universities favour the socially committed
G. Be a dreamer	H. Limit your choices
I. Payment issues	J. Peer pressure

Read the opening paragraph and answer the following questions.

6 Which word is closest in meaning to "satisfying"?

....

7 What is the most important benefit of volunteering?

....

8 Which word is closest in meaning to "it does not matter"?

....

Read paragraphs 1 and 2. Which words go in the gaps 9 to 16? Choose the words from the list and write them in the spaces provided.

advantages	career	expenses	expand	graduate	high	horizons
locals	maximize	skills	universal	sympathetic	volunteers	willing

9 .... 13 ....

10 .... 14 ....

11 .... 15 ....

12 .... 16 ....

17 Read paragraphs 3 and 4 and then read statements A to H. Identify the four statements that are correct.

a Colleges insist on experience as a volunteer for entry to certain courses.

b There are specific scholarships for former volunteers.

c Colleges do not only consider exam grades when selecting students.

d Experience as a volunteer shows you are committed to the world around you.

e Organizations that help others receive enough support from the government.

f It is best to start volunteering early in life.

g Volunteering leads to success in life.

h Volunteering can help you to make a difference

Choose the correct answer from A, B, C or D.

18 The main purpose of the text is to:

- **A.** narrate a story
- **B.** describe a job
- **C.** explain a problem
- **D.** argue a point of view.

19 The intended audience for this text is probably:

- **A.** teachers
- **B.** parents
- **C.** volunteers
- **D.** students.

20 The writer's point of view of volunteering is:

- **A.** balanced
- **B.** impersonal
- **C.** biased
- **D.** positive.

21 The meaning of the text is:

- **A.** contradictory
- **B.** clear
- **C.** ambiguous
- **D.** perfect.

Social and communication skills

ATLs

Your school might have a community service programme. Working in pairs, plan a poster to promote the benefits of volunteering as part of a school-based project in your local community. Together decide which points from the list below you would choose to emphasize. Justify your choices. Plan your poster and find visuals and text to communicate your ideas effectively.

Reasons for volunteering

1 Improves your emotional well-being
2 Improves your physical health
3 Develops your self-confidence
4 Expands your social network
5 Helps you develop new skills
6 Puts your existing skills to work
7 Advances your future career
8 Gives you new career options
9 Makes a difference in causes that are important to you
10 Other (add your own ideas here)

In this activity you can develop the following social skills:

- Work effectively with others
- Work collaboratively in teams
- Delegate and share responsibility for decision-making
- Help others to succeed
- Build consensus
- Use appropriate forms of writing for different purposes and audiences
- Use a variety of media to communicate with a range of audiences
- Interpret and use effectively modes of non-verbal communication

Oral activity: Role play and drama

What is a role play?

Personal Information Sheet

First name: ______

Preferred Name/Nickname: ______

Birthday: ______

Married? ______

Children (names and ages): ______

Home: ______

Home city: ______

Former profession: ______

3 things you love: ______

3 things you hate: ______

The farthest I have ever travelled from home is:

______

My favourite place in the world is: ______

What is your favourite kind of music? ______

What is your favourite hobby? ______

What have been the most important moments in your life?

______

______

Role play is a speaking activity in which two or more people put themselves into other characters' shoes for a short time and express the thoughts and opinions of those characters. The role play will take place within a given situation. A simple example of a role play would be an improvised dialogue between members of a family who cannot agree where to go on holiday.

Language students particularly can benefit from the practice because the improvisations can develop fluency and thinking skills in imaginary situations that are outside the normal classroom experience.

While the role play is taking place the rest of the class can observe and judge the action. At the end students can vote in favour of or against a character or their opinions.

Role play works best when you prepare your ideas and language before you start. Role plays make use of cue cards which contain the basic ideas you need to explore.

For instance, imagine you are going to conduct a role play in which service volunteers visit an old people's home. Each volunteer is assigned a "buddy", a resident. There is a "getting to know you" session for all buddies and volunteers. Imagine you are the resident. You have a lifetime of stories. Invent a completely new identity for yourself. Fill in the Personal Information Sheet here to create this new identity. You will use this as a cue card.

In pairs take turns to ask each other questions to find out as much a possible about your "buddy".

Thinking skills ATLs

When we think about volunteering in the community, is it right to concern ourselves with the welfare of animals when there are so many people who need help?

To answer this question use the following critical thinking skills:

- interpret existing data
- evaluate evidence and arguments
- recognize and evaluate propositions
- draw reasonable conclusions and generalizations
- test generalizations and conclusions
- revise understanding based on new information and evidence
- consider ideas from multiple perspectives.

Role play: Applying for a volunteer post

Read the announcement below from a local hospital looking for volunteers. They are willing to accept young people for these very rare opportunities if they can display all the right characteristics. Conduct a role play between a candidate and three interviewers. There are examples of cue cards for the three interviewers and the candidate that you could use to help you to organize your role play. At the end of each role play the interviewers must decide whether to accept the candidate or not. Explain your decision to the candidate.

Volunteers wanted

We are currently seeking volunteers to provide a highly valued service to our patients. You may be a student or retiree, or just someone who has some time to give. Volunteers come from many backgrounds and walks of life and we recognize and value every volunteer's unique ability. The role of a volunteer at Chorlton Nursing Home is to help provide a positive experience for residents and to make a significant difference daily to them, their family and friends, and staff. The volunteer recognizes diversity by treating all people with dignity and respect.

Contact the Services Manager, Linda Felix on (08) 4255 XXXX or email lindafelix@chorltonresidential.net

You may be asked to come to the hospital to discuss your application.

Cue cards

Interviewer A: Basics

Tell us about yourself.
How much time do you have some available?
What is your interest in volunteering?
Why do you want to make a difference?
What do you hope to gain from your volunteer experience?

Social skills ATLs

There are some useful social skills you can develop during the development and rehearsal of the role play:

- Listen actively to other perspectives and ideas
- Encourage everyone to contribute
- Help all members of the group to succeed
- Give and receive meaningful feedback

Interviewer B: Possible areas of service.

Ask the candidates to pick four possible areas they would be interested to help with. Ask the candidates to justify their choices.

Possible responses	Yes/No/Maybe	Candidate's justifications
Talk with patients.		
Assist with patients' meals.		
Arrange and refresh patients' flowers.		
Deliver newspapers and magazines.		
Escort patients from reception.		
Make up patient information packs.		
Tidy patient rooms.		

Interviewer C: Evidence of social skills

Ask the candidate to give examples of social skills and note evidence they provide.

Possible responses	Yes/No	Evidence provided/examples given
Facing new challenges		
Learning new skills and abilities		
Following instructions clearly		
Sharing and working as a member of a team		
Having a happy, enthusiastic approach to life		
Caring about others		

Cue card for volunteer (possible questions to the interviewers)

What days and times can I volunteer?

In which departments can I volunteer?

What are some of the volunteer roles?

What qualities are you looking for in a volunteer?

What problems should I be aware of?

What responsibilities should I be aware of?

How do the staff and patients view volunteers?

Assess the presentations given by your classmates. Use the following table to guide your assessment.

Peer assessment

In small groups, assess the role plays given by your classmates. You can use the rubrics below as a basis for your comments.

	Good	Improvement possible	Needs some improvement	Needs a lot of improvement
Eye contact	Makes good eye contact with audience.	Makes eye contact with the audience most of the time.	Sometimes makes eye contact with the audience.	Does not make eye contact with the audience.
Enthusiasm	Shows great enthusiasm for the topic.	Shows enthusiasm for the topic.	Shows some enthusiasm for the topic.	Shows little enthusiasm for the topic.
Preparation and organization	Very prepared and well organized.	Mostly prepared and well organized.	Somewhat prepared and organized.	Not very prepared or organized.
Clear speech	Speaks very clearly and is very easy to understand.	Speaks clearly most of the time and is fairly easy to understand.	Sometimes speaks clearly and is sometimes easy to understand.	Does not speak clearly and is quite difficult to understand.
Knowledge of topic	Shows excellent understanding of the topic.	Shows good understanding of the topic.	Shows some understanding of the topic.	Shows little understanding of the topic.

Self-management skills ATLs

You cannot always expect positive feedback from your peer assessments. However, you can learn from the experience.

Practice resilience

Learn how to "bounce back" after adversity, mistakes and failures.

Practice "failing well" and dealing with disappointment and unmet expectations.

Learn how to use the rubrics like the ones above to find out where you need to improve, and make plans not to make the same mistakes twice.

Exam tip

If you are wondering what to say about a photograph here are three things to talk about.

Context: When and where was the photograph taken? What background detail can you describe? What does it tell us about the Anglophone world?

Text: What is happening in the picture? Describe the people and what they are doing.

Subtext: What is the message of the picture? Why did the photographer take the picture?

Finally how does the photo relate to the designated theme?

The themes are

- identities
- experiences
- human ingenuity
- social organization
- sharing the planet.

Internal assessment (SL)

Take a look at the visual stimulus here. The image relates to the theme of the chapter, "Social organization".

Brainstorming

In pairs, discuss and answer the following questions.

- What is the main idea in the photograph? How does it relate to the title of the section, "Community"?
- What do you see in foreground of the photograph? What does it tell you about why the photograph was taken?
- What is happening and why?
- What is happening in the picture? How does the action relate to the title of the chapter, "Volunteering"? What does it tell us about English-speaking communities?

Presenting

Based on your answers to the questions above, prepare a four-minute presentation on the photograph.

Remember that the presentation should not only include description of the photograph, but should also connect it to the theme social organization, the topic of volunteering and an Anglophone culture. Present your photograph and topic to your classmates.

Internal assessment (HL)

The Secret Diary of Adrian Mole, Aged 13¾ is written as the diary of a teenager growing up in the English Midlands in the 1980s. Adrian is self-obsessed and full of self-doubt. Nevertheless, he believes himself to be an intellectual and superior to the people around him. Adrian is also hopelessly in love with a girl at his school, Pandora Braithwaite.

Note

In your internal assessment, the literary extract will not exceed 300 words. You will be shown two, one from each of the works of literature studied in class.

The Secret Diary of Adrian Mole, Aged 13¾

by Sue Townsend

Monday January 19th

I have joined a group at school called the Good Samaritans. We go out into the community helping and stuff like that. We miss Maths on Monday afternoons. Today we had a talk on the sort of things we will be doing. I have been put in the old age pensioners' group.

Can't wait for next Monday. I will get a cassette so I can tape all the old fogies' stories about the war and stuff. I hope I get one with a good memory.

... Pandora smiled at me in school dinner today, but I was choking on a piece of gristle so I couldn't smile back. Just my luck!

Wednesday January 21st

...

I went to see old Mr Baxter after tea. My father dropped me off on his way to play badminton. Mr Baxter's house is hard to see from the road. It has got a massive overgrown privet hedge all round it. When I knocked on the door a dog started barking and growling and jumping up at the letter-box. I heard the sound of bottles being knocked over and a man swearing before I ran off. I hope I got the wrong number.

I saw Nigel on the way home. He told me Pandora's father is a milkman! I have gone off her a bit.

Nobody was in when I got home so I fed the dog, looked at my spots and went to bed.

Saturday January 24th

Today was the most terrible day of my life. ...

Bert Baxter is not a nice old age pensioner! He drinks and smokes and has an Alsatian dog called Sabre. Sabre was locked in the kitchen while I was cutting the massive hedge, but he didn't stop growling once.

But even worse than that! Pandora is going out with Nigel!!!!! I think I will never get over this shock.

Monday January 26th

I had to leave my sick-bed to visit Bert Baxter before school. It took me ages to get there, what with feeling weak and having to stop for a rest every now and again, but with the help of an old lady who had a long black moustache I made it to the front door. Bert Baxter was in bed but he threw the key down and I let myself in. Sabre was locked in the bathroom; he was growling and sounded as if he was ripping up towels or something.

Bert Baxter was lying in a filthy-looking bed smoking a cigarette, there was a horrible smell in the room, I think it came from Bert Baxter himself. The bed sheets looked as though they were covered in blood, but Bert said that was caused by the beetroot sandwiches he always eats last thing at night. It was the most disgusting room I have ever seen (and I'm no stranger to squalor).

Bert Baxter gave me ten pence and asked me to get him the Morning Star from the newsagent's. So he is a communist as well as everything else! Sabre usually fetches the paper but he is being kept in as a punishment for chewing the sink.

The man in the newsagent's asked me to give Bert Baxter his bill (he owes for his papers, £31.97), but when I did Bert Baxter said, 'Smarmy four-eyed git', and laughed and ripped the bill up. I was late for school so I had to go to the school secretary's office and have my name put in the late book. That's the gratitude I get for being a Good Samaritan! I didn't miss Maths either! Saw Pandora and Nigel standing close together in the dinner queue but chose to ignore them.

...

Midnight

Goodnight Pandora my treacle-haired love.

XXXXXXXXX

Friday January 30th

That filthy commie Bert Baxter has phoned the school to complain that I left the hedge-clippers out in the rain! He claims that they have gone all rusty. He wants compensation. I told Mr Scruton, the headmaster, that they were already rusty but I could tell he didn't believe me. He gave me a lecture on how hard it was for old people to make ends meet. He has ordered me to go to Bert Baxter's and clean and sharpen the hedge-clippers. I wanted to tell the headmaster all about horrible Bert Baxter but there is something about Mr Scruton that makes my mind go blank. I think it's the way his eyes pop out when he is in a temper.

On the way to Bert Baxter's I saw my mother and Mr Lucas coming out of a betting shop together. I waved and shouted but I don't think they could have seen me. I'm glad Mr Lucas is feeling better.

Bert Baxter didn't answer the door. Perhaps he is dead.

Pandora! You are still on my mind, baby.

Brainstorming

Discuss the following questions then summarize your discussion in point form.

- What attitudes does Adrian show towards volunteering in the community? How does Adrian feel towards his "buddy", Bert Baxter?
- Adrian does not seem to have much luck with or take much pleasure from volunteering? What is your explanation for this?
- On the evidence of the text, how would you assess Adrian's skills as a volunteer helper? Justify your answers. If you were in Adrian's position how do you think you would react? Explain your answer.

Presenting

Based on your answers to the questions above, prepare a four-minute presentation on the text.

Make your presentation to your classmates. Students listening to the presentation should prepare individual questions about the text which they can ask you at the end of your presentation. They also can use the peer assessment chart on page 143 to assess the presentation.

Assess the presentations given by your classmates.

Paper 1: Instructions

What is a set of instructions?

A set of written instructions explains how to make, do or complete something. Clear written instructions should describe a set of procedures, such as a recipe, or guidelines for assembling a product from a kit. Instructions are usually set out in a logical step-by-step fashion. Instructions should be easy to read but writing them often takes considerable precision. Study the picture and use it to explain why it is so important to be able to give clear, unambiguous instructions.

Transfer skills ATLs

In the picture on the left the driving instructor is giving a set of instructions to the learner driver.

Can you think of other instances in the world beyond school in which the ability to create clear, unambiguous instructions is an essential professional skill?

In groups brainstorm this question and find as many instances from diverse professions as you can.

Writing to a specific audience: tone and style

When giving instructions you are writing as an expert in the field. Address the readers directly, but politely. Do not sound too bossy! There are a number of different levels of formality for the advice you want to give, so you may need to qualify your verbs. Use modal verb phrases such as: "may", "might", "can", "could", "ought to", and so on. They can help you to achieve the correct level of politeness towards your audience.

Communication skills ATLs

Using a variety of organizers for academic writing tasks

In this book we have already used a number of graphic organizers to help you to plan the structure of a particular text type. What about the kinds of instructions that are being described here? Choose the best way to plan a set of instructions. Would you use

a) a hierarchy
b) a classification table
c) a flow chart?

Also use the following communication skills to plan what you want to write.

- Organize and depict information logically.
- Structure information effectively into a set of instructions.
- Paraphrase your thoughts accurately and concisely.
- Produce texts to build understanding.
- Make effective planning notes.
- Write a specific purpose and audience.

Structure

Remember in the real world a lot of people hate reading instructions, and will only do so when they are hopelessly lost. Your readers may become impatient, frustrated or even angry, so phrase each step as if your reader has just asked, "What should I do next?" Answer directly with a simple verb phrase, such as "Add two cups of flour." A precise verb helps the reader know what to do.

Remember to:

- explain each step of the operation
- limit the amount of information in each step
- use bullet points or numbers.

Features

Instructions should have four parts: title, introduction, main body and conclusion.

Title: Your title should explain in plain language what you are writing about and why your reader should read the document.

Introduction: Your introduction should include the topic you will discuss and the background or context. For example, you may need to give a list of ingredients or equipment required.

The main body: This will give your readers a road map to follow and will explain to them each step to take. The body of your instructions could be organized chronologically.

Conclusion: Your conclusion should tell the reader what they can do now that they have finished making or building the product.

Now read this set of instructions on how to write a formal letter.

Example: A set of instructions for writing formal letters

In English there are a number of conventions you should follow when writing formal or business letters.

Addresses

a) Your address
Write your return address in the top right-hand corner of the letter.

b) The address of your correspondent
Write your correspondent's address should be written on the left, starting below your address.

c) Date

Write the date on the right or the left on the line after the address you are writing to.

Salutation or greeting

a) Dear Sir or Madam,
Use this salutation if you do not know the name of the person you are writing to.

b) Dear Mr Khan,
If you know the name, use the title (Mr, Mrs, Miss or Ms, Dr, etc.). Use the surname only. Use Ms, which is for married and single women, if you are writing to a woman and do not know.

Closing your letter:

a) Yours Faithfully
If you do not know the name of the person, end the letter this way.

b) Yours Sincerely
If you know the name of the person, end the letter this way.

c) Your signature
Sign your name, then print it underneath the signature. If you think the person you are writing to might not know whether you are male of female, put you title in brackets after your name.

Other style tips

Always write as simply and as clearly as possible.

Do not make the letter any longer than necessary.

Use formal language.

Do not use contractions.

Communication skills ATLs

Do these instructions for writing a formal letter comply with the guidelines? To answer this question, consider each of the points in the table below.

Features of instructions
How well do the instructions address a specific audience?
How appropriate is the tone and style used to address the audience?
How clear and effective is the structure?
Does the writer use all the typical features of a set of written instructions?
Comment on the effectiveness of: The title The introduction The main body The conclusion
What improvements to the set of instructions would you suggest to the writer?

Exam tip: writing

Choosing the correct question.

Always choose the question for which you are able to formulate the best answer.

Here are some questions to help you to decide the meaning of "best".

- Do I understand exactly what I have to do?
- Do I understand the purpose of the text?
- Do know who is the intended audience for the the text?
- Do know which text type best addresses the purpose, audience and context of the text?
- Can I handle the features of the type of text?
- Can I write in the correct register?

If you can answer yes to all these points, then you should probably answer that question!

Now test yourself.

Look at the three practice writing tasks opposite. Which question will you answer?

Justify your choice.

Writing activity: Instructions

Here are three opportunities to practice writing sets of instructions.

Plan, draft, revise and redraft one of these stimuli.

Exam tip:

At Standard Level you should write between 250 and 400 words.

At Higher Level you should write between 450 and 600 words.

Remember to use the conventions for writing a set of instructions that you have learned about in this section.

1. There is increasing poverty, and a larger number of young families are having to cope on very low incomes. Your school social service programme is asking students to contribute low-cost recipes for a cookbook entitled *Meals on a shoestring budget*.

Set of instructions	Blog entry	Email

2. In this section you practiced a role play in which student candidates applied to participate in a volunteer programme at a residential centre for the elderly. As there are so many applicants, the managers decide to explain to applicants how to apply and how to conduct themselves at interviews.

Brochure	Set of instructions	Email

3. For the last two years you have been visiting an elderly person in the community as a part of your school's social service programme. However, you are now leaving your community to go to university. You have developed an excellent relationship with your buddy and want to ensure that the next volunteer can be as useful as possible.

Email	Speech	Set of instructions

Having read the prompts above, which text type have you chosen for each? Why?

Brainstorming

Follow the steps below.

1. Reflect on everything you have learned in this section. Choose your focal point and your point of view. What information do you want to emphasize?
2. Generate ideas to be used in your text. Research additional material to support your opinion.
3. What else do you need to think about? Language and register? Audience? Context and text type?
4. Sort your ideas into a logical order. Choose examples to support your ideas.

Planning

You could use a chart like the one below to help you plan your set of instructions. Think about what measures you will take to make sure make your instructions are clear and effective.

	Have I completed this aspect of my instructions satisfactorily?
Title:	
Introduction:	
Main body:	
Conclusion:	
Other special features of the text type: (headings, bullets, title, etc.)	
Audience:	
Purpose:	
Tone and level of formality	

Write a draft of the body of your set of instructions. Write an eye-catching title.

Re-read the completed draft of your set of instructions. Remember you will be assessed on three criteria: criterion A, language; criterion B, message; criterion C, conceptual understanding (including audience, context and purpose). Make any necessary changes.

Conclusion to research question A

What are the benefits of volunteering in your local community?

1. Now that you have completed this section what are your thoughts and reactions to the question above?
2. What justifications would you give for your answers?
3. What more would you need to know before you can come to a definitive conclusion about the statement?

Conceptual understanding

Peter has a great business idea but he needs to communicate his message to his friend and partner, Anna. Here is the message: "I have a cool idea for that phone app."

The **coding** of a message involves the creation of a message by a sender, or messenger, in this case Peter. In the process of encoding, Peter uses verbal language, for example, words, symbols signs or images, which he believes the recipient, Anna, will understand clearly.

Peter could use different channels for the communication: words and numbers, visual images, facial expressions, signals and/or actions. Additionally, if face-to-face with Anna, he could also use non-verbal language (for example, body language, hand gestures, facial expressions). In each case we can represent the act of communicating a message like this.

The **decoding** of a message is a process of interpretation and translation of the meaning of the coded message. In our example, effective communication is accomplished only if Anna receives the message and she understands Peter's meaning in the way he intended. However, it is still possible for Anna to understand a different meaning to what Peter was trying to convey.

- Is the meaning of Peter's message clear?
- In what ways might Anna misinterpret Peter's message?
- What is the difference between a message and its meaning?
- When you are writing to someone, how can you make sure your message is clearly understood? List at least 10 different things you can do.

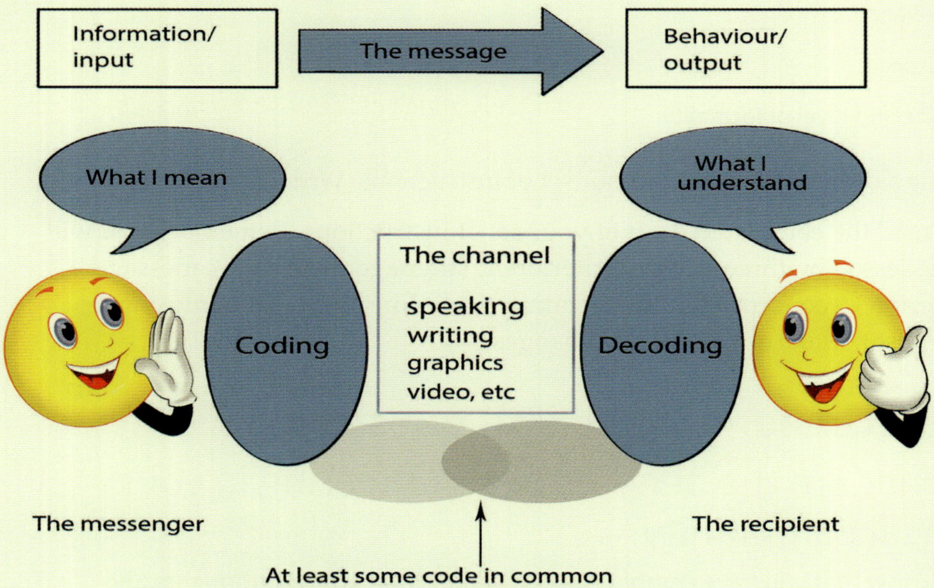

A TOK Moment

What are the limits of translation when communicating ideas from one language into another?

We can see it is already complicated communicating ideas from a sender to a receiver using the same language. What happens when we try to communicate ideas from one language to another using translation?

Translate a pop lyric from your own language and culture. Go through the steps below.

Step 1: Literal translation

Take a short pop rap or rock song lyric in English.
Make a literal translation (word for word) of the song into your Language A. Do not attempt to make a "good" translation.

List some of the major differences between your Language A and English in terms of:

Word order	Vocabulary	Grammar items	Idioms and images

Does a literal translation feel right? Use the table to help you to analyze your thoughts and findings.

Step 2: Liberal translation

You are now going to write a "good" version of the translation. How can you change the literal version to make it sound more fluent in your Language A?

Make the changes and record them using the same chart to help you.

Word order	Vocabulary	Grammar items	Idioms and images

Step 3: Free translation

Now try to compose a lyric in your Language A to go with the original song. How many of the original ideas of the English lyric are you able to keep? How much of the original cannot be translated?

Consider this question: Are certain ideas untranslatable because of language or because of cultural differences between different societies in different parts of the world?

So, is our understanding of the world limited by the language, or languages, we speak?

In other words, from a TOK perspective, is language a very limited ***way of knowing***?

Listening comprehension

Click the icon to practice the listening section of Paper 2. After you have listened to an audio track you will complete an accompanying activity. In this exercise you will find a short piece of text with five gaps in it. Find suitable words from the recording to fill the gaps. You should be able to complete each gap using no more than four words.

Section B: Social engagement

Research question B:

To what extent do we need to participate in a global community?

1. What are your first thoughts and reactions to the question above?
2. What justifications would you give for your answers?
3. What more would you need to know before you can come to a definitive conclusion about the question?

Before you read

On this page you can see two photographs. Each one communicates a different message about volunteering. Study the first photo.

- What kinds of preparations would you have to make before taking a gap year?
- What qualities would you need to take a gap year?

Now look at the second photo.

- What skills do you think you could learn on a gap year?
- What service to others could you provide on a year abroad?

Volunteering overseas: To Gap Year or not to Gap Year?

1 Universities generally consider productive Gap Year students to be valuable members of their college community. As a result of the tremendous formative experiences that have shaped their personalities and interests, such students tend to be more mature, confident, and purposeful about returning to academic life. Universities comment favourably on students' greater sense of identity, enhanced inter-personal and communication skills, and on their social skills as both potential team-players, and future leaders and managers.

2 Universities value all kinds of productive Gap Year activities, including paid or volunteer work, community service, travel, language study, caring for sick family members, taking short-term courses, gaining work experience in a particular field, attempting extreme physical challenges like mountain-climbing, developing skills in a particular sport, fulfilling National Service obligations – or any combination of these relevant hands-on Gap Year experiences definitely enhance students' chances of acceptance onto certain desirable courses, such as medicine, veterinary medicine and law.

3 The willingness shown by many universities to defer a student's admission offer in order to enable them to take a Gap Year is testament to the high value that they place on the experience. Productive Gap Year students seem to interview much more successfully for highly selective courses. We have seen several cases of students being unsuccessful when they applied during their final year of High School, but then being accepted when re-applying during a Gap Year, with considerably more relevant experience and purpose.

4 A point to note, however, is that universities really take note of what candidates have actually achieved during their Gap Year. So it doesn't particularly enhance a student's chances of being accepted if they simply declare their intention to undertake great things. Anyone can intend anything. However, if students are able to draw on their actual Gap Year experiences in their application essays or personal statements, they are seen as bringing real-world experiences and skills to the table.

5 Some universities have even created their own bridging programs for students they have admitted. For example, Princeton and Tufts Universities are so supportive of Gap Years that they recently announced the launch of in-house programs that will provide financial assistance to students who would otherwise be unable to afford a Gap Year.

6 My final note on the value of a Gap Year is on the value to future employers. Anecdotally, we have heard from both our alumni and employers that a student's Gap Year experiences are often an eagerly pursued topic during job interviews. Many employers want hard evidence of teamwork, communication and language skills, leadership, innovation, or problem solving. A Gap Year can teach practical skills better than any academic course. And in today's global, mobile world, these are the qualities that can make a prospective employee stand out in interview.

Mallika Ramdas
Head of University Advising
UWCSEA Dover

Communication skills (ATLs)

The text you have just read is an essay. Reflect on this introduction to essay writing before you answer the questions below.

What is an argumentative essay?

An essay is a piece of writing that analyses a topic or issue. Fundamentally, an essay allows the writer to defend an opinion on a particular matter. This opinion is called a thesis.

A successful argumentative essay must achieve four things:

1. An essay must address a topic. An essay should be about "something" such as volunteering, taking a gap year, finding the right college course.
2. An essay answers a question, for example, "What are the benefits of volunteering?" or "What is the point of going to university?"
3. An essay (usually) takes the form of an argument. Very broadly, an essay can be for or against an issue. Alternatively the essay can take a balanced view reflecting on both sides of an argument.
4. An essay must reach a conclusion.

Analyze the quality of the essay by answering these questions:

- Does the essay address a clear topic?
- Does the essay answer a question?
- Does the essay follow a logical argument?
- Does the essay have a clear conclusion?

Reading comprehension

In the essay above the paragraph headings A to F are missing. Choose the correct heading from the list below for each paragraph.

A The meaning of a Gap Year

B Going with the trend

C Improved prospects

D The value of experience

E Postponing your application

F What you can do

G Only actual experience counts

H Learning life's lessons

I Disadvantages

J Living abroad

Answer the following questions.

7. Which phrase in paragraph 1 explains why universities think gap year students may have great potential?
8. Which phrase in paragraph 2 explains why gap year students may have greater chances of getting a place on very popular college courses?
9. What two qualities allow previous applicants to successfully reapply for a course after a gap year?
10. Which schemes show that certain universities have adopted the concept of the gap year?
11. Which phrase in paragraph 6 suggests that some skills learned on a gap year are more useful than those acquired at college?

HL extension (HL)

The essay writer wants to be even-handed in her assessment of gap year programmes. She mentions the advantages and a few of the drawbacks for students. Go through the essay again and make lists of the five best arguments in favour of taking a gap year. Find evidence from the text for each argument.

Oral activity: Role play or semi-scripted drama

In this role play a student and his/her parents discuss taking a gap year. They have opposing views. One member of the team can play a student who would really love to take a gap year. One or two members of the group can play the role of the parent or parents. The rest of the group can help with the preparations and act as critical observers during the rehearsals and performance.

You should plan the whole conversation in advance and create cue cards to help you organize what you want to say. Use the advice in the previous section of this chapter to help you to produce your cue cards. Read the background information and arguments below and make helpful notes. Each "team" should make at least five points in support of the point of view they hold.

The student

You have a great opportunity to volunteer for six months in a developing country. The organization you will work with has an excellent ethical reputation. It also has a first-class volunteer programme with an experienced local volunteer coordinator and excellent, safe on-site accommodation.

You will work in the community school helping the local teachers with English classes. You could also run your own study groups in other relevant subjects according to the needs and wishes of the students.

You can contribute to different community projects. These activities include: well-digging resources to villagers to allow them maintain water-wells; water distribution for irrigation; providing filters for drinking water; improving health care; organizing microloans; caring for animals for food and income generation; gardening and fish-pond projects; beekeeping and honey production; fair-trade projects selling clothing and craft products to local and overseas markets

Consequently, you will have a chance to develop any number of skills and gain practical experience of subjects taught at university level.

Thinking and social skills ATLs

In this activity there are opportunities to develop the following skills:

- Generate novel ideas and consider new perspectives
- Use visual diagrams to generate new ideas and inquiries
- Consider multiple alternatives, including those that might be unlikely or impossible
- Create novel solutions to authentic problems
- Make unexpected or unusual connections between objects and/or ideas
- Make guesses, ask "what if" questions and generate testable hypotheses
- Apply existing knowledge to generate new ideas
- Create original works and ideas; use existing works and ideas in new ways
- Work effectively with others
- Practice empathy
- Help others to succeed
- Take responsibility for one's own actions
- Manage and resolve conflict, and work collaboratively in teams
- Make fair and equitable decisions
- Listen actively to other perspectives and ideas
- Negotiate effectively
- Encourage others to contribute

The parents

The parents do not like the idea of their son or daughter taking a gap year. Here are some things they say.

"A gap year can put you in deep debt once you have graduated from college."

"A year out can mess with your head, and may lead you to think that you can travel forever and forget about college altogether."

"If you are away from the classroom, you will forget everything you learned at school. You will fall behind the rest of your classmates."

"The university might not accept you, if you take a year off."

"Who is paying for this? We are! So we will decide what you do."

"If you take a year off school, you will lose out socially. Students that are your age will be one year ahead, and have already established relationships with other students."

"Taking a gap year means more than making plans. You will have to make them work. It will prove a lot more difficult than you originally expected."

"We worry about the lack of safety. You will have to travel alone. Even if you travel abroad in a group, you can put yourself in a very dangerous position."

"You might change all your plans for your education and your future career."

Listening comprehension

Click the icon to practice the listening section of Paper 2. In this exercise, you must match the opening halves of four sentences with their correct endings. The matching halves will form a true sentence in the context of the recording.

Tip

Tips on successful classroom role-play

Role-play work best when you prepare before you start. Make sure you have prepared the **arguments** you are going to use.

You may want to make a note of your arguments on a cue card. You may need time to "get into" the role by thinking about the character you are going to play and rehearsing how best to express the **opinions** the character might hold.

When each person is ready you can act out the role-play in front of your audience.

In order to engage your audience, give the a "while-watching" task such as deciding which arguments are strongest, or who has the best logical argument.

Internal assessment (SL)

Take a look at the visual stimuli below. The images relate to the theme of the chapter: "Social organization".

Brainstorming

In pairs, choose one of the photographs, then discuss and answer the following questions.

1. What is the main idea in the photograph? How does it relate to the title of the section, "Social relationships"?
2. What do you see in the background of the photograph? What does the background tell you about the location and context of the photograph?
3. Look at the foreground of the photograph. Describe the person or people you can see.
4. What is happening in the picture? How does the photograph relate to the topic of the chapter, "Volunteering"? How does it relate to an Anglophone culture?

Presenting

Based on your answers to the questions above, prepare a four or five-minute presentation on the photograph.

Remember that the presentation should not only include description of the photograph, but should also connect it to the theme social organization and the topic of volunteers in an Anglophone society. Present your photograph and topic to your classmates.

Peer assessment

Assess the presentations given by your classmates. Use the SL IA criteria to guide your assessment.

	IA (SL)
Criterion A	Language
Criterion B	1. Message: visual stimulus 2. Message: conversation
Criterion C	Interactive skills: communication

Suggest ways in which your classmates can improve their presentation techniques.

Internal assessment (HL)

The Color Purple

by Alice Walker

Taking place in the 1930s, the story focuses on the lives of a variety of African-American women. In this section of the novel, a missionary couple, Samuel and Corrine, and their children, Olivia and Adam, befriend the letter writer, a young woman called Nettie. With few prospects of her own, Nettie agrees to accompany Samuel and Corrine to West Africa to undertake missionary work. Whenever she finds time, Nettie writes to her sister, Celie, whom she has not seen for several years. In the letters from Africa Nettie describes her life and work among the Olinka people, and gradually reveals that she is becoming disillusioned with her volunteer work.

Dear Celie,

It has been a long time since I had time to write. But I always, no matter what I'm doing, I am writing to you. Dear Celie, I say in my head in the middle of Vespers, in the middle of the night, while cooking, Dear, dear Celie. And I imagine that you really do get my letters and that you are writing back to me: Dear Nettie this is what life is like from me.

We're up at 5 o'clock for a light breakfast of millet porridge and fruit, and the morning classes. We teach the children English, reading, writing, history, geography, arithmetic and the stories in the bible. At 11 o'clock we break for lunch and household duties. From one until four it is too hot to move, though some of the mothers sit behind their hut and sew. At 4 o'clock we teach the older children and at night we are available for adults. Some of the older children are used coming to the Mission school, but the smaller ones are not. Their mothers sometimes drag them here, screaming and kicking. They are all boys. Olivia is the only girl.

The Olinka do not believe girls should be educated. When I asked a mother why she thought this, she said:

A girl is nothing to herself; only to her husband can she become something.

What can she become? I asked.

Why, she said, the mother of his children.

But I am not the mother of anybody's children, I said, and I am something.

You are not much, she said. The missionaries drudge.

It is true that I work harder here than I ever dreamt I could work, and that I sweep out the school and tidy up after service, but I don't feel like a drudge. I was surprised that this woman, whose Christian name is Catherine, saw me in this light.

She has a little girl, Tashi, who plays with Olivia after school. Adam is the only boy who will speak to Olivia at school. They are not mean to her; it is just–what is it? Because she is where they are doing "boys things" they do not see her. But never fear, Celie, Olivia has your stubbornness and clearsightedness, and she is smarter than all of them, including Adam, put together.

Why can't Tashi come to school? She asked me. When I told her the Olinka don't believe in educating girls. She said, quick as a flash, they are like White people at home who don't want coloured people to learn.

Oh, she's sharp, Celie. At the end of the day when Tashi can get away from all the chores her mother assigns her, she and Olivia secret themselves in my hut and everything Olivia has learnt she shares with Tashi. To Olivia right now Tashi alone is Africa. The Africa she came beaming across the ocean hoping to find. Everything else is difficult for her.

Brainstorming

Discuss the following questions then summarize your discussion in point form

1. What are the main topics of Nettie's letter to her sister, Celie?
2. What attitudes does Nettie show towards her job as a volunteer teacher?
3. Nettie seems not to agree with the Olinka people's attitudes to girls and their education. What does she say about these issues? Do you agree with her?
4. Do you think the organization that is engaging Nettie as a volunteer is treating her fairly? Give reasons for your answer.
5. In the book Nettie knows she will be volunteering in the Olinka village for a long time. What advice would you give to Nettie to help her make the most of her time as a volunteer?

Note

In your internal assessment, the literary extract will not exceed 300 words. You will be shown two, one from each of the works of literature studied in class.

Presenting

Based on your answers to the questions above, prepare a four or five-minute presentation on the text.

Make your presentation to your classmates. Students listening to the presentation should prepare individual questions about the text which they can ask you at the end of your presentation.

Peer assessment

Assess the presentations given by your classmates. Use the rubrics on page 143 to guide your assessment.

Suggest ways in which your classmates can improve their presentation techniques.

	Personal essay	Thesis-driven essay
Prompt	Title	Question
Opening	Opening remark or observation	Thesis
Body	Narrative or supporting paragraphs	Supporting paragraphs
Ending	Final thought	Conclusion
Audience	Depends on context	Formal relationship
Language	Formal, semi-formal, informal	Formal
Pont of view	First person	Third person

Paper 1: Essays

As we have seen, an essay can be a piece of writing in which you state your ideas on a topic. The essay is an essential communication tool, especially in school. The ability to write well-written, well-organized essays will serve you well now, in college and in later life. A good essay demonstrates that you can communicate your ideas clearly, and persuade an audience that your opinions are logical and trustworthy.

Writing for a specific audience

If writing for a teacher on a formal subject, you should aim to write a **thesis-driven** essay using formal language and in the third person. If writing for a general audience on a personal experience or subject, you can write a **personal essay** with a first-person narrative.

Analyzing an essay

The reading comprehension text on page 155, "Volunteering overseas: To Gap Year or not to Gap Year" is an essay. Read it again and analyze its effectiveness as an essay. To do so answer the following questions and give evidence for your answers.

- Do you think the introduction does a good job introducing the topic?
- Does the opening paragraph grab your attention?
- Can you identify a clear thesis statement in the introduction? If yes, what is it?
- Is the main body of the essay effective?
- Does each of the paragraphs in the body present one single idea?
- Is there a clear topic phrase or sentence in each of the supporting paragraphs?
- Write down the topic phrase or sentence you can find for each of the paragraphs.
- Does each topic phrase or sentence relate to the thesis statement?
- Are there reasons, examples, or different explanations to support each topic sentence?
- Is the use of connectors effective or would you suggest adding more connectors?
- Is there a conclusion? If yes, write it down.
- Does the conclusion relate to the thesis statement?
- Is there a final thought? If yes, write it down.

Structure

For a formal argumentative essay you will need to use a thesis-driven structure. You will also need to cite evidence and use formal language to communicate your opinions. Look at the opening paragraph below. What is the thesis here?

Many teenagers spend their time messing with their phones, watching TV, or playing computer games. However, other teenagers are doing amazing things. Two such examples are Alex Lin, who recycles and refurbishes e-waste and Malala Yousafzai, who has made a stand for girls' education. They both want to make their community, and the world, a better place.

You will need to divide your argumentative essay into a series of supporting paragraphs. Each paragraph will focus on a single supporting point that supports your thesis. You should express each point clearly in a topic sentence. This will help your readers to focus on the main idea of each of your paragraphs.

A personal essay may have an opening statement, a story in the middle to illustrate your point and a final thought on the subject, explaining what you have learned from the experience.

Writing activity: Essays

Here are three opportunities to practice writing essays.

Plan, draft, revise and redraft one of these stimuli.

1. You have been asked to write an essay for your school magazine on either the benefits or disadvantages of taking a gap year. Use the material you have read in this section to build a coherent thesis and supporting arguments. You may choose to represent either point of view. Make sure that the thesis-driven essay is clearly structured and is written in an appropriate register for the audience.
2. Write an essay on the subject of volunteering in the community. You may choose to write either a thesis-driven argumentative essay in which you argue a particular point of view. Alternatively, write a personal essay based on your own experiences. In either case, make sure that the essay is clearly structured and is written in an appropriate register for the audience.
3. Study the poster below. Imagine you have already been on a gap year and during your time abroad you have experienced one or more of the events depicted in the poster. As a very recent alumnus of your school, your former English teacher asks you to write an essay for your school magazine directed at current DP students. Write your personal essay entitled "Take a gap year and experience life as you have never seen it before!"

Make sure that the essay is clearly structured and is written in an appropriate register for the audience.

Brainstorming

Follow the steps below.

1. Reflect on everything you have learned in this section. Choose your focal point and your point of view. What information do you want to emphasize?

Exam tip:

At standard level you should write between 250 and 400 words.

At higher level you should write between 450 and 600 words.

Communication skills ATL

Using mental models

Whatever you are writing, your text should have a structure. For example, thesis-driven texts such as a formal essay will structure its arguments to lead and guide your reader along down a specific path.

On this page you will find two different charts to help you to organize your essays. These "mental models" can help you plan your writing more clearly.

You can also use the same mental modal when you plan similar writing tasks in other subjects.

2. Generate ideas to be used in your text. Research additional material to support your opinion.
3. What else do you need to think about? Language and register? Audience? Context and text type?
4. Sort your ideas into a logical order. Choose examples to support your ideas.

Planning

You could use a chart like the ones below to help you plan your essay. Think about what measures you will take to make sure make your essay is clear and effective.

	Thesis-driven essay
Prompt	Question
Opening	Introduction and thesis
Body	Topic of supporting paragraphs
Ending	Conclusion
Audience	Formal relationship
Language	Formal
Pont of view	Third person

	Personal essay
Prompt	Title
Opening	Introduction with opening remark or observation
Body	Narrative sequence or topic of supporting paragraphs
Ending	Final thought
Audience	Depends on context
Language	Semi-formal, informal
Pont of view	First person

Self-management skills ATLs

Two of the greatest assets of a good writer are the self-discipline to complete a task on time and a critical eye to be able to redraft a piece of writing.

Once you have finished the first draft of your essay, re-read it critically and then write a new and much improved draft.

Learn to practice the skill of redrafting in all your written work.

Create a draft of the body of your essay. Write an eye-catching title.

Drafting

Re-read the completed draft of your essay. Remember you will be assessed on three criteria: criterion A, language; criterion B, message; criterion C, conceptual understanding (including audience, context and purpose). Make any necessary changes.

Conclusion to research question B

To what extent do we need to participate in a global community?

1. Now that you have completed this section what are your thoughts and reactions to the question above? What conclusions have you come to?
2. What justifications would you give for your answers?
3. What more would you need to know before you can come to a definitive conclusion about the question?

A TOK moment

How do we know (evaluate) whether a community project has meaning/is worth engaging with?

In the extract from *The Color Purple*, the narrator, Nettie, is clearly unhappy with her volunteer placement. She did not know enough about the organization she was going to work for, nor did she have a clear idea whether the work she was going to do would be useful and effective.

This leads us to pose the question: How do we know about things that are far away or that we cannot experience directly?

What is the purpose of the poster above? What elements of the poster help the reader to understand its meaning?

Now look at the TOK diagram below. Decide which ways of knowing would help you to decide whether you should engage with a particular community project

How many of these ways of knowing would be valuable in answering the question? Which ways of knowing would be the most valuable? Justify your answers.

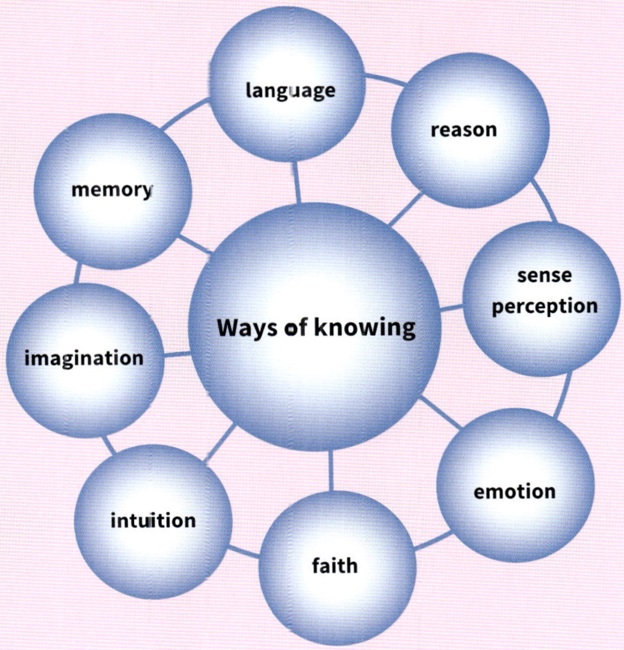

Section C: Social relationships

Research question C:

Is it still possible to be a global citizen?

1. What are your first thoughts and reactions to the question above?
2. What justifications would you give for your answers?
3. What more would you need to know before you can come to a definitive conclusion about the statement?

Before you listen

Study the poster promoting the values of global citizenship. Which of these values are promoted in your school? In what ways are they promoted?

Make a list of all the activities in your school that promote the values of global citizenship. Are there any other values that your school promotes which have not been illustrated in the poster?

Listening comprehension

Global citizenship education

Listen to the speech on global citizenship and answer the following questions.

Choose the correct answer from A, B, C or D.

1 According to the speech, our world …
- A is expanding in size and volume
- B is shrinking in size and volume
- C is becoming more interconnected
- D is dividing into small factions.

2 The speaker believes …
- A we face the same problems but not everyone will be affected
- B we face a variety of problems affecting us all
- C we will not all face the same problems
- D some of us will face more problems than others.

3 The speaker asks us to think about …
- A how to solve our problems
- B how to ask the right questions.
- C where to look for answers
- D whom to ask for answers.

4 The speaker asks whether basic education …
- A can answer our questions
- B can teach us basic skills
- C can meet our educational needs
- D can prompt the right questions.

5 The speaker thinks the policies of businesses and governments can …
- A affect all of us
- B have only local effects
- C affect our education
- D change the way we think.

6 The speaker asks us to change …
- A our behaviour towards society
- B our way of thinking about global issues
- C the way we see the world
- D our behaviour and our ideas.

Listen to the speech and identify whether, according to the speaker, these statements are true or false.

7 According to the speech, we must find a new approach to education.

8 According to the speaker, education on environmental issues is less important than developing a social conscience.

9 The speaker thinks education should have a humane and moral dimension.

10 The speaker believes education can answer the most important scientific questions for us.

11 The speech suggests we connect all the new ideas of the 21st century together.

12 The speaker believes that education is the fundamental tool for affecting global change for the better.

13 What is the speaker's thesis?

14 Name three points the speaker makes to support her thesis.

15 What conclusion does the speaker come to?

16 What is the speaker's final thought?

17 In your opinion how convincing is the speech? Evaluate it on a scale of 1 to 5, where 1 is "very convincing". Give reasons and evidence for your answers.

Exam tip: listening techniques

You will only have a limited number of opportunities to listen to the Paper 2 recordings. Make sure that you use your time well. Be an active listener. For example, when you are uncertain which is the correct multiple choice answer, make a note of the two most likely answers so you can choose the correct answer on a second listening.

HL extension HL

18. ***Fill in the missing blanks with words from the recording.***

We must give future generations a different kind of (__a__). They will need more than reading, (__b__) and arithmetic. Children will require the (__c__) to solve the global issues they will be facing. They will need to look after the (__d__). Children must learn about and stand up for justice and (__e__) rights. Children will need to be able to live together and resolve (__f__) peacefully. Unfortunately, (__g__) education cannot solve these problems.

Choose the correct answer from A B C or D.

19. Global citizenship education requires students to participate in ...
- **A.** community projects
- **B.** political projects
- **C.** media projects
- **D.** academic projects.

20. The word "proactive" describes students that ...
- **A.** acquire new knowledge
- **B.** acquire essential skills
- **C.** participate in their learning
- **D.** challenge their teachers.

21. The speaker believes that Global Citizenship Education will help students ...
- **A.** get into better universities
- **B.** have better job prospects
- **C.** acquire greater knowledge
- **D.** become more socially aware.

Oral activity: Role play

An important question for international education is "How do we promote global cooperation and understanding in culture, education, human rights, and environmental protection while respecting and understanding the world's many local and national identities?"

Look up the lyrics for John Lennon's song "Imagine".

This song promotes the idea of global citizenship that, in turn, promotes values such as these.

Diverse World	Global Issues	Values and Attitudes	Identity	Participation
Descriptions of a diverse world	Social Justice, Sustainable Development, Environment	What we think and believe	A sense of belonging to a group beyond immediate living area or situation	Working together and making a contribution
e.g. multicultural, international, cosmopolitan, multilingual	e.g. human rights, climate change, equality and diversity	e.g. being responsible for, being open to different perspectives, accepting difference	e.g. being part of a wider community, united, belonging to the world	e.g. collective responsibility, colunteering, supporting others

On the other hand, in some Anglophone countries we are seeing a rise in nationalist values as seen in the UK's Brexit vote and the election of Donald Trump in the USA.

Study these two sets of values.

Nationalists ...
1. see their country and its culture as unique and worth preserving
2. want to live in a stable and coherent moral order
3. think their governments should put their citizens' interests first
4. see patriotism as a virtue
5. think citizens have a duty to love and serve their country
6. have a sense of national identity and history
6. mistrust people with different values
7. oppose immigration and globalization

Internationalists ...
1. identify with people beyond national boundaries
2. want to live in a world that accepts change
3. think governments should put international concerns first
4. see internationalism as a virtue
5. think citizens have a duty to love and serve all humankind
6. have a sense of transnational identity and a common history
7. try to understand those with different values
8. welcome and participate in immigration and globalization

In small groups, imagine you are going to take part in a televised discussion. One person could play the part of the presenter/moderator and the others form two teams: one defending nationalism, the other defending internationalism. The purpose of the discussion is to find common ground and points that all parties can agree on.

Before you start, each team should prepare by giving examples, evidence or explanations for the eight debating points above. This may involve further research and preparation.

The role play requires you to reach a consensus. You should try to achieve full agreement; however, if you cannot all agree, a consensus allows you to approve a majority decision.

When your group has finished your discussions, you should summarize your findings and present them to the class.

Social skills ATLs

Role-playing exercises let us explore new ideas and concepts from different perspectives. This is because role-playing exercises allow us to adopt opinions and positions that we might not normally hold. By acting out a role in an empathetic manner we may come to see other people's points of view in a new light. In a role play you need to:

- practice empathy
- listen actively to others' perspectives and ideas
- manage and resolve conflict.

We can also learn that the world is a complex place with complicated problems that need more thought than our initial instinctive reactions can provide.

Internal assessment (SL)

Take a look at the visual stimuli below. The images relate to the theme of the chapter: "Social organization".

Peer assessment

Assess the presentations given by your classmates. Use the SL IA criteria to guide your assessment.

	IA (SL)
Criterion A	Language
Criterion B	1. Message: Visual stimulus 2. Message: conversation
Criterion C	Interactive skills: communication

Suggest ways in which your classmates can improve their presentation techniques.

Brainstorming

In pairs, choose one of the photographs, then discuss and answer the following questions.

- What is the main idea in the photograph? How does it relate to the theme of this section, "Social organization".
- What do you see in background of the photograph? What does the background tell you about the location and context of the photograph?
- Look at the foreground of the photograph. Describe the person or people you can see.
- What is happening in the picture? How does the action relate to the topic of this section, "Global citizenship"? How does it relate to an English-speaking community?
- Do you agree with the message of the photograph? Give reasons.

Presenting

Based on your answers to the questions above, prepare a four-minute presentation on the photograph.

Remember that the presentation should not only include description of the photograph, but should also connect it to the themes of social organization and the topic of global citizenship with focus on an Anglophone culture. Present your photograph and topic to your classmates

Internal assessment (HL)

Stargirl

by Jerry Spinelli

Stargirl Caraway is a new student at Mica High. Her clothes are eccentric, as are her mannerisms. She has a pet rat that she carries around in a bag that has a picture of a Sunflower on it. She becomes the confidante and girlfriend of the narrator, Leo Borlock, but is treated with suspicion by many students. In their eyes Stargirl makes a huge mistake when she cheers for both teams at a competitive basketball match. Even worse, she runs to the aid of an injured player on the visiting team. When Mica's team lose, Stargirl is blamed. When Stargirl puts a note on the school bulletin board proclaiming her love for Leo, the other students ostracize him along with Stargirl. In this scene Leo begs Stargirl to conform to the unwritten norms of the community.

Days passed. I continued to avoid Stargirl. I wanted her. I wanted them. It seemed I could not have both, so I did nothing. I ran and hid.

But she did not give up on me. She hunted me down. She found me in the TV studio after school one day. I felt fingers slipping down the back of my neck, grabbing my collar, pulling me backward. The crew was staring. "Mr. Borlock," I heard her say, "we need to talk." Her voice told me she was not smiling. She released my collar. I followed her out of the room. In the courtyard a couple cooing on the bench beneath the palmetto saw us coming and bolted, so that's where we sat.

"So," she said, "are we breaking up already?"

"I don't want to," I said.

"So why are you hiding from me?"

Forced to face her, forced to talk, I felt my gumption rising. "Something's gotta change," I said. "That's all I know."

"You mean like change clothes? Or change a tire? Should I change a tire on my bike? Would that do it?"

"You're not funny. You know what I mean."

She saw I was upset. Her face got serious.

"People aren't talking to me," I said. I stared at her. I wanted it to sink in. "People I've known ever since we moved here. They don't talk to me. They don't see me."

She reached out and lightly rubbed the back of my hand with her fingertip. Her eyes were sad. "I'm sorry people don't see you. It's no fun not being seen, is it?"

I pulled my hand away. "Well, you tell me what it's like. Doesn't it bother you that nobody talks to you?" It was the first time I had openly mentioned the shunning to her.

She smiled. "Dori talks to me. You talk to me. Archie talks to me. My family talks to me. Cinnamon talks to me. Senor Saguaro talks to me. I talk to me." She cocked her head and stared at me, waiting for a responding smile. I didn't give it. "Are you going to stop talking to me?"

"That's not the question," I said.

"What is the question?"

"The question is", I tried to read her face but I could not, "what makes you tick?"

"Now I'm a clock!"

I turned away. "See, I can't talk to you. It's all just a big joke."

She put my face between her hands and turned me to her. I hoped people were not watching from the windows. "Okay, serious now. Go ahead, ask me the tick question again. Or any other, any question at all."

I shook my head. "You just don't care, do you?"

That stumped her. "Care? Leo, how can you say I don't care? You've gone with me to places. We've delivered cards and flowers. How can you say-"

"That's not what I mean. I mean you don't care what people think."

"I care what you think. I care."

"I'm talking about the school, the town. I'm talking about everybody."

She sniffed around the word. "Everybody?"

"Right. You don't seem to care what everybody thinks. You don't seem to know what everybody thinks. You..."

She broke in: "Do you?"

I thought for a moment. I nodded sharply. "Yeah. Yeah, I think I do know. I'm in touch with everybody. I'm one of them. How could I not know?"

"And it matters?"

"Sure, it matters. Look", I waved my arm at the school around us, "look what's happening. Nobody talks to us. You can't just not give a crap what anybody thinks. You can't just cheer for the other team and expect your own school to love you for it." Words that I had been thinking for weeks rolled off my tongue now. "Kovac, Kovac, for God's sake. What was that all about?"

She was baffled. "Who's Kovac?"

"Kovac. The guy from Sun Valley. The basketball star. The guy who broke his ankle."

She was still baffled. "What about him?"

"What about him? What about you? What were you doing out there on the floor with him with his head in your lap?"

"He was in pain."

"He was the enemy, Stargirl! Susan. Whatever. The enemy!" She stared dumbly back at me. She had blinked at "Susan." "There were a thousand Sun Valley people there. He had his own people to take care of him, his own coaches, his own teammates, his own cheerleaders' laps. And you had your own team to worry about." I was screeching. I got up and walked away. I came back, leaned into her. "Why?" I said. "Why didn't you just let him be taken care of by his own people?"

She looked at me for a long time, as if in my face she could find herself explained. "I don't know," she said dimly at last. "I didn't think. I just did."

I pulled back. I was tempted to say, Well, I hope you're satisfied, because they hate you for what you did, but I didn't have the heart.

Now I was feeling sorry for her. I sat back down beside her. I took her hand. I smiled. I spoke as gently as I could.

"Stargirl, you just can't do things the way you do. If you weren't stuck in a home school all your life, you'd understand. You can't just wake up in the morning and say you don't care what the rest of the world thinks."

Her eyes were wide, her voice peepy like a little girl's. "You can't?"

Brainstorming

In small groups, discuss the following questions then summarize your discussion in point form.

1. What are the main causes of the arguments between Leo and Stargirl?
2. What attitudes does Stargirl show towards her own school and the students from Sun Valley school?
3. What attitudes does Leo show towards the other students and to Stargirl? Do you agree with him? Give reasons.
4. What advice would you give Leo about his relationship with Stargirl?
5. What advice would you give Stargirl about her relationship with Leo?
6. According to this passage, is it possible to be a member of a local community and simultaneously be a global citizen?

Presenting

Based on your answers to the questions above, prepare a four-minute presentation on the text.

Make your presentation to your classmates. Students listening to the presentation should prepare individual questions about the text which they can ask you at the end of your presentation.

Peer assessment

Assess the presentations given by your classmates. Use the HL IA criteria to guide your assessment.

	IA (HL)
Criterion A	Language
Criterion B	1. Message: literary extract 2. Message: conversation
Criterion C	Interactive skills: communication

Suggest ways in which your classmates can improve their presentation techniques.

Note

In your internal assessment, the literary extract will not exceed 300 words. You will be shown two, one from each of the works of literature studied in class.

Exam tip: Internal assessment SL and HL

When preparing for your individual oral assessment, you cannot bring any additional resources, such as a laptop, mobile phone or class notes, into the preparation room. Your teacher will give you a piece of paper on which to make notes – a maximum of 10 bullet points. You may bring these notes into the interview room and use them for reference. But when you present your thoughts on the visual or the literary extract, remember to speak naturally. Do not just read out your bullet points.

> **Exam tip**
>
> At standard level you should write between 250 and 400 words.
>
> At higher level you should write between 450 and 600 words.

> **Exam tip**
>
> Always choose the most natural text type for the task; that is, the most suitable for the purpose, context and audience of the task. Otherwise, you may lose marks for criterion C: conceptual understanding (including audience, context and purpose).

Paper 1 practice

Here are three opportunities to practice writing for Paper 1.

Plan, draft, revise and redraft one of these stimuli.

1. This year your school is making a big effort to promote the Creativity Action and Service programme to its IB students. As editor of the school newspaper write a text with the title, *Why we all need to undertake Service*. Choose one of the text types below to offer your opinions on the subject.

An essay	A set of instructions	A play script

2. Your school is offering grants to two graduating students to undertake their own Gap Year project. Students will be sponsored to participate for six months in an overseas development project of their choice. Choose one of these three text types to apply for one of the sponsored places.

A set of instructions	An email	An essay

3. The editor of your school magazine has asked you to contribute a suitable text entitled, *How to be a Global Citizen*. The purpose of the text is to give practical advice to younger students. Choose one of these three text types to express your point of view on this matter.

An interview	A set of instructions	An essay

Brainstorming

Global citizenship outlooks

Follow the steps below.

1. Reflect on everything you have learned in this section. Choose your focal point and your point of view. What information do you want to emphasize?
2. Generate ideas to be used in your text. Research additional material, such as the poster opposite, to support your opinion.
3. What else do you need to think about? Language and register? Audience? Context and text type?
4. Sort your ideas into a logical order. Choose examples to support your ideas.

Planning

Think about the concepts below when you plan your written text. Think about what measures you will take to make sure make your text communicates its message clearly and effectively:

- context
- audience
- purpose

Drafting

Individually, write a draft of your text. Remember to include any special features of the text type, such as an eye-catching title, headlines, by-lines or layout.

Re-read the completed draft of your opinion column.

Remember you will be assessed on three criteria: criterion A, language; criterion B, message; criterion C, conceptual understanding (including audience, context and purpose). Make any necessary changes.

Conclusion to research question C

Is it possible to be a global citizen?

1. Now that you have completed the section, what do you now think is the answer?
2. To what extent have your opinions on the subject changed since the beginning of this chapter? To what extent have your opinions remained the same?
3. Justify your answers.

Conclusion to the chapter

How can individuals participate in their community?

- Now that you have completed the chapter, what are your conclusions about the research question?
- To what extent have your opinions on the subject changed since the beginning of this chapter?

Justify your answers.

In particular, you may want to consider this question: In the long term how can participation in the communities we belong to enrich our lives and the lives of others?

Beyond the classroom

You can use the information you have learned and the communication skills you have developed in this chapter for practical purposes beyond the classroom.

CAS

Service

Community service is vital part in many communities. Many small organizations rely on people with community spirit to survive. The work can include tutoring children, assisting the elderly, looking after animals at animal shelters, performing environmental restoration or helping with civic beautification. In all cases, unpaid volunteers perform work that would not otherwise be accomplished.

Many people engage in community service out of a spirit of altruism, or a desire to connect with their communities. For DP students, completion of community service is essential for graduation, in which case your school or local organizations will often help to organize community service opportunities. Community service can be a great way to learn more about the place in which you live and the communities you are part of.

Here are just a few of the goals that volunteering can help you achieve:

- build self-esteem or confidence
- learn or develop skills
- enhance work experience
- be active and improve your health
- meet new people or broaden your social set
- make a difference in someone's life
- express gratitude for help you may have received in the past or "give back"
- support a cause you feel strongly about
- feel needed and valued which is satisfying in itself
- make a difference within your own community.

Create a series of inspirational posters promoting the benefits of volunteering. Relate the material to existing or potential volunteer projects within your school.

Suggested reading

The Diary of Adrian Mole Aged 13 3/4 by Sue Townsend

Stargirl by Jerry Spinelli

Make Lemonade by Virginia Euwer Wolff

The Color Purple by Alice Walker

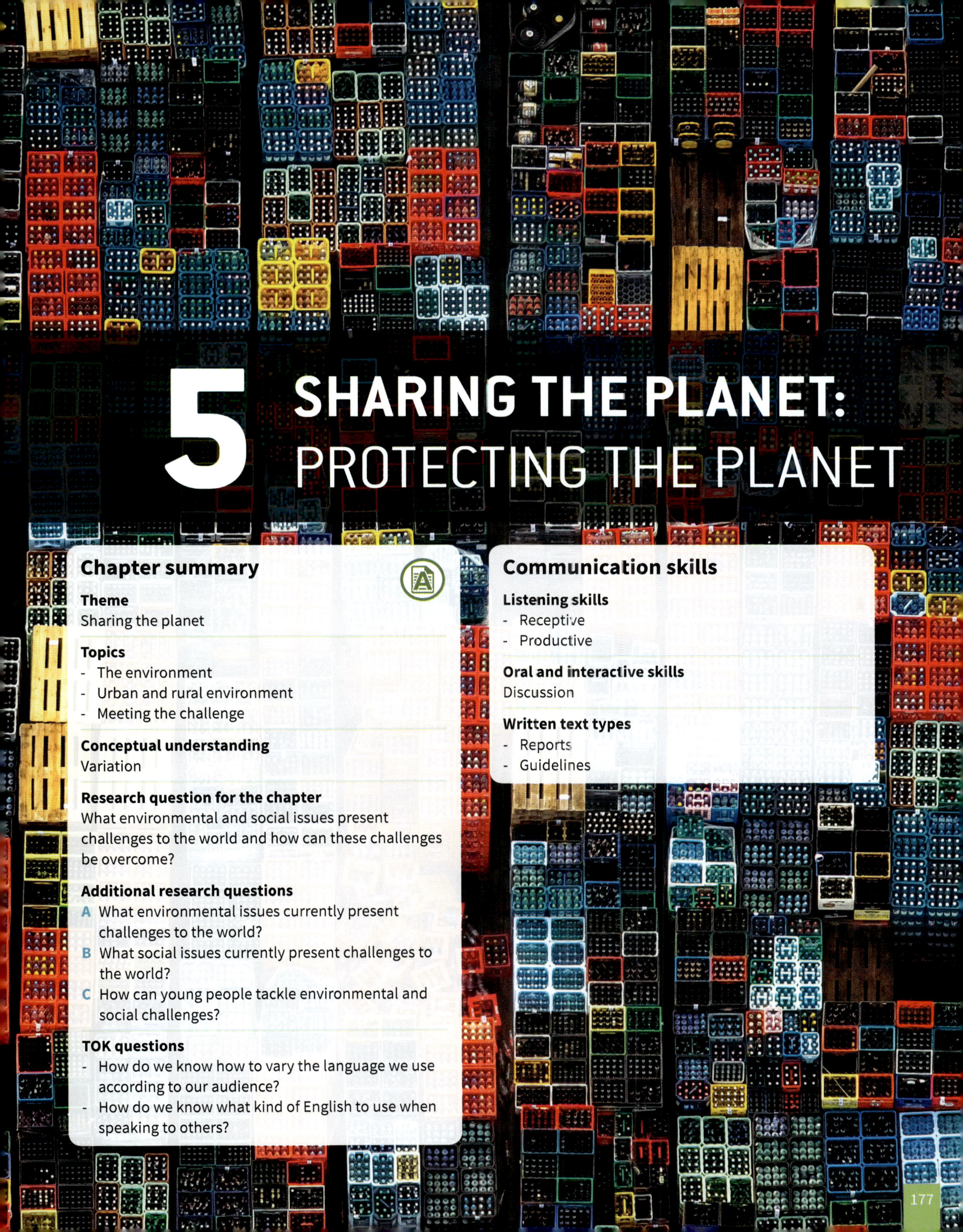

5 SHARING THE PLANET: PROTECTING THE PLANET

Chapter summary

Theme
Sharing the planet

Topics
- The environment
- Urban and rural environment
- Meeting the challenge

Conceptual understanding
Variation

Research question for the chapter
What environmental and social issues present challenges to the world and how can these challenges be overcome?

Additional research questions
A What environmental issues currently present challenges to the world?
B What social issues currently present challenges to the world?
C How can young people tackle environmental and social challenges?

TOK questions
- How do we know how to vary the language we use according to our audience?
- How do we know what kind of English to use when speaking to others?

Communication skills

Listening skills
- Receptive
- Productive

Oral and interactive skills
Discussion

Written text types
- Reports
- Guidelines

Research question for the chapter:

What environmental and social issues present challenges to the world and how can these challenges be overcome?

1. What are your first thoughts and reactions to the question above?
2. What justifications would you give for your answer?
3. What more would you need to know before you can come to a definitive conclusion about the question?

Study the pictures below. What environmental issues do they illustrate?

In groups make lists of the biggest environmental challenges facing us in the 21st century. Organize your ideas into different categories. Be prepared to present your ideas to the rest of the class.

Imagine the Earth in 50 years' time and think about your future children. What kind of world would you like them to inherit? What environmental problems will they face and how might they be overcome?

Section A: The environment

Research question A:

What are today's biggest environmental challenges to the world?

1. What are your first thoughts and reactions to the question above?
2. What justifications would you give for your answers?
3. What more would you need to know before you can come to a definitive conclusion about the question?

Communication skills (ATLs)

How much do you know about the issues facing your local environment? You might want to conduct an Internet search.

- Collaborate with peers using a variety of digital environments and media.

Once you have completed your search discuss your findings.

- Negotiate ideas and knowledge with peers and teachers

When you have completed your research and discussed your ideas, think about how best to communicate your findings.

- Share ideas with multiple audiences using a variety of digital environments and media

Before you read

Think about the local environment in which you live. Can you find specific examples of the issues listed below in your area?

Deforestation | Energy production | Food | Global warming | Industrialization

Poor housing | Pollution | Transportation | Waste | Water shortage

In groups, discuss how the problems affect your community. Which problems are the easiest or the least complicated to solve?

When you have finished your assessment, justify your answers

https://inhabitat.com/why-we-need-earth-day-7-most-pressing-environmental-problems-we-need-to-solve/

Happy Earth Day: The World's 6 Most Pressing Environmental Issues

by Charley Cameron

At Inhabitat, every day is Earth Day. We work each and every day to bring the latest news on the many exciting ways to inhabit the Earth in a smarter, greener, more sustainable way. So this Earth Day, we're considering the most important environmental issues, and a few of the steps we can take to create a healthier future for ourselves, our communities and of course, the Earth.

1. ______________

We can't live without it, and thankfully much of the Earth is made up of it. Yet we face major problems where the life-sustaining liquid is concerned. While there is technically enough available for all 6.8 billion of us, one-fifth of the world's population live in areas of scarcity.

Poor quality not only poses supply problems, but also has a huge, inevitable impact on marine life. Whether it's through pollution from industry, or ill-regulated efforts to drill for yet more oil we're increasingly filling our rivers, seas and oceans with toxic waste. Life in our seas is suffering tremendously.

2. ____________

This has long posed a threat to our Earth. Trees cover 30 percent of the planet's land, and give vital protection from sandstorms and flooding, as well as provide natural habitats for wildlife. They are one of our greatest resources for offsetting some of our carbon emissions, and without the tree canopy we leave areas vulnerable to intense heat. This drives further climate change. Yet every single year we lose an area the size of Panama, cleared to make way for farmland.

3. ____________

Agricultural production comes with a hefty carbon footprint. Damage is caused by the loss of trees. Fertilizers pollute our water, and pesticides kill our bees. However, demand is expected to rise sharply — by 2050 a population of 8.9 billion will eat, on average, a diet with 340 calories more than the 2001 average of 2790 calories. Other studies show that demand will double by that same date. Some of this projected increase is attributed to an expectation that populations, which currently have inadequate access to nutrition, will see improvements in the coming decades.

4. ____________

In the US alone we've made the Gulf of Mexico toxic with oil, we've caused earthquakes in the Midwest while fracking for natural gas, and we've blasted the tops off mountains in Virginia looking for coal. In the course of harvesting non-renewable resources we're releasing all manner of toxic gases into the atmosphere, driving climate change and creating a hazardous environment for all living beings. The fact that we're destroying the planet is a pretty good reason to give pause and change course. Yet massive corporations continue to look for fossil fuels.

5. ____________

Studies show young people are driving less, but we aren't going to be doing without cars any time soon. As long as urban developments are built to be unwalkable, we're going to have to find a way for everyone to be able to get from a to b and back again without destroying the planet. As it stands, a full 20 percent of US greenhouse gas emissions come directly from cars.

6. ____________

As a growing population, we have a lot of stuff. From consumer electronics to clothing to diapers, a worrying proportion of our 'stuff' is made using finite resources, and only to be used for a relatively short amount of time before being tossed into landfill.

Everything on this list is a contributing factor to the problem and yet we still have elected officials who argue that it isn't 'real.' A poll by Yale University said the majority of participants agreed that a rise in temperatures was causing an increasing number of extreme weather events and natural disasters. Earlier this year sea levels were predicted to rise 20-80 inches by 2100. As a result, 3.7 million residents are at risk from floodwaters. It's time for climate change deniers to finally give in to the evidence.

Happy Earth Day!

Reading comprehension

In the text, the paragraph headings 1 to 6 are missing. Choose the correct heading for each paragraph from the list below.

Deforestation | Food policies | Pollution | Water shortages | Unnecessary waste | Poor housing | Industrialization | Global warming | Overpopulation | Energy production | Desertification | Transportation policies

Choose the correct answer from A, B, C or D.

7. In line 19, the phrase "carbon footprint" means:
   - A. coal production
   - B. the production of greenhouse gases
   - C. an amount of greenhouse gases produced
   - D. pollution.
8. Bees are in danger because for which two reasons?
   - A. Deforestation
   - B. Global warming
   - C. Overpopulation
   - D. Pest control chemicals

Identify if the sentences below are true or false. Provide a quotation to support your answer. Base your answers on information that appears between line 26 and 32.

9. US industry is not the main source of pollution in seas around Mexico.
10. There is a relationship between the extraction of oil and air pollution.
11. The energy industry is now taking a more ecologically friendly approach to climate change.

Answer the following questions.

12. What is the planning defect mentioned between lines 33 and 37 that prevents the banning of cars?
13. Which phrase between lines 38 and 40 describes something that "cannot renew itself in a sustainable manner"?
14. Which phrase between lines 38 and 40 means "put into the trash"?
15. Give the two **general** consequences of global warming mentioned between lines 41 and 46.
16. Give the two **specific** consequences of global warming mentioned between lines 41 and 46.

Exam tip

Skimming and scanning a reading text for meaning

Skimming

When you first read a text, do not try to understand immediately every single word or idea. Skim the text. In other words read it quickly to understand the overall meaning.

When skimming a text, ask yourself

- what is the main idea in the text
- what is the main purpose of the text
- how is the text organized
- what are the main subtopics of the text
- how does the writer achieve this aim or purpose?

In the exercise opposite, use skimming techniques to find answers 1 to 6.

Scanning

Scanning a text involves reading to find specific information. If you have first skimmed the text and understand "the big picture", you will find it much easier to locate specific pieces of information.

When answering comprehension questions, more often than not, you are asked to scan the text to find specific answers.

In the exercise opposite, questions 7 to 16 require you to scan the text.

Oral activity: Discussion

Here are some of the environmental issues listed in the article Happy Earth Day. Imagine you are running your local council and are faced with each of the problems. How do you decide which are the most important environmental problems to solve? How do you decide what to do?

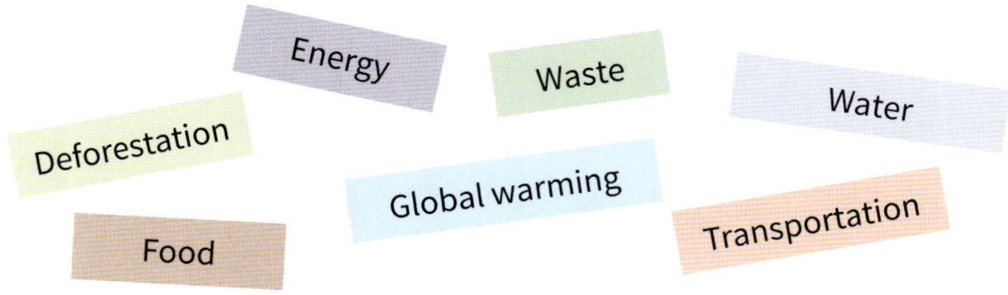

In groups, look at the list of ideas below on ways to combat these environmental issues. Once you have understood the solutions, match them to the problems listed above. Some solutions may be useful for more than one problem.

1. Adopt renewable resources such as solar and wind power.
2. Block imports of low-cost industrially produced crops.
3. Cut domestic and commercial use of lighting.
4. Deselect politicians who insist that carbon dioxide emissions do not pose a threat to our environment.
5. Develop urban farming initiatives by converting areas into fruitful green spaces.
6. Encourage people to carry a far lower carbon footprint.
7. Encourage the use of reusable and recyclable materials such as coffee cups and shopping bags.
8. Ensure access in areas facing widespread pollution, waste and drought.
9. Ensure that the right crops are grown where they are needed.
10. Improve infrastructure.
11. Pass laws to make recycling obligatory.
12. Pedestrianize urban developments.
13. Prevent waste.
14. Set up local recycling centres and promote their use.
15. Promote the use of electric bicycles.
16. Provide clean supplies to areas which need them.
17. Provide more education about where food comes from and how it is made.
18. Provide more education about where wood comes from and how it is produced.
19. Provide municipal recycling programmes.
20. Reduce and eliminate emissions of all kinds.
21. Reduce meat consumption.
22. Start replanting programmes.
23. Stop destroying environments.
24. Support sustainable and managed production of woodland.
25. Take steps to regulate drilling, fracking and mining.
26. Use hybrid electric technologies in vehicles.
27. Work together towards a greener, more sustainable future.

Once you have matched the problems to their potential solutions, hold a group discussion to choose which you think is the single most important solution for each problem.

Present and justify your choices by giving clear reasons.

Social skills

ATLs

A group discussion is a conversation about a particular topic. In language B, your discussion will have a practical purpose. It could be to answer a question, solve a problem or conflict, create a plan of action, or organize an event.

A discussion group is small to allow everyone to take part. A group of two or three generally does not need a leader or chairperson; no single person should dominate the discussion. If the group includes five or more people, it may be helpful to choose a chairperson who can manage the discussion and make sure everyone's voice is heard.

Sometimes the members of a discussion group will disagree. At this point you will need to demonstrate negotiation skills. It is best to have procedures to come to a common solution, or point of view. It is a really important social skill to be able to discuss and negotiate in order to find areas of mutual agreement.

Negotiation skills and procedures

Opening the discussion

- Clarify things you don't understand.
- Find out what each member of the group thinks.

Putting forward ideas

- Make suggestions.
- Propose solutions.
- Look at advantages and disadvantages of all ideas

Agreement

- Make choices.
- Agree on what to do.
- Agree on how to do it.

Peer assessment

In small groups, assess the presentations given by your classmates. You may use the rubrics below as a basis for your comments.

	Good	Improvement possible	Needs some improvement	Needs a lot of improvement
Eye contact	Makes good eye contact with audience.	Makes eye contact with the audience most of the time.	Sometimes makes eye contact with the audience.	Does not make eye contact with the audience.
Enthusiasm	Shows great enthusiasm for the topic.	Shows enthusiasm for the topic.	Shows some enthusiasm for the topic.	Shows little enthusiasm for the topic.
Preparation and organization	Very prepared and well organized.	Mostly prepared and well organized.	Somewhat prepared and organized.	Not very prepared or organized.
Clear speech	Speaks very clearly and is very easy to understand.	Speaks clearly most of the time and is fairly easy to understand.	Sometimes speaks clearly and is sometimes easy to understand.	Does not speak clearly and is quite difficult to understand.
Knowledge of topic	Shows excellent understanding of the topic.	Shows good understanding of the topic.	Shows some understanding of the topic.	Shows little understanding of the topic.

Internal assessment (SL)

Take a look at the visual stimulus here. The image relates to the theme of the chapter: "Sharing the planet".

Exam tip: Internal assessment (SL)

Remember in the examination you will be able to choose between two images.

However, you will not know which of the five themes will be presented, nor will you have seen the visual stimulus before.

Social skills ATLs

Cooperative learning

Cooperative learning involves working in small groups to reach a common goal.

It may help with your preparations for the internal assessment if you work together in small groups and discuss the visual stimulus and the accompanying questions.

Working cooperatively may enable you to use techniques and find answers that you might not have found by working alone.

At the same time you can learn to listen to other perspectives and ideas, make positive contributions to discussions and work towards a common goal.

Brainstorming

In pairs, discuss and answer the following questions.

- What is the main idea in the photograph? How does it relate to the title of the section, "The environment".
- What do you see in the background of the photograph? What does the background tell you about the location and context of the photograph? How does the photograph relate to an English-speaking community?
- Look at the foreground of the photograph. Describe the person or people you can see.
- If you had the power, what one thing would you do to improve the lives of the children in the picture? Explain your reply.
- What is happening in the picture? How does the action relate to the theme of the chapter: "Sharing the planet"?

Presenting

Based on your answers to the questions above, prepare a four-minute presentation on the photograph.

Remember that the presentation should not only include description of the photograph, but should also connect it to the themes of sharing and protecting the planet in an Anglophone culture. Present your photograph and topic to your classmates.

Peer assessment

Assess the presentations given by your classmates. Consider the SL IA criteria as a guide in your assessment.

	IA (SL)
Criterion A	Language
Criterion B	1. Message: Visual stimulus 2. Message: Conversation
Criterion C	Interactive skills: Communication

Suggest ways in which your classmates can improve their presentation techniques.

Internal assessment (HL)

Read the passage and answer the questions that follow.

Love Canal—A Brief History

Love Canal is an abandoned canal project branching off of the Niagara River about four miles south of Niagara Falls. It was also the name of a fifteen-acre, working-class neighborhood of around 800 single-family homes built next to the canal. From 1942 to 1953, the Hooker Chemical Company began using the partially dug canal as a chemical waste dump. At the end of this period, the contents of the dump consisted of around 21,000 tons of toxic chemicals, including at least twelve that are known carcinogens. Hooker capped the 16-acre hazardous waste landfill in clay and sold the land to the Niagara Falls School Board.

Public awareness of the disaster began in the late 1970s. Investigative newspaper journalists and grassroots door-to-door health surveys began to reveal a series of inexplicable illnesses—epilepsy, asthma, migraines, and abnormally high rates of birth defects and miscarriages in the Love Canal neighborhood.

As it turns out, heavy rains in the late 1970s caused the chemicals to leak into the basements and yards of neighborhood homes, as well as into the playground of the elementary school which was built directly over the canal. Apathetic New York State officials were slow to act but quick to dismiss the activists (most of whom were working-class women who lived in the neighborhood) as a collection of hysterical housewives. However, President Jimmy Carter declared a state of emergency in 1978 and the federal government relocated 239 families.

This left 700 families, even though tests conducted by the NYS Department of Health revealed that toxic substances were leaking into their homes. After another hard battle, activists forced Carter to declare a second state of emergency in 1981, and the remaining families were relocated at cost of $17 million.

Love Canal symbolizes the environmental disaster caused by untold numbers of toxic waste disposal sites scattered throughout America. Lawmakers have used the Love Canal disaster to push for new legislation to hold polluters financially responsible for cleaning up their toxic waste sites. The result was the 1980 Comprehensive Environmental Response, Compensation, and Liability Act—better known as Superfund. A less well-known but equally important outcome of Love Canal was the emergence of a militant, grassroots "environmental justice" movement.

Note box

In your internal assessment, the literary extract will not exceed 300 words. You will be shown two, one from each of the works of literature studied in class.

Brainstorming

In small groups, discuss the following questions then summarize your discussion in point form.

- What was the sequence of events at Love Canal between 1940 and 1980?
- What were the causes of the environmental disaster at Love Canal?
- What were the environmental and social consequences of the pollution?
- What lessons can be learned from this story?
- How is the story of Love Canal linked to the theme of protecting the planet?
- If your community were faced with a similar environmental disaster to the one at Love Canal, what would be your reaction? What action would you take?

Peer assessment

Assess the presentations given by your classmates. Consider the HL IA criteria as a guide in your assessment.

	IA (HL)
Criterion A	Language
Criterion B	1. Message: literary extract 2. Message: conversation
Criterion C	Interactive skills: communication

Suggest ways in which your classmates can improve their presentation techniques.

Presenting

Based on your answers to the questions above, prepare a four-minute presentation on the content of the text.

Make your presentation to your classmates. Students listening to the presentation should prepare individual questions about the text which they can ask you at the end of your presentation.

Paper 1: Guidelines

Guidelines are texts that help you to make choices when deciding on a course of action. When you are faced with a problem or decision, guidelines set out standard routines or good practice that you can follow. Unlike instructions, they do not simply give orders. Guidelines suggest solutions and procedures. They may also offer explanations for the actions suggested.

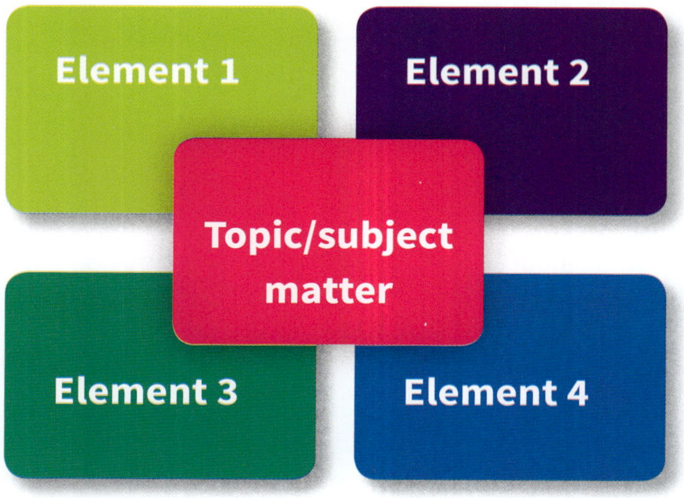

Look at the guidelines on the next page: *10 tips to Keep your Recycling Clean and Marketable*.

How has the writer organized the information?

- Identify the main topic.
- List the elements or subtopics. How are the subtopics organized?

Guidelines are organized around a topic or a specific subject. You can organize guidelines as if you were defining an issue.

For example, if you were writing guidelines on the topic of "What university course to take?" what would be the four different elements to take into account when advising your audience?

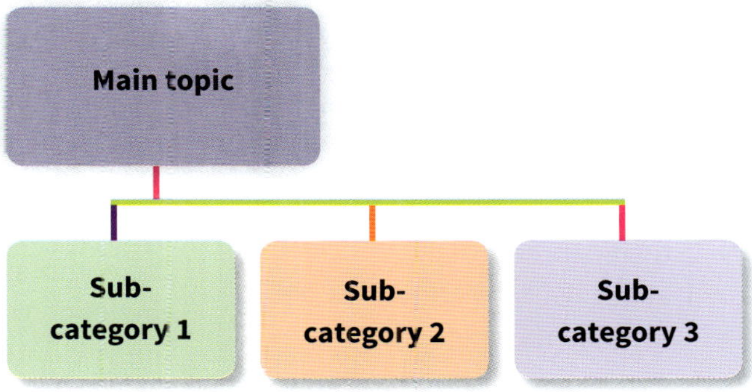

Alternatively your guidelines can help your readers to take a big problem and break it down into smaller subcategories. For instance, if the main topic you are advising on is recycling, you might want to give advice about recycling different materials.

Guidelines can be written in any style, depending on the topic, context and the relationship between you, as writer, and your audience. Study the set of guidelines below and then answer the questions that follow.

10 Tips to Keep your Recycling Clean and Reusable

Recycling that is either contaminated with trash or mixed with different types of recyclable material will either be trashed or sold as a much lower value material to recycling companies.

Please use the following recycling tips to help maximize our community's efforts.

1. **DO NOT PUT YOUR RECYCLING IN PLASTIC BAGS** – It cannot be processed at the recycling center and will either be emptied by hand (expensive!) or thrown in the trash (a real bummer - you went to all that trouble to separate it).
2. No loose plastic bags of any kind – they get tangled up in the equipment. Most grocery stores will recycle grocery bags.

Sorting out your trash

3. Don't flatten cartons or cans – these items are separated based on their dimension and the machines separate flat material with the paper.
4. DO attach plastic screw-top lids to plastic containers.
5. Remove metal lids from glass containers – then the metal will go with the metal, not the glass.
6. Shredded paper should go in your compost cart rather than recycling as at the recycling center it gets tangled in the machinery.

Preparing your trash

7. Plastic food containers and plastic cups are trash. Please be careful they can get flattened in transportation and wind up with the paper.
8. Do not put scrap metal in your recycling bin. It can be dropped off at Western's Trash & Recycle Center (fees may apply).
9. Frozen food boxes and the containers inside are trash – these materials are simply not recyclable.
10. Rinse it! Be respectful of the folks who handle the material.

Communication skills ATLs

Writing guidelines

- Use clear main headings to tell the reader what the instructions are about.
- Number the stages or points to help organize the steps in a set of instructions.
- Use sub-headings to break down and organize the guidelines according to different features or subcategories.
- Break down instructions into small steps so each section is easy to follow with enough detail to help the reader.
- Highlight any materials needed using bullet points.
- Add useful diagrams, illustrations or photographs to help the reader to understand your advice.

Exam tip

At standard level you should write between 250 and 400 words.

At higher level you should write between 450 and 600 words.

Analyzing a set of guidelines

What do you notice about these guidelines?

A. What do you notice about the language used to address the audience?

Comment on:

- the complexity of the sentences used
- the level of formality
- the vocabulary used.

B. Comment on the organization of the text.

- Identify the main topics.
- Identify how the subtopics are organized.

Writing activity: Guidelines

Here are two opportunities to practice writing guidelines.

Plan, draft, revise and redraft one of these stimuli.

1. A recent report stated, "Litter is one of the first signs of social decay. If we don't care about litter on our street, in our parks or on our high streets, we are unlikely to care about other environmental issues that negatively impact on our lives, our communities and society".

   You and your friends are very concerned about the amount of litter in your local community. Write a set of guidelines for residents pointing out the effects of litter on different aspects of life: health, local community, tourism or the local economy. Write a set of guidelines suggesting ways of reducing, or even eliminating, litter in your area.

2. Working in groups or pairs, plan, draft and present a set of guidelines on one or more of the following topics:

   - Top 10 sustainability tips for schools
   - Top 10 energy conservation tips for schools
   - Setting up or improving a school's recycling programme
   - Going green – how to make our homes more eco-friendly
   - Talking the talk – guidelines for a greener lifestyle
   - Guidelines for organizing an environmental awareness event
   - Dealing with e-waste

Brainstorming

Follow the steps below.

1. Reflect on everything you have learned in this section. Choose your focal point and your point of view. What information do you want to emphasize?

2. Generate ideas to be used in your text. Research additional material to support your opinion.

3. What else do you need to think about? Language and register? Audience? Context and text type?
4. Sort your ideas into a logical order. Choose examples to support your ideas.

Planning

You might want to use a chart like the one below to help you plan your set of guidelines. Think about what measures you will take to make sure your set of guidelines is well written and effective.

Make sure to use all the conventions and formatting associated with a set of guidelines.

Consider the context in which you are writing. What is the publication? Who is the audience? What level of formality will you use to address your audience?

Planning your guidelines	
The language used	
• Types of sentence used	
• The level of formality	
The organization of the text	
• Identify the main topic.	
• List the elements or subtopics.	
• How will you organize subtopics?	

Write a draft of the body of your interview. Write an eye-catching title.

Re-read the completed draft of your guidelines and revise where necessary.

Self-assessment skills ATLs

Remember your written work will be assessed against three criteria:

- Criterion A: language
- Criterion B: message
- Criterion C: conceptual understanding

(including audience, context and purpose).

How well do you understand these criteria?

Make sure you have a copy of the relevant assessment criteria for either SL or HL writing (Paper 1).

Assess your writing against these criteria. In this way you can see what you have achieved and what you need to do next to move to the next band of achievement

For example, you score a "6" in criterion B: message. Examine the criterion and ask yourself, "What must I do to reach band 7/8?" .

Conclusion to research question A

What are today's biggest environmental challenges to the world?

1. Now that you have completed this section what are your thoughts and reactions to the question above?
2. What justifications would you give for your answers?
3. What more would you need to know before you can come to a definitive conclusion about the statement?

A TOK Moment TOK

How do we know what is "good" and what is "bad"?

If there are so many geographical varieties and variations of English, how do we know what is "good" and what is "bad" English?

Which ways of knowing can you use in order to decide what is "good" and "bad" language?

Would you use the same ways of knowing to decide what is "good" and what is "bad" behavior?

Listening comprehension

Click the icon to practice the listening section of Paper 2. After you have listened to an audio track you will complete an accompanying activity. In this exercise, you will read a 'letter to the editor'. There are six gaps which you must fill with words or phrases from the text. Do not write a word or phrase that is not in the audio recording even if it makes sense.

Conceptual understanding: Variation

Read this article in class. What seems to be the message of the text? Do you agree with the writer's point of view?

What is "good English" and what is "bad English"?

When we think about the countries and the places around the world where English is used. It is not surprising that there are so many varieties of English.

Throughout the English-speaking world there are enough differences between different versions of the English language that someone may not always understand exactly what someone from the other country is saying. What are these differences?

Pronunciation differences

The different varieties of English sound different. For example, when you compare Australian, British, Indian, Caribbean and American English there are major pronunciation differences in the vowel sounds.

Differences in spelling and vocabulary

Not only do the types of English sound different, but there are also varieties of spelling, especially between American and British English. In some ways, the spelling reflects the difference in pronunciation. For instance, Americans use the world "airplane". In Great Britain, the word is "aeroplane", pronounced with an audible "o" sound. In American English, verbs pronounced "-ize" will always be written with an "-ize". However, in UK English, they typically end in "-ise" – realize and organize versus realise and organise.

Differences in vocabulary

Each English-speaking country has its own local vocabulary. For instance, Australia has several terms that are not used elsewhere in the English-speaking world, such as "evo" (evening) and "arvo" (afternoon). Also, Australians use some phrases that are combinations of British and American terms, such as "rubbish truck." Rubbish is commonly used in the UK, and truck is commonly used in the US.

Grammar distinctions

In the UK, it is perfectly acceptable to use a collective noun as a plural word ("Liverpool are winning"), whereas in the US collective nouns are almost always singular ("the army is coming").

Section B: Urban and rural environments

Research question B:

What are the causes and solutions to global poverty?

1. What are your first thoughts and reactions to the question above?
2. What justifications would you give for your answers?
3. What more would you need to know before you can come to a definitive conclusion about the question?

Before you listen

The poster below sets out the United Nations Millennium Development Goals for 2015. Imagine that a charitable foundation is offering to donate $5,000,000 to an organization in order to support one of these Millennium Development Goals. In small groups decide how you would spend the money in your own community. Decide what your priorities would be and then make a decision you can all agree on.

Listening comprehension

In Conversation: Professor Ruby Hassan talks to Margaret Carrol about the evolution of the United Nations Millennium Development Goals

Listen to this extract from a radio programme and answer the questions that follow.

Choose the correct answer from A, B, C or D.

1. The UN Millennium Goals were designed to help the world's

   A. children
   B. poorest
   C. illiterate
   D. hungry

2. The UN Millennium Goals have helped reduce poverty by:

   A. a quarter
   B. a third
   C. a fifth
   D. a half.

3. The radio broadcast focuses on the reasons for the _________ of the UN Millennium Goals.

   A. failure
   B. popularity
   C. success
   D. breakdown

4. Prof. Hassan explained that the new Millennium Goals were easy to:

   A. put into practice
   B. finance
   C. adapt to each country
   D. read and understand.

5. Identify the four true sentences below.

   A. The Millennium Goals helped to concentrate the actions of governments and donors.
   B. Governments started to develop programs with different aims and different goals.
   C. Not all countries have eliminated poverty to the same degree.
   D. The Millennium Goals have helped to protect many children.
   E. From a practical point of view the Millennium Goals have been very motivational.
   F. The reduction in poverty is mainly a result of the Millennium Goals.
   G. Donors could measure their success against a clear target for each goal.
   H. The policies have helped to reduce the number of people needing treatment for AIDS/HIV,

Answer the following questions.

6. Why is Prof. Hassan so excited by the improvements in living standards for the Earth's population in the ten years up to 2015?
7. What is different about the Development Goals for 2030?
8. What will the next segment of the show discuss?

Which words go in the gaps? Read the summary of the text then choose the words from the recording and write them in the spaces below.

In this broadcast the ____(9) ____ of '*In conversation*' discussed the UN Millennium Goals with Professor Ruby Hassan. The purpose of the goals was to bring about a reduction in global ____(10) ____ . It has been argued that the adoption of the goals was a ____(11) ____ for the subsequent improvements. Professor Hassan said that the goals set in 2000 were ____(12) ____. By contrast the list of goals drawn up in 2005 were easy to ____(13) ____ . Because of this, governments and donors ____(14) ____ money and resources where they could be used most effectively.

HL extension

HL

Imagine that you are a listener to this radio broadcast. After the show you decide to write a letter to the editor in which you express your concerns about Professor Hassan's statements about the UN Development Goals for 2030. Using information from the recording, explain why you think the Millennium Goals have been so successful and offer an alternative set of Development Goals to be adopted by the UN. Write between 100 and 150 words.

Exam tips

Practicing listening

Always follow the examiner's instructions carefully.

Focus precisely on what you are asked to do to complete the types of questions.

The most likely question types are:

- true/false
- multiple choice
- gap-filling
- matching
- short answer questions.

Listen for the specific information you want.

Listen and make notes at the same time.

If you do not know the answer to a question, attempt it but do not waste time; move quickly onto the next one.

Do not panic if you think the topic is too difficult or the speaker is talking too fast; relax and tune in.

Attempt all questions; there are no penalties for incorrect answers.

Always check your answers.

Oral activity: Discussion

Causes of poverty: some facts

- Almost half the world — over 3 billion people — lives on less than $2.50 a day.
- Nearly a billion people entered the 21st century unable to read a book or sign their names.
- 1 billion children live in poverty (1 in 2 children in the world).
- 640 million children live without adequate shelter.
- 400 million have no access to safe water.
- 270 million have no access to health services.
- 10.6 million died in 2003 before they reached the age of 5 (or roughly 29,000 children per day).
- Less than 1% of what the world spent every year on weapons was needed to put every child into school by the year 2000 and yet it didn't happen.
- The GDP (Gross Domestic Product) of the 41 Heavily Indebted Poor Countries (567 million people) is less than the wealth of the world's 7 richest people combined.

Source: http://www.globalissues.org/issue/2/causes-of-poverty

Research skills ATLs

In order to find out more about the topic, practice your **Information literacy skills**.

- Find, interpret and judge information .
- Collect, record and verify data.
- Access information to be informed and inform others.
- Make connections between various sources of information.
- Create new information.
- Present information in a variety of formats and platforms.

Brainstorming

Here are a series of questions concerning global poverty. Discuss some or all of them and come to an agreed conclusion about each one.

You may choose to answer the questions in any order.

- Are the world's poor solely responsible for their situation?
- Is poverty influenced by multinational corporations and international institutions?
- Are the governments of poor nations and their people often powerless in the face of such enormous external influence?
- Do the governments of poor countries have policies that actually harm successful development?
- In the global context, we are relatively wealthy while the majority struggle. So are we, as individuals, to blame?

Peer assessment

Although group presentations are not assessed at SL or HL, you can evaluate the presentations given by your classmates using the rubrics on page 183.

Presenting

Each group presents its conclusions and justifications.

Internal assessment (SL)

Take a look at the visual stimuli below. The images relate to the theme: "Sharing the planet".

Brainstorming

In pairs, choose one of the photographs, then discuss the following questions.

- What is the main idea in the photograph? How does it relate to the title of the section, "Urban and rural environments" and an English-speaking community?
- What do you see in the background of the photograph? What does the background tell you about the location and context of the photograph?
- Look at the foreground of the photograph. Describe the person or people you can see.
- What is happening in the picture? How does the action relate to the title of the chapter, "Protecting the planet"?
- If you were in a position of power, what policies would you pursue to improve the lives of the children in the picture?

Presenting

Based on your answers to the questions above, prepare a four-minute presentation on the photograph.

Remember that the presentation should not only include a description of the photograph, but should also connect it to the topic of protecting the planet in an Anglophone culture. Present your photograph and topic to your classmates.

Internal assessment (HL)

To Kill a Mockingbird

To Kill a Mockingbird is a both a coming-of-age story and an anti-racist novel. It is is set during three years (1933–35) of the Great Depression in the fictional "tired old town" of Maycomb, Alabama. All the townsfolk were suffering from the harsh economic conditions and the lack of local employment opportunities. This passage describes the home of the Ewell family – one of the poorest families in town.

Every town the size of Maycomb had families like the Ewells. No economic fluctuations changed their status—people like the Ewells lived as guests of the county in prosperity as well as in the depths of a depression. No truant officers could keep their numerous offspring in school; no public health officer could free them from congenital defects, various worms, and the diseases indigenous to filthy surroundings.

Maycomb's Ewells lived behind the town garbage dump in what was once a Negro cabin. The cabin's plank walls were supplemented with sheets of corrugated iron, its roof shingled with tin cans hammered flat, so only its general shape suggested its original design: square, with four tiny rooms opening onto a shotgun hall, the cabin rested uneasily upon four irregular lumps of limestone. Its windows were merely open spaces in the walls, which in the summertime were covered with greasy strips of cheesecloth to keep out the varmints that feasted on Maycomb's refuse.

The varmints[1] had a lean time of it, for the Ewells gave the dump a thorough gleaning every day, and the fruits of their industry (those that were not eaten) made the plot of ground around the cabin look like the playhouse of an insane child: what passed for a fence was bits of tree-limbs, broomsticks and tool shafts, all tipped with rusty hammer-heads, snaggle-toothed rake heads, shovels, axes and grubbing hoes, held on with pieces of barbed wire. Enclosed by this barricade was a dirty yard containing the remains of a Model-T Ford (on blocks), a discarded dentist's chair, an ancient icebox, plus lesser items: old shoes, worn-out table radios, picture frames, and fruit jars, under which scrawny orange chickens pecked hopefully.

One corner of the yard, though, bewildered Maycomb. Against the fence, in a line, were six chipped enamel slop jars holding brilliant red geraniums, cared for as tenderly as if they belonged to Miss Maudie Atkinson[2], had Miss Maudie deigned to permit a geranium on her premises. People said they were Mayella Ewell's.

Nobody was quite sure how many children were on the place. Some people said six, others said nine; there were always several dirty-faced ones at the windows when anyone passed by. Nobody had occasion to pass by except at Christmas, when the churches delivered baskets, and when the mayor of Maycomb asked us to please help the garbage collector by dumping our own trees and trash.

To Kill A Mockingbird, Harper Lee

[1] troublesome wild animals, pests

[2] An old and respectable resident of Maycomb

Brainstorming

In small groups, discuss the following questions then summarize your discussion in point form.

- What do we learn about the Ewell's lifestyle from the passage?
- Use the detail in the passage to describe the Ewells's home.
- What do the geraniums tell us about Mayella Ewell?
- What do we learn about the Ewell children from the passage?
- In your opinion what could be done to help the Ewell children escape from poverty?

Presenting

Based on your answers to the questions above, prepare a four-minute presentation on the text.

Make your presentation to your classmates. Students listening to the presentation should prepare individual questions about the text which they can ask you at the end of your presentation.

Peer assessment

Assess the presentations given by your classmates. Use the HL IA criteria to guide your assessment.

	Internal assessment (SL and HL)
Criterion A	Language
Criterion B	1. Message: literary extract 2. Message: conversation
Criterion C	Interactive skills: communication

Suggest ways in which your classmates can improve their presentation techniques.

Exam tip: Internal assessment (HL)

The individual oral (HL) assesses the degree to which you are able to:

- communicate clearly and effectively in a range of contexts and for a variety of purposes
- understand and use language appropriate to a range of interpersonal and inter-cultural contexts
- understand and use language to express and respond to a range of ideas with fluency and accuracy
- identify, organize and present ideas on a range of topics
- understand, analyze and reflect within the context of presentation and conversation.

Your oral will have three parts.

Part 1: Presentation

You will present your extract.
You should put the extract into context, but spend most of the time presenting the events, ideas and messages in the passage.
(3–4 minutes)

Part 2: Follow-up questions

Your teacher will ask questions about the content of the extract and ask you to explain in greater detail the ideas which you presented in part 1.
(4–5 minutes)

Part 3: General discussion

You continue to a general discussion using one or more of the five themes of the syllabus as a starting point.
(5–6 minutes)

Paper 1: Reports

A report is written in order to present facts or findings often as a basis for further action. Here are two types of report:

- an evaluative report
- a leading report.

Writing for a specific audience: tone and style

Reports are written for a specific professional purpose and for a specific audience. They use formal English; however, the language must be straightforward so that the reader can understand the ideas contained in the report and act on them, as required.

To be completely successful a report must ensure that the intended audience:

- understands everything without difficulty
- accepts the facts, findings, conclusions and recommendations
- decides to take the recommended course of action.

Write an evaluative report

As part of its CAS programme, your school is supporting a school for a group of 10 refugee children. Your English class has raised the equivalent of $1000. You can spend the money either on clothes or on English Lessons. Write an evaluative report explaining how the money should be spent.

Evaluative reports

Evaluative reports can be written about present issues and future solutions. They can set out an existing problem, discuss different solutions and leave the readers to come to their own conclusions. Evaluative reports include consumer reports which analyse a variety of similar goods and services so that the buyer can make the best decision.

For this kind of comparative task, put the two items side by side and find characteristics that can be compared. These characteristics can be similarities or differences, or both. Conclude by stating your choice and justifying it on the basis of the relative strength of the two options.

You could use a table like the one below to plan this type of report.

Topic	Evaluative report	
	Item A	Item B
Characteristic 1		
Characteristic 2		
Characteristic 3		
Conclusions	Strengths of each suggestion Weaknesses of each suggestion	

Leading reports

A leading report examines a problem or explains a situation and leads the readers to a specific conclusion. It is used for making plans and solving problems. Usually an organization commissions someone to research and write a report. As a result of the report, the readers will decide whether to accept the recommendations.

Such a problem-driven report sets out to resolve an issue or present a point of view, which is stated at the beginning of the text. The leading report should start with the statement of the issue, explore the benefits and end with a conclusion about what action you would like the reader to take. Here is a possible structure:

- Define the issue.
- Present a series of factors or benefits.
- State a conclusion.

You could use a table like the one below to plan this type of report.

Write a leading report

On a recent holiday abroad you visited a sustainable environmental project and were very impressed by the work of the NGO. Now that you are back at school, you would would like your school to support the organization. Write a leading report. Explain clearly how your school's support will directly benefit the organization and the community it supports. Remember your leading report should: present the NGO and its work, present a series of reasons for supporting the NGO, state benefits for your school, state a conclusion.

	Your ideas	Evidence, examples or explanations
Introduction: Topic and issue		
Argument 1		
Argument 2		
Argument 3		
Conclusions Solutions, recommendations, actions to be taken		

Writing activity: reports

Here are two opportunities to practice writing different kinds of reports.

Plan, draft, revise and redraft one of these stimuli.

1. Your English teacher has asked you to recommend two books that highlight some aspect of children in need for younger students. The books should highlight social or environmental issues. Write an evaluative report comparing the two books.
2. In your school, DP students participate in a variety of community services for CAS, and may support a variety of overseas development projects as well. You have been asked to write an annual leading report for one of the organizations that you support. Your report should include the core aims of the organization, your school's achievements this year in partnership with them, and your aims concerning any future involvement.

Exam tip

At standard level you should write between 250 and 400 words.

At higher level you should write between 450 and 600 words.

Self-management skills ATLs

In each chapter of this book you have written tasks to complete. Are you making progress? Is your written English improving? Make sure that you are learning effectively and efficiently. Study this list of self-management tips. Decide which points are most helpful and utilize them!

- Consider personal learning strategies. What can you do to become a more efficient and effective learner?
- Identify weaknesses of personal learning strategies.
- Identify and develop new skills, techniques and strategies for effective learning.
- Be more flexible in your choice of learning strategies.
- Find good models of working to imitate.
- Keep a journal to record reflections.

Brainstorming

Follow the steps below.

1. Reflect on everything you have learned in this section. Choose your focal point and your point of view. What information do you want to emphasize?
2. Generate ideas to be used in your text. Research additional material to support your opinion.
3. What else do you need to think about? Language and register? Audience? Context and text type?
4. Sort your ideas into a logical order. Choose examples to support your ideas.

Planning

What kind of report are you writing? You could use one of the tables on pages 198 and 199 to help you plan your report. Remember your report should be written using formal language appropriate to the context, purpose and audience for the report.

Write a draft of the body of your report. Write an eye-catching title.

Make sure to use all the conventions and formatting associated with a report.

Consider the context in which you are writing. What is the publication? Who is the audience? What level of formality will you use to address your audience?

Drafting

Re-read the completed draft of your written interview and revise as necessary.

Remember you will be assessed against three criteria: criterion A, language; criterion B, message; criterion C, conceptual understanding (including audience, context and purpose).

Conclusion to research question B

What are the causes and solutions to global poverty?

1. Now that you have completed this section what are your thoughts and reactions to the question above?
2. What justifications would you give for your answers?
3. What more would you need to know before you can come to a definitive conclusion about the question?

A TOK moment

TOK

How do we know what kind of English to use when speaking to others?

We all use language in different ways depending on the speaker, the context and the audience.

Ourselves as speakers

We have seen that there are clear geographical and social variations in English. We observe wide differences in dialect and accent depending on the country and region in which it is spoken. By the same token, the social, educational and economic position that a person grows up in affects their choice of language. The way we speak English also depends on whether we use it as a first or as an additional language.

Age also affects a person's language. Older people also often use words and phrases commonly used when they were young. The young often invent their own words and phrases. For example, popular media and music can be a source of new words and phrases for younger people.

It has also been noted that males and females also use language in slightly different ways. This may be due to the different roles that each has in society. Moreover, no two people can ever have exactly the same way of using a language. Each person has particular words and phrases, or ways of saying them. This individual use of language is called an idiolect.

Speaking in context

Some work-related language is technical, and this is called jargon. A person's job or profession affects the jargon they use at work. For example, a university professor of languages will use jargon that a flower-seller would not, and vice versa. Interestingly, men and women from the same professions do not show much variation in their language when talking about technical matters.

Speaking to an audience

Who we are speaking to is also likely to affect the language we use. We speak less formally to our friends than to our doctor, or someone of importance less familiar to us. A sociolect is a language variety that occurs as a result of belonging to a particular kind of social group. For instance in places like schools, groups of friends often share special words and phrases.

It is surprising that given all this information we are still capable of making instantaneous decisions about deciding how to use a language when speaking to a specific person in a specific context and for a specific purpose. Look at these ways of knowing.

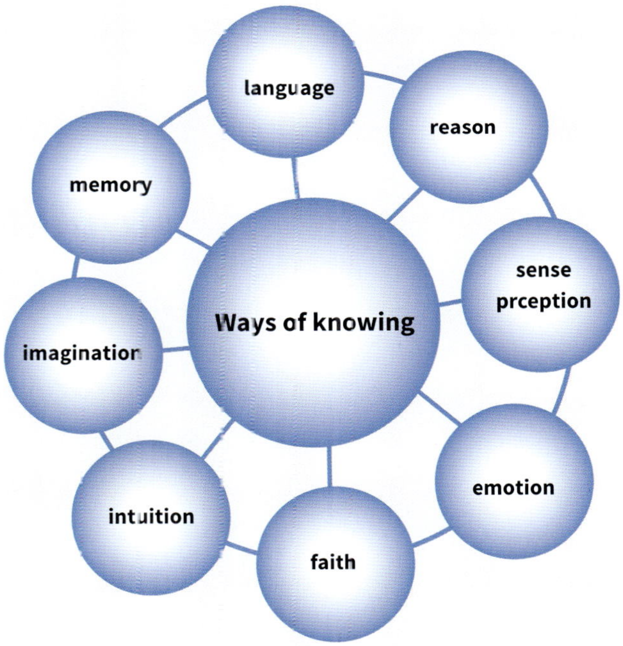

Which are the most important when deciding what variety of English to use?

Section C: Meeting the challenge

Research question C:

How can young people tackle environmental and social challenges?

1. What are your first thoughts and reactions to the question above?
2. What justifications would you give for your answers?
3. What more would you need to know before you can come to a definitive conclusion about the statement?

Thinking skills ATLs

During this activity you will have the opportunity to analyze and evaluate issues and ideas.

- Practice careful observation in order to recognize problems.
- Gather and organize relevant information to formulate an argument.
- Interpret data.
- Evaluate evidence and arguments.
- Recognize and evaluate propositions.
- Draw reasonable conclusions and generalizations.

Before you read

Examine the poster below.

The idea behind the workshop to improve participants' leadership skills is excellent. But, realistically, is there enough time to achieve real results? Imagine you are going to organize a similar workshop at your own school. In a group, discuss at least five improvements you could make to the original workshop programme. At the end of your discussion present the ideas you have agreed on. Be prepared to justify and explain your choices to the class.

What do you think about the aims of the workshop? Do you think the organizers have allowed enough time to cover all the topics and teach all the skills advertised?

Justify your answers.

Current Issues and Youth Activism

"GIV gave me the hope and optimism that I needed to try and work on issues that I thought could not be fixed. Thank you for making me feel that I can make a difference in our state, country, and world."

-A 2015 CIYA graduate

Want to change the world? This Institute is for you! You'll be empowered and inspired in this ten-day program focused on the big issues affecting people in Vermont and around the world in 2016. From critical issues impacting Vermont towns, to pressing U.S. social issues, to exciting and complex global issues, we'll cover it all.

We'll also give you the leadership, activism, communication and organizing skills to get involved and create real change on any issue! You'll join young people from other countries to explore the problems and daily challenges impacting young people everywhere, and learn how to turn your ideas into action.

Every Governor's Institute is as unique and special as the students who attend. But they all share some common attributes. They all focus on YOU, the student, and the topics you love. They're all very concentrated, blasts of learning, discovery and thought, all rolled up into more fun than you think could even be possible. All will introduce you to inspiring mentors and Vermonters your age who you'll probably stay in touch with for years to come. Every Institute is held on a college campus in Vermont and gives you the chance to try out living in a college setting and try on potential careers and futures in the areas that interest you.

A typical day includes:

- Intensive Issue Groups on Politics, Access to Justice, Global Issues, Leadership & Climate Change
- Honest, Direct Discussions with Politicians, Activists, Issue Experts & Today's Change-Makers
- Mock Congress, Model United Nations and Local Democracy Simulations and Role Plays
- Teambuilding Challenges, Leadership & Activism Skills Workshops, and Arts Activities
- Fun Evening Activities: Drumming, a Barn Dance, Campfires, Sports, Open Mic Night & Banquet

Participants will also swim in the nearby rivers and lake, build & paddle rafts, march in the July 4th town parade, attend a celebration BBQ, hike, visit local community organizations & have a Farmer's Market lunch!

For more information visit www.giv.org

Reading comprehension

1. Find a word between lines 1 and 5 which is similar in meaning to "motivated".
2. What local matters will be addressed at the conference?
3. What national issues will be assessed?
4. Which set of skills will not be directly taught at the conference?
   a. Communication skills
   b. Internationalism
   c. Leadership skills
   d. Activism

Find the word or phrase between lines 8 and 17 that could meaningfully replace the words below.

5. affecting
6. characteristics
7. concentrate
8. Find a phrase which suggests that the skills acquisition process will be very intensive.
9. Find a phrase in the text between lines 11 and 17 which explains why the programme is so motivating to its target audience.
10. Which practical knowledge and life skills does the course offer in addition to those related to youth activism?

HL extension HL

If this programme were available at a college near your home, would you be interested in applying? Write a response using any appropriate text type. Justify your answer by giving at least five reasons and justifications. Write a final thought or conclusion. Write between 250 and 450 words.

Thinking skills ATLs

The programme also lists a variety of activities to increase participants' knowledge, skills and personal development. Work in pairs and from the lists on lines 18 to 27 in the text find at least one activity which will develop each of the elements of learning listed below.

Knowledge	
• Political issues • Environmental issues • Social issues • International issues • Human rights issues	
Learning skills	
• Thinking skills • Communication skills • Self-management skills • Research skills • Social skills	

Oral activity: planning your own youth activist programme!

Imagine your school or community group has the opportunity to develop a two-day residential workshop for DP students to develop skills to make a lasting impact in their community. You have been asked to help develop the programme.

Brainstorming

In groups, decide which ideas and topics you would like to discuss.

- What are the essential social and environmental issues you would like to discuss?
- What skills would you like to develop?
- What fun activities would you include for team and relationship building?

Imagine you can use your school facilities for a whole weekend. Decide what additional facilities and resources you will need to make your ideas work.

What teaching and learning methods would you suggest to interest and motivate participants?

Use the four headings below to organize your ideas.

Issues to examine	Skills to develop	Fun activities	Teaching and learning methods

Planning and drafting

Draw up a complete timetable of events. Then draw up a two-day agenda for your workshop with a clear opening, a varied set of interactive learning experiences and a closing event.

Presenting

Present your ideas and your agenda to the rest of the class. You can use visuals to make the presentation interesting and persuasive.

Record your presentation in whatever format you wish so you can use it in the writing component of this section.

Thinking skills ATLs

When planning your workshop you will need to employ critical thinking skills. You need to:

- analyze complex ideas by dividing them into their constituent parts
- consider ideas from multiple perspectives
- propose and evaluate a variety of solutions
- come to mutually agreed solutions.

You will also need to generate new ideas.

To create something original:

- use brainstorming and visual diagrams to generate new ideas and inquiries
- create novel solutions to authentic problems
- make guesses, ask "what if" questions and generate testable hypotheses.

Internal assessment (SL)

Take a look at the visual stimulus below. The image relates to the theme of the chapter: "Sharing the planet".

Brainstorming

In pairs, discuss and answer the following questions.

- What is the main idea in the image? How does it relate to the topic of this section of this chapter, "tackling social and environmental issues" in an Anglophone community?
- What do you see in background of the image? What does the background tell you about the location and context of the image?
- Look at the foreground of the image. Describe the people you can see.
- What is happening in the image? How does the action relate to the theme of this chapter, "sharing the planet"?

Presenting

Based on your answers to the questions above, prepare a four-minute presentation on the photograph.

Remember that the presentation should not only include a description of the image, but should also connect it to the topic of tackling social and environmental issues in an English-speaking community. Present your image and topic to your classmates.

Peer assessment

Assess the presentations given by your classmates. Use the SL IA criteria to guide your assessment.

	Internal assessment (SL)
Criterion A	Language
Criterion B	1. Message: visual stimulus 2. Message: conversation
Criterion C	Interactive skills: communication

Suggest ways in which your classmates can improve their presentation techniques.

Internal assessment (HL)

Lord of the Flies

William Golding

During a war sometime in the future, a transport plane carrying a group of English boys is shot down over the Pacific or Indian Ocean. It crashes in thick jungle on a deserted island. Two of the surviving boys, Ralph and Piggy, discover a large conch shell, which can be used as a kind of trumpet. Ralph blows the conch and boys between the ages of 6 and 12 come out of the jungle onto the beach, including a group of choirboys led by Jack. The boys meet and introduce themselves. On the island they face a huge number of social issues, as they have almost no tools or technological resources. In order to organize themselves they decide to have a democratic vote to appoint a leader.

Jack spoke.

"We've got to decide about being rescued."

There was a buzz. One of the small boys, Henry, said that he wanted to go home.

"Shut up," said Ralph absently. He lifted the conch. "Seems to me we ought to have a chief to decide things."

"A chief! A chief!"

"I ought to be chief," said Jack with simple arrogance, "because I'm chapter chorister and head boy. I can sing C sharp."

Another buzz.

"Well then," said Jack, "I--"

He hesitated. The dark boy, Roger, stirred at last and spoke up.

"Let's have a vote."

"Yes!"

"Vote for chief!"

"Let's vote--"

This toy of voting was almost as pleasing as the conch. Jack started to protest but the clamor changed from the general wish for a chief to an election by acclaim of Ralph himself. None of the boys could have found good reason for this; what intelligence had been shown was traceable to Piggy while the most obvious leader was Jack. But there was a stillness about Ralph as he sat that marked him out: there was his size, and attractive appearance; and most obscurely, yet most powerfully, there was the conch. The being that had blown that, had sat waiting for them on the platform with the delicate thing balanced on his knees, was set apart.

"Him with the shell."
"Ralph! Ralph!"
"Let him be chief with the trumpet-thing."
Ralph raised a hand for silence.
"All right. Who wants Jack for chief?"
With dreary obedience the choir raised their hands.
"Who wants me?"
Every hand outside the choir except Piggy's was raised immediately. Then Piggy, too, raised his hand grudgingly into the air.
Ralph counted.
"I'm chief then."
The circle of boys broke into applause. Even the choir applauded; and the freckles on Jack's face disappeared under a blush of mortification. He started up, then changed his mind and sat down again while the air rang. Ralph looked at him, eager to offer something.
"The choir belongs to you, of course."
"They could be the army--"
"Or hunters--"
"They could be--"
The suffusion drained away from Jack's face. Ralph waved again for silence.
"Jack's in charge of the choir. They can be--what do you want them to be?"
"Hunters."
Jack and Ralph smiled at each other with shy liking. The rest began to talk eagerly.

Note

In your internal assessment, the literary extract will not exceed 300 words. You will be shown two, one from each of the works of literature studied in class.

Brainstorming

In small groups, discuss the following questions then summarize your discussion in point form.

- Explain the process by which the boys elect their leader. Illustrate the steps with quotations from the text.
- What social, thinking and communication skills do the boys demonstrate in the discussions before the election?
- What social problems will the new leader have to solve?
- What possible problems might occur between Ralph and Jack as a result of the election?
- How do you think you would react if you found yourself in a similar situation?

Presenting

Based on your answers to the questions above, prepare a four-minute presentation on the text.

Make your presentation to your classmates.

Students listening to the presentation should prepare individual questions about the text which they can ask you at the end of your presentation.

Peer assessment

Assess the presentations given by your classmates. Use the HL IA assessment criteria in the Language B guide to guide your assessment. Suggest ways in which your classmates can improve their presentation techniques.

Paper 1 practice

Here are three opportunities to practice writing for Paper 1.

Plan, draft, revise and redraft one of these stimuli.

Exam tip

At standard level you should write between 250 and 400 words.

At higher level you should write between 450 and 600 words.

1 You recently attended an international youth conference. Read the statement made by one of the participants.

> "From this conference we learned that saving our planet and lifting people out of poverty are part of the same issue. I feel full of energy having met with international students, who are from many different parts of the world and yet have very similar ideas."

Write an appropriate text outlining the main events of the conference and your evaluation of it. Choose one of these three text types to complete the task.

a) A report | b) A set of guidelines | c) A magazine article

2 The local council has announced plans to fell a line of 100-year-old trees in order to improve traffic flow immediately outside your school. You and a group of friends organized a meeting to oppose the council's plans. You have now drawn up a plan of action which you wish to submit to your school management. Choose one of these three text types to put forward your plan.

a) A set of guidelines | b) A formal letter | c) A report

Exam tip: Paper 1

The aim of paper 1 is to assess how well you can communicate in writing.

You will need to show that you can choose the correct text type, register and style for the task.

You also need to show that you understand the concepts of audience, context, and purpose and how they inform the choice of text type.

3 You are becoming increasingly concerned about the low levels of recycling and increases in litter at school. You wish to encourage younger students to do more to participate in existing recycling programmes and to take more initiatives for themselves. Write a suitable text which would persuade your target audience to take greater responsibility for their environment. Choose one of these three text types to express your ideas.

a) A report | b) A leaflet | c) A set of guidelines

Brainstorming

Follow the steps below.

1. Reflect on everything you have learned in this section. Choose your focal point and your point of view. What information do you want to emphasize?
2. Generate ideas to be used in your text. Research additional material to support your opinion.
3. What else do you need to think about? Language and register? Audience? Context and text type?
4. Sort your ideas into a logical order. Choose examples to support your ideas.

Remember to include any special features of the text type, such as headlines, by-lines or layout.

Drafting

Re-read the completed draft of your text.

Remember you will be assessed against three criteria: criterion A, language; criterion B, message; criterion C, conceptual understanding (including audience, context and purpose). Make any necessary changes.

Listening comprehension

Click the icon to practice the listening section of Paper 2. After you have listened to an audio track you will complete an accompanying activity. In this matching exercise, you will put twelve statements into different categories.

Conclusion to research question C

How can young people tackle environmental and social challenges?

1. Now that you have completed this section what are your thoughts and reactions to the question above?
2. What justifications would you give for your answers?
3. What more would you need to know before you can come to a definitive conclusion about the statement?

Research and self-management skills ATLs

Combatting environmental issues

In groups, re-examine the various methods suggested in this section to combat environmental issues.

To what extent have you encountered these issues and challenges in your own life and in your community?

Decide what governments can do to solve these problems.

Decide what we can do as individuals to solve these problems.

Conclusion to the chapter

Having completed the chapter, reflect on its key research question:

What environmental and social issues present challenges to the world and how can these challenges be overcome?

When we began the chapter, you debated this research question. Now that you have completed the chapter, answer the following questions.

- In this chapter what have you learned about today's environmental and social challenges and the methods of overcoming them?
- What don't you still understand about the topic?
- What questions do you have?
- What more would you like to know about the subject?
- What could you do to find answers to these questions?

Beyond the classroom

You can use the information you have learned and the communication skills you have developed in this chapter for practical purposes beyond the classroom.

CAS

Service learning

Ideas for service learning related to this chapter include ways to create awareness of a global issue

Topics could include: Poverty, Child Labour, Terrorism, Youth Movements, HIV/AIDS, International Conflict, Immigration, Human Trafficking, Climate Change, Food Security, School Quality, Landmines, Religion, Democracy, Bullying, Energy, Refugees, & the Environment.

Some skills you may use while creating awareness include:

- undertaking new challenges
- planning and initiating activities
- working collaboratively with others
- showing perseverance and commitment
- engaging with issues of global importance
- considering ethical implications

Speak to your service coordinator to find out how such a project could meet your school's expectations for CAS.

Creativity: Using text types

In this chapter you have learned how to write guidelines and reports. Now use these skills to write articles for your school magazine or another outlet.

Practice by writing a set of guidelines for younger students advising them how to best make use of your school's recycling programme.

Alternatively write guidelines for younger students to help them in their school life. The guidelines could be humorous in tone and intent giving your audience an alternative view of school life

Alternatively, if you want to change some aspect of your school, try your hand at report writing. It is one way of persuading people of your point of view and an important tool in real life.

Suggested reading

Lord of the Flies by William Golding

Hoot by Carl Hiaasen

Under the Weather: Stories About Climate Change ed. Tony Bradman

Breathe by Sarah Crossan

Watership Down by Richard Adams

The Word for World is Forest by Ursula Le Guin

Exodus by Julie Bertagna

Cosmic by Frank Cottrell Boyce

The Last Wild Trilogy by Piers Torday

6 IDENTITIES: WHO WE ARE!

Chapter summary

Theme
Identities

Conceptual understanding
- Context

Topics
- Beliefs and values
- Language and identity
- Subcultures

Research question for the chapter
How do language and culture contribute to forming our identity?

Additional research questions for each section

A Do different Anglophone cultures share the same values?
B In what ways does language shape our identity?
C In what ways does belonging to a certain subculture define us, if at all?

TOK question
To what extent does the language we use reflect our identity?

Communication skills

Listening skills
- Receptive
- Interactive

Oral and interactive skills
- Receptive: listening to a talk/listening to presentations
- Productive: presenting to classmates, writing a proposal, writing a speech
- Interactive: presentation

Written text type(s)
- Proposal
- Speech

Research question for the chapter:

How do language and culture contribute to forming our identity?

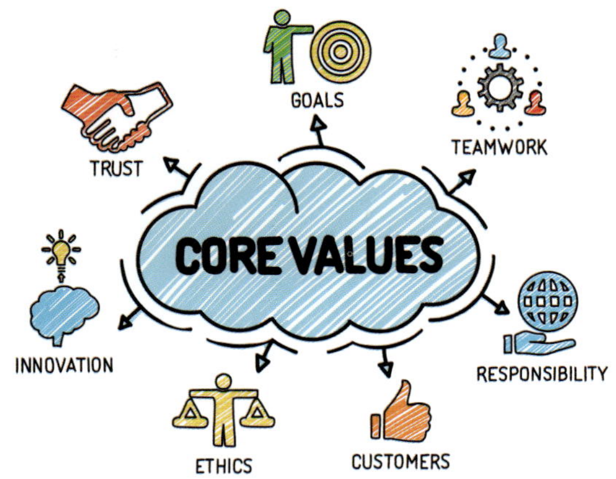

Thinking and communication skills ATLs

This activity involves reflection, higher-order thinking in the form of creation and the ability to express oneself in a coherent and persuasive manner.

What, in your opinion, do these images represent?

- Divide the class into four groups. Each group should choose one of the images above.
- With your group, generate a list of ideas and initial thoughts that came to your mind when you first saw the picture, and write them around your chosen picture.
- Connect your ideas by drawing lines between ideas that have something in common and write a sentence on the line that explains this connection.
- Elaborate on any of the ideas/thoughts you have written so far by adding new ideas that expand, extend, or add to your initial ideas.
- Share your picture and ideas with the other groups.

Section A: Are you living your life in accordance with your values?

Research question A:

Do different Anglophone cultures share the same values?

Before you read

Pick a country other than your own. How are beliefs and values in that country similar to, or different from, your own culture?

In groups of four:

- list three thoughts/ideas that you have about the topic
- pose two questions that you have about the topic
- give one analogy that explains the similarities or the differences between those beliefs and values and your own
- share your thoughts, questions and analogy with the larger group.

Do you think we choose our own values or are they instilled in us? Read the blog entry below to learn more about personal values and how they affect us.

https://www.psychologytoday.com/blog/the-power-prime/201205/personal-growth-your-values-your-life

Your Values, Your Life

Your values form the foundation of your life. They dictate the choices you make and determine the direction that your life takes. Your values will influence decisions related to your relationships, career, and other activities you engage in. Despite this importance, few people choose their values. Instead, they simply adopt the values of their parents and the dominant values of society. In all likelihood, the values that you internalized as a child remain with you through adulthood. Unfortunately, these values may also have created a life that is carrying you down a path that is not the direction you want to go at this point in your life.

What were the values you were raised with? What values are you presently living in accordance with? Are they the same or different? Do your values bring you happiness?

Deconstructing Your Values

To truly understand what values you possess and live by, you must deconstruct them until you are able to clearly see what exactly you value and why you hold those values. Looking openly and honestly at the way you were raised is the first step in identifying the values that you instilled growing up. What did your parents value and what values did they impress upon you—achievement, wealth, education, religion, status, independence, appearance? Think back to your childhood and ask yourself several questions: What values were emphasized in the way your parents lived their lives? What values were stressed in your family? What values were reflected in the way you were rewarded or punished? For example, were you rewarded for being highly ranked in your high school class and for winning in sports, or were you rewarded for giving your best effort and for helping others?

Your next step in the deconstruction process involves looking at your present life and the values your life reflects. In responding to these questions, you should ask yourself what values underlie your answers. What do you do for a living—are you a corporate employee, a business owner, a teacher, salesperson, caterer, or social worker? A common question that people in social gathering ask is, what do you do for a living? For example, though a bit of a generalization, it is probably safe to say that someone who becomes an investment banker has different values than someone who becomes an elementary school teacher. What those underlying values might be may vary, but one might assume that the investment banker values money, while the teacher values education and helping children.

Where do you live—do you live in a high-rise apartment in a city, in the suburbs, or in the country—and what values led you there? What activities do you engage in most—cultural, physical, religious, political, social—and what values are reflected in those activities? What do you talk about mostly—politics, religion, the economy, other people—and what does that tell you about your values?

Finally, perhaps the most telling question reflecting what you value is: What do you spend your money on—a home, cars, travel, clothing, education, art, charity? Because money is a limited resource for most people, they will use their money in ways that they value most. Over and above what people say and other indicators in their life, where they spend their hard-earned money says the most about their values.

You can then ask yourself whether your current values are the same as those you grew up with. Have you gone through a period of examination and reconsideration? Have you consciously chosen to discard some values from your upbringing and adopt new ones?

Now that you have deconstructed your life and have a clear idea of what you value, you can see the values upon which you have created your life. You can see whether those values contribute to your dissatisfaction or bring you happiness. Look at which aspects of your life contribute to your unhappiness—your career, marriage, lifestyle—and ask yourself what values underlie those parts of your life.

Popular Culture and Values

A recurring theme that runs throughout my work is that inadvertently buying into the values that predominate popular culture, for example, winning, status, power, appearance, and conspicuous consumption, is a leading cause of life dissatisfaction. The popular culture in America today—as reflected in our various media—no longer has the time, attention span, or energy to devote to weighty and deep issues such as values. It is much easier to focus on the superficial "things" in our culture. Thus, the pursuit of wealth and material goods has become the dominant "value" in much of our society in the mistaken belief that these values will bring people happiness.

One of the most powerful ways in which this "value" was impressed on you was in how you learned to define success. Popular culture typically defines success as winning, wealth, status, physical appearance, and popularity—the more money and power you have and the more attractive and popular you are, the more successful you would be. Growing up with these definitions, success was largely unattainable for most people. At the same time, our culture made losing even more intolerable to contemplate—being poor, powerless, unattractive, and unpopular is simply unacceptable. With these restrictive definitions, you may have believed, like so many others, that you were caught in the untenable situation of having little opportunity for success and great chance for failure.

Blindly having accepted society's narrow definitions of success and failure takes away your power to decide how you wish to define them. By buying into popular culture's limiting definitions of success and failure rather than choosing definitions based on your own values, you can't become truly successful and happy because you are forced down a path that is, for most people, impossible to attain and that is not truly yours. You may become successful in the eyes of society, but you probably won't feel like a success yourself. And this path certainly won't bring you meaning, happiness, or real success in your life.

I'll explore how to "reconstruct" your values in a future post.

https://www.psychologytoday.com/blog/the-power-prime/201205/personal-growth-your-values-your-life

Reading comprehension

Skim through the text quickly to get a feeling of what it is about.

What is the text's overarching idea?

Lines 1–19

Answer the following questions.

1. How do values affect a human being?
2. Which phrase between lines 1 and 15 shows that people do not usually select their own values?
3. Whose values do people usually take on?
4. How does the author perceive our retaining of childhood values?
5. Which word between lines 1 and 19 is closest in meaning to "now"?

Lines 20–92

Match the first part of the sentence with the appropriate ending on the right.

6. Analyzing our values
7. The values we gained growing up
8. Reward and punishment
9. Our choice of career
10. When we value helping children, we

a. is key to comprehending them.
b. are making assumptions about our values.
c. are probably educators.
d. conceals our values.
e. condone the value of success.
f. often reflect the values our parents held dear.
g. indicates the values we hold dear as adults.
h. should be analyzed first.
i. should be identified and categorized.
j. shows how much we possess them.

Oral activity

Having read the blog entry, and in the same groups of four you formed for the 'Before you read' exercise, reflect on how your understanding of the topic has changed:

- Discuss three new thoughts/ideas that you have gained about the topic.
- Pose two new questions that you think will help improve your understanding of the topic.
- Choose a different analogy that better expresses the similarities and differences in perceiving beliefs and values in an Anglophone culture and your own.
- Share your thoughts, questions and analogy with the larger group.

Communication skills ATLs

Ability to present ideas in a logical, coherent and convincing manner is the aim of this activity. By developing this ability, you will become a better speaker and writer.

Find the words in the text which mean the following:

11. directed
12. participate
13. mirrored
14. scrutiny
15. abandon
16. shaped
17. add
18. motivate

Lines 93–144

Choose the correct phrases from the text to complete the following sentences. Base your answers on the information as it appears in the text.

19. We are often dissatisfied because we opt for ...
20. For us, Americans, discussing important issues is not ...
21. Because American society mistakenly believes superficial things bring people happiness, ...

To whom or to what do the following words refer?

22. this value (line 111)
23. them (line 132)
24. that (line 138)

State whether the following statements are true or false. Justify your answer with a relevant brief quotation from the text.

25. Success is achievable for a good number of people.
26. Anticipating failure is effortless and bearable.
27. The meaning of failure and success in society is broad.

Listening comprehension

Click the icon to practice the listening section of Paper 2. After you have listened to an audio track you will complete an accompanying activity. In this exercise you will practice multiple choice questions. There are always three options. There is one correct answer and two distractors.

Internal assessment (SL)

Take a look at the visual stimulus here. The image relates to the theme of the chapter: "Identities".

1. In pairs, answer the following questions.
   a. What do you see in the visual stimulus?
   b. How does the main theme of the visual stimulus relate to the theme "identities"?
   c. How does the picture relate to the text on values that you read earlier?
   d. How does the picture relate to an Anglophone culture? Think of what you have learned of the values of the American society that you have seen in the text you read earlier. You may also wish to explore how those values are similar to, or different from, values held in your own culture.
2. Based on your answers to the questions above, prepare a four-minute presentation on the visual stimulus. Remember that the presentation should not only include description of the stimulus, but should also connect it to the theme "identities", the topic "beliefs and values" and an English-speaking culture.
3. Present your visual stimulus and topic to your classmates.

Peer assessment

In groups of four, assess the presentations given by your classmates. Use the assessment criteria in the Language B Guide to focus your feedback:

Criterion A: Language

A. Is the vocabulary used appropriately? Is it varied?

B. Are the grammatical structures correct? Are they mainly simple? Are any complex structures used?

C. Is pronunciation clear? What about intonation? Does it help you understand the focus of their presentation?

Criterion B: Message

A. Is the presentation connected to the visual stimulus?

B. Are the ideas relevant to an Anglophone culture?

Criterion C: Interactive skills – communication

A. How well-presented and clear are the ideas?

B. Are the ideas presented in depth?

Suggest ways in which your classmates can improve their presentation techniques.

Note

This is an effective formative assessment tool that will help you to reflect on your classmates' performance in order to help each other improve. The purpose of peer assessment is to help you to reflect on the feedback given from your peers and use it to improve your presentation skills.

Internal assessment (HL)

a. Divide into five groups. Each group is to read only one of the chapters from Mark Twain's *The Five Boons of Life* on pages 222 and 223.

b. In your group, prepare a presentation that focuses on the following:
   1. the characters, events, ideas or themes presented in your chapter
   2. how the chapter may be connected to the previous and/or the following chapters
   3. the message, or moral, of the chapter.

c. Present your chapter to the larger group.

Peer assessment

In groups of four, assess the presentations given by your classmates. Use the assessment criteria in the Language B Guide to focus your feedback:

Criterion A: Language

Is the vocabulary used appropriately? Is it varied?

A. Are the grammatical structures correct? Are they mainly simple? Are any complex structures used?

B. Is pronunciation clear? What about intonation? Does it help you understand the focus of their presentation?

Criterion B: Message

A. Is the presentation connected to the group's chapter?

B. Does the presentation reveal understanding of that chapter?

Criterion C: Interactive skills – communication

A. How well-presented and clear are the ideas?

B. Are the ideas presented in depth?

Suggest ways in which your classmates can improve their presentation techniques.

Note

This type of assessment is directly connected to metacognition as it helps you to reflect on the benchmarks used in the internal assessment, develop your understanding of the assessment criteria, and reflect on your performance and aim to improve it.

Note

In your internal assessment, the literary extract will not exceed 300 words. You will be shown two, one from each of the works of literature studied in class.

Note

Criterion B is divided into the following:

1. Message: visual stimulus (SL) or literary extract (HL)

2. Message: conversation

As the conversation part happens in the formal IA, you do not see reference to it in the peer assessment boxes. For further information about Criterion B2 and what is expected of you in parts 2 and 3 of the IA, refer to the IA assessment criteria in the Language B guide.

The Five Boons of Life w

CHAPTER I

In the morning of life came a good fairy with her basket, and said:

"Here are gifts. Take one, leave the others. And be wary, chose wisely; oh, choose wisely! for only one of them is valuable."

The gifts were five: Fame, Love, Riches, Pleasure, Death. The youth said, eagerly:

"There is no need to consider"; and he chose Pleasure.

He went out into the world and sought out the pleasures that youth delights in. But each in its turn was short-lived and disappointing, vain and empty; and each, departing, mocked him. In the end he said: "These years I have wasted. If I could but choose again, I would choose wisely.

CHAPTER II

The fairy appeared, and said:

"Four of the gifts remain. Choose once more; and oh, remember – time is flying, and only one of them is precious."

The man considered long, then chose Love; and did not mark the tears that rose in the fairy's eyes.

After many, many years the man sat by a coffin, in an empty home. And he communed with himself, saying: "One by one they have gone away and left me; and now she lies here, the dearest and the last. Desolation after desolation has swept over me; for each hour of happiness the treacherous trader, Love, had sold me I have paid a thousand hours of grief. Out of my heart of hearts I curse him."

CHAPTER III

"Choose again." It was the fairy speaking.

"The years have taught you wisdom – surely it must be so. Three gifts remain. Only one of them has any worth – remember it, and choose warily."

The man reflected long, then chose Fame; and the fairy, sighing, went her way.

Years went by and she came again, and stood behind the man where he sat solitary in the fading day, thinking. And she knew his thought:

"My name filled the world, and its praises were on every tongue, and it seemed well with me for a little while. How little a while it was! Then came envy; then detraction; then calumny; then hate; then persecution. Then derision, which is the beginning of the end. And last of all came pity, which is the funeral of fame. Oh, the bitterness and misery of renown! target for mud in its prime, for contempt and compassion in its decay."

CHAPTER IV

I"Choose yet again." It was the fairy's voice.

"Two gifts remain. And do not despair. In the beginning there was but one that was precious, and it is still here."

"Wealth – which is power! How blind I was!" said the man. "Now, at last, life will be worth the living. I will spend, squander, dazzle. These mockers and despisers will crawl in the dirt before me, and I will feed my hungry heart with their envy. I will have all luxuries, all joys, all enchantments of the spirit, all contentments of the body that man holds dear. I will buy, buy, buy! deference, respect, esteem, worship – every pinchbeck grace of life the market of a trivial world can furnish forth. I have lost much time, and chosen badly heretofore, but let that pass; I was ignorant then, and could but take for best what seemed so."

Three short years went by, and a day came when the man sat shivering in a mean garret; and he was gaunt and wan and hollow-eyed, and clothed in rags; and he was gnawing a dry crust and mumbling:

"Curse all the world's gifts, for mockeries and gilded lies! And miscalled, everyone. They are not gifts, but merely lendings. Pleasure, Love, Fame, Riches: they are but temporary disguises for lasting realities – Pain, Grief, Shame, Poverty. The fairy said true; in all her store there was but one gift which was precious, only one that was not valueless. How poor and cheap and mean I know those others now to be, compared with that inestimable one, that dear and sweet and kindly one, that steeps in dreamless and enduring sleep the pains that persecute the body, and the shames and griefs that eat the mind and heart. Bring it! I am weary, I would rest."

CHAPTER V

The fairy came, bringing again four of the gifts, but Death was wanting. She said:

"I gave it to a mother's pet, a little child. It was ignorant, but trusted me, asking me to choose for it. You did not ask me to choose."

"Oh, miserable me! What is left for me?"

"What not even you have deserved: the wanton insult of Old Age."

Paper 1 – Text type: Proposal (Professional)

The general purpose of any proposal is to persuade someone to do something in a professional context. For example, you can write a proposal to your school board to convince them to spend more on extracurricular activities or to suggest a new summer camp. Your proposal must explain what you are planning, how you plan to do it, when you plan to do it, how much it is going to cost and what the benefit will be.

As with all written communication, your audience is very important and so is the context. A proposal is a formal piece of writing, and this should be reflected in the way you address the person/organization you are writing the proposal for. Depending on context, you may also need to use facts, technical language and figures to convince your audience to support your plan.

Here are a few cardinal rules that should be taken into consideration when writing a proposal:

1. Use subheadings to break down your proposal into clear sections.
2. Give a concise introduction to your project, identifying the aims, or what problems it will address.
3. Explain your objective, methods, timeline, or budget when needed.
4. Conclude by emphasizing the benefits of your proposed idea if needed.
5. Take a clear stand in your proposal and set a positive tone.
6. Avoid language such as: "might", "could", "ought", "may", "should", "hope", "it appears".
7. Remember to support your argument with evidence.
8. Use formal language and be very polite.
9. Avoid exaggerated or emotional expressions.

Look at the following example showing how a proposal is structured.

Process improvement

Situation: ← Uses subheadings throughout

Customer calls to our helpline are currently answered by an assistant who asks the customer if they are calling to report a new problem or to check the status of a previously reported issue. If the customer is calling about a previously reported issue, the assistant asks the customer for the Incident ID #. The assistant then places the customer on hold, calls a customer service representative, advises the representative of the reason for the call (new problem or Incident ID #), and transfers the caller.

Proposed solution:

The role of the assistant who answers the call could easily be replaced by ← Begins by describing the problem and the focus of the proposal
an automated system, which would allow the customer to press 1 for a new problem or 2 for a previously reported issue. If the customer pressed 2, they

would be prompted to enter their Incident ID #. The caller would then be routed to a customer service representative, along with the Incident ID #, if applicable, which would be passed along via the phone system.

Steps involved:

1 Purchase a new phone routing system that would allow these capabilities.

2 Program and test the new routing system. ← Mentions the methods

3 Convert Incident ID #s from a combination of letters and numbers to numbers only.

4 Communicate the new workflow to customer service representatives.

Benefits:

- The new process would eliminate the need for assistants to answer customer calls, freeing them up for other tasks. Each assistant typically answers 30 calls per day. At an average of 42 seconds per call, this would give each assistant an additional 21 minutes per day. ← Explains the benefits of the proposed idea
- Customer service would be enhanced, as the first voice that would greet the customer would be that of the customer service representative who will ultimately assist them.

Potential obstacles:

- The cost of the new phone routing system (approximately $700 dollars). This cost would be miniscule compared with the savings over time associated with the additional capacity of the assistants.
- The time associated with programming and testing and developing the new ID system (48 total man-hours). Again, the time saved by implementing the new procedure would more than make up for this initial investment. ← Explains the potential problems
- Resistance of customers who do not prefer dealing with an automated system. No solution is going to please every customer, but most consumers today expect to be greeted with an automated system when calling a business. One option is to allow customers to press 0 if they're unsure how to answer the automated questions.
- Customer service issues with early callers whose ID # still contains numbers and letters. The above solution concerning the 0 option would eliminate this problem as well. ← The language used is impersonal and courteous throughout

Conclusion:

As you can see from the above, not only will customer service be improve, but the suggested solution will also ensure that assistants have more time to do constructive work . ← Concludes by restating the benefits

Writing activity

Refer to the blog entry , "Your values, your life" on page 216 and change it into a proposal to be given to a town council in the United States.

The aim of the proposal is to improve understanding of values in that town.

Brainstorming

In pairs:

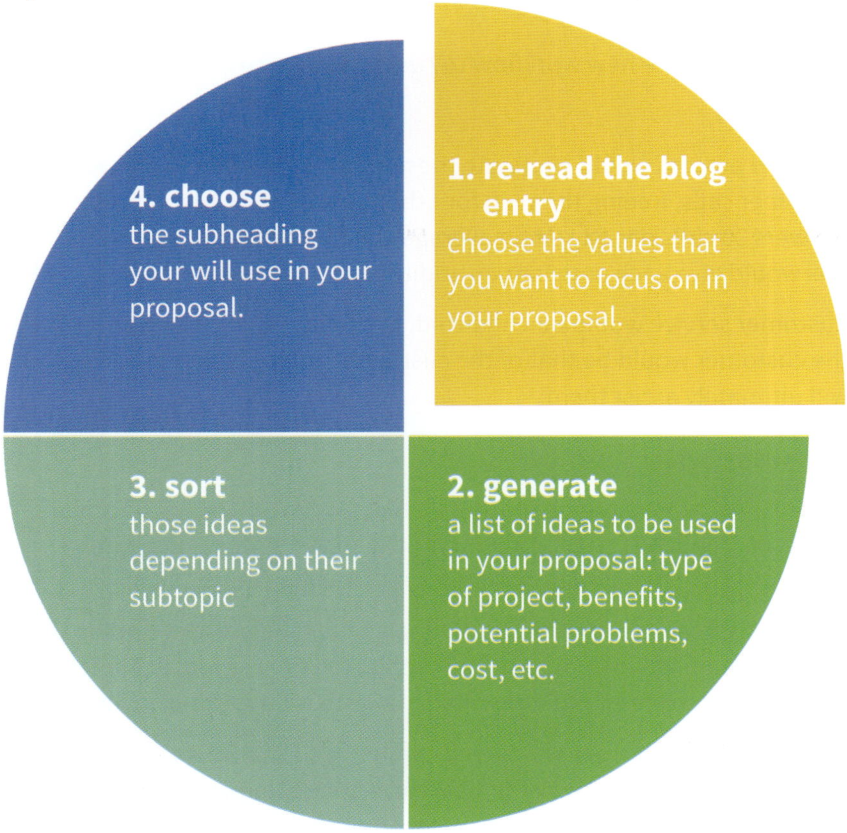

Planning

In pairs:

1. decide how you will approach the town council. Will the proposal be embedded in an email, or in a letter to the editor?
2. decide the tone and style of your proposal: What is the best way to address the town's council?
3. decide how you are going to order your subtopics: Which should go first? Which should appear last? What should appear in the middle? Does your chosen order ensure that your ideas will be coherent and your writing will flow smoothly?

Drafting

Individually, write a draft of the body of your proposal.

When you are done, revise this draft: does it make sense?

Add your introduction and your conclusion to the body. Re-read what you have written: do the transitions make sense? Are your paragraphs well connected? How polite, coherent, and relevant to the topic is your proposal?

Re-read the complete draft of your proposal for the last time. Make any necessary changes.

Paper 1 practice (HL/SL)

Your school is investing in a new library. As President of the Student Council, you know what students would like to change in the library and how those changes will help them use the library more. Suggest how the library can be improved to your school board and mention the benefits to be gained from those improvements.

Note

As you can see, the text type is not mentioned. However, the context provided directs you to writing a proposal. It is your responsibility to choose whether you will present this in a proposal format or you will embed it in a letter or an email.

Self-management skills ATLs

One of the main tenets of self-management is affective skills. By reflecting on what you have learned and what you still need to learn, you will develop mindfulness by being aware of the issue at hand and focusing intently and solely on that issue.

Conclusion to research question A

Having completed Section A of this chapter, reflect on the section's research question:

Do different Anglophone cultures share the same values?

In groups of four, discuss the following:

- What have you learned so far?
- What do you still want to know?

A TOK moment

TOK

Changes in language and word use reflect our shifting values, UCLA psychologist reports

A new UCLA analysis of words used in more than 1.5 million American and British books published between 1800 and 2000 shows how our cultural values have changed.

The increase or decrease in the use of certain words over the past two centuries – a period marked by growing urbanization, greater reliance on technology and the widespread availability of formal education – reveals how human psychology has evolved in response to major historical shifts, said Patricia Greenfield, a distinguished professor of psychology at UCLA and the author of the study.

For instance, the words "choose" and "get" rose significantly in frequency between 1800 and 2000, while "obliged" and "give" decreased significantly over these two centuries. "Choose" and "get" indicate "the individualism and materialistic values that are adaptive in wealthier urban settings," while "obliged" and "give" "reflect the social responsibilities that are adaptive in rural settings," Greenfield said.

Usage of "get" declined between 1940 and the 1960s before rising again in the 1970s, perhaps reflecting a decline in self-interest during World War II and the civil rights movement, she noted.

Greenfield also observed a gradual rise in the use of "feel" and a decline in the use of "act," suggesting a turn toward inner mental life and away from outward behavior. She found a growing focus on the self, with the use of "child," "unique," "individual" and "self" all increasing from 1800 to 2000.

Over the two centuries, the importance of obedience to authority, social relationships and religion in everyday life seems to have waned, as reflected in the decline of "obedience," "authority," "belong" and "pray."

"This research shows that there has been a two-century-long historical shift toward individualistic psychological functioning adapted to an urban environment and away from psychological functioning adapted to a rural environment," Greenfield said. "The currently discussed rise in individualism is not something recent but has been going on for centuries as we moved from a predominantly rural, low-tech society to a predominantly urban, high-tech society."

1. Skim through the article and reflect on your understanding of how use of language reflects our values.
2. In groups of four, discuss the following questions:
   - How would you define "values" in relation to identities?
   - How would you define "language" in relation to identities?
   - How does our use of language reflect our values? Is the reverse true: do our values also affect the way we use language?

Section B: Language and identity

Research question A:

In what ways does language shape our identity?

Before you read

Individually, think:

- How do you define your identity?
- Does your mother tongue shape your identity? If so, how?
- Does speaking another language further shape your identity?

In pairs, discuss:

- any questions or elements that puzzle you about the way in which language affects identity.

In groups, decide:

- how you can best explore this topic to find answers to your questions.

Now read the following text about the extent to which language affects our perceptions of our identity, then decide if the text answers any of your questions or just adds more puzzles to the ones you have already identified.

How Much Does the Language We Speak Shape our Identity?

Will speaking a foreign language change the way you see the world?

"She cloaked herself in another language, played in its brocade shades of meaning discovered deep pockets of puns, Surprise linings of double entendre."

Ronnie Scharfman

A white English-speaking child, growing up in the apartheid period in South Africa, I knew at a very young age that I wanted to write. I realized even then that in order to do this it was necessary to know who one was. What else was I going to write about? The other alternative and perhaps equally appealing, was to become an actress, but even then I felt I needed to discover who I was. How did one find out such a thing? Who was I? In what tradition would my work follow?

I felt it necessary to leave the country where I was born, to put on the cloak of other languages (as my friend Ronnie Scharfman has written so eloquently), ones that were not my mother tongue. I wanted to leave my home, my mother, and a land of injustice and racial divide.

I lived first in Switzerland, and then in Italy. I went on to France where I eventually did my studies in psychology and finally to America the country that George Bernard Shaw famously said is separated from England by a common language.

Did the fact that I learned to speak French fluently and to some lesser degree Italian, help me to find myself? I have written of the loneliness of finding myself in a strange French family at seventeen. Speaking a foreign language presents, of course, many difficulties: the frustration of not being understood, and the feeling of being stupid, reduced to a smaller vocabulary, without the familiarity with the expressions, the fine tuning of your own language. It is almost impossible to really appreciate poetry for example, in another language, or so it seems to me.

Yet ultimately and despite the difficulties involved, I do believe one becomes different, other, speaking another language. A language where the words do not have the echoes from our childhood, where the vocabulary is not associated with childhood connotations enables us to look at life in a slightly different way. We even move differently, gesture differently, even perhaps walk differently. In some ways this new identity is liberating.

I remember a patient at the Salpêtrière, the big mental hospital in France where Freud worked with Charcot and where I was doing an internship, coming up to speak to me in English. The doctors were amazed; the woman had been silent or almost silent for so long. Her English was not very good, but she would not speak to anyone else in French but somehow felt free enough to speak to me in this foreign language which must have seemed less threatening to her. We think too of Anna O, Breuer's famous patient who coined the term "talking cure" who lost her own language, German, for a while but was still able to read Italian and French and translate them into English.

Somehow speaking a foreign language, it [-17-] became possible to voice certain opinions, to speak of matters which might have seemed [-18-] in English. Is that because the French are less squeamish about certain matters?

And when I learned the lovely language of Italy, and felt there [-19-] welcome even in my reduced capacity to express myself, I think I [-20-] again.

Of course, our identities are formed in so many different ways: by the people around us, the books we read, our heroes and heroines, and above all perhaps by the work we do, but speaking a foreign language can lead one to create a different [-21-] and help to understand who we are.

Adapted from https://www.psychologytoday.com/gb/blog/dreaming-freud/201411/how-much-does-the-language-we-speak-shape-our-identity

Reading comprehension

Answer the following questions.

1. Which word between lines 1 and 7 is closest in meaning to "immersed"?
2. What did the author discover when she was a child?
3. What, according to the writer, is of utmost importance if one wants to become a writer or an actor?
4. How is South Africa described between lines 9 and 30?
5. What did the writer find truly difficult when speaking a foreign language?

Find the words in the text which mean the following.

6. to a similar degree
7. tempting
8. expressively
9. demoted
10. eventually
11. connected
12. to some extent
13. intimidating
14. articulate
15. prudish

16. ***From statements A to J, select the five that are true according to the text.***

- **A.** The writer lived in different countries around the world as a child.
- **B.** The writer felt somewhat deserted when she lived in France.
- **C.** The writer believes people change when they speak an additional language.
- **D.** The patient at Salpêtrière spoke to Freud in English instead of French.
- **E.** The patient at Salpêtrière spoke French as a first language.
- **F.** The term "talking cure" was invented by a speaker of German as a first language.
- **G.** Speaking a foreign language facilitates the articulation of viewpoints about some topics.
- **H.** Speaking a foreign language hinders the communication of one's opinions.
- **I.** Identities are molded in a number of ways.
- **J.** Our idols primarily shape our identities.

Which words go in the gaps between lines 89 and 108?

acceptable	changed	disguise	gradually	less
more	rapidly	swapped	taboo	world

17. ______________________ **20.** ______________________

18. ______________________ **21.** ______________________

19. ______________________

HL extension HL

Choose the correct answer from A, B, C, or D.

1. "She cloaked herself in another language" (line 3) indicates that speaking another language:
- **A.** makes us feel strange
- **B.** disguises our true personalities
- **C.** broadens our perspectives
- **D.** surprises us.

2. "deep" (line 5) means:
- **A.** meaningless
- **B.** profound
- **C.** grave
- **D.** facile.

3. According to Shaw, England and the United States share a(n):
- **A.** culture
- **B.** ocean
- **C.** etymology
- **D.** language.

4. According to the writer, speaking a foreign language:
- **A.** is easy despite the many obstacles one encounters
- **B.** is generally frustrating
- **C.** adds to one's dim-wittedness
- **D.** is exasperating when others do not comprehend.

To whom or to what do the following words refer? Make notes.

5. this (line 13)
6. such a thing (line 20)
7. ones (line 26)
8. where (line 69)
9. her (line 81)
10. them (line 84)

Listening comprehension

Mother Tongue by Amy Tan

Listen to the audio clip provided of Amy Tan discussing how the language we grow up with affects our entire lives.

From the options given, choose the one that best fits in the blank to complete the summary with information from the listening text.

Although Amy Tan is an author, she claims the extent of her knowledge of linguistic variation is **a.** (objective/ literary/ subjective). She enjoys examining how language **b.** (abuses/ forms/ inhibits) different shapes and ideas. She has grown up using **c.** (special/ similar/ distinct) variations of English and she became aware of how **d.** (similar/ dissimilar/ unusual) that was when she was scheduled to give a talk about her novel *The Joy Luck Club* as it was the first time she used standard English **e.** (in front of/ with/ in addition to) her mother.

Choose the correct answer from A, B, C, or D.

1. When listening to her speaking with her mother, Tan's husband:
   - A. was surprised that she used a different type of English.
   - B. acted normally because it was the kind of English she used with him.
   - C. thought she had created a special type of English to be used with her mother.

2. The English used by Tan's mother:
   - A. does not reflect the quality of what she has to say.
   - B. is not good enough to shop in department stores.
   - C. does not influence people's perceptions of her.

3. When she speaks to people:
   - A. the majority say they understand Tan's mother.
   - B. a minority says they do not understand Tan's mother.
   - C. some do not take her seriously, or ignore her.

4. The English of Tan's mother:
   - A. limited Tan's possibilities.
   - B. affected Tan's use of English.
   - C. shaped Tan's perception of life.

5. Tan ________ describing her mother's English as "broken" or "limited".
   - A. likes
   - B. flinches at
   - C. is afraid of

6. In the past, Tan acted as if her mother's English:
   - A. was a source of embarrassment.
   - B. was imperfect.
   - C. meant people would think she was imperfect too.

HL extension HL

Complete the conversation below by choosing the most appropriate option as per the information provided in the recording.

Jane and Heidi are having a conversation about how language shapes the human being.
Jane: I recently heard a speech by Amy Tan who believes that the language spoken by immigrant families affects their children [a.]__________ (far more than/ much less than/ perhaps as much as) the language spoken by peers.
Heidi: Yes, I heard the same speech. Tan even claimed that her language skills were [b.] (less impressive/ as good as/ maybe a little better) than her mathematical knowledge when she was at school. She believed that was because Math had definitive answers, whereas English relied mostly on [c.]__________ (contradicting rules/ meaning formation/ grammatical limitations) and that was difficult for her because of her mother's perception of language.
Jane: That is so true. The same applies to analogies, right? Imagine how difficult it would be if your ability to answer language questions was [d.]__________ (dependent on/ independent of/ detached from) your ability to think about similar situations in your own experience!
Heidi: it's really amazing that she chose writing as a profession. She did mention that that was because of her [e.]__________ (conformist/ obliging/ defiant) character.

Choose the correct answer from A, B, C, or D.

1. Tan used the type of English her prospective audience would:
   a. avoid.
   b. identify with.
   c. single out.
2. The translated Chinese used in Tan's books is best described as:
   a. descriptive.
   b. simplified.
   c. weak.
3. Tan's aim behind using different variations of English in her books is to:
   a. convey things that cannot be captured in language exams.
   b. show what language ability tests reveal.
   c. capture her mother's language & gain her approval.

Research skills ATLs

The discussion on the left promotes good research practices such as comparing, contrasting and validating information, which in turn improve higher-order thinking.

Discussion

From what you have read in this section, to what extent do you think the languages we speak affect our identity?

In groups:

- list a number of ways in which the languages we speak may or may not affect the way we perceive ourselves
- do some research about the ways your language is identified
- discuss whether those ways should be seen in a positive or negative light
- pick one point from your list that you think has the most effect on how we perceive ourselves and explain it to the other groups.

Internal assessment (SL)

Examine the visual stimulus here. The image relates to the theme of the chapter: "Identities".

Brainstorming

In groups of three, discuss the following questions.

A. What is the picture communicating to you?

B. Whose viewpoint, if any, is missing from the picture?

C. How will you relate the picture to the theme "identities" and the topic "language and identity"?

D. How does the picture relate to an Anglophone culture? Think of what you have learned so far about how language shapes identity.

Presenting

Based on your answers to the questions above, prepare a four-minute presentation on the picture.

Remember that the presentation should not only include description of the picture, but should also connect it to the theme "identities", the topic "beliefs and values" and an English-speaking culture.

Use your answers to the questions above to map out your presentation. The following should help you:

1. Address the focus of the picture.
2. Describe the picture in no more than 30 seconds.
3. Connect the picture to the relevant theme and topic.
4. Address the topic: define it, mention how it is perceived in Anglophone cultures, highlight how similar or different this perception is to that in your own culture. Make sure your presentation is precise and concise; you have only four minutes.
5. Decide on who will say what: this is a group presentation and all participants should get the chance to speak.

Present to your classmates.

Conceptual understanding: Context

Imagine that your teacher asked you to give this presentation in a video call to a group of English-speaking students who live in another country. How would you change your presentation to make it more appropriate to the new context? How would the language (register) and the style of the presentation change? Why?

Peer assessment

In groups of four, assess the presentations given by your classmates. Use the assessment criteria in the Language B Guide to focus your feedback:

Criterion A: Language

1. Is the vocabulary used appropriately? Is it varied?
2. Are the grammatical structures correct? Are they mainly simple? Are any complex structures used?
3. Is pronunciation clear? What about intonation? Does it help you understand the focus of their presentation?

Criterion B: Message

A. Is the presentation connected to the visual stimulus?

B. Are the ideas relevant to an Anglophone culture?

Criterion C: Interactive skills – communication

A. How well-presented and clear are the ideas?

B. Are the ideas presented in depth?

Suggest ways in which your classmates can improve their presentation techniques.

Internal assessment (HL)

Before you read the short story below, examine the following:

Divide into five groups. Each group should focus on one of the characters below:

Tamara

Wanda

Roger

Mr. Gilman

The Borden sisters

In your group, prepare a four-minute presentation in which you:

1. draw a visual representation of your assigned character
2. describe your character's physical and personality traits
3. conclude by creating a diagram to express what you, as a group, think about the character's personality and identity.

Present to your classmates.

Note

In your internal assessment, the literary extract will not exceed 300 words. You will be shown two, one from each of the works of literature studied in class.

Conceptual understanding

The use of register and language in general differs depending on certain concepts. Two important concepts are perspective and context. When the perspective changes, the kind of language used changes and so does register. For example, the language used by the group describing Tamara may differ greatly from that used by the group describing Mr. Gilman depending on how the group perceives the character.

Does context affect the use of language in the same way. If so, how?

Peer assessment

After each presentation, hold a short, whole-class discussion session in which you address the following:

1. How clear was the description of the group's assigned character? How well was the presentation connected to the extract given?
2. How has the presentation improved your understanding of identity?

Suggest ways in which the group can improve their focus on the excerpt and their presentation techniques.

Note

The peer assessment above is an effective formative assessment tool that will help you to reflect on your classmates' performance in order to help each other improve. The purpose of peer assessment is to help you to reflect on the feedback given from your peers and use it to improve your presentation skills.

Extract from DRESSING UP FOR THE CARNIVAL

By CAROL SHIELDS

All over town people are putting on their costumes.

Tamara has flung open her closet door; just to see her standing there is to feel a squeeze of the heart. She loves her clothes. She knows her clothes. Her favorite moment of the day is this moment, standing at the closet door, still a little dizzy from her long night of tumbled sleep, biting her lip, thinking hard, moving the busy hangers along the rod, about to make up her mind.

Yes! The yellow cotton skirt with the big patch pockets and the hand detail around the hem. How fortunate to own such a skirt. And the white blouse. What a blouse! Those sleeves, that neckline with its buttoned flap, the fullness in the yoke that reminds her of the morris dancers she and her boyfriend Bruce saw at the Exhibition last year.

Next she adds her new straw belt; perfect. A string of yellow beads. Earrings of course. Her bone sandals. And bare legs, why not?

She never checks the weather before she dresses; her clothes are the weather, as powerful in their sunniness as the strong, muzzy early morning light pouring into the narrow street by the bus stop, warming the combed crown of her hair and fueling her with imagination. She taps a sandaled foot lightly on the pavement, waiting for the number 4 bus, no longer just Tamara, clerk-receptionist for the Youth Employment Bureau, but a woman in a yellow skirt. A passionate woman dressed in yellow. A Passionate, Vibrant Woman About To Begin Her Day. Her Life.

Roger, aged thirty, employed by the Gas Board, is coming out of a corner grocer's carrying a mango in his left hand. He went in to buy an apple and came out with this. At the cash register he refused a bag, preferring to carry this thing, this object, in his bare hand. The price was $1.29. He's a little surprised at how heavy it is, a tight seamless leather skin enclosing soft pulp, or so he imagines. He has never bought a mango before, never eaten one, doesn't know what a mango tastes like or how it's prepared. Cooked like a squash? Sliced and sugared like a peach? He has no intention of eating it, not now anyway, maybe never. Its weight reminds him of a first-class league ball, but larger, longer, smooth skinned, and ripely green. Mango, mango. An elliptical purse, juice-filled, curved for the palm of the human hand, his hand.

He is a man of medium height, burly, divorced, wearing an open-necked shirt, hurrying back to work after his coffee break. But at this moment he freezes and sees himself freshly: a man carrying a mango in his left hand. Already he's accustomed to it; in fact, it's starting to feel lighter and drier, like a set of castanets which has somehow attached itself to his left arm. Any minute now he'll break out into a cha-cha-cha right here in front of the Gas Board. The shriveled fate he sometimes sees for himself can be postponed if only he puts his mind to it. Who would have thought it of him? Not his ex-wife Lucile, not his co-workers, not his boss, not even himself.

And the **Borden sisters** are back from their ski week in Happy Valley. They've been back for a month now, in fact, so why are they still wearing those little plastic ski passes on the zipper tabs of their jackets? A good question. I SKIED HAPPY MOUNTAIN these passes say. The Bordens wear them all over town, at the shopping center, in the parking lot. It's spring, the leaves are unfolding on the hedges in front of the post office, but the Borden girls, Karen and Sue, still carry on their bodies, and in their faces too, the fresh wintry cold of the slopes, the thrill of powder snow and stinging sky. (The air up there chimes with echoes, a bromide of blue.) It would be an exaggeration to say the Borden sisters swagger; it would be going too far. They move like young ponies, quivery and thoughtful, with the memory of expended effort and banked curves. They speak to each other in voices that are loud and musical, and their skin, so clear, pink, bright, and healthy, traps the sunshine beneath its surface. With one hand, walking along, they stroke the feathering-out tops of hedges in front of the post office, and with the other they pull and tug on those little plasticized tags—I SKIED HAPPY MOUNTAIN. You might say it's a kind of compulsion, as though they can't help themselves.

And then there's **Wanda** from the bank who has been sent on the strangest of errands. It happened in this way: Mr. Wishcourt, the bank manager where Wanda works, has just bought a new baby carriage for his wife, or rather, for their new baby son, Samuel James. The baby carriage was an impulsive lunch-hour purchase, he explains to Wanda, looking shamefaced but exuberant: an English pram, high-wheeled, majestically hooded, tires like a Rolls-Royce, a beauty, but the fool thing, even when folded up, refuses to fit in the back of his Volvo. Would she object? It would take perhaps three-quarters of an hour. It's a fine day. He'll draw her a plan on a sheet of paper, put an X where his house is. He knows how she loves walking, that she gets restless in the afternoon sometimes, sitting in her little airless cage. He would appreciate it so much. And so would his wife and little Sam. Would she mind? He's never before asked her to make coffee or do personal errands. It's against his policy, treating his employees like that. But just this once?

Wanda sets off awkwardly. She is, after all, an awkward woman, who was formerly an awkward girl with big girlish teeth and clumsy shoulders. The pram's swaying body seems to steer her at first, instead of her steering it. Such a chunky rolling oblong, black and British with its wambling, bossy, outsized keel. "Excuse me," she says, and "Sorry." Without meaning to, she forces people over to the edge of the sidewalks, crowds them at the street corners, even rubs up against them with the big soft tires.

All she gets back are smiles. Or kindly little nods that say: "It's not your fault" or "How marvelous" or "What a picture!" After a bit she gets the hang of steering. This is a technical marvel she's pushing along, the way it takes the curbs, soundlessly, with scarcely any effort at all. Engineering at its most refined and comical. Her hands rest lightly on the wide white handlebar. It might be made of ivory or alabaster or something equally precious, it's so smooth and cool to the touch.

By the time Wanda reaches Pine Street she feels herself fully in charge. Beneath the leafy poplars, she and the carriage have become a single entity. Gliding, melding, a silvery hum of wheels and a faint, pleasing adhesive resistance as the tires roll along suburban asphalt. The weight of her fingertips is enough to keep it in motion, in control, and she takes the final corners with grace. Little Sam is going to love his new rolling home, so roomy and rhythmic, like a dark boat sailing forward in tune with his infant breathing and the bump-dee-bump of his baby heart.

She stops, leans over, and reaches inside. There's no one about; no one sees her, only the eyes inside her head that have rehearsed this small gesture in dreams. She straightens the blanket, pulling it smooth, pats it into place. "Shhh," she murmurs, smiling. "There, there, now."

Mr. Gilman is smiling too. His daughter-in-law, who considers him a prehistoric bore, has invited him to dinner. This happens perhaps once a month; the telephone rings early in the morning. "We'd love to have you over tonight," she says. "Just family fare, I'm afraid, leftovers."

"I'd be delighted," he always says, even though the word leftovers gives him, every time she says it, a little ping of injury.

At age eighty he can be observed in his obverse infancy, metaphorically sucking and tonguing the missing tooth of his life. He knows what he looks like: the mirror tells all—eyes like water sacks, crimson arcs around the ears, a chin that betrays him, the way it mooches and wobbles while he thrashes around in his head for one of those rumpled anecdotes that seem only to madden his daughter-in-law. Better to keep still and chew. "Scrumptious," he always says, hoping to win her inhospitable heart, but knowing he can't.

Today he decides to buy her flowers. Why-oh-why has he never thought of this before! Daffodils are selling for $1.99 a half dozen. A bargain. It must be spring, he thinks, looking around. Why not buy two bunches, or three? Why not indeed? Or four?

They form a blaze of yellow in his arms, a sweet propitiating little fire. He knows he should take them home immediately and put them in water for tonight, but he's reluctant to remove the green paper wrapping which lends a certain legitimacy; these aren't flowers randomly snatched from the garden; these are florist's flowers, purchased as an offering, an oblation.

There seems nothing to do but carry them about with him all day. He takes them along to the bank, the drugstore, to his appointment with the foot specialist, his afternoon card club at the Sunset Lodge. Never has he received more courteous attention, such quick service. The eyes of strangers appear friendlier than usual. "I am no worse off than the average person," he announces to himself. He loses, gracefully, at canasta, then gets a seat on the bus, a seat by the window. The pale flowers in his arms spell evanescence, gaiety. "Hello there," a number of people call out to him. He is clearly a man who is expected somewhere, anticipated. A charming gent, elegant and dapper, propounding serious questions, bearing gifts, flowers. A man in disguise.

Paper 1 – Speech (Mass media)

A speech is addressed to a listening audience. The speaker wishes to make an impact, hold the attention of the audience and convince them of an idea. In order achieve this, speakers use a variety of techniques that help make their speeches convincing.

When writing a speech, you must consider who will be listening to you and what aspects of your topic are best suited to meet the needs of your audience. Therefore, you need to consider the angle you will take to best suit that group. Be clear about your purpose – is it, for example, to persuade, inform, demonstrate, entertain, or welcome? Is it a combination of these?

Make sure you connect with your audience. Use direct address but be careful with the use of the pronouns. How you address your audience can radically affect your relationship with them. Which form of address is appropriate for your speech?

Here are a few cardinal rules that should be taken into consideration when writing a speech:

1. Have a clear introduction: begin by greeting your audience, grabbing their attention and making sure they understand the topic. You will then need to give a one sentence summary of your speech topic and your point of view or angle. You also want to convince your audience that you have credibility – the right to speak on the topic. You can do this by citing your qualifications or expertise. Next, briefly outline the key points you are going to cover. Explain the benefit for the audience. What's in your speech for them? Why will they want to hear what you have got to tell them?

2. The main body of your speech can be a reasoned argument. It will contain supporting paragraphs with topic sentences, supporting examples or evidence and explanations.
3. Conclude your speech by re-stating the main arguments using different words. The final sentence should be a clincher or call to action.
4. Always maintain contact with your audience.
5. Use rhetoric that is appropriate to your audience.

Look at the following example of a structured speech. Can you identify the cardinal rules given above?

Discovering Your Identity

Layo Olayiwola was the Keynote Speaker at ACD's and Vanguard Connect's Discovering Your Identity Event on Saturday, 3rd January. Read the full text of her "Discovering Your Identity" speech as prepared for delivery below:

I feel very deeply honored and privileged to give the keynote address for this event, given the many impressive achievements of my peers both here on the panel and in the audience. I am grateful to Brenda King and Laura Marrast, the program coordinator at ACD, for being so proactive in making this event possible.

The process of discovering one's identity is seemingly unending. Just when you think you know who you are, or have figured out your place in the world, things change and you find yourself back at square one.

Going to university is an incredibly significant event – it could be the first time that you've left home, it could be the first time that you've done your own shopping, cooking and cleaning, it could be the first time that you've shared a room with a stranger – and this last point is particularly important given the wide range of personalities (some wonderful, some strange) you encounter.

Studying away from home is highly challenging: How do you confront a roommate that steals your belongings? How do you negotiate between your educational, social and personal needs? How do you survive in an environment where knowing who you are is crucial to selecting the right classes, friends, job opportunities and overall direction in life?

First things first, don't panic. It's okay if you've had a few hiccups. Part of the great thing about going to university is that perceived mistakes can teach you important things about yourself and life in general.

Understanding your identity, seeking out opportunities that refine your identity and maximizing upon the uniqueness of your identity can lead to positive outcomes throughout your university and post-university life.

So in this address I'm going to briefly speak about the importance of knowing who you are, cultivating your identity and getting the most out of your unique self.

Every now and again I have this epiphany. I stop absolutely everything that I'm doing and I embark upon a journey to discover myself. Sometimes this journey is a few minutes long, but sometimes these epiphanies evolve into epic journeys. It was one such epiphany, coupled with a cheap plane ticket that led me to spend a weekend in Istanbul.

The one thing you should never do when visiting Istanbul is go alone, particularly as a female. Not knowing this crucial piece of information, I went to Istanbul alone, on a quest to discover my identity but I ended up becoming very skilled in the art of rejecting marriage proposals.

My grand quest was doomed to fail from the start for several key reasons:

- We live in a dynamic world and the formation of one's identity is a process, not a single event. A greater understanding of your identity is dependent on interactions with other people in real world contexts as this best represents the reality in which we live.

- There are many factors that contribute to the formation of your identity. Some of these factors are genetic, some only emerge in specific situations, whilst others require patience to perceive and understand.

Thus, a weekend trip to Istanbul did not offer enough time or the right environment for the complex nature of my identity to be fully understood. Seeing as your identity is built up over time, it is important to give yourself the time and space to meditate upon what really makes you tick.

When I was at school I was convinced that I was going to be a doctor. I wasn't particularly thrilled by or interested in science, but I had this driving ambition and so I ended up taking a lot of science classes.

I soon reevaluated that decision in light of the fact that I actually did not enjoy taking science classes and I was rather bad at conducting experiments. I would be that person who was first to come in and set up, but last to leave, and with results that completely undermined the hypothesis. I think the only way that I did well was by writing very elaborate justifications to explain my unexpected results, and by being very strategic in selecting my lab partner. One thing that remains with me today from those science classes, is the notion of the scientific method – the idea that new knowledge of the world can be gained through experimentation and observable results.

Similarly by observing the decisions that you make and your reactions to events, it is possible to construct an accurate idea of your identity. Some people choose to write journals, or blog or maintain active profiles on social media sites; the sum of all this data is really useful in understanding who you are, as well as who you project yourself to be to your family, peers and the wider public.

This fuller understanding permits you to work on aspects of your identity and develop interests or characteristics that really define who you are. Sometimes this refining of self can lead you outside your comfort zone, but think of yourself as a piece of gold. Without going through an intensive purification process, it is impossible to get high quality gold. So also, without deepening your experience of the world, it is difficult to allow yourself to grow into the person that you want to be.

Understanding your identity and refining that identity are processes that go on indefinitely. There is no finishing line or timestamp or expiry date by which you must have finished discovering yourself. The beauty of this whole process is that you have countless opportunities to influence the development of your unique self and get the most out of life.

The formation of your identity is not a neutral process. Think of yourself like a rare gem, formed over centuries of pressure. Your identity emerges from years of decision-making and interactions with others. If you don't take an active role in understanding yourself and seeking out opportunities that refine your identity then someone else will.

Albert Camus, the influential philosopher, famously stated: man is the sum of all his decisions. Whilst that statement can feel quite oppressive, seeing as we don't always make the best decisions, it reinforces the importance of decision-making in constructing your identity. Taking control of who you are will lead to you making informed choices that you are comfortable with.

Ultimately having an identity, which feels authentic to you, will allow you to naturally flourish in whatever you pursue whilst drawing out the best in those around you.

As I conclude this talk, I want to leave you with one key image that best captures the ideas I have been expressing:

Your identity can be compared to an iceberg.

Apart from being the villains of the film, The Titanic, icebergs are fascinating in that they are impossible to comprehend in a single glance. Only 10% of an iceberg lies above the surface of water, thus in order to get a fuller understanding of the nature of an iceberg, you have to dive really deep. So also, you may only be able to perceive the very tip of your identity, but by diving deep and mindfully trying to understand yourself, refine yourself and make decisions that bring out the best of yourself, it is possible to achieve more in life, live a happier life and get a fuller understanding of the unique contributions that you can make to the world.

Thank you.

Writing activity

Write a speech to be delivered in your town's hall in which you explain your point of view on how the languages we speak affect our identity.

Brainstorming

In pairs:

1. reflect on everything you have learned in this section
- Choose your focal point and your stance: what would you like to emphasize in your speech?

2. generate
- Generate a list of ideas to be used in your speech.

3. sort
- Sort those ideas depending on their main topic.
- Decide on examples to use.
- Research some facts to support your ideas.

4. choose & establish
- Pick the ideas you will use in your speech.
- Determine how you will establish yourself as an authority on the topic.

Planning

In pairs:

1. make sure you have researched the topic sufficiently.
2. decide how you will grab your audience's attention: What should appear in your introduction? What is your conclusion? Connect these to the stance and approach you have chosen in the "brainstorming" stage.
3. decide the tone and style of your speech: do you know who your audience is? What is the best way to address this audience? What emotive and persuasive words and phrases will help you to support your ideas?
4. decide how you are going to order your ideas: which should go first? which should appear last? What should appear in the middle? Does your chosen order ensure that your ideas will be coherent and your writing will flow smoothly?
5. decide how you will incorporate the examples that will support your argument.

Drafting

Individually, write a draft of the body of your speech.

When you are done, revise this draft: does it make sense?

Add your introduction and your conclusion to the body. Re-read what you have written: does the transition make sense? Are your paragraphs well connected? How interesting and persuasive is your speech?

Presenting

Re-read the complete draft of your speech for the last time. Make any necessary changes.

Paper 1 practice (HL/SL)

You wish to explain to a number of your schoolmates the importance of speaking more than one language and how this ability will help them better understand who they are.

You were given the prompt above and the following text types to choose from:

Letter to the editor | **email** | **speech**

Which of those text types will best help you achieve the communicative purpose given in the prompt above? Why?

Using your chosen text type, write the task.

Thinking skills ATLs

Reflection in this exercise will help you to develop your critical thinking abilities by assessing how what you have learned has led to more questions and areas that need to be answered and explored.

Conclusion to research question B

Having completed Section B of this chapter, reflect on the section's research question:

In what ways does Language shape our identity?

In groups of four, discuss the following:

- What have you learned so far?
- What do you still want to know?

A TOK moment TOK

Role of Language in Identity Formation

People that have [a] multilingual background face complex issues in adapting and assimilating their language to [the] cultural identity that they want to be identified with. People create their linguistic structure so as to bear a resemblance to those of the group with [whom] from time to time they wish to identify. Cultural identity is defined as the product of social and historical background that is constructed when individuals categorize themselves as a group, in addition to social context and ethnically accustomed communicative structures in a particular society (Jung and Lee, 2004). Language serves as a tool that embraces one's identity and operates as a mean of uniting a cultural community that share the same collective identity.

In the process of identity formation, language functions as a tool that holds the cultural identity that the language resembles. Professor Ngugi Wa Thiong'o, an African scholar and Kenyan author claims that "language is a carrier of culture" (cited in Ka'ili and Ka'ili). He explains that the [distinctive] qualities that a culture possessed, for example, its own value, custom, principles, faith, ideologies and the ways of life, are embedded in its own language [...].

However, the role language plays in influencing cultural identity is debatable because there are some cases in which the individuals do not identify themselves as a group in a particular ethnicity even though they master the language of that ethnicity. Jung and Lee (2004) in their study about the ethnic identities of Korean American students found that most of their research subjects identify themselves as a person that has a strong Korean background although they are fluent in English and were born in U.S. They identify themselves as either Korean American or Korean, but not American.

https://brightkite.com/essay-on/the-roles-of-languages-in-culture

Research about the role of language in the formation of one's identity.

1. Look up the definitions of culture and identity in a dictionary and compare them to what is given above. What do you think the relationship between culture and identity is? How does language influence, or not, our cultural identity?
2. In groups of four, discuss the following questions:
   A. How would you define 'identity' in relation to the languages you speak?
   B. How would you define 'culture' in relation to the languages you speak?
   C. How does our notion of 'identity' and 'culture' affect your understanding of the role language plays in defining both?

Section C: Subcultures

Research question C:

In what ways does belonging to a certain subculture define us if at all?

Before you read

1. ***Below is a list of subcultures that may be found in the Anglophone world today.***

- How many are you familiar with?
- Look up any terms you do not know.
- Do you perceive these subcultures in a positive or negative light?
- Justify your answers.

Everyday subculture examples

- Beatniks – the beat generation of the 1950s and 1960s
- Cosplay – a group involved with wearing costumes and role play
- Cybergoth – a mix of goth and rave culture with energetic music and bright, futuristic clothing
- Fandom – can be fans of movies, a celebrity, or any shared interest
- Goth – characterized with dark hair, eyeliner, nail polish and clothes
- Grunge – includes fans of alternative rock prominent in the 1990s
- Hip hop – started in South Bronx in the 70s, includes break dancing, graffiti, DJs combining two songs and rap music
- New Age – a spiritual and metaphysical movement including holistic health and parapsychology
- Otherkin – a group who view themselves as partly or totally non-human
- Skater – a skateboarding subculture
- Skinhead – early skinheads were not politically involved, but the subculture has evolved to include those who are racially motivated, as in the ideology of white supremacy
- Survivalism – people who actively prepare for disasters of all kinds
- Trekkie – Star Trek fans
- Vampire culture – alternative lifestyle based on vampires
- Zazou – a French subculture during World War II, characterized by wearing flashy clothing and dancing to bebop and swing

http://examples.yourdictionary.com/subculture-examples.html

1. Have any of the subcultures you listed earlier made the list?
2. Are there any of the subcultures you could add to the list?
3. Sort all those subcultures into their main characteristics: music, fashion, technology, politics, free speech, and so on.
4. Which subculture do you find most interesting? Conduct some research into it and present your findings to your classmates.

Now read the following text about subcultures then answer the questions that follow it.

Geeks, MOPs, and sociopaths in subculture evolution

Subcultures are dead. I plan to write a full obituary soon.

Subcultures were the main creative cultural force from roughly 1975 to 2000, when they stopped working. Why?

One reason—among several—is that as soon as subcultures start getting really interesting, they get invaded by muggles, who ruin them. Subcultures have a predictable lifecycle, in which popularity causes death. Eventually—around 2000—everyone understood this, and gave up hoping some subculture could somehow escape this dynamic.

Today I realized that the muggles who invade and ruin subcultures come in two distinct flavors, mops and sociopaths, playing very different roles. This thought was influenced by Venkatesh Rao's Gervais Principle, an analysis of workplace dynamics. Rao's theory is hideous, insightful nihilism; I recommend it.

The birth of cool

Before there is a subculture, there is a scene. A scene is a small group of creators who invent an exciting New Thing—a musical genre, a religious sect, a film animation technique, a political theory. Riffing off each other, they produce examples and variants, and share them for mutual enjoyment, generating positive energy.

The new scene draws fanatics. Fanatics don't create, but they contribute energy (time, money, adulation, organization, analysis) to support the creators.

Creators and fanatics are both geeks. They totally love the New Thing, they're fascinated with all its esoteric ins and outs, and they spend all available time either doing it or talking about it.

If the scene is sufficiently geeky, it remains a strictly geek thing; a weird hobby, not a subculture.

If the scene is unusually exciting, and the New Thing can be appreciated without having to get utterly geeky about details, it draws mops. Mops are fans, but not rabid fans like the fanatics. They show up to have a good time, and contribute as little as they reasonably can in exchange.

Geeks welcome mops, at first at least. It's the mass of mops who turn a scene into a subculture. Creation is always at least partly an act of generosity; creators want as many people to use and enjoy their creations as possible. It's also good for the ego; it confirms that the New Thing really is exciting, and not just a geek obsession. Further, some money can usually be extracted from mops—just enough, at this stage, that some creators can quit their day jobs and go pro. Full-time creators produce more and better of the New Thing.

The mop invasion

Fanatics want to share their obsession, and mops initially validate it for them too. However, as mop numbers grow, they become a headache. Fanatics do all the organizational work, initially just on behalf of geeks: out of generosity, and to enjoy a geeky sub-society. They put on events, build websites, tape up publicity fliers, and deal with accountants. Mops just passively soak up the good stuff. You may even have to push them around the floor; they have to be led to the drink. At best you can charge them admission or a subscription fee, but they'll inevitably argue that this is wrong because capitalism is evil, and also because they forgot their wallet.

Mops also dilute the culture. The New Thing, although attractive, is more intense and weird and complicated than mops would prefer. Their favorite songs are the ones that are least the New Thing, and more like other, popular things. Some creators oblige with less radical, friendlier, simpler creations.

Mops relate to each other in "normal" ways, like people do on TV, which the fanatics find repellent. During intermission, geeks want to talk about the New Thing, but mops blather about sportsball and celebrities. Also, the mops seem increasingly entitled, treating the fanatics as service workers.

Fanatics may be generous, but they signed up to support geeks, not mops. At this point, they may all quit, and the subculture collapses.

The sociopath invasion

A subculture at this stage is ripe for exploitation. The creators generate cultural capital, i.e. cool. The fanatics generate social capital: a network of relationships—strong ones among the geeks, and weaker but numerous ones with mops. The mops, when properly squeezed, produce liquid capital, i.e. money. None of those groups have any clue about how to extract and manipulate any of those forms of capital. Enter sociopaths.

The sociopaths quickly become best friends with selected creators. They dress just like the creators—only better. They talk just like the creators—only smoother. They may even do some creating—competently, if not creatively. Geeks may not be completely fooled, but they also are clueless about what the sociopaths are up to.

Mops are fooled. They don't care so much about details, and the sociopaths look to them like creators, only better. Sociopaths become the coolest kids in the room, demoting the creators. At this stage, they've extracted the cultural capital.

https://meaningness.com/geeks-mops-sociopaths

Reading comprehension (HL/SL)

Lines 1–32

Answer the following questions.

1. Which word between lines 1 and 8 is closest in meaning to "overrun"?
2. What effect do muggles have on a subculture?
3. To what does "this dynamic" (line 13) refer?
4. What types of muggles are there?
5. What, according to the text, is a scene?
6. Which word between lines 21 and 32 is closest in meaning to "worship"?

Lines 33–88

Choose the correct phrases from the text to complete the following sentences.

Base your answers on the information as it appears in the text.

7. Creators and fanatics are captivated by …
8. Mops are interested when …
9. The difference between mops and fanatics is that the mops are …
10. A subculture is created by …
11. Large numbers of people enjoying the New Thing …
12. Creators can turn professional when money is …
13. Mops become a nuisance when …
14. Because they are generous, …

To whom or to what do the following words refer?

15. they (line 45)
16. their (line 75)
17. the ones (line 76)
18. which (line 81)
19. they (line 87)

Lines 89–112

State whether the following statements are true or false and justify your answer with a relevant brief quotation from the text.

20. A subculture is manipulated after the fanatics quit.
21. Creators know how to get and exploit cultural, social and liquid capital.
22. Sociopaths may generate some cultural capital proficiently.
23. Mops mistake sociopaths for creators.
24. Sociopaths strip creators of their rank.

HL extension

HL

Find the words in the text which mean the following.

1. expected
2. sooner or later
3. alternatives
4. mysterious
5. bizarre
6. endorse
7. at the beginning
8. organize
9. certainly
10. weaken
11. disgusting
12. babble
13. removed

Choose the correct answer from A, B, C, or D.

14. The tone used in 'plan to write a full obituary soon' is:

A. sarcastic
B. morose
C. benevolent
D. bitter.

15. The writer thinks that Rao's Principle is:

A. horrible yet perceptive
B. not worthy because it advocates nothingness
C. just a theory
D. skeptical about the lifecycle of subcultures.

16. "they have to be led to the drink" (line 68) indicates that mops are:

A. creators
B. parasites
C. imposters
D. frauds.

17. Mops ruin the subculture because they:

A. refuse to pay subscription fees
B. are too attracted to the New Thing
C. think the New Thing is not for them
D. remain attached to their 'normal' things.

18. Draw a visual metaphor of the rise and decline of a subculture using ideas from the text.

Research and thinking skills

ATLs

In our modern world, research involves more than comparing and contrasting data. A huge importance is placed on validating this data, especially in a world in which information is available at the click of a button. These research skills will also help you improve your metacognition and higher-order thinking through the use of synthesis and evaluation.

Oral activity

"She cloaked herself in
another language,
played in its brocade
shades of meaning
discovered deep pockets
of puns,
Surprise linings of
double entendre."

Ronnie Scharfman

In groups, brainstorm a list of different meanings of the verse above and then use the following script skeleton to explore each one:

1. I am thinking of ... 'speaking a foreign language'... from the point of view of [the viewpoint you've chosen. E.g. a monolingual, a multilingual, a third culture kid]
2. I think ... describe the topic from your viewpoint. Be an actor - take on the character of your viewpoint
3. A question I have from this viewpoint is ... ask a question from this viewpoint

Wrap up: What new ideas do you have about the topic that you didn't have before? What new questions do you have?

Internal assessment (SL)

Examine the visual stimulus below. The image relates to the theme of the chapter: "Identities".

You have been given this visual stimulus and asked to prepare a four-minute presentation on the topic the stimulus highlights, which is connected to the theme 'identities'.

In groups of four, prepare your presentation and present it to your classmates.

The mind map below should remind you of the ground rules that you have to observe when preparing a presentation.

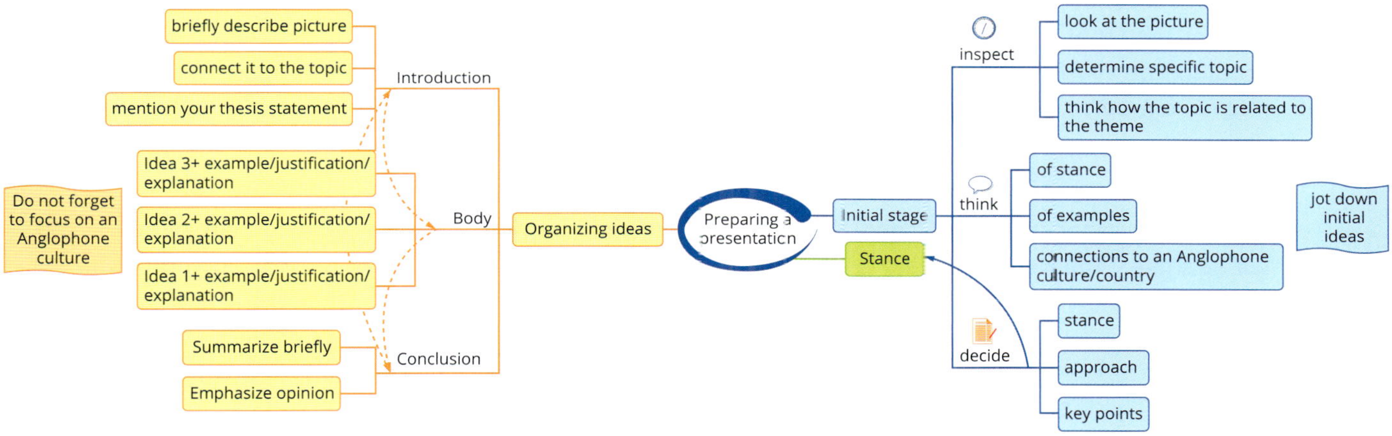

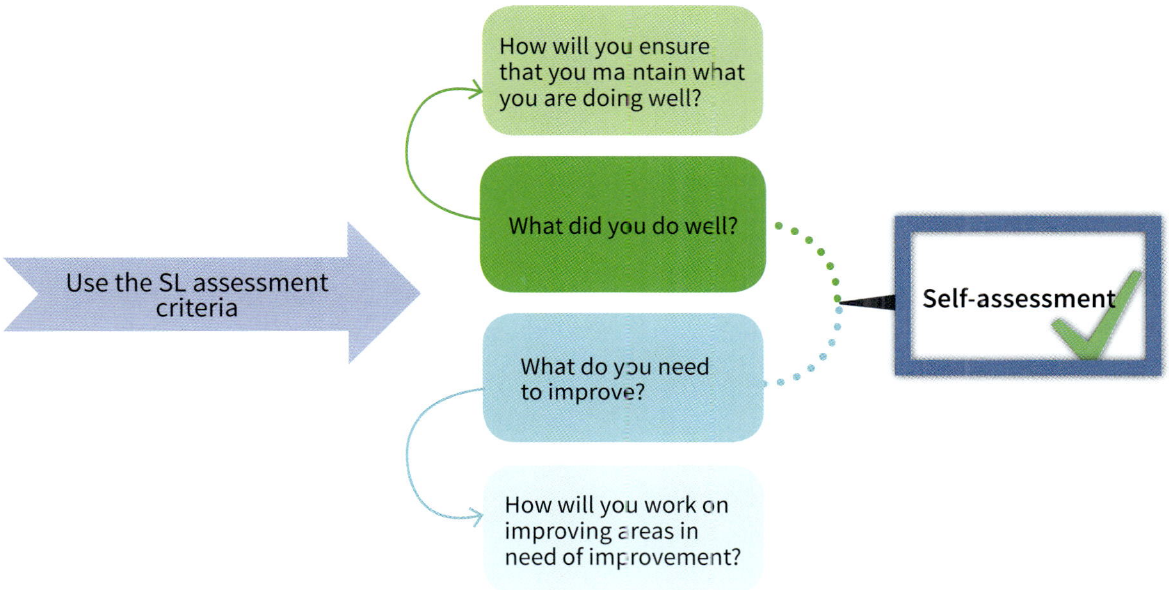

Internal assessment (HL)

Divide into groups. One group should read the story and write down their impressions of the teenage narrator and his friends. The other group should write down their impressions of the older generation: the narrator's parents and Georgie's father.

Cyberpunk

By Bruce Bethke

The snoozer went off at seven and I was out of my sleepsack, powered up, and on-line in nanos. That's as far as I got. Soon's I booted and got–

CRACKERS/BUDDYBOO/8ER

–on the tube I shut down fast. Damn! Rayno had been on line before me, like always, and that message meant somebody else had gotten into our Net– and that meant trouble by the busload! I couldn't do anything more on term, so I zipped into my jumper, combed my hair, and went downstairs.

Mom and Dad were at breakfast when I slid into the kitchen. "Good Morning, Mikey!" said Mom with a smile. "You were up so late last night I thought I wouldn't see you before you caught your bus."

"Had a tough program to crack," I said.

"Well," she said, "now you can sit down and have a decent breakfast." She turned around to pull some Sara Lees out of the microwave and plunk them down on the table.

"If you'd do your schoolwork when you're supposed to you wouldn't have to stay up all night," growled Dad from behind his caffix and faxsheet. I sloshed some juice in a glass and poured it down, stuffed a Sara Lee into my mouth, and stood to go.

"What?" asked Mom. "That's all the breakfast you're going to have?"

"Haven't got time," I said. "I gotta get to school early to see if the program checks." Dad growled something more and Mom spoke to quiet him, but I didn't hear much 'cause I was out the door.

I caught the transys for school, just in case they were watching. Two blocks down the line I got off and transferred going back the other way, and a coupla transfers later I wound up whipping into Buddy's All-Night Burgers. Rayno was in our booth, glaring into his caffix. It was 7:55 and I'd beat Georgie and Lisa there.

"What's on line?" I asked as I dropped into my seat, across from Rayno. He just looked up at me through his eyebrows and I knew better than to ask again.

At eight Lisa came in. Lisa is Rayno's girl, or at least she hopes she is. I can see why: Rayno's seventeen–two years older than the rest of us– he wears flash plastic and his hair in The Wedge (Dad blew a chip when I said I wanted my hair cut like that) and he's so cool he won't even touch her, even when she's begging for it. She plunked down in her seat next to Rayno and he didn't blink.

Georgie still wasn't there at 8:05. Rayno checked his watch again, then finally looked up from his caffix. "The compiler's been cracked," he said. Lisa and I both swore. We'd worked up our own little code to keep our Net private. I mean, our Olders would just blow boards if they ever found out what we were really up to. And now somebody'd broken our code.

"Georgie's old man?" I asked.

"Looks that way."

In your groups, prepare a four-minute presentation based on your reading. Take into consideration the questions below.

Describe your impressions of *Cyberpunk's* narrator and his friends. Which words or phrases in the text prove that your image is correct?

How does the language used in the extract reflect the narrator's subculture?

What would you do if you were in the narrator's shoes?

Describe your impressions of the narrator's parents and Georgie's father. Which words or phrases in the text prove that your image is correct?

Which words in the text would the narrator's parents find difficult to understand? Does the same apply to Georgie's father?

What would you do if your own parents acted like Georgie's father?

Present to your classmates.

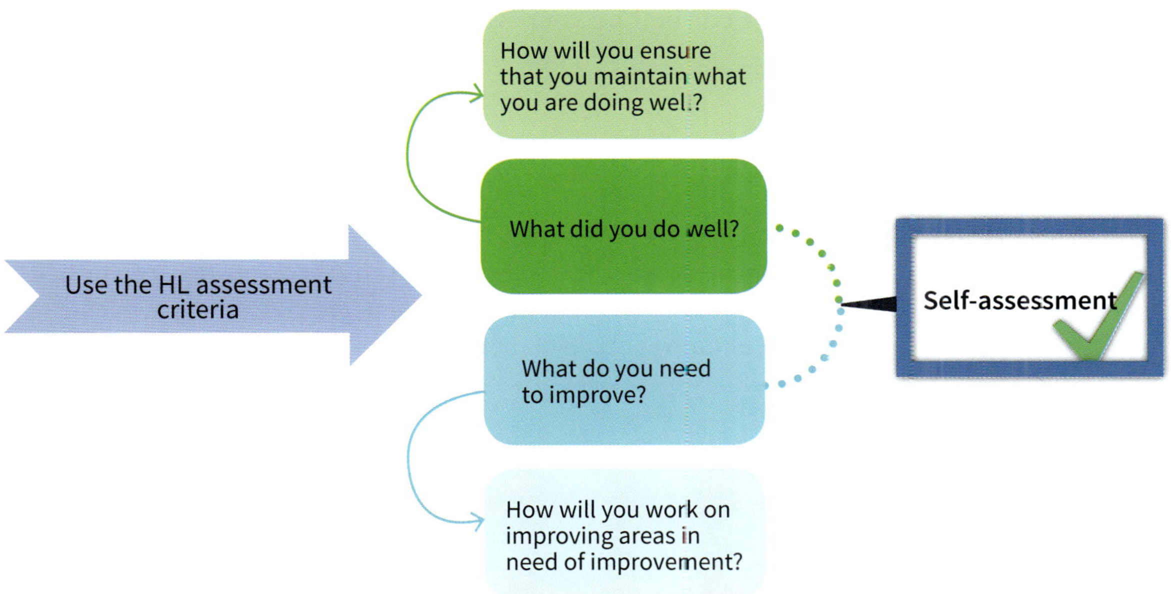

Paper 1 practice (HL and SL)

Proposal/ Speech

In this chapter, we have covered writing speeches and proposals. You are now invited to practice those two text types further.

Consider the following prompts.

1. You have innovative ideas regarding the learning of a foreign language and how it can be improved at your school by integrating information technology. You wish to introduce your ideas to the administration of the school.
2. You noticed that many of the international students at your school spend their break time alone because they find it difficult to communicate with others in English. You wish to inform your school community about this issue and suggest ways in which those students can be encouraged to communicate with their peers.

Speech **Proposal**

A. Which of the text types above best suits each prompt? Why? Justify your choice.
B. Choose one of the prompts above and practice your writing.

Listening comprehension

Click the icon to practice the listening section of Paper 2. After you have listened to an audio track you will complete an accompanying activity. In this exercise you will read a number of statements that may have been said by Paul or Cathy or both of them. You must identify who said what.

Conclusion to research question C

Having completed Section C of this chapter, reflect on the section's research question:

In what ways does belonging to a certain subculture define us, if at all?

In groups of four, discuss the following two questions:

- What have you learned so far?
- What do you still want to know?

Beyond the chapter

In this chapter, we examined how language may affect our identity or knowledge of self. However, this chapter is just the tip of the iceberg, for you may also wish to consider the following:

1. Nelson Mandela once said "If you talk to a man in a language he understands, that goes to his head. If you talk to him in his own language, that goes to his heart." To what extent do you think this should encourage people to learn foreign languages?
2. Does speaking a foreign language increase intellectuality? Examine this question in relation to Agatha Christie's famous fictional detective Poirot.
3. When writers self-translate their work, do they convey the same ideas in both languages? Think in terms of *The Prophet* by Jibran.

Conclusion to the chapter

Having completed the chapter, reflect on its research question:

How do language and culture contribute to form our identity?

In groups of four, discuss the following two questions:

- What have you learned so far?
- What do you still want to know?

A TOK moment

TOK

Hippy glossary

Hippies had to develop a whole new language to communicate their daily experiences for which there were no precedents. Many of the words passed around among hippies were from other cultures, particularly India. Karma, yoga, ashram, mantra were typical of the exotic words introduced into everyday speech in the '60s. If you're looking for a name, please go to the section on famous hippies.

- Be-In: One of the first gatherings of hippies, January 14, 1967 was at the Polo field in Golden Gate Park. It was called "A Gathering of the Tribes." In attendance were the Grateful Dead, the Jefferson Airplane, Timothy Leary, Allen Ginsberg, and thousands of hippies with painted faces, beads, bells, robes, etc. The Diggers were there giving out free food. There was no big reason to be there, other than to be there, hence a Be-In. An event where you groove on everyone else.
- Blast: A really great party or time. British origin? "We had a blast at the Stones concert!"
- Bread: Money. "Hey man, gotta any bread for the groceries?"
- Bummer: A bad thing.
- Cat: A male person who's hip. Beatnik term adopted by hippies.
- Cop out: Escape from responsibility. "Don't cop out when your bro is in need."
- Drag: Bummer, something definitely unenjoyable.
- Fad: A popular craze, a temporary fashion.
- Flaky: Someone unreliable, untrustworthy.
- Freak Flag: Long Hair
- Gig: A concert or a job. Something to do.
- Groovy!: Very pleasing, wonderful.
- Hip: Aware of what's going on. Knowledgeable. "I'm hip to what's happening." Something cool or groovy. "Those are the hippest love beads I've ever seen!"
- Hype: To promote something excessively. "This book sure hypes hippies!"
- Mellow out!: Calm down! Equal to chill out!
- Pigs: Derogatory name for police.
- Primo: First quality stuff. "Those buds were primo!"
- Put On: A joke on somebody. "Is that story real or are you just putting me on?"
- Rap: To have a friendly discussion.
- Rip Off: To steal, or have something stolen. "Someone ripped off my last lid!"
- Selling Out: To sacrifice one's counter-culture ideals for acceptance by society or material gain.
- Stoked: Totally happy about something.
- Tapped Out: Out of money. "I'd lend you the dough, but I'm all tapped out."
- Ticked Off: Also Teed-Off, Ticked... upset, angry.
- Totaled: Completely destroyed. "Bummer! I totaled my car, and I got no insurance!"

http://www.hipplanet.com/books/atoz/glossary.htm

1. Read the text above and reflect on your understanding of the hippy terms used.
2. Group those words into emotive, persuasive, and informative. Which of the three groups has the most amount of words? What does this indicate about evolution of the language used by subcultures?
3. Have any of those terms moved into mainstream English? Why do you think that is the case?
4. In groups of four, discuss the following questions:
   - To what extent does language affect emotion?
   - Is language biased?

Beyond the classroom

CAS

Experience 1

For your CAS project, you are thinking of teaching a foreign language to the less fortunate to improve their transferable skills and the likelihood of them getting better jobs in the future. As part of this project, you want to address your principal/mayor/town council president to convince them to support the project. Write your speech.

Reflect on the speech you have written: which of the CAS outcomes has writing the speech helped you achieve? How?

Experience 2

Design three greeting cards that demonstrate the importance of speaking a foreign language.

Reflect on the process of designing your greeting cards: which of the CAS outcomes has designing the cards helped you achieve? How?

Experience 3

As part of your CAS project, you want to improve language learning at your school. Propose a summer programme to your head of school in which you outline your aims and how they will be achieved.

Reflect on the process of writing your proposal: which of the CAS outcomes has writing the manifesto helped you achieve? How?

CAS learning outcomes

- LO1: Identify own strengths and develop areas for growth
- LO3: Demonstrate how to initiate and plan a CAS experience
- LO2: Demonstrate that challenges have been undertaken, developing new skills in the process
- LO4: Show commitment to and perseverance in CAS experiences
- LO5: Demonstrate the skills and recognize the benefits of working collaboratively
- LO6: Demonstrate engagement with issues of global significance
- LO7: Recognize and consider the ethics of choices and actions

Suggested reading list

- *The Joy Luck Club* by Amy Tan
- *A Clockwork Orange* by Anthony Burgess
- *Journeys* by Minfong Ho
- *The Outsiders* by S.E. Hinton
- *The Noughts and Crosses trilogy* by Malory Blackman
- *The Perks of Being A Wallflower* by Stephen Chbosky

Suggested films

- Captain Fantastic
- Peace, Love & Misunderstanding
- Lost in Translation
- A Borrowed Identity
- Brave

7 EXPERIENCES: FACING LIFE'S CHALLENGES

Chapter summary

Theme
Experiences

Topics
Life stories, rites of passage, customs and traditions

Conceptual understanding
Purpose

Research question for the chapter
Does our past shape our present and our future?

Additional research questions

A To what extent do historical events shape our life stories?
B To what extent do customs and traditions shape our present and future?
C To what extent are we shaped by the rites of passage we undergo on our journey from adolescence to adulthood?

TOK questions

- What ways of knowing do we employ to learn about the past?
- What are the functions of language and how do we use them to communicate about the past?

Communication skills

Listening skills

- Receptive
- Interactive

Oral and interactive skills
Debate

Written text type(s)

- Public commentary
- Editorial
- Letters to the editor

Research question for the chapter:

Does our past shape our present and our future?

1. What are your first thoughts and reactions to the question above?
2. What justifications would you give for your answer?
3. What more would you need to know before you can come to a definitive conclusion about the question?

Study the diagram below and discuss the research question in class. You may want to think about all the different influences that can affect you on your journey to adulthood.

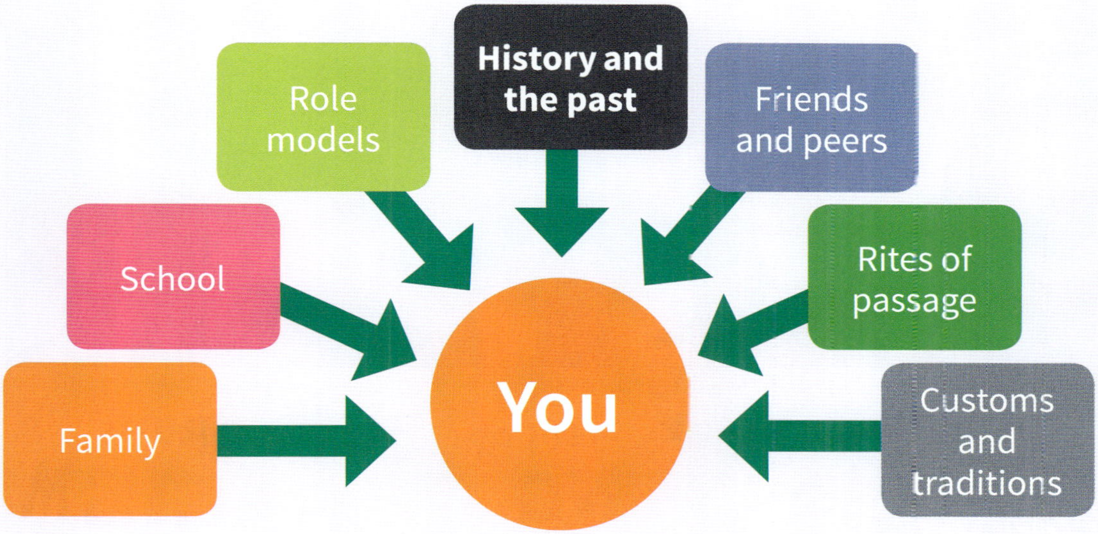

1. Are there any other influences which you want to add to this list?
2. Which of these influences are the most important?
3. Which of these influences are the least important?
4. Are there items on this list which are beyond our powers to control?

In this chapter you are going to examine some of these issues and have opportunities to debate them.

Section A: Life stories

Research question A:

To what extent do historical events shape our life stories?

1. What are your first thoughts and reactions to the question above?
2. What justifications would you give for your answers?
3. What more would you need to know before you can come to a definitive conclusion about the question?

Before you read

Look at the pictures of different protesters in the last 100 years.

1. In what historical context do you think each picture was taken?
2. In four groups discuss each of the pictures. What are the life stories of the people involved in each photograph? What has happened to make each group protest?
3. Do you see the protesters as people who should be admired and whose example should be followed? Or are they just troublemakers?
4. Are these protests still relevant today? Or are they just part of history?

Rosa Parks – A Great American Role Model

1. ______________________

Rosa Louise McCauley was born in Tuskegee, Alabama, on February 4, 1913. Rosa moved to Montgomery, Alabama, at age 11. She left school at 16, early in 11th grade, because she needed to care for her dying grandmother. In 1932, at 19, she married Raymond Parks, who worked as a barber and was a long-time member of the National Association for the Advancement of Colored People (NAACP).

2. ______________________

Raymond and Rosa became respected members of Montgomery's large African-American community. Co-existing with white people in a city governed by "Jim Crow" (segregation) laws, however, was fraught with daily frustrations: Black people could attend only inferior schools, could drink only from designated water fountains, could borrow books only from the "black" library, among other restrictions. In December 1943 Rosa also joined the Montgomery chapter of the NAACP, and she became their secretary. She worked closely with chapter president Edgar Daniel (E.D.) Nixon.

3. ______________________

On Thursday, December 1, 1955, the 42-year-old Rosa Parks was commuting from a long day of work by bus. Segregation was written into local law; the front of a Montgomery bus was reserved for white citizens, and the seats behind them for black citizens. However, it was only by custom that bus drivers had the authority to ask a black person to give up a seat for a white rider. At one point on the route, a white man had no seat because all the seats in the designated "white" section were taken. So the driver told the riders in the four seats of the first row of the "colored" section to stand, in effect adding another row to the "white" section. The three others obeyed. Parks did not.

4. ______________________

"People always say that I didn't give up my seat because I was tired," wrote Parks in her autobiography, "but that isn't true. I was not tired physically… No, the only tired I was, was tired of giving in." Eventually, two police officers approached the stopped bus and arrested Parks.

5. ______________________

Parks used her one phone call to contact her husband and word of her arrest spread quickly. E.D. Nixon was there when Parks was released on bail later that evening. Nixon had hoped for years to test the validity of segregation laws. He would use Rosa's trial to do this. Another idea arose as well: The black population of Montgomery would boycott the buses on the day of Parks' trial.

6. ______________________

On December 5, Parks was found guilty of violating segregation laws, given a suspended sentence and fined $10 plus $4 in court costs. Meanwhile, black participation in the boycott was much larger than even optimists in the community had anticipated. Nixon formed a committee to manage the boycott, and they elected Reverend Dr. Martin Luther King Jr.–new to Montgomery and just 26 years old–as the MIA's president.

7. ______________________

As appeals and related lawsuits went all the way up to the U.S. Supreme Court, the boycott engendered anger and aggression in much of Montgomery's white population and Nixon's and Dr. King's homes were bombed. The violence didn't deter the boycotters or their leaders, however, and the drama in Montgomery continued to gain attention from the national and international press.

8. ______________________

On November 13, 1956, the Supreme Court ruled that bus segregation was unconstitutional; the boycott ended December 20, a day after the Court's written order arrived in Montgomery. Parks—who had lost her job and experienced harassment all year—became known as "the mother of the civil rights movement."

Adapted from http://www.history.com/topics/black-history/rosa-parks

Reading comprehension

In the text the section headings 1 to 8 are missing. Choose the correct heading from the list below for each paragraph.

A. An Explanation
B. Segregation
C. The Verdict and Aftermath
D. The Bus Ride
E. Early Life
F. The Judgment
G. Education
H. Solidarity with Rosa
I. Gaol Time
J. The Roots of Activism
K. A Violent Reaction
L. Rosa and Martin Luther King

Find words or phrases in Paragraphs 2 and 3 that correspond to the phrases 9 to 12 .

9. made complicated by
10. specific
11. traveling home
12. set aside

13. ***Reread Paragraph 4. From statements a to f, select the four that are true. Write the appropriate letters in the boxes provided.***

A. Rosa phoned E.D. Nixon in order to raise enough money to get out of jail.

B. E.D. Nixon wanted Rosa's help to fight for justice because she was an excellent role model for the civil rights movement.

C. Nixon's plan was to use Rosa's case to fight the segregation laws.

D. At the same time the black population of Montgomery started a successful campaign to avoid using the buses.

E. Rosa was found guilty because of her bus protests.

F. Martin Luther King formed the Montgomery Improvement Association and became its president.

G. The homes of Nixon and King were destroyed in fire-bombings.

H. The U.S. Supreme Court supported the verdict of the Montgomery courts.

I. Rosa Parks became a role model for the followers of the civil rights movement.

Thinking skills (ATLs)

Now that you have completed the reading exercises, think again about the research question for this section: *To what extent do historical events shape our life stories?* What conclusions do you come to?

Why did Rosa Parks refuse to move seats?

Was it because …

a. she was tired at that moment
b. she wanted to change the world
c. she was influenced by the past
d. history dictated the moment
e. all or some of these answers?

Give your opinion and justify it. In class discuss which recent historical events may shape your own life stories. What conclusions do you come to?

HL extension (HL)

Imagine you are Rosa Parks speaking to a reporter. Retell the story of your bus ride home and your arrest. Also explain what happened as a result of your arrest. Write between 100 and 150 words.

Research and communication skills (ATLs)

Look at the technical legal vocabulary and work out the meanings of any vocabulary you do not know.

appeal	bail	guilty	lawsuit
plaintiff	rule	Supreme Court	suspended sentence
unconstitutional	validity	violation	written order

Using all the vocabulary in the list above write a chronological summary of the legal process which explains why the Rosa Parks case was central to the civil rights movement.

Oral activity: debate

Can one person change the world?

Think about Rosa Parks' part in the story of the civil rights movement in the USA. There are at least two ways of viewing her story.

- Rosa Parks made history.
- History made Rosa Parks.

Here are some points in support of both sides of the argument.

It is possible for one person to change the world. Example: Rosa Parks made history.	**One person alone can never change the world. Example: History made Rosa Parks.**
• We have witnessed in many cultures and throughout history that it only takes one person to initiate change. • Religious and political leaders, writers and philosophers have ideas that can change the way we think. • Individuals such as scientists and technologists can change the world. It is through their innovations that global developments occur. • One individual can be a role model and inspiration for millions.	• Nelson Mandela and Gandhi were not alone. The people were behind them and were part of a much larger movement. • Politicians need an army to change things. • In this world there is too much corruption for things to change. • The rich have more money than some countries spend on the welfare of their people. So how can an individual change the world?

Conducting the debate

Appoint a moderator and create two teams of four or five, one to support each side of the argument. All members of the team should work on the opening speeches. Two people from each team should deliver the first two speeches.

All other students, whether they are in a team or not, should prepare a one-minute speech reflecting their own views on the subject. Remember to think about how the case of Rosa Parks relates to these two arguments.

Hold the debate and, at the end, take a vote.

Listening comprehension

Click the icon to practice the listening section of Paper 2. After you have listened to an audio track you will complete an accompanying activity. In this gap-filling exercise, you will find a list of twelve nouns. There are only six gaps. Choose the correct noun to fit each gap.

Research skills — ATLs

- Each team should undertake further research on the subject of Rosa Parks.
- Each team should undertake research on the question, "Do individuals make history or do the forces of history turn individuals into symbols of a political or social movement?" Each team should do their own research on other figures who have played an important role in major historical events.

Internal assessment (SL)

Take a look at the visual stimulus. The image relates to the theme of the chapter, "Experiences".

Brainstorming

In pairs, discuss and answer the following questions.

- What is the main idea in the photograph? How does it relate to the title of the section, "Life stories".
- What do you see in the background of the photograph? What does the background tell you about the location and context of the photograph? What does it convey about an English-speaking community?
- Look at the foreground of the photograph. Describe the person or people you can see.
- What is happening in the picture? How does the action relate to the theme of the chapter, "Experiences"?

Presenting

Based on your answers to the questions above, prepare a four-minute presentation on the photograph.

Remember that the presentation should not only include description of the photograph, but connect to the topic of role models in an Anglophone culture. Present your photograph and topic to your classmates.

Peer assessment

In small groups, assess the presentations given by your classmates. You may use the rubrics below as a basis for your comments.

	Good	Improvement possible	Needs some improvement	Needs a lot of improvement
Eye contact	Makes good eye contact with audience.	Makes eye contact with the audience most of the time.	Sometimes makes eye contact with the audience.	Does not make eye contact with the audience.
Enthusiasm	Shows great enthusiasm for the topic.	Shows enthusiasm for the topic.	Shows some enthusiasm for the topic.	Shows little enthusiasm for the topic.
Preparation and organization	Very prepared and well organized.	Mostly prepared and well organized.	Somewhat prepared and organized.	Not very prepared or organized.
Clear speech	Speaks very clearly and is very easy to understand.	Speaks clearly most of the time and is fairly easy to understand.	Sometimes speaks clearly and is sometimes easy to understand.	Does not speak clearly and is quite difficult to understand.
Knowledge of topic	Shows excellent understanding of the topic.	Shows good understanding of the topic.	Shows some understanding of the topic.	Shows little understanding of the topic.

Internal assessment (HL)

I Have a Dream, Martin Luther King

On 28 August 1963, on the steps of the Lincoln Memorial, before 200,000 people, Martin Luther King Jr, gave his famous "I have a dream" speech during The March on Washington for Jobs and Freedom. In his speech Martin Luther King called for an end to racism in the United States and called for civil and economic rights for all African Americans. All the television networks covered the event live so in his speech King was able to address the whole country. This moment would become a turning point in the history of the USA.

And so even though we face the difficulties of today and tomorrow, I still have a dream. It is a dream deeply rooted in the American dream.

I have a dream that one day this nation will rise up and live out the true meaning of its creed: "We hold these truths to be self-evident, that all men are created equal."

I have a dream that one day on the red hills of Georgia, the sons of former slaves and the sons of former slave owners will be able to sit down together at the table of brotherhood.

I have a dream that one day even the state of Mississippi, a state sweltering with the heat of injustice, sweltering with the heat of oppression, will be transformed into an oasis of freedom and justice.

I have a dream that my four little children will one day live in a nation where they will not be judged by the color of their skin but by the content of their character.

I have a dream today!

I have a dream that one day, down in Alabama, with its vicious racists, with its governor having his lips dripping with the words of "interposition" and "nullification" – one day right there in Alabama little black boys and black girls will be able to join hands with little white boys and white girls as sisters and brothers.

I have a dream today!

I have a dream that one day every valley shall be exalted, and every hill and mountain shall be made low, the rough places will be made plain, and the crooked places will be made straight; "and the glory of the Lord shall be revealed and all flesh shall see it together."

This is our hope, and this is the faith that I go back to the South with.

With this faith, we will be able to hew out of the mountain of despair a stone of hope. With this faith, we will be able to transform the jangling discords of our nation into a beautiful symphony of brotherhood. With this faith, we will be able to work together, to pray together, to struggle together, to go to jail together, to stand up for freedom together, knowing that we will be free one day.

And this will be the day – this will be the day when all of God's children will be able to sing with new meaning:

My country 'tis of thee, sweet land of liberty, of thee I sing.

Land where my fathers died, land of the Pilgrim's pride,

From every mountainside, let freedom ring!

Peer assessment

Assess the presentations given by your classmates. Consider the HL IA criteria as a guide in your assessment.

	IA (HL)
Criterion A	Language
Criterion B	1. Message: literary extract 2. Message: conversation
Criterion C	Interactive skills: communication

Suggest ways in which your classmates can improve their presentation techniques.

Brainstorming

In small groups, discuss the following questions then summarize your discussion in point form.

- What is the topic of the speech?
- What techniques does the speaker use to communicate his message so effectively?
- If you had been in the crowd when the speech was made, what emotions might you have felt? Explain your answer.
- On the evidence of the text, why do you think Martin Luther King was able to change the course of history?

Presenting

Based on your answers to the questions above, prepare a four-minute presentation on the content of the text.

Make your presentation to your classmates. Students listening to the presentation should prepare individual questions about the text which they can ask you at the end of your presentation.

Paper 1: Editorials

Editorials are mass media texts. They express the view of the senior leadership of a newspaper. They are unsigned and are the voice of the news organization. Editorials can offer an opinion or present a collective point of view on some topical subject. They can explore a whole range of newsworthy issues, events and ideas. They can inform, entertain or persuade.

Editorials are designed to stimulate public debate, and readers are invited to send letters to the editor in order to comment on the topic. Such letters may be printed in the newspaper.

Structure

Like any form of persuasive writing, an editorial has specific characteristics that help the readers follow the writer's reasoning. While content may vary, an editorial should always include a headline, introductory paragraph, a main body consisting of supporting paragraphs and a conclusion.

Headline: The headline grabs the readers' attention and persuades them to read the piece. If the headline is neither interesting nor relevant, no one will read the text.

Introductory paragraph: The purpose of the introduction is to capture the attention of the readers and make them want to read further. The introduction may also explain the context and background to the topic being discussed.

Communication skills ATLs

Kickers

Journalists often use an attention grabber (sometimes referred to as a "kicker").

- This "kicker" may be a provocative rhetorical question about a topical issue: "Do you really need a university degree?"
- An introductory paragraph can begin with a dramatic moment in a news story: "Yesterday the Supreme Court ruled that bus segregation was unconstitutional."
- Sometimes the editor will use a quote to start.
- Alternatively, the "kicker" could be a striking fact or statement, "Rosa Parks, the Alabama seamstress considered the one-woman catalyst for the civil rights movement, died in much the same way she changed the world: quietly."

Why do you think this device is called a "kicker"?

Practice writing "kickers" in all your essays. It can make your writing much more vivid and readable.

The introduction will also contain the main idea or thesis that the writer wishes to explore. Now look at these three examples of opening paragraphs. How does the editor begin each one? What techniques does the writer use to grab the reader's attention? What is the main idea/thesis of each editorial?

Example A

Young or old, it pays to stay active. Take what enjoyment you can from life and help your fellows. Just ask 8-year-old Liam Green, a Cub Scout with Shelburne Falls Cub Scout Pack 85, and his two buddies, Ray Dyer and Grayson Bishop.

Or if you don't believe them, because you think they are too young to know about such things, then ask 99-year-old Dorothy Wright of Greenfield. They may not seem to have a lot in common, but they agree about this.

The Recorder, Vermont, USA

Example B

In the late 1960s, Virginia Slims cigarette advertising told women, "You've come a long way, baby." Women have come even further since then, but equality remains elusive.

A program at Valparaiso University last week examined the role of female stereotypes in the media—especially advertising, movies and television—in depriving girls of the positive role models they need to help finally attain equality.

North West Times, Indiana, USA

Example C

TEACHERS play a critical role in our state, helping to shape the minds of our children and assist them to reach their full potential.

They deserve all the appropriate resources and protection required for the mission of inspiring a love for learning. But they aren't the most important influence in a child's life.

That role falls to parents, who must provide their children with the basic tools and support needed to become moral and productive citizens. Parents must ensure their children arrive at school with a foundation teachers can build on.

The Advertiser, South Australia

The main body and supporting paragraphs: The middle section consists of a number of paragraphs that expand the main topic of the article into subtopics. The paragraphs should link with your angle and in fact prove your point of view. There are different structures you can use for this.

- A "one-sided" approach: Each section of the feature emphasizes a single point to support your angle. For example, your angle might be, "X is a great but vulnerable character". Make sure to give examples for each point you make. This is similar to a thesis-driven text.
- A "balanced" approach: There are two sides to the issue or problem. Give both sides of the argument with supporting evidence.

Conclusion: A conclusion should tie everything together and sum up the editorial. The concluding paragraph should leave a lasting impression by:

- reminding the reader of the article's main idea; you can return to your question/statement at the start of the editorial
- suggesting an appropriate course of action or making a recommendation
- if writing about a person, explaining that person's future plans.

You can save an unexpected piece of information until the last paragraph.

Tone and style: If you choose to write an editorial, you must consider the relationship between you, as the writer and expert opinion, and your readership. You therefore need to use appropriate vocabulary and register. Now read the editorial below and then comment on its effectiveness using the chart on the following page.

Remember Rosa Parks on the 60th anniversary of the Montgomery bus boycott: editorial

Editorial Board
December 03, 2015

The 60th anniversary this week of Rosa Parks' historic refusal to give up her seat and move to the back of a bus is an opportunity to honor a dedicated activist who helped break the grip of racial segregation.

The ensuing 381-day bus boycott against Montgomery, Alabama's segregated city bus system would also usher a little-known minister, the Rev. Martin Luther King Jr., onto the national stage.

When she was arrested, Parks, then 42, was described as a mild-mannered seamstress. But she was more than that. Parks and her husband, Raymond Parks were leaders in the Montgomery National Association for the Advancement of Colored People and long had been active in trying to get Alabama to treat black people fairly.

And she was quite a fighter. On some earlier occasions, Parks had refused to follow the directions of white bus drivers to pay at the front of the bus and board in the back where blacks were supposed to sit. And she had at least one previous run-in with the same bus driver, James Blake, who had her arrested Dec. 1, 1955 for failing to give up her seat to a white man.

Parks has been quoted as saying that she was too tired to relinquish her seat, but she later said that it was more than just that -- her very soul was tired.

"I was not tired physically, or no more tired than I usually was at the end of a working day ... No, the only tired I was, was tired of giving in," she wrote in her autobiography, "Rosa Parks: My Story."

Her brave stance would lead to a U.S. Supreme Court decision to ban segregation on public transportation, but Parks paid a heavy price for demanding equal treatment. She and her husband lost their jobs and they were forced to move to Detroit.

All this week, cities across America will honor Parks who died in 2005 at the age of 92.

But the best way to honor her is to continue to do the work she made part of her life: Bring equal justice to all, including those killed in our cities' streets or in encounters with police, protect the right to vote and treat all people fairly. Parks worked for nothing less.

Analyzing an editorial	
Structure of the editorial	How effective and clear is the headline?
Introduction	How does the introduction capture the attention of the readers? How does it make them want to read further?
The main body	Does the editorial take a one-sided or a balanced approach to the subject matter? Give evidence. How are the paragraphs organized?
Conclusion	What conclusion does the editorial reach?
Language	Comment on the tone and style of the editorial. Is the language appropriate to subject matter and the readership? Give evidence.

Writing activity: editorials

Here are three opportunities to practice writing editorials.

Plan, draft, revise and redraft one of these stimuli.

1. You have been asked to write an editorial for your school magazine to celebrate International Human Rights Day. Using the information in the texts above, write your editorial explaining the significance of either Rosa Parks or Martin Luther King as a person who was able to change human history.
2. Using the texts and exercises in this section, write an editorial for a teenage magazine entitled "Are yesterday's role models still relevant today?"
3. What real life challenges do students face in your school? Imagine you are the editor of your school newspaper. Write an editorial about one of the major challenges faced by students. Identify the cause of the problem and offer a solution.

You may wish to watch the video entitled The Rosa Parks Legacy available at https://www.youtube.com/watch?v=cNzQW_lwOko.

Alternatively, use your own research material.

Exam tip

At standard level you should write between 250 and 400 words.

At higher level you should write between 450 and 600 words.

Conclusion to research question A

To what extent do historical events shape our life stories?

1. Now that you have completed this section what are your conclusions and reactions to the question above? What useful lessons about life have you learned from this section?
2. What justifications would you give for your answers?
3. What more would you need to know before you can come to a definitive conclusion about the research question?

A TOK moment

What ways of knowing do we employ to learn about the past? In your opinion, which are the most reliable ways of knowing about the past? Which ways of knowing are the least reliable? Justify your answers.

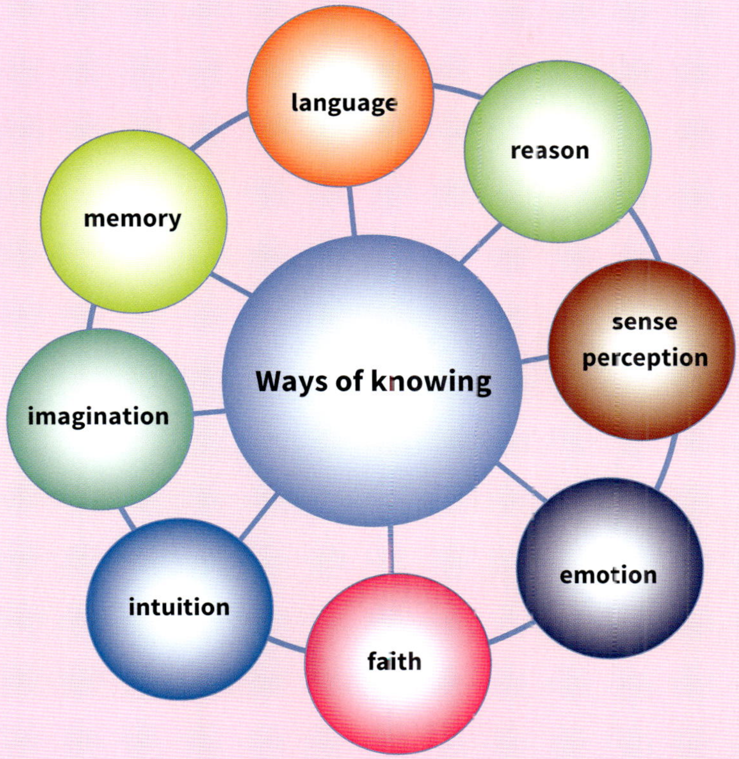

Our research question for this section is "To what extent do historical events shape our life stories?" However, this raises another question, "How do we know what happened in the past?"

Consider the story of Rosa Parks. How do we know whether her story, as reported in the text, is true or not?

In a time when "fake news" is an increasing and alarming development, the ability to tell truth from lies and "alternative facts" is an essential skill. Look at the TOK ways of knowing in the diagram. Decide which are the most important to help you to know whether the information in the article you read earlier in this section is trustworthy or not.

Once you have completed this exercise, repeat it by looking at a contemporary news article in which the truth or the facts are disputed. Don't believe every word of what you read. Research multiple sources to ensure that the news is indeed true.

Section B: Customs and traditions

Research question B:

To what extent do customs and traditions shape our present and future?

1. What are your first thoughts and reactions to the question above?
2. What justifications would you give for your answers?
3. What more would you need to know before you can come to a more definitive conclusion about the statement?

Before you read

Study the poster and read the quotations.

"Uniforms may work for police officers, soldiers and neo-nationalists, but they have no place in schools. Kids should wear what they want, their schools should let them – and then everyone could get on with some actual learning." Emma Jacobs, student

"There is a huge opportunity for (members of the armed forces) who have served their country in uniform to serve their country in our schools. They have many of the virtues that parents across the country feel have disappeared from our schools and need to be restored: self-discipline, a sense of purpose and a belief in the importance of working as a team." Michael Gove, former UK Secretary of State for Education

1. On the topic of uniforms and dress codes, which speaker do you think is right?
2. What is the relationship between school uniform and a school's customs and traditions?
3. Can it ever be right to protest against the customs and traditions of a school?

Justify your opinions.

Zulaikha Patel: How we all wish we were you

Azad Essa

During her school's weekend fair, a 13-year-old South African student, Zulaikha Patel, and her fellow classmates staged a silent protest against their school's hair policy, which targeted and restricted how black girls wear their hair to school.
The following opinion piece from a South African newspaper praises the girl's actions and claims that she should be a role model for all young people.

I don't think I have ever seen anything quite like it.

The little girl – now known to all as Zulaikha Patel – standing with her fellow students in front of a row of three white males, refusing to back down, calling on them to follow through with their threats to arrest them – all because of their hair.

"Take us all," she said, for half a dozen girls at the school. "They want to take us to prison … take us all."

It was an act of extraordinary courage that left us tingling. Who were these brave girls and how had they shown such resilience in the face of authority?

I watched the video on a loop on Instagram. I didn't dare to blink.

She protested unconcerned about "her career" or "that promotion"; undaunted by future mortgage payments and outstanding car loans.

She is a free spirit, asking only for the right to be herself.

For Zulaikha – her resolve was as natural as the curls on her head. It was earnest, determined and uncomplicated.

In the photo we see her standing tall with steely eyes, arms outstretched and fists folded above her irresistible afro in a defiance of an antiquated, warped and racist policy. It will be studied for years to come.

We learnt later that Zulaikha had been previously put in detention for her hair. That she had to leave three schools because her hair challenged the system. Her sister said she was continually mocked, her hair described as "exotic" and looking like a "cabbage". She would come home in tears. It is remarkable then that she didn't look to mend the "problem".

I know I would have.

Many of us have changed our behaviour, assimilated, changed the way we speak so we fit in, or have avoided drawing attention to ourselves. And if we protest, our interest in taking on prejudice will be decided after a cost-benefit assessment: based on time and place, potential to win and lose, and current energy levels.

We are all in awe of Zulaikha, because we wish to hell we could have all been her growing up. We wish we could be her, as a grown up.

While so many of us were trying as children, and then as adults, to make the world work for us, we forgot that world already belonged to each and every one of us. We've been left so insecure and desperate to "make it", we've been wired to forgo anything, including ourselves.

I wondered after watching the clip another five times: what if there hadn't been a video to record the sublime protest initiated by the girls of the school? The reported narrative would have never gone viral. It would not have brought the school to its knees, its policies into the spotlight. It might not have brought politicians and policymakers into the discussion. Zulaikha might have found herself immediately suspended, or expelled, maybe jailed. It might have all been in vain.

We don't know, as per her sister's admission, how all of this attention will impact on Zulaikha. She is just a 13-year-old after all, acting on her own accord. And this is not a fight she was ever meant to fight.

But she has provided a most memorable lesson.

Justice, it turns out, simply needs people to speak out against injustice.

And it's apt, that it would take a child to make us remember that.

Reading comprehension

Identify whether the sentences below are true or false and justify your answer with a relevant brief quotation from the text.

> **Exam tip: True/false with justification**
>
> When deciding whether a statement is true or false, remember that the justification you give has to be an **exact quote** from the text!

		True	False
1.	The writer has frequently seen similar acts of protest and defiance.		
Justification:			
2.	Zulaikha was one of several protesters.		
Justification:			
3.	The girls were refusing to obey the school's uniform code.		
Justification:			
4.	The protesters believed that they could be sent to jail for their demonstration at school.		
Justification:			
5.	The writer knew the girls personally.		
Justification:			
6.	Zulaikha was also protesting to improve her future job prospects.		
Justification:			
7.	The protesters were demanding the right to their own identity.		
Justification:			
8.	The writer believes the protest will not leave a lasting impression on viewers.		
Justification:			

Answers these questions.

9. Name two ways that Zulaikha had been punished for her hair in her previous schools.

10. Which phrase between lines 15 and 26 shows that Zulaikha was determined not to change her appearance?

Choose the correct answer from A, B, C or D.

11. The writer's generation did not protest against racism because they wanted to …

A. get the approval of their peers and employers
B. acquire a more socially acceptable accent
C. draw much more attention to themselves
D. put their personal interests first.

12 The writer thinks the teenage protesters should be …

A. role models for their own generation
B. role models for the next generation
C. role models for her own generation
D. role models for everyone.

13. The writer believes her generation has fought against prejudice …

A. too much
B. as much as possible
C. when it suited them
D. when they were forced to.

14. The writer believes social media …

A. increased opposition to the protest
B. made little impact on the protest
C. forced the school to change its policies
D. made a huge impact on the public.

15. The writer says the protesters have …

A. been successful in changing school policies
B. made little impact on school policies
C. harmed their own futures
D. created a public debate on school policies.

16. The writer believes that Zulaikha …

A. will adapt her ideas to the school ethos
B. faces an uncertain future
C. will become a celebrity in the future
D. will have a great academic future.

17. Which sentence best summarizes the writer's final thought on the protest?

A. And this is not a fight she was ever meant to fight.
B. But she has provided a most memorable lesson.
C. Justice, it turns out, simply needs people to speak out against injustice.
D. And it's apt, that it would take a child to make us remember that.

Research and thinking skills (ATLs)

Do you think women like these anti-Apartheid demonstrators from an earlier generation of South Africans were role models for Zulaikha Patel and her friends? Do you think Zulaikha Patel was influenced by the customs and traditions of protest in South Africa?

To what extent is it right to protest against customs and traditions that oppress certain groups within society?

HL extension (HL)

Imagine you are one one of the protesting schoolgirls. Tell the story of your school protest from your point of view. Explain the background to the protest. Describe the events on the day of the protest. Analyze the effectiveness of the protest.

Oral activity: Debating

In education there are two distinct camps. Both groups believe that schools have a huge influence on the lives of their students.

- One group of educators, parents, and students are in favour of schools with strict customs and traditions, and codes of behaviour. They believe that students become better adults by learning to follow traditional sets of values and rules, and thereby developing self-discipline.
- Liberal critics oppose very strict schools with their formal uniforms and authoritarian ethos. They believe that students need to operate in a school with a non-traditional ethos. In such a learning environment students can learn how to take responsibility for their own decisions.

The arguments about dress codes of both groups are summarized below.

Authoritarian ethos	Liberal ethos
1. Schools, like society in general, must have rules in order to function.	1. School rules interfere with self-expression. Students should be free to express their own sense of identity.
2. Students need to dress and behave in ways appropriate to the culture in which they live.	2. School rules can be arbitrary and undemocratic. Teachers have no right to decide what is "appropriate" clothing or appearance.
3. Schools want their students to appear tidy and behave well.	3. Schools should not favour one set of cultural values over another.
4. Schools do not want their students to wear clothes with inappropriate or offensive language or insignia (such as gang colours).	4. Schools should promote a multicultural sense of identity or school spirit.
5. It is easier to have strict rules and dress codes uniform in order to enforce what students can and can't do.	5. The wearing of school uniforms may give students the message that conformity is a way to prevent conflict.
6. School uniforms helps to create a united school spirit.	6. Uniforms are associated with the military and the police and schools should not be seen in the same light.
7. If everyone's uniform is identical intruders and outsiders can be more readily identified and students on field trips are more easily spotted.	7. Students need to learn to think, not just obey.
8. Dress codes help students to realize people's talents are not defined by their outward appearance.	8. The whole concept of wearing school uniform is now outdated.
9. Peer pressure can lead families and students to spend money that they cannot afford on fashionable clothes and accessories.	9. Uniforms are expensive. They need replacing as students grow. The uniform is frequently only available from an expensive school shop rather than from inexpensive retailers.
10. The wearing of a school uniform prevents the formation of cliques defined by their clothes and appearance.	10. Students can be bullied because their school uniform identifies them as being from a "rival" school.

The statement for debate is: "We believe that schools have the authority to impose a dress code on their students."

Conducting the debate

Appoint a moderator and create two teams of four or five, one to support each supporting side of the argument.

All members of the team should work on the opening speeches. Two people from each team should deliver the first two speeches.

All other students, whether they are in a team or not, should prepare a one-minute speech reflecting their own views on the subject.

How does the case of the South African schoolgirls relate to these two arguments?

Hold the debate and, at the end, take a vote.

Internal assessment (SL)

Take a look at the visual stimulus below. The image relates to the theme of the chapter: "Experiences".

Brainstorming

In pairs, discuss and answer the following questions.

- What is the main idea in the photograph? How does it relate to the title of the section, "Customs and traditions"?
- What do you see in background of the photograph? What does the background tell you about the location and context of the photograph?
- Look at the foreground of photograph. Describe the person or people you can see.
- What is happening in the picture? How does the content relate to the theme of the chapter, "Experiences"?

Presenting

Based on your answers to the questions above, prepare a four-minute presentation on the photograph.

Remember that the presentation should not only include description of the photograph, but should also connect to the topic of role models in an English-speaking society. Present your photograph and topic to your classmates.

Peer assessment

Assess the presentations given by your classmates. Use the SL IA criteria to guide your assessment:

	Internal assessment (SL)
Criterion A	Language
Criterion B	1. Message: visual stimulus 2. Message: conversation
Criterion C	Interactive skills: communication

Suggest ways your classmates can improve their presentation techniques.

Internal assessment (HL)

Speak

by Laurie Halse Anderson

The summer before her freshman year of high school, the narrator, 15-year-old Melinda Sordino is raped at a party. Melinda calls the police but does not know what to say and runs home. The police break up the party and arrest some students. Melinda does not tell anyone what happened to her. Consequently, when she starts at Merryweather High School, her peers refuse to speak to her. Melinda stays silent and sinks into depression.

As Melinda's depression deepens, she begins to withdraw from her parents and other authority figures, particularly an unsympathetic social studies teacher that Melinda calls "Mr Neck". He sees her silence as merely a means of getting attention and he is determined to get Melinda to speak in class. In spite of her difficulties, Melinda has befriended her lab partner, David Petrakis, who encourages her to find alternative ways to protest against her treatment.

NO JUSTICE, NO PEACE

There is no way I'm reading my suffragette report in front of the class. That wasn't part of the original assignment. Mr Neck changed it at the very last second because he wants to flunk me or hates something, or me. But I've written a really good report and I'm not going to let an idiot teacher jerk me around like this.

I ask David Petrakis for advice. We come up with a Plan. I get to class early, when Mr Neck is still in the lounge. I write what I need to on the board and cover the words with a suffragette protest sign. My box from the copy shop[1] is on the floor.

Mr Neck walks in. He grumbles that I can go first. I stand suffragette tall and calm. It is a lie. My insides feel like I'm caught in a tornado. My toes curl inside my sneakers, trying to grip the floor so I won't get sucked out the window.

Mr Neck nods at me. I pick up my report as if I'm going to read it out loud. I stand there, papers trembling as if a breeze is blowing through the closed door. I turn around and rip my poster off the blackboard.

THE SUFFRAGETTES FOUGHT FOR THE RIGHT TO SPEAK. THEY WERE ATTACKED, ARRESTED, AND THROWN IN JAIL FOR DARING TO DO WHAT THEY WANTED. LIKE THEY WERE, I AM WILLING TO STAND UP FOR WHAT I BELIEVE NO ONE SHOULD BE FORCED TO GIVE SPEECHES. I CHOOSE TO STAY SILENT.

The class reads slowly, some of them moving their lips. Mr Neck turns around to see what everyone is staring at. I nod at David. He joins me at the front of the room and I hand him my box.

David: "Melinda has to deliver her report to the class as part of the assignment. She made copies everyone can read." He passes out the copies. They cost me $6.72 at the office-supply store. I was going to make a cover page and color it, but I haven't gotten much allowance recently, so I just put the title at the top of the first page.

My plan is to stand in front of the class for the five minutes I was given for my presentation. The suffragettes must have planned out and timed their protests, too. Mr Neck has other plans. He gives me a D and escorts me to the authorities.

I forgot about how the suffragettes were hauled off to jail. Duh. I go on a tour of the guidance counselor's office, Principal Principal's, and wind up back in MISS[2]. I am back to being a Discipline Problem again.

I need a lawyer. I showed up every day this semester, sat my butt in every class, did some homework, and didn't cheat on tests. I still get slammed in MISS. There is no way they can punish me for not speaking. It isn't fair. What do they know about me?

1 photocopy shop
2 detention

Brainstorming

In small groups, discuss the following questions then summarize your discussion in point form.

- Explain in detail Melinda's task, her problem with it and her plan to solve her dilemma.
- How do Melinda's problems relate to the suffragettes whose protests she is presenting?
- Is the teacher being fair to Melinda? Is he a good role model for his students? Justify your answers.
- What appears to be the school's ethos when dealing with students like Melinda?
- By the end of the passage how much do we sympathize with Melinda?

Note

In your internal assessment, the literary extract will not exceed 300 words. You will be shown two, one from each of the works of literature studied in class.

Presenting

Based on your answers to the questions above, prepare a four-minute presentation on the photograph.

Make your presentation to your classmates. Students listening to the presentation should prepare individual questions about the text which they can ask you at the end of your presentation.

Peer assessment

Assess the presentations given by your classmates using the HL IA assessment criteria in the Language B guide.

Suggest ways your classmates can improve their presentation techniques.

Paper 1: Letters to the editor

If you feel strongly about an issue in a newspaper, and you want to let the public know what you think, writing a letter to the editor can be an effective way to communicate your ideas to a wider public. In your letter you may wish to take a position for or against an issue, or suggest a new way of thinking.

The reason for writing a letter is to make a clear impression and have the reader take note of your ideas. You need to be able to express an opinion, to defend an argument, or to increase awareness of an issue. You may try to convince readers by using emotion, reason, or a combination of the two.

Letters to the editor are usually short and tight, rarely longer than 450 words. Therefore you will have to communicate your ideas in a clearly organized manner. This will need planning.

Structure

Salutation: Begin with the addressee's title above the salutation line. For example:

The Editor
The Daily Newspaper,

Dear Editor,

Opening paragraph: Identify the article or the issue you wish to discuss. State your opinion on the matter.

Middle paragraphs: Support your opinion with a series of supporting points. Explain what will happen if something isn't done to solve the problem.

Closing paragraph: Make a closing remark (a clincher) to summarize your point of view. Explain why your approach or solution is relevant. Simply end with "Yours faithfully,"

Style and language

It has been said that any formal letter is like a wedding: there are certain conventions that have to be followed. One set of conventions relate to form and layout. The other relates to language and register. Study the table below.

The conventions of formal letter writing	Required	Not acceptable
Form and layout	• Addresses • Date • A formal greeting • A polite and formal close • Signing off with your name	• Smileys
Language and register	• Grammatical accuracy • Correct spelling • Unemotional and factual • A polite tone • Correct punctuation • Paragraphing • Formal vocabulary and phrasing	• Exaggeration • Informal language • Contractions • Idiomatic language • Abbreviations • SMS spellings • Deliberate misspellings/slang e.g. "gonna" • Swearing

Now read the letter to the editor below and then, using the information in the chart on the previous page, comment on its effectiveness.

The Editor,
Anytown News

Dear Sir or Madam,

I have to agree with your editorial on June 15th. The majority rules and, in my opinion, a vote of seventy-eight percent in favour of uniforms at Anytown High School is more than enough to implement a formal dress code in our schools. Those who don't like it should stop moaning and accept the result.

Personally I'm all for uniforms, at least in the high school. Unlike the school's present unworkable voluntary policy, a uniform is a clear, coherent rule, easy to follow and to enforce.

Moreover, I would ask whether the people against uniforms have seen how some of the high school students dress!!!!! Like you, I also believe the move from a formal dress code at school to an informal "come as you like" attitude has had a rotten impact on the youngsters in our town where job opportunities are scarce ;-(. For many children wearing school uniform is the only time in life where they learn values. They certainly don't learn them at home!

I admit that I too sometimes rebelled against the school dress code in my last years at school. However, over the years, I have seen the need to dress for an occasion, whether for a job interview, a professional meeting or just to go out to dinner.

Additionally I would like to point out that, for many local families, the price of regular teenage clothes is unaffordable these days, and uniforms, especially at my shop in the Lower Arcade, are so much cheaper.

Yours etc.
Anne Other (Mrs.)

When you have finished your analysis, write a reply to the letter giving your own views on the subject. Use the techniques for writing a letter to an editor that you have learned in this section.

Which of these formal features does the writer use correctly?

- Addresses
- Date
- A formal greeting
- A polite and formal close
- Signing off with a full name

Comment on the writers use of language and register.

- Grammatical accuracy
- Correct spelling
- Unemotional and factual content
- A polite tone
- Correct punctuation
- Paragraphing
- Formal vocabulary and phrasing

Does the writer use any of these techniques which are inappropriate for a formal letter?

- Emoticons
- Exaggeration
- Informal language
- Contractions
- Idiomatic language
- Abbreviations
- SMS spellings
- Deliberate misspellings/ slang, e.g. "gonna"
- Swearing

Overall, on a scale of 1–10 how successful is the letter to the editor?

Suggest improvements to the form and content of the letter so that it is more appropriate for its purpose.

Exam tip: Rewriting

Some students believe that rewriting anything is a waste of time and effort. This is simply not true. Always be prepared to rewrite what you have written.

Three tips are: Reread! Check! Rewrite!

Writing activity: Letters to the editor

Here are three opportunities to practice writing letters to the editor.

Plan, draft, revise and redraft one of these stimuli.

Note

At standard level you should write between 250 and 400 words.

At higher level you should write between 450 and 600 words.

1. You see the following headline, picture and story in your local paper. Write a letter to the editor in which you set out your views on the subject.

Schoolboys, 14, who were banned from wearing shorts to school on the hottest day of the year wear SKIRTS instead

But the UK school in Brighton, East Sussex, said it wasn't part of uniform code. In protest, the boys arrived the following day wearing pleated navy skirts.

George, Jesse, Kodi and Michael, all 14, chose cooler clothing which is part of the official uniform – a pleated navy skirt They were eventually allowed to wear skirts as they are part of agreed school uniform.

2. Write a letter to the editor in response to the text *Zulaikha Patel: How we all wish we were you* by Azad Essa. You may wish to agree or disagree with the writer's point of view. Remember to give your opinion on the school's customs and traditions. Write a clear conclusion.
3. Reread the letter from Mrs. Anne Other concerning school uniforms. Write a letter to the editor of Anytown News in which you respond to her letter and the opinions expressed in it. Remember to give your own justified opinions and write a clear conclusion.

You may wish to watch a news report of the protest about hair policies available at http://www.onenewspage.com/video/20160831/5434873/South-Africa-Girls-Fight-Racist-Hair-Policy.htm.

Planning: Checklist for a letter to the editor

The tables below will help you to plan your letter.

Context

Audience for the text		
Purpose of the text		
Approach to the topic	Logical	
	Emotional	
	Both	
Language	Very formal	
	Formal	
	Informal	
	Casual	

Content

	Content	Evidence, examples
Salutation		
Opening paragraph and thesis		
Middle paragraph 1 and supporting points		
Middle paragraph 2 and supporting points		
Middle paragraph 3 and supporting points		
Closing paragraph and final thought		

Listening comprehension

Click the icon to practice the listening section of Paper 2. After you have listened to an audio track you will complete an accompanying activity. In this multiple-choice exercise, you must answer four questions which summarize the contents of the audio text.

Conceptual understanding: Purpose

There are many ways of defining and classifying "language". For example, we can use grammar to describe the "rules" by which a language operates. Alternatively, we can classify language by looking at the ways we use it to communicate: its purpose.

If we understand the purpose of a text, we can also understand the writer's motives for communicating to his or her audience. For instance, when writing about the past do we simply narrate a set of events? Probably not.

A sophisticated written text may perform different communicative functions. These include:

- instructing or telling others what to do
- describing people, places and objects
- narrating stories and events
- explaining processes and motives
- persuading others of a point of view.

In order to understand this concept, look at the news report on page 283 about the student protest in South Africa and analyse the text according to its different communicative functions.

1. Read the text and find examples of these different functions in the text. Record your results in a table like the one below. If possible, use different coloured highlighters to show the different functions in the text. For instance, you might highlight the narrative in blue, and so on. Some sentences may have more than one function. For example, a sentence might both describe someone and also narrate an event.

Narrative	Description	Explanation	Instructions	Persuasion
Which sentences tell the story?	Which sentences describe people and places?	Which sentences explain why events have happened, or are happening?	Which sentences tell you what to do or to think?	Which sentences try to change your point of view?

2. Having completed the analysis, what would you say is the overall purpose of the text?

   A. Instruct, or tell others what to do
   B. Describe certain people, places and objects
   C. Narrate certain events
   D. Explain processes and motives
   E. Persuade the audience of a point of view
   F. More than one of these

Explain your answer.

3. Imagine the content of the text was used differently. It could be:

   - a leaflet to be handed out at a protest
   - the body of a petition supporting the girls' protest
   - the text of a poster supporting students' rights.

How would you use the information in the news report differently? What would be the purpose of the new text?

13-year-old Zulaikha Patel Is Taking A Stand Against School Policies That Frown At Natural Black Hair

All over the world, many black women have experienced discrimination at school and work because of their natural hair. But, what happens in an African country where black people are told not to wear their natural hair?

Zulaikha Patel, a 13-year-old student of Pretoria Girls' High School in South Africa has stood up for herself and her friends when she was asked to tame her natural hair "afro" because it was "exotic."

Pretoria Girls' High was originally an all white school during apartheid, but since 1990, it has been integrated to include all races.

Tired of being told to straighten their hair, Zulaikha and her fellow classmates staged a silent protest against their school's hair policy, which targets and restricts how black girls wear their hair to school.

Zulaikha's elder sister, Amira Patel, said that Zulaikha had changed school three times because of her hair and that other children had laughed at her and called her hair "cabbage".

She also noted that the school's code of conduct was biased and one-sided and was not a system that could fit everybody.

Malaika Eyoh, another student at Pretoria said, "I had recently cut my hair, so it was a small afro and I was repeatedly called out of class by one of the members of staff, who called my hair incorrect, said my hair was untidy, not fit for school and once threatened to cut my hair with scissors," she said.

She explained that black girls were repeatedly called out of class for having untidy hair when their hair is natural or their hair being incorrect or constantly met with snide remarks from teachers, like their hair needs to be tamed.

A petition to end school's alleged practices has got more than 20,000 signatures.

A TOK moment TOK

In this section we have seen what happens when two cultures clash.

To what extent could such clashes be avoided by being able to see the another person's point of view?

In class debate this TOK question: To what extent is our perspective determined by our membership of a particular culture?

What can we do to overcome the boundaries created by our own culture?

Conclusion to research question B

To what extent do customs and traditions affect our future?

1. Now that you have completed this section what are your conclusions and reactions to the question above? What useful life lessons have you learned from this section?
2. What justifications would you give for your answers?
3. What more would you need to know before you can come to a more definitive conclusion about the research question?

Section C: Rites of passage

Research question C:

To what extent are we shaped by the rites of passage we undergo on our journey from adolescence to adulthood?

1. What are your first thoughts and reactions to the question above?
2. What justifications would you give for your answers?
3. What more would you need to know before you can come to a definitive conclusion about the question?

Before you listen

In small groups or pairs consider these questions:

Can a role model change the way you look? Can a role model change the way you think? Can a role model change the way you act? In short, can a role model help you to change your life?

Critical-thinking and social skills ATLs

Here is an opportunity to use your critical thinking skills.

Work together and undertake these stages of critical thinking.

- Analyze and evaluate these issues and ideas.
- Evaluate evidence and arguments.
- Draw reasonable conclusions and generalizations.
- Test generalizations and conclusions.
- Organize your conclusions in a logical manner to formulate an argument.

When you have finished share your ideas with the rest of your class.

Listening comprehension

Jackie Robinson: role model

Listen to Tommy, a professional basketball player, talking about a visit to Notre Dame University and Jacky Robinson's significance as a role model.

Jackie Robinson slides into base, 1948

1. ***From statements A to H, select the five that are true according to the interview.***

A. Tommy had offers from a large number of universities.

B. Tommy's coaches were not sure if he should apply for Notre Dame.

C. Tommy was surprised by O'Farrell's suggestion to apply to Notre Dame University.

D. According to Tommy, he had already visited a number of universities when he went to visit Notre Dame.

E. Tommy was shocked by what he saw during his visit to the university campus.

F. Tommy knew that if he chose Notre Dame he would not find many students from similar social backgrounds in his classes or his teams.

G. Tommy realized that Jackie Robinson had faced similar, and even greater, challenges at college earlier.

Choose the correct answer from A, B, C, or D. Write the letter in the box provided.

2. Faced with a decision about accepting a place at the university, Tommy …

A. accepted without hesitation.

B. asked his basketball coach.

C. delayed making a decision.

D. wondered what to do for the best.

Exam tip: Multiple-choice questions

Answering multiple-choice questions is not as easy as it looks. The four alternative answers are often very close in meaning. Therefore, always read the question carefully. Listen to the text carefully to find the sentence or sentences which contain the answer you need. Eliminate the answers that are wrong. Only then will you be able to decide which answer is correct.

Creative thinking skills (ATLs)

Positive role models can help us to uncover our potential and overcome barriers. But are the role models we adopt at 16 the same ones we have when we are 40?

While you discuss this question use the following skills:

- Generate novel ideas and consider new perspectives.
- Use brainstorming and visual diagrams to generate new ideas and inquiries.
- Consider multiple alternatives.
- Arrive at new understandings.

3. According to Tommy, he was …
   - A. one of eight Black students in his year group.
   - B. one of eight Black students at the university.
   - C. one of eight Black students in his basketball team.
   - D. one of eight Black students in his academic classes.

4. Tommy thought of going to Notre Dame as a rite of passage because …
   - A. he would be going on a long journey
   - B. it would be an experience that would change him
   - C. he would go out to combat racism and prejudice
   - D. he would need to overcome bad luck.

5. According to Tommy, he used the role model of Jackie Robinson to help him ….
   - A. to train as hard as possible
   - B. to overcome any sense of isolation
   - C. to seek great financial rewards
   - D. to find peace within himself.

6. Tommy believes that the decision to attend Notre Dame was …
   - A. one of the best things he ever did.
   - B. the key to his later sporting and business successes.
   - C. a way of celebrating the achievements of Jackie Robinson.
   - D. one of the worst mistakes he ever made.

HL extension (HL)

Imagine you are the 18-year-old Tommy Hawkins visiting Notre Dame University for the very first time. What would have happened that day? To what extent was the visit to Notre Dame a rite of passage for Tommy Hawkins? Who would you have met? What would have been your thoughts, emotions and reactions to the visit? Write a 200-word diary entry recording the day's events and your reactions to them. The best answers will reflect on the challenges of the day and the influence of Jackie Robinson's example on Tommy.

Oral activity: Debate

Is going to university the biggest rite of passage teenagers face on their way to adulthood?

Introduction and preparation

In Tommy Hawkins' story, he described going to university as a kind of *rite of passage* from adolescence to adulthood.

But is leaving home and arrival at college the only rite of passage young people face on the journey to maturity? Clearly there is no one single event that marks the beginning and the end of the journey. There are both formal and informal transformative events along the way.

So what exactly is a rite of passage?

A rite of passage can be a ceremony or event that marks the change from one phase of life to another. So the term is often used to describe various moments of transition from adolescence to adulthood, such as beginnings and endings, initiations, and the forming of relationships.

Certain societies conduct formal ceremonies or tests of character at which a youth is formally invested with adult status in a community. The purpose of such rites of passage is to transmit a community's core values and confer adult responsibilities to the young people being initiated. At the same time the community also creates a common bond between the generations.

There are also a number of informal rites of passage, particularly in Anglophone cultures. Study the following list and decide which of these events can be described as a rite of passage.

18th birthday	Doing military service
21st birthday	Going away to college
Adopting a role model	High school graduation
A first kiss	Moving house
A first serious relationship	Obtaining a driving license
Becoming a teenager at 13	Taking a part-time job

What other events would you add to your list?

In groups use the ideas in this section on rites of passage to prepare a debate: "Is going to university the biggest rite of passage teenagers face on their way to adulthood?"

Conducting the debate

Appoint a moderator and create teams. One team should propose the motion that going away to college is the most important rite of passage facing young people. The other teams should each adopt an alternative rite of passage and argue its merits.

All members of the team should work on the opening speech .

All other students should prepare a one-minute speech on the subject reflecting the views of their team.

Hold the debate and, at the end, take a vote.

Research skills ATLs

Conduct research into such formal initiation ceremonies around the world. Find out where and why they are carried out. Describe the stages of one such initiation.

What initiation rites exist in your own society?

Present your findings to the class. In doing so use the following skills:

- Access information to be informed and inform others
- Make connections between various sources of information
- Create new information
- Present information in a variety of formats and platforms

Internal assessment (SL)

Take a look at the visual stimuli below. The images relate to the theme of "Experiences".

Brainstorming

In pairs, choose one of the images then discuss and answer the following questions.

- What is the main idea in the photograph? How does it relate to the title of the section, "Rites of passage" and an Anglophone culture.
- What do you see in background of the photograph? What does the background tell you about the location and context of the photograph?
- Look at the foreground of the photograph. Describe the person or people you can see.
- What is happening in the picture? How does the action relate to the theme of the chapter, "Experiences"?
- How do you relate the picture to events in your own life?

Presenting

Based on your answers to the questions above, prepare a four-minute presentation on the photograph.

Remember that the presentation should not only include description of the photograph, but should also connect it to the the topic of role models in an English-speaking community. Present your photograph and topic to your classmates.

Peer assessment

Assess the presentations given by your classmates using the SL IA assessment criteria in the Language B guide.

Suggest ways your classmates can improve their presentation techniques.

Exam tip: SL oral

In the SL Internal assessment you can choose either picture.

In the course of the two years you should practice the oral assessment as often as you can.

You can practice the presentation part of the oral using any of the visual stimuli found in this book.

Record yourself and assess your performance against the SL IA criteria in the Language B guide.

Even when the results are below par, you can learn to measure your strengths and weaknesses and learn from each effort.

Begin to practice your oral presentation skills early in the course. Such a gradualist approach will enable you to gain confidence in public speaking skills.

Internal assessment (HL)

Slaughterhouse 5 – Kurt Vonnegut

Little green men from the planet Tralfamadore have kidnapped Billy Pilgrim. The Tralfamadoreans see in four dimensions; this means they see time. As they pass through a time warp in their flying saucer the creatures are attempting to teach Billy how the universe works when seen in the 4th dimension. They also try to teach Billy that the universe is made of forces over which neither they nor human beings have any control.

'Welcome aboard, Mr. Pilgrim,' said the loudspeaker. 'Any questions?' Billy licked his lips, thought a while, inquired at last: 'Why me?' 'That is a very Earthling question to ask, Mr. Pilgrim. Why you? Why us for that matter? Why anything? Because this moment simply is. Have you ever seen bugs trapped in amber?'

'Yes.'

Billy in fact, had a paperweight in his office which was a blob of polished amber with three ladybugs embedded in it.

'Well, here we are, Mr. Pilgrim, trapped in the amber of this moment. There is no why.'

(...)

'Where am I?' said Billy Pilgrim.

'Trapped in another blob of amber, Mr. Pilgrim. We are where we have to be just now- three hundred million miles from Earth, bound for a time warp which will get us to Tralfamadore in hours rather than centuries.'

'How-how did I get here?'

'It would take another Earthling to explain it to you. Earthlings are the great explainers, explaining why this event is structured as it is, telling how other events may be achieved or avoided. I am a Tralfamadorian, seeing all time as you might see a stretch of Rocky Mountains. All time is all time. It does not change. It does not lend itself to warnings or explanations. It simply is. Take it moment by moment, and you will find that we are all, as I've said before, bugs in amber.'

'You sound to me as though you don't believe in free will,' said Billy Pilgrim.

'If I hadn't spent so much time studying Earthlings,' said the Tralfamadorian, 'I wouldn't have any idea what was meant by "free will." I've visited thirty-one inhabited planets in the universe, and I have studied reports on one hundred more. Only on Earth is there any talk of free will.'

Billy Pilgrim says that the Universe does not look like a lot of bright little dots to the creatures from Tralfamadore. The creatures can see where each star has been and where it is going, so that the heavens are filled with rarefied, luminous spaghetti. And Tralfamadorians don't see human beings as two-legged creatures, either. They see them as great millipedes with babies' legs at one end and old people's legs at the other,' says Billy Pilgrim.

Note

In your internal assessment, the literary extract will not exceed 300 words. You will be shown two, one from each of the works of literature studied in class.

Brainstorming

In small groups, discuss the following questions then summarize your discussion in point form.

- How does Billy Pilgrim face the challenges of being kidnapped by creatures from outer space?
- In what ways can Billy's experience be considered a rite of passage?
- What do we learn about the way the Tralfamadoreans understand time?
- Do you agree with the Tralfamadoreans that we are "bugs in amber" and have no choice about what happens to us?
- How do you think you would react in the same circumstances?

Creative thinking skills ATLs

When thinking about the HL stimulus questions, use your creativity and imagination.

Generating novel ideas and considering new perspectives

- Use brainstorming and visual diagrams to generate new ideas and inquiries
- Consider multiple alternatives, including those that might be unlikely or impossible
- Make unexpected or unusual connections between objects and/or ideas
- Make guesses, ask "what if" questions and generate testable hypotheses

Presenting

Based on your answers to the questions above, prepare a four-minute presentation on the text.

Make your presentation to your classmates. Students listening to the presentation should prepare individual questions about the text which they can put ask you at the end of your presentation.

Peer assessment

Assess the presentations given by your classmates using the HL IA assessment criteria in the Language B guide.

Suggest ways your classmates can improve their presentation techniques.

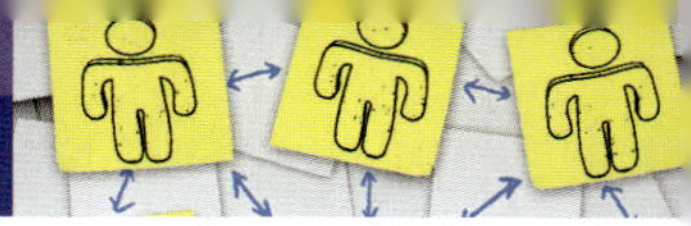

Paper 1

Respond to one of the following options. Write 250 to 400 words (SL) or 450 to 600 words (HL).

1. A politician known for having extremist views on nationalism and immigration has recently given a speech in a city near you. There was a very large counter demonstration in which you and your friends participated. Choose one of the text types below to express your opinion publicly and to state reasons for your protest.

   a) Opinion column **b)** Letter to the editor **c)** Proposal

2. It is a tradition at your school to hold a leavers' day at which graduating students dress up and act in an exuberant manner to celebrate the end of their time at school. This year, however, the celebrations to mark this rite of passage have got out of hand and there has been a certain amount of damage to school property. The school has decided to ban future leavers' day celebrations. Choose one of these three text types to give your opinion about this decision.

   a) Flyer **b)** Opinion column **c)** Letter to the editor

3. There has been a debate in your national parliament about the need to remove any form of gender stereotyping from the national education system. One suggestion has been put forward that only mixed school sports teams should be allowed to participate in schools sports. Choose one of these three text types to express your point of view on this matter.

   a) Letter to the editor **b)** Interview **c)** Opinion column

Exam tip: Responding to the question

In paper 1 you will score well if you can do these things.

1. Demonstrate your conceptual understanding by responding appropriately in a written task using an appropriate text type.
2. Use the appropriate language, register and format for the, audience, purpose and context.
3. Demonstrate that you can produce a coherent and organized response to the question.

Conclusion to research question C

To what extent are we shaped by the rites of passage we undergo on our journey from adolescence to adulthood?

1. Now that you have completed this section what conclusions have you come to about the research question? What useful life lessons have you learned in this section?
2. What justifications would you give for your answers?
3. What more would you need to know before you can come to a more definitive conclusion about the question?

Conclusion to the chapter

Having completed the chapter, reflect on its key research question:

Does our past shape our present and future?

When we began the chapter, you debated this research question.

Now that you have completed the chapter, answer the following questions.

To what extent have your opinions changed since the beginning of the chapter? Justify your answers.

In particular, you may want to consider this issue: What opportunities and challenges will the 21st century bring you?

What else would you like to know about the subject?

Beyond the classroom

You can use the information you have learned and the communication skills you have developed in this chapter for practical purposes beyond the classroom. You can use the persuasive communication skills you have developed while learning to write editorials and letters to the editor. Try using these skills while writing essays and other persuasive texts in school.

Think about issues which concern you that you read about in the local or national press. Write letters to the editor to express your opinions.

CAS

Service

Create a series of inspirational posters based on the 10 different attributes of the IB learner profile. Find one famous role models to illustrate each characteristic.

Creativity: debating club

Join or set up a debating club. Debating is a fantastic way of engaging with a broad range of contemporary social and ethical issues. It offers the opportunity to develop public speaking skills which will be useful when you enter college and, eventually, the workforce.

- Pick a regular day and time to meet each week and ensure you let other students know about the activity.
- Create relevant debates around ethical issues or matters that really affect your lives as local, national and global citizens.
- Create awareness. Promote debates, blog about them, create podcasts, and report them for your school magazine.
- Invite guest speakers to debate with.
- Hold debates in front of the school community and beyond.

Creativity: using text types

In this chapter you have learned how to write editorials and letters to the editor.

Now use these skills to write for, or to, your school magazine.

Suggestions for further reading

God Bless You, Mr Rosewater by Kurt Vonnegut

Speak by Laurie Halse Anderson

To Kill a Mockingbird by Harper Lee

Cry, the Beloved Country by Alan Paton

Claudette Colvin: Twice Toward Justice by Phillip Hose

The Watsons Go to Birmingham by Christopher Paul Curtis

Brown Girl Dreaming by Jacqueline Woodson

The Noughts and Crosses Trilogy by Malorie Blackman

Martin's Big Words: The Life of Dr. Martin Luther King Jr. (Big Words) by Doreen Rappaport, & Bryan Collier (Illustrator)

Rosa by Nikki Giovanni and Bryan Collier (Illustrator)

8 HUMAN INGENUITY: SCIENTIFIC AND TECHNOLOGICAL INNOVATION

Chapter summary

Theme

Human ingenuity

Topics

- Communication and media
- Scientific innovation
- The future of humanity

Conceptual understandings

Meaning

Research question for the chapter

How do developments in science and technology influence our lives?

Additional research questions for each section

A How can developments in science and technology create a better world for us all?

B How might scientific innovation influence our future lives?

C How might scientific innovation change the human species?

TOK questions

- Can the meaning of a text change over time?
- What does "meaning" mean?

Communication skills

Listening skills

- Receptive
- Productive

Interactive skills

- Discussion
- Negotiation

Written text types

Advertisements

Brochures/newsletters/flyers/leaflets

Chapter research question:

How do developments in science and technology influence our lives?

1. What are your first thoughts and reactions to the question above?
2. What justifications would you give for your answer?
3. What more would you need to know before you can come to a definitive conclusion about the question?

Now look at the diagram below. In this chapter we are going to look at three aspects of the general research question.

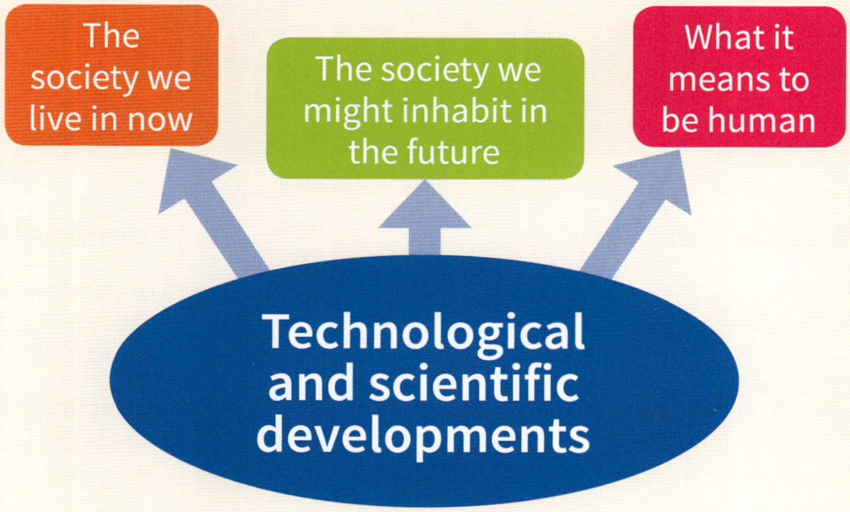

Before you begin the chapter, brainstorm your thoughts on these three question.

A. How can developments in science and technology create a more sustainable world now?

B. How might future developments in science and technology influence any future society we live in?

C. How might future scientific and technological innovation change the human species?

Section A: Technological innovation

Research question A:

How can developments in science and technology create a better world for us all?

1. What are your first thoughts and reactions to the question above? Make a list of points.
2. What reasons would you give for your answers?
3. What more would you need to know and what would you need to do before you could come to a definitive conclusion about the statement?

Social skills ATLs

Working effectively with others

Group work gives you the opportunity to practice collaborating effectively with others to achieve a common purpose.

As a group, practice the following skills while discussing the questions on this page.

- Listen actively to other perspectives and ideas
- Put forward your own ideas
- Share responsibility for decision-making
- Help others to succeed
- Resolve conflict
- Build consensus
- Make fair and equitable decisions
- Take responsibility for any group failures

When you have finished the task, ask yourselves these self-assessment questions:

- How effectively did I give helpful feedback to other contributors?
- How effective was the feedback I received from others in the group?
- How well did I ask for help when I needed it?
- Did I always take responsibility for my own actions when working within the group?
- What one thing could I have done to improve the quality of the group's work?

Before you read

Look at the picture below. In it, an early 19th-century artist imagines life in the 21st century. Work in groups to discuss and find answers to the following questions.

- What new technologies does the artist predict?
- Which of these innovations have come into use?
- Overall, how accurate has the artist been in imagining the future?
- How have the successful innovations predicted by the artist changed people's lives in the 21st century?

Overall what can the picture teach us about predicting the future of scientific and technological innovations?

Finally, make your own predictions about how mobile phones will continue to help economies to grow in the 21st century.

Africa calling: mobile phone revolution to transform democracies

Zoe Flood

Lower smartphone prices are creating a digital revolution in Africa, allowing mobile phone users to access the Internet at unprecedented levels. The number of smartphone connections across the continent almost doubled over the last two years, reaching 226 million. Prices have dropped from an average of $230 in 2012, to $160 in 2015, and to $130 in 2017. Many in Africa took up mobiles with great enthusiasm at the start of the last decade. There are more mobile phones than adults in most African countries, with the number of subscriptions in Kenya, for example, surging from 330,000 in 2001 to 38m in 2016, in a country with a population of nearly 45 million.

In recent years, mobile Internet access is acting as a new game-changer. All over the continent mobile networks are transforming public services in education, energy and water management for the better.

In addition, as handsets and data become more affordable greater accessibility to mobiles is also changing the way in which politics are being conducted. "This is having a huge democratizing effect," says John Githongo, one of Kenya's leading anti-corruption campaigners. "The growth in access to smartphones has led to the creation of more durable activist networks."

He stresses how the mobile technology revolution has given a voice to citizens. "We are already witnessing a transformation in the way people relate to their governments, as we have seen recently protest movements can spring up from a single post on the Internet that captured the imagination of the public."

This growth has also fuelled an expansion in the number of start-up companies looking to ride the mobile wave on the continent in areas such as healthcare and business.

In Ghana, the Mobile Technology for Community Health initiative aims to improve healthcare for pregnant mothers by providing time-specific information about their pregnancies and childcare each week. A separate application enables nurses to collect patient data and upload records to a centralized database to track the progress of patents and identify those who are due for care.

A programme in Nigeria known as Smart has halved the waiting time for the early diagnosis of HIV infection in infants.

Hand phones have also transformed the way business is conducted. Few advances have been as successful as M-Pesa, introduced in Kenya in 2007. Seven in 10 adults in Kenya use M-Pesa, making 9m transactions daily. The service has become a popular alternative to cash for numerous businesses and government agencies and offers everyone from grocers to mechanics a safer way to transfer their money.

Safaricom is funding numerous start-ups looking for markets outside Kenya. These include iCow, a "virtual midwife" for cows that helps farmers to maximise their herd's breeding potential by tracking their fertility cycle. M-Kopa, a firm that sells 500 units of small, solar-powered lighting units a day in Kenya, Uganda, Tanzania and Ghana and aims to have sold a million units by the end of next year.

Mteto Nyati, chief executive of MTN South Africa predicts their online retail operation will be another next big thing: "My sense is that the e-commerce space is going to be key going forward in Africa. But any e-commerce needs to be connected with some kind of logistics – we need to solve logistics challenges. We can do the transactions – people are comfortable using mobile devices. But how do you deliver the goods?"

Su Kahumbu Stephanou, the founder of iCow, says there is reason to be optimistic about Africa's digital prowess: "The mobile will help Africa close the digital divide with the rest of the world. We have only begun to scratch the surface in terms of exploiting the huge potential there is in this field.

https://www.theguardian.com/world/2016/aug/08/africa-calling-mobile-phone-broadband-revolution-transform-democracies#img-7

Reading comprehension

In this exercise you must read the text carefully and identify true and false statements.

The sentences below are either true or false. Tick [√] the correct response then justify it with a relevant brief quotation from the text.

	True	False
1. Mobile phone connections have doubled in price in since 2012.		
Justification:		
2. There were more mobile phones than adults in Kenya in 2016.		
Justification:		
3. Mobiles phones are transforming people's lives.		
Justification:		
4. Political pressure groups are much better connected as a result of mobile phone networks.		
Justification:		
5. Governments are now less able to control their citizens.		
Justification:		
6. The mobile phone industry is attracting new, innovative businesses.		
Justification:		
7. The public can now submit their medical records via their mobile phones.		
Justification:		
8. In Nigeria mobile phone technology allows medical staff to reduce the number of HIV positive babies.		
Justification:		

Find the definition in the right-hand column that best describes the business in the left-hand column.

Company
9. M-Pesa
10. Safaricom
11. iCow
12. MKopa
13. MTN

Description
A. A manufacturer of solar power units
B. A mobile money transfer system
C. An information service for dairy farmers
D. A tourist information centre
E. An exporter of solar lamps
F. A virtual dairy farmer
G. An online vendor
H. A transport company
I. An Internet bank
J. An investment company

Answer the following short-answer questions.

14. According to Mteto Nyati, what is the biggest single problem facing online sellers of goods?

....

15. According to Su Kahumbu Stephanou how is the mobile phone improving Africa's economic competitiveness with the rest of the world?

....

Choose the correct answer from A, B, C, or D. Write the letter in the answer box provided.

16. What does the phrase, 'We have only begun to scratch the surface' in the concluding paragraph suggest about Africa's digital future?

A. The future of the African economy lies in agriculture.

B. All future developments will need a great deal of hard work.

C. There is huge potential for growth in the coming years.

D. They must look for new opportunities currently hidden from sight.

Listening comprehension

Click the icon to practice the listening section of Paper 2. In this listening exercise, you will read ten statements. Only five are true – identify them.

Oral activity: Discussion and negotiation

In Language B, your discussions should always have a practical purpose. This could be to answer a question, solve a problem or conflict, create a plan of action, or organize an event.

Ideally every discussion should have a straightforward procedure that everyone can follow.

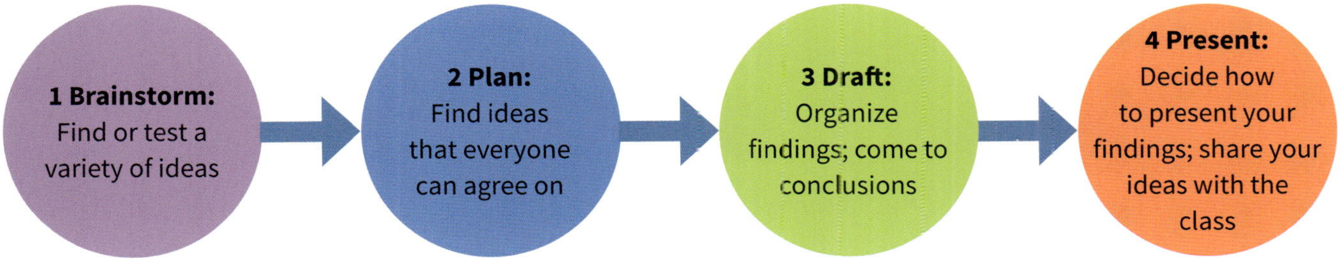

The small size of the discussion group should allow everyone to take part. However, once the number reaches five, it may be helpful to choose a chairperson who can manage the discussion, and make sure everyone's voice is heard. Sometimes the group will be in general agreement about the task, so the discussion may focus on how to present the conclusions.

What is a negotiation?

However, sometimes the members of your group will not agree. At this point you will need to demonstrate negotiation skills and procedures to come to a solution you can all work with.

A negotiation is a discussion about a particular topic in which the members of the group come to conclusions they can all agree on.

If there is disagreement, listen carefully to the alternative points of view.

In order to find compromise, you may need to use a more complex set of social and thinking skills.

Brainstorming

- Define the task
- Clarify things you don't understand
- Find out what each member of the group thinks

Planning

- Make suggestions
- Propose solutions
- Find broad ideas that everyone can agree on

Social and communication skills ATLs

When you negotiate, you have to make sure that you are open and honest. If you approach a negotiation without being open, your partner will know that you're trying to take advantage of them and they'll be less likely to work with you.

You might be very committed to your point of view, but you need to be able to see your partner's points of view as well. Your partner is going to be as committed as you are. If you can practice empathy you'll be more likely to find a compromise that works for everyone.

- Look at advantages and disadvantages of all ideas
- Debate the strength of the suggestions
- If members suggest very different solutions, find outcomes that give each member a portion of what they want.
- Make choices that the entire group can agree on.
- Come to conclusions

Presenting

- Agree on what information to present
- Agree on how to present it
- Present your conclusions

Discussion with negotiated outcomes: allocating resources

Constructive discussions involve problem solving and decision-making. How would you solve the following problem?

A telecoms company installs new cell towers in a various regions of a developing country.

The company only has the financial means to install cell towers in one village each year. Do they put the tower in village A or village B this year? The former is relatively accessible and already has partial mobile network coverage. The latter is remote and has no mobile coverage at all.

Work in three groups.

Groups 1 and 2 should represent each of the villages A and B.

Group 3 should represent the telecoms company.

Brainstorming

The community groups will each need to create a proposal. Each group should first discuss, and then create a series of arguments for their proposal.

The group representing the telecoms company should create a series of questions to put to each community group.

In all cases all the groups will have to use negotiation skills.

Area A		Area B	
Relatively accessible (300 km from the capital)	Dense population (500,000)	Remote (1000km form the capital)	Widely scattered population (1,000,000)
Enjoys partial mobile coverage	Some industry but high levels of urban poverty	No mobile coverage at present	Communities of subsistence farmers
Population speaks the national language	Extensive but poorly maintained transport links	Population speaks a variety of minority languages	Unexploited natural resources
Community politically stable	Some bank branches	Community vulnerable to external political influences	Almost no banks
25% of population own mobile phones	Opportunities for increasing small business	3% of the population own land lines	Opportunities for improving agriculture
30% literacy	Low cost of installation of a new cell tower	Population largely illiterate	High cost (twice the cost of Area A) of installation of cell towers

Planning

For the two teams put all your supporting points in a logical order. Make sure you can back up your arguments with examples and explanations. How will you introduce your village? How will you conclude?

At the end of the presentations your committee must make a decision. They can only provide one network to one region this year. The committee members should put their questions in a logical order.

Each village should make sure that their arguments are as convincing as possible.

How will the members of the committee justify their decision? What criteria will the committee members use to decide which village should receive the mobile connection this year? Create a set of criteria by which they can judge the arguments of each village fairly and transparently.

Presenting

Each village and the telecoms company should present their argument to the committee.

At the end of the presentations the committee should pose their questions. After this the committee and the villagers can negotiate the best outcome for everyone in the two communities. However, if there is no agreement, at the end of the day the committee will have to make a decision.

Social skills ATLs

In this exercise you will really have to use your social skills to the maximum.

How to work effectively with others

- Work collaboratively in a team
- Build and develop relationships
- Practice empathy
- Listen actively to other perspectives and ideas
- Manage and resolve conflict within the group
- Share responsibility for decision-making
- Build consensus
- Make fair and equitable decisions

Peer assessment

In small groups, assess the discussion or the final presentation given by your classmates. You may use these rubrics as a basis for your comments:

Oral communication skills

	Good	Improvement possible	Needs some improvement	Needs a lot of improvement
Eye contact	Has good eye contact with audience.	Has eye contact with the audience most of the time.	Sometimes has eye contact with the audience.	Does not have eye contact with the audience.
Enthusiasm	Shows great enthusiasm for the topic.	Shows enthusiasm for the topic.	Shows some enthusiasm for the topic.	Shows little enthusiasm for the topic.
Preparation and organization	Very prepared and well organized.	Mostly prepared and well organized.	Somewhat prepared and organized.	Not very prepared or organized.
Clear speech	Speaks very clearly and is very easy to understand.	Speaks clearly most of the time and is fairly easy to understand.	Sometimes speaks clearly and is sometimes easy to understand.	Does not speak clearly and is quite difficult to understand.
Knowledge of topic	Shows excellent understanding of the topic.	Shows good understanding of the topic.	Shows some understanding of the topic.	Shows little understanding of the topic.

Internal assessment (SL)

Take a look at the visual stimulus below. The image relates to the theme of "Human ingenuity".

Brainstorming

In pairs, discuss and answer the following questions:

A. What is the main idea in the visual stimulus? How does it relate to the themes of the section, "Media and communication"?
B. What do you see in background of the visual stimulus? What does the background tell you about the location and context of the photograph? How does the image portray an English-speaking community?
C. Look at the foreground of the visual stimulus. Describe the people you can see.
D. What is happening in the picture? How does the action relate to the theme of the chapter, "Human ingenuity"?

Planning

Based on your answers to the questions above, prepare a four-minute presentation on the photograph.

Remember that the presentation should not only include a description of the photograph, but should also connect it to the topic of "Media and communication" in an Anglophone culture. Present your photograph and topic to your classmates. Remember that in the actual examination you will have 15 minutes to prepare your presentation.

Peer assessment

Assess the presentations given by your classmates. Use the SL IA criteria to guide your assessment:

	Internal assessment (SL)
Criterion A	Language
Criterion B	1. Message: visual stimulus 2. Message: conversation
Criterion C	Interactive skills: communication

Suggest ways in which your classmates can improve their presentation techniques.

Self-management skills ATLs

Prepare and practice the individual oral with a partner

From time to time, use an Internet search to select a range of visual stimuli linked to the five themes you study during the course. Label each visual according to theme.

For the SL individual oral, a "visual stimulus" may be a photo, a poster, an illustration or an advertisement.

An effective visual stimulus:

- is clearly relevant to one of the five themes in the course
- offers sufficient visual text for you to describe a scene or situation
- allows you to offer a personal interpretation
- is clearly connected to an Anglophone culture

Use your collection of visuals to practice presenting and discussing the visuals you have collected.

This will give you insight into the procedures before the formal assessment takes place.

Note

In your internal assessment, the literary extract will not exceed 300 words. You will be shown two, one from each of the works of literature studied in class.

Internal assessment (HL)

Read the following poem. Then answer the questions that follow.

The Telephone Call

*A **scam** is a term used to describe any dishonest scheme that makes an attempt to take money or goods from an unsuspecting person. These days, scammers use phone technology to give the impression that members of the public can gain large amounts of money. People receive phone calls or emails asking them to give their confidential bank details in order receive a large cash prize. The scammers then use this information to steal the victim's savings. With the world becoming more connected thanks to the Internet, the number of scams has increased.*

This poem describes a scam with a difference.

They asked me `Are you sitting down?
Right? This is Universal Lotteries',
they said. `You've won the top prize,
the Ultrasuper Global Special.
What would you do with a million pounds?
Or, actually, with more than a million-
not that it makes a lot of difference
once you're a millionaire.' And they laughed.

`Are you OK?' they asked –`Still there?
Come on, now, tell us, how does it feel?'
I said `I just . . . I can't believe it!'
They said, 'That's what they all say.
What else? Go on, tell us about it.'
I said `I feel the top of my head
has floated off, out through the window,
revolving like a flying saucer.'

'That's unusual' they said. 'Go on.'
I said 'I'm finding it hard to talk.
My throat's gone dry, my nose is tingling.
I think I'm going to sneeze – or cry.'
`That's right' they said, `don't be ashamed
of giving way to your emotions.
It isn't every day you hear
you're going to get a million pounds.

Relax, now, have a little cry;
we'll give you a moment . . . ' 'Hang on!' I said.
`I haven't bought a lottery ticket
for years and years. And what did you say
the company's called?' They laughed again.

'Not to worry about a ticket.
We're Universal. We operate
a Retrospective Chances Module.

Nearly everyone's bought a ticket
in some lottery or another,
once at least. We buy up the files,
feed the names into our computer,
and see who the lucky person is. '
`Well, that's incredible' I said.
`It's marvellous. I still can't quite . . .
I'll believe it when I see the cheque.'

`Oh,' they said, `there's no cheque.'
`But the money?' `We don't deal in money.
Experiences are what we deal in.
You've had a great experience, right?
Exciting? Something you'll remember?
That's your prize. So congratulations
from all of us at Universal.
Have a nice day!' And the line went dead.

Fleur Adcock

Brainstorming

In small groups, discuss the following questions then summarize your discussion in point form.

1. What is unusual about the telephone call described in the poem?
2. Describe and explain the different emotions the narrator experiences at the different stages of the phone call?
3. In your opinion, what motivates the caller to make such phone calls?
4. On the evidence of the text, what is the meaning of the poem? What is the poet's message?
5. How would you react to a similar phone call? Explain and justify your answer.

Planning

Based on your answers to the questions above, prepare a four-minute presentation on the photograph.

Make your presentation to your classmates. Remember that in the actual examination you will have 20 minutes to prepare your presentation.

Students listening to the presentation should prepare individual questions about the text. They can put these questions to you at the end of your presentation.

Peer assessment

Assess the presentations given by your classmates. Use the HL IA criteria to guide your assessment:

	Internal assessment (HL)
Criterion A	Language
Criterion B	1. Message: literary extract 2. Message: conversation
Criterion C	Interactive skills: communication

Suggest ways in which your classmates can improve their presentation techniques.

Self-management skills ATLs

By now you will have completed a number of HL and or SL Internal Assessment practice activities. How well are you doing? How can you improve? Study carefully the assessment criteria published in the *IB Language B Guide* for first examinations in 2020. Examine the marks you receive for each criterion. How do you move onto the next grade level? For example, if you usually score 5 for criterion A, Language, how can you move onto the next grade band? Read the grade descriptors and find out what is expected of you. Consult your teacher to find out which specific aspects of your language you need to improve.

Paper 1: Advertisements

What is advertising copy?

Advertising aims to grab the interest of the prospective customers, and to persuade them to make a purchase, all within a few short seconds. Advertising copy can be found in print, radio, or television advertising messages and is used to grab the attention of potential customers.

Print adverts make use of both linguistic and visual text. Full-page colour ads can be found in feature magazines. Advertising copy is the written or spoken part of an advert.

In the advert on the left, how has the writer organized the text?

Remember the magazine readers do not have to look at the advertisements, so your ad needs to persuade your readers to take an interest within a few short moments. How does the advert on the left grab the readers' attention?

Magazine ads do more than just sell products; they promote ideas, suggest ideal worlds, reinforce public opinions, and entertain.

- What is the subtext/underlying message of the advertisement?
- How persuasive is the advertisement? Give reasons.

Adverts also reflect the culture and values of the society we live in.

Look at the advertisement on the left. What does it tell you about the culture and values of its time?

Writing to a specific audience

Effective advertising copy must grab the audience's attention and make the readers react to it.

- Always visualize the kind of people you want to buy the product.
- Keep in mind the ideal reader that will buy your product while you are writing.
- Write down what you know about the person and think about how to sell your product to them.
- Use the same level of formality as if you were talking to your customers in person.

Research skills

ATLs

In the modern world you will be bombarded by information far more subtle than the advertisement on the previous page. When you interact with media you will need to interpret data very carefully. Here are some skills you will need to be able to use:

- Evaluate information from a variety of sources and media (including digital social media and online networks)
- Demonstrate an awareness of media interpretations of events and ideas (including digital social media)
- Make informed choices about personal viewing experiences
- Understand the impact of media representations and modes of presentation
- Compare, contrast and draw connections from a variety of (multi)media resources

Analysis of advertisement A

Now look at this advertisement. You are going to examine some of the psychological techniques used to persuade the reader to buy a product or service. It may be useful to first think about the following:

1. The social context in which the advertisement appeared.
2. The message of the advertisement.
3. The subtext of the advert. What is the unspoken message behind the words and picture?

Advertisers use TOK to persuade their audiences to buy the products they are promoting. Which of these techniques can you find in advertisement A?

A. They make the product sound attractive by appealing to the readers' sense of taste, smell and sight.
B. They make emotional appeals to the readers. They stimulate their desires.
C. They create positive emotional associations, such as happiness and satisfaction, with the product.
D. They support their emotional appeals with logic.
   - They stress how the product or service will benefit the customers.
   - They give practical advice. They talk about what job the product does and how it works.
   - They can mention free stuff that comes with the product or the service.
   - They explain where to buy the product or find more information.

Conceptual understanding: Meaning

Advertisers need to make sure their audiences understand the meaning of their messages. Meaning can be achieved in a variety of different ways. For example, the advert below encourages young people to use the services of the Bank of Africa to pay their National Health Insurance Fund (NHIF) contributions. The advertisers use a number of linguistic techniques to convey the exact meaning of the text.

How many of the techniques mentioned in the list below can you find in the advertisement?

When you have completed the task, make a list and share them with your class.

Structure and language techniques for advertisements

- **A.** Use clear and simple sentences.
- **B.** Use lots of one and two syllable words.
- **C.** Use short paragraphs.
- **D.** Use bullet points/lists.
- **E.** Address your ideal customer directly.
- **F.** Personalize the message by using 'you' and 'your'.
- **G.** Use command forms to make your writing more direct. "Call now!"
- **H.** Use simple comparisons: metaphors and similes to help your readers to understand complex ideas

Writing activity: Advertising copy

Here are three opportunities to practice writing up advertising copy.

Plan, draft, revise and redraft one of these stimuli.

1. Your school wishes to increase the number of IB diploma students attending your school. Create some advertising copy to appeal to both potential students and their parents. The focus for the advertising campaign should be preparing students for life and work in the 21st century. In your copy, as well as promoting all the specific benefits for studying at your school, you should detail all the advantages of the IB diploma over your national examination system in helping students to prepare for all the technological and social changes in the decades ahead.
2. Your local tourist board is holding a student competition to create convincing Internet advertising copy for a local tourist attraction. The successful advertisement will appear on the website of the tourist board. Your advertisement should promote the specific attraction and your region and should appeal to an international audience.
3. Reread Text A: Africa calling: mobile phone revolution to transform democracies. Create a recruitment advertisement for one of the technology companies mentioned in the text. Your advertisement will address young people such as the ones depicted in the photograph opposite looking for a first job. Your advertisement should explain the specific aims of the technology company, describe the jobs on offer as well as describe the qualities needed by applicants.

Exam tip

At Standard Level you should write between 250 and 400 words.

At Higher Level you should write between 450 and 600 words.

Brainstorming

During the first stage write down as many ideas as you can about the product or service you are advertising. What are the important qualities you wish to emphasize?

1. Reflect on everything you have learned in this section
   - Choose your focal point and your point of view. What information would you like to emphasize?

→

2. Generate
   - Generate ideas to be used in your text.
   - Research additional material and, if necessary, facts to support your opinion.

Creative thinking skills

ATLs

Writing is a very creative process. Almost every text that you write involves you making choices and deciding how to make the text as effective and clear as possible.

Therefore, during the initial stages of planning and writing the first and then second drafts of a text, it is always useful to be as flexible as possible in your thinking. That way you can see your writing from new angles and continue to improve. For example, try to see your text from the point of view of your readers. Will they understand exactly the message you want to convey?

While composing your text:

- use brainstorming and visual diagrams to generate new ideas and inquiries
- consider multiple alternatives,
- make unexpected or unusual connections between objects and/or ideas
- make guesses, ask "what if" questions and generate testable hypotheses
- make comparisons; create metaphors and similes.

Planning

Magazine ads do more than just sell products; they promote ideas, suggest ideal worlds, reinforce public opinions, and entertain.

What will be the subtext/underlying message of your advertisement?

Write a draft of the body of your advertisement.

Write an eye-catching title.

Make sure to use all the conventions and formatting associated with advertising copy.

Which of these techniques will you use?

A. Use clear and simple sentences.

B. Use lots of one and two syllable words.

C. Use short paragraphs.

D. Use bullet points/lists.

E. Address your ideal customer directly.

F. Personalize the message by using 'you' and 'your'.

G. Use command forms to make your writing more direct. "Call now!"

H. Use simple comparisons: metaphors and similes to help your readers to understand complex ideas

Consider the context in which you are writing. What is the publication? Who is the audience? What level of formality will you use to address your audience?

Drafting

Reread the completed draft of your advertising copy and revise as necessary.

Remember you will be assessed on three criteria: **Criterion A:** Language, **Criterion B:** Message, **Criterion C:** Conceptual understanding (including audience, context and purpose).

Conclusion to research question A

How can developments in science and technology create a better world for us all?

Now that you have completed the section, what do you think is the answer?

- To what extent have your opinions on the subject changed since the beginning of this chapter? To what extent have your opinions remained the same?
- What big ideas have you learned about scientific and technological innovation in this section? Justify your answers.

A TOK moment: Language, meaning and context

TOK

Can the meaning of a text change over time?

Look at the advert. To the 21st-century reader the text might look old-fashioned and out of date.

But what impact did the advertisement have when it was first published in 1953?

In the exercise below you are going to examine whether a change of context changes the meaning of a text even though the language is unchanged.

In groups use the table below to analyse the advertisement by identifying its key features and considering their impact on readers in the past and now.

As you complete the chart, you might like to think about how changes in medical knowledge have changed our understanding of the advertisement.

Six features of an advertisement	Identify or describe the actual features in the advertisement above	Explain the intended impact of each feature on readers in the 1950s	Explain the impact of each feature on today's readers
The picture of the "consumer"			
The picture of the product			
The headline			
The personal endorsement			
The medical claims			
The slogan			

Conclusions

1 What was the overall meaning of the text in the 1950s?

2 What is the overall meaning of the text today?

3 What lessons about time and meaning will you take away from this exercise?

Section B: Scientific innovation

Which developments in science and technology might have the most profound effect on the society we live in?

Developments in science and technology in the 21st century are already having an effect the way people live, connect and communicate. Technological and scientific revolutions are bringing huge economic changes, as well as improvements to healthcare systems, education and transport. Entirely new sciences, based on microprocessors, telecommunications, bio-technology and nanotechnology, now exist. Their countless innovations are transforming the lives of all who have access to them.

Research question B:

How might scientific innovation influence our future lives?

1. What are your first thoughts and reactions to the question above? Make a list of points.
2. What reasons would you give for your answers?
3. What more would you need to know and what would you need to do before you could come to a definitive conclusion about the question?

Before you read

Examine the images here.

What advances in science and technology are being suggested by each image? In your opinion, which invention would have the most positive benefit for society? Which invention is potentially the most dangerous? Discuss your choices with the rest of your class.

http://www.sciencefocus.com/feature/future/future-technology-22-ideas-about-change-our-world

Future technology: Ten ideas to change our world

Ex: The sonic fire-fighter

Drones could direct loud noises at the trees to deal with forest fires. Sound is made up of pressure waves; they can be used to disrupt the air supply surrounding a fire. This cuts off the supply of oxygen to the fire. At the right low frequency, the fire simply dies out.

1. ______________________________

Imagine travelling on land at the same speed as a commercial jet airliner. Passengers would travel at up to 1000 kilometers per hour through a vacuum tunnel, propelled by compressed air.

2. ______________________________

Such ships would be filled with helium, and could also fly for thousands of kilometers while burning less fuel than an aeroplane. These airborne freighters could also replace long-haul freight trucks and cargo ships and could also be used for tourism. Tourists could take trips into space in specially designed space balloons.

3. ______________________________

Engineers are developing cars that can measure alcohol levels by sniffing a driver's breath or scanning the blood in their fingertips via the steering wheel. The device would immobilize the car if levels were too high.

4. ______________________________

Neuroscientists will develop the means of making surgical adjustments to the wiring of the human brain. The process will triple the human IQ, enabling individuals to become "super-geniuses". Such individuals will be able to combine the mathematical power of the supercomputer with enhanced emotional intelligence. Such individuals could become the greatest administrators, politicians and legal minds on the planet.

5. ______________________________

Driverless trucks would be cheaper to run than regular lorries, driving more smoothly using less fuel. Computers never get tired or need breaks, so they would be more efficient, making longer and faster journeys moving in convoys.

6. ______________________________

By 2050, 80 per cent of the world's population may be living in cities – creating a huge demand for food. So three-tier vertical farms could be fabricated at sea or on lakes close to cities. They would have solar panels on top to provide energy. The middle tier would grow fruit and vegetables using nutrients in liquid. Excess nutrients and plant matter would drop into an enclosed pond to feed fish farmed there.

7. ______________________________

City restaurants produce millions of tonnes of waste every year, so what do we do with it? Town planners and engineers are collaborating to develop practical recycling systems that will convert all such waste into biofuels for heating buildings.

8. ______________________________

An aerogel is a material that's full of tiny holes Those pores are so small – between 20 and 50 nanometers – that gas molecules can't squeeze through them. As a result, aerogels can't conduct heat, creating a material with incredible temperature-resistant properties.

9. ______________________________

Such a computer would be able to analyse a scientific problem and simulate countless scenarios in hours rather than years. Although humans would still need to feed the machine with data, it would be able to create new theories independently. This would be a huge forward step in the way we carry out research.

Listening comprehension

Click the icon to practice the listening section of Paper 2. After you have listened to an audio track you will complete an accompanying activity. In this exercise you will read ten statements. Identify the five true statements.

Reading comprehension

Match the headings A–L with the paragraphs 1–9 above.

A. Artificial water

B. Breathalyzer cars

C. Food power

D. Magnetic transport systems

E. Near-perfect insulation

F. Self-driving trucks

G. Space airships

H. Supersonic trains

I. Surgically-enhanced intelligence

J. The Artificial Intelligence Calculator

K. The sonic fire-fighter

L. Vertical agriculture

Find a word in the 'choices' column that is closest in meaning to the word in the text. There is one word per paragraph.

Paragraph	Word	Choices		Answer
10.	propelled	A) compelled B) motivated	C) pushed D) encouraged	
11.	airborne	A) floating B) flying	C) moving D) hovering	
12.	scanning	A) measuring B) rating	C) valuing D) ranking	
13.	enhanced	A) rectified B) corrected	C) valued D) improved	
14.	efficient	A) well-organized B) effective	C) competent D) capable	
15.	fabricated	A) aimed B) designed	C) intended D) constructed	
16.	convert	A) renovate B) translate	C) transform D) recondition	
17.	conduct	A) transmit B) direct	C) hold D) broadcast	
18.	scenarios	A) risks B) locations	C) dramas D) possibilities	

HL extension HL

How might these future developments in science and technology influence future society? Make a note of the potential benefits and drawbacks of each innovation.

Innovation	Benefits for society	Drawbacks for society
Supersonic trains		
The sonic fire-fighter		
Space balloons		
Breathalyzer cars		
Surgically-enhanced intelligence		
Self-driving trucks		
Floating farms		
Food power		
Near-perfect insulation		
The Artificial Intelligence Calculator		

Creative thinking skills ATLs

One purpose of these interactive orals is to allow you to explore new ideas and look at the concepts you are learning from new perspectives.

A negotiation can show you how to resolve conflict and make compromises.

In an interactive oral you may need to adopt opinions and positions that you might not normally hold or believe in. However, by acting out a role in an empathetic manner you may come to see other people's points of view in a new light.

Oral activity: Discussion with negotiated outcome

Imagine your group is made up of civil servants, business people and scientists charged with advising your government on investment policy for scientific research.

Re-examine the list of innovations you have read about in this section. In groups re-examine the potential benefits and drawbacks for society of each innovation by comparing notes or completing the HL extension exercise on the previous page. When you have finished, give each innovation a rating of 1 to 5, where 1 is the highest score. Recommend to your government the innovations with the greatest social benefit for the citizens of your country.

Brainstorming

Before you start, define the meaning of the concept of a "benefit to society". Then, in your groups, choose one innovation from the list you have made which you think would be the most beneficial to society. The purpose of the discussion will be to come to a conclusion you can all agree on. So be prepared to negotiate and compromise during your discussions.

Planning

After you have made your choice, design a visual to show your understanding of the concept. You must justify your choice by listing its benefits for society, and also explain how any possible drawbacks could be minimized.

Put your ideas into the best possible order.

Create a formal introduction and conclusion with a final thought.

Presenting

Present your choice and your visual to the rest of your class, explaining in detail what benefits your innovation will have for people in the future.

You may wish to record the discussion and/or the presentation. You may want to use the recording as a prompt for one of the writing exercises later in the chapter.

Peer assessment

In small groups, assess the discussion or the final presentation given by your classmates. You may use the rubrics on page 302 as a basis for your comments.

Internal assessment (SL)

Take a look at the visual stimulus below. The image relates to the theme of "Human ingenuity".

Brainstorming

In pairs, discuss and answer the following questions.

- What do you see in background of the picture? What does the background tell you about the location and context of the picture?
- Look at the foreground of the picture. Describe the object(s) you can see.
- What is happening in the picture? How relevant is this to an Anglophone culture?
- What is the main idea in the picture? How does it relate to the theme of the chapter: "Human ingenuity"?

Presenting

Based on your answers to the questions above, prepare a four-minute presentation on the image.

Remember that the presentation should not only include a description of the photograph, but should also connect it to the topic of scientific and technological innovation in an English-speaking culture. Present your image and topic to your classmates. Remember that in the actual examination you will have 15 minutes to prepare your presentation.

Peer assessment

In small groups, assess the presentations given by your classmates. Use the SL assessment criteria in the Language B guide as a basis for your comments.

Internal assessment (HL)

Read the extract from* Flowers for Algernon *and then answer the questions that follow.

Flowers for Algernon

Context

The story Flowers for Algernon is told through a series of diary entries written by Charlie Gordon, a man with severe learning difficulties who previously worked as an unskilled janitor. Two neuroscientists, Dr Strauss and Dr Namur, select Charlie to undergo a surgical procedure to enhance his intelligence. The technique has already been successful on a laboratory mouse, Algernon. The surgery on Charlie is also a success, and he becomes a super-genius, and he starts to research the procedure he and Algernon have undergone. However, Algernon suddenly declines. Charlie realizes that his own intelligence increase is also only temporary.

June 4: LETTER TO DR STRAUSS (copy)

Dear Dr Strauss:

Under separate cover I am sending you a copy of my report entitled, The Algernon-Gordon Effect: A Study of Structure and Function of Increased Intelligence,' which I would like to have you read and have published.

As you see, my experiments are completed. I have included in my report all of my formulae, as well as mathematical analysis in the appendix. Of course, these should be verified.

Because of its importance to both you and Dr Nemur (and need I say to myself, too?) I have checked and rechecked my results a dozen times in the hope of finding an error. I am sorry to say the results must stand. Yet for the sake of science, I am grateful for the little bit that I here add to the knowledge of the function of the human mind and of the laws governing the artificial increase of human intelligence.

I recall your once saying to me that an experimental failure or the *disproving* of a theory was as important to the advancement of learning as a success would be. I know now that this is true. I am, sorry, however, that my own contribution to the field must rest upon the ashes of the work of two men I regard so highly.

Yours truly,

Charles Gordon

encl: report.

Note

In your internal assessment, the literary extract will not exceed 300 words. You will be shown two, one from each of the works of literature studied in class.

June 5 I must not become emotional. The facts and the results of my experiments are clear, and the more sensational aspects of my own rapid climb cannot obscure the fact that the tripling of intelligence by the surgical technique developed by Drs Strauss and Nemur must be viewed as having little or no practical applicability (at the present time) to the increase of human intelligence.

As I review the records and data on Algernon, I see that although he is still in his physical infancy, he has regressed mentally. Motor activity is impaired; there is a general reduction of glandular activity; there is an accelerated loss of co-ordination.

There are also strong indications of progressive amnesia.

As will be seen by my report, these and other physical and mental deterioration syndromes can be predicted with statistically significant results by the application of my formula.

The surgical stimulus to which we were both subjected has resulted in an intensification and acceleration of all mental processes. The unforeseen development, which I have taken the liberty of calling the Algernon-Gordon Effect, is the logical extension of the entire intelligence speed-up. The hypothesis here proven may be described simply in the following terms: Artificially increased intelligence deteriorates at a rate of time directly proportional to the quantity of the increase.

I feel that this, in itself, is an important discovery.

As long as I am able to write, I will continue to record my thoughts in these progress reports. It is one of my few pleasures. However, by all indications, my own mental deterioration will be very rapid.

I have already begun to notice signs of emotional instability and forgetfulness, the first symptoms of the burnout.

June 10 Deterioration progressing. I have become absentminded. Algernon died two days ago. Dissection shows my predictions were right. His brain had decreased in weight and there was a general smoothing out of cerebral convolutions as well as a deepening and broadening of brain fissures.

I guess the same thing is or will soon be happening to me. Now that it's definite, I don't want it to happen.

I put Algernon's body in a cheese box and buried him in the backyard. I cried.

Brainstorming

In small groups, discuss the following questions then summarize your discussion in point form.

- Why is Charlie writing to Dr. Strauss in the first extract?
- What conclusions does Charlie come to about the experiment in the letter to Dr. Strauss?
- In the diary entry of June 5th what side effects does Charlie report in Algernon and what conclusions does he come to?
- Comment on and explain the changes in language used by Charlie in the course of the diary entry of June 10th.
- How does the extract relate to the title of the section, "Scientific innovation"?

Presenting

Based on your answers to the questions above, prepare a four-minute presentation on the contents of the text. Present to your classmates. Remember that in the actual examination you will have 20 minutes to prepare your presentation.

Students listening to the presentation should prepare individual questions about the text. They can put these questions to you at the end of your presentation.

Peer assessment

In small groups, assess the presentations given by your classmates. Use the HL IA assessment criteria in the Language B guide as a basis for your comments.

Thinking and Social skills ATLs

Brainstorming in groups

Brainstorming can help you escape your usual ways of thinking.

Brainstorming in groups allows you to combine an informal approach to problem solving with creative thinking.

It allows you to come up with thoughts and ideas that can seem a bit crazy. Some, but not all, of these ideas can become original, imaginative responses solutions to a problem or a question. Remember, you are trying to find new possibilities. So during brainstorming sessions, you should avoid criticizing any new ideas.

However, you will need to evaluate your ideas at the end of the brainstorming session.

Then you will be able sort out the most useful ideas from the rest.

Paper 1: Flyers, leaflets, pamphlets & newsletters

Flyers

A flyer, also known as a handbill, is usually produced to market a product or an event to a relatively small audience. It offers a limited amount of information. For example, flyers might be used to advertise a community meeting or a new restaurant. Flyers are handed out or hung in public places. Alternatively they are sent out as email attachments.

Flyers are also used as:

- announcements of events, especially concerts or club openings.
- product information for shops and businesses, such as special offers at a supermarket or the services offered by a small business.
- factsheets handed out at meetings or conferences.

Here is a sample flyer.

Anytown Valley Community College
STUDENT AMBASSADOR PROGRAMME

ARE YOU INTERESTED IN...

... TAKING AN ACTIVE ROLE IN COLLEGE ACTIVITIES?

... GIVING TOURS OF THE CAMPUS?

... PROMOTING COLLEGE LIFE?

... RECRUITING STUDENTS FROM LOCAL PRIMARY AND MIDDLE SCHOOLS?

... PROMOTING COLLEGE EVENTS IN THE LOCAL COMMUNITY?

DO YOU HAVE

A strong commitment to diversity

Ability to work individually and with others

Ability to plan, organize, and lead a variety of activities and events

Skill of identifying and resolving problems and conflicts

Strong organizational abilities

Strong interpersonal and public speaking skills

Ability to create posters and flyers

IF SO, APPLY TO BE AN AVCC STUDENT AMBASSADOR

SUBMIT YOUR APPLICATION

TO:
LAURA VAUGHN
COMMUNITY SERVICES MANAGER
SENIOR SCHOOL OFFICE
02426 28XXXX
lv@avcc.edu.com

Critical thinking skills ATLs

In the previous section, you looked at and analyzed advertisements. In what ways are flyers and leaflets similar to advertisements? In what ways are they different?

Gather some examples and then analyze and evaluate the different text types.

- Practice careful observation in order to recognize similarities and differences.
- Gather and organize relevant information to formulate an argument.
- Create your own criteria by which to make comparisons.
- Interpret data and evidence.
- Evaluate evidence.
- Draw reasonable conclusions and generalizations.

Leaflets

Leaflets are better designed than flyers using colour printing and better quality paper. Their design should catch the attention of prospective customers and consumers, and deliver a convincing message to them.

The main purpose of a leaflet is to persuade, often in order to

- promote a service or organization
- market and sell a product.
- educate, inform, persuade, or entertain your intended audience
- mobilize people to support a cause and to spread a message.

Leaflets are often inserted into local newspapers or posted directly into letterboxes.

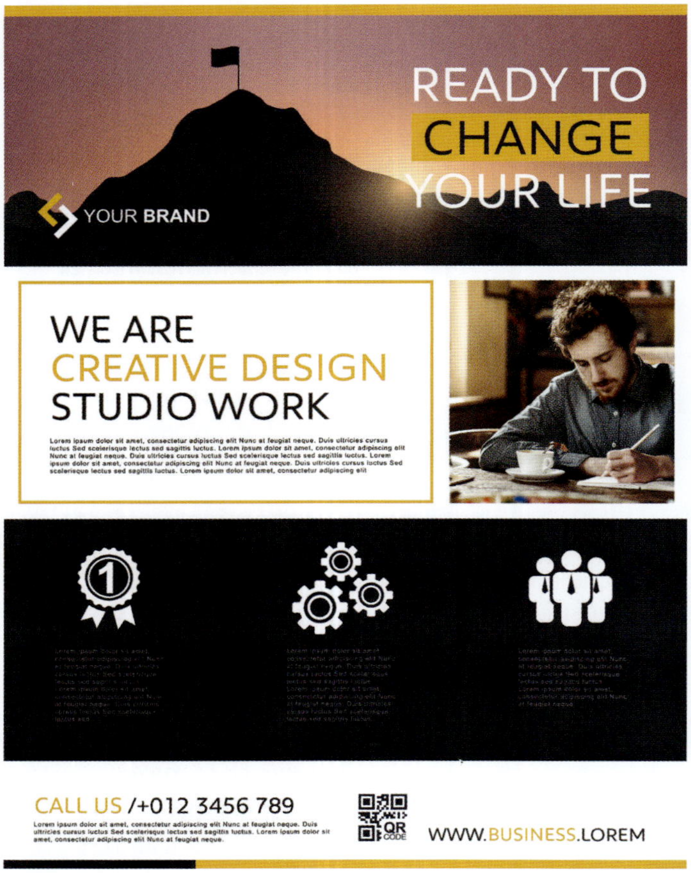

Pamphlets

A pamphlet is an unbound booklet. It may consist of a single sheet of paper or a few folded pages. It will give more detail than a flyer and is often used to promote awareness.

Newsletters

Newsletters are publications that are distributed by businesses, charitable organizations, societies, clubs and community bodies.

A newsletter will contain information on specific topics that interest their specific audience. They contain the latest information the sender wants the audience to know.

They are also an effective way to maintain contact and keep the audience informed, involved and interested.

Study the newsletter here.

- What is the subject matter of the newsletter?
- What is the purpose of this newsletter?
- Who is audience for the newsletter?
- What are the special features of the newsletter used to interest the audience?

Language and style

Flyers, leaflets, pamphlets and newsletters are mass-media documents and will have a mass audience. In some cases, the audience will be known, in others the audience will be strangers to the writer.

You need to think about the audience you are writing for. If your flyer or newsletter targets an audience of your peers, you could use more familiar language. In such cases, you will want to be informative but use relatively informal language.

On the other hand, if your task involves targeting the general public, then your language will depend on the task itself.

If you want a more personal relationship with the audience, such as promoting an event, or marketing a product, then you can be less formal in your use of register.

If your purpose is to persuade an audience you do not know of a particular point of view, then it is best to be more polite and formal. For example, if you were creating a document to convince an audience to donate money to a cause, would you use formal or informal language?

Writing activity: Flyers, leaflets, pamphlets and newsletters

Here are opportunities to practice writing flyers, leaflets, pamphlets and newsletters.

Plan, draft, revise and redraft using one or more of the examples 1–8 below to practice writing flyers, leaflets, pamphlets and newsletters.

As we have seen, publicity material can have different purposes, depending on the subject matter and the intended audience. Study the list of potential purposes of various publications below. Complete the chart by identifying the audience and purpose of the following eight texts. Your teacher may wish you to justify your responses.

Exam tip

At Standard Level you should write between 250 and 400 words.

At Higher Level you should write between 450 and 600 words.

Audience and purposes of flyers, leaflets, pamphlets and newsletters

Text	Audience	Purpose (Note: A text may have more than one purpose.)	Justification
1. A leaflet to promote a science fiction film festival at your local cinema	A) An audience of your peers B) A familiar group with shared interests C) Strangers with specific shared interests D) The general public	A) To inform B) To persuade C) To market and sell D) A call to action E) Other (specify) …	
2. A pamphlet from the local heath authority to promote a new initiative on healthy living	A) An audience of your peers B) A familiar group with shared interests C) Strangers with specific shared interests D) The general public	A) To inform B) To persuade C) To market and sell D) A call to action E) Other (specify) …	
3. A flyer from a school advertising its annual science fair for young inventors	A) An audience of your peers B) A familiar group with shared interests C) Strangers with specific shared interests D) The general public	A) To inform B) To persuade C) To market and sell D) A call to action E) Other (specify) …	
4. A newsletter from your local organic shop advertising the arrival of new products and giving details of upcoming talks on low-tech farming	A) An audience of your peers B) A familiar group with shared interests C) Strangers with specific shared interests D) The general public	A) To inform B) To persuade C) To market and sell D) A call to action E) Other (specify) …	

5. A flyer by a local DJ advertising a multimedia gig at a club.	A) An audience of your peers B) A familiar group with shared interests C) Strangers with specific shared interests D) The general public	A) To inform B) To persuade C) To market and sell D) A call to action E) Other (specify) ...	
6. A newsletter from school to parents giving details of new energy-efficient technologies installed in school buildings	A) An audience of your peers B) A familiar group with shared interests C) Strangers with specific shared interests D) The general public	A) To inform B) To persuade C) To market and sell D) A call to action E) Other (specify) ...	
7. A leaflet from a community college detailing information technology courses for the coming year	A) An audience of your peers B) A familiar group with shared interests C) Strangers with specific shared interests D) The general public	A) To inform B) To persuade C) To market and sell D) A call to action E) Other (specify) ...	
8. A pamphlet from a community group protesting against the nearby construction of a high-speed railway	A) An audience of your peers B) A familiar group with shared interests C) Strangers with specific shared interests D) The general public	A) To inform B) To persuade C) To market and sell D) A call to action E) Other (specify) ...	

For this exercise, only the text will be graded. However, you should also pay close attention to formatting and layout to improve the quality of the message and to make sure your meaning is clear.

1. Reflect on everything you have read in the table on pages 323 and 324.
   - Choose your focal point and your point of view. What information would you like to emphasize?

2. Generate
   - Generate ideas to be used in your text.
   - Research additional material and, if necessary, facts to support your opinion.

Drafting

Reread the completed draft of your chosen text type and revise as necessary.

Remember you will be assessed on three criteria: **Criterion A:** Language, **Criterion B:** Message, **Criterion C:** Conceptual understanding (including audience, context and purpose).

Conclusion to research question B

How might scientific innovation influence our future lives?

1. Now that you have completed this section what are your thoughts and reactions to the question about?
2. What justifications would you give for your answers?
3. What big ideas have you learned about scientific and technological innovation in this section?

Section C: The future of humanity

Research question C:

How might future scientific and technological innovation change the human species?

Look at the picture below and then answer the following questions.

1. What are your first thoughts and reactions to this section's research question?
2. What justifications would you give for your answers?
3. What sort of innovations might change the human body in the years to come? Could we all become superhuman?

Before you listen

You are going to listen to a recording of a radio programme which discusses an innovation that may allow us to control the content of our dreams.

Here are four common dreams and their proposed explanations:

A. You're being chased

There's an issue you need to confront but are not sure how to do so. Your pursuer is an aspect of your own character (which is why you can't escape it) trying to bring something to your attention.

B. Your teeth fall out or crumble

The only time in our lives when our teeth fall out is when we're children – having dreams in which this occurs signals you are lacking in confidence.

C. You're unprepared for an exam

Exams are about judging our ability to perform, so this dream shows you're actively examining your life. People who have this dream tend to be self-critical. It requires being able to accept your talents by celebrating your achievements.

D. You're falling

This is about the need to let go of something. You might be trying to micromanage someone. The message from the dream is to relax and let go.

From: http://www.independent.co.uk/life-style/health-and-families/features/can-we-control-our-dreams-2300240.html

Research skills ATLs

Many people suffer from nightmares.

But scientists now claim to have found a way to let people take control of their dreams using a variety of different techniques.

Psychologists now believe there may be ways to increase people's ability to control their dreams.

Use your research skills to explore this idea.

- Collect and analyze data to identify solutions and make informed decisions.
- Process data and report results.

Present your findings to your English class.

1 Conduct a survey in your class to see which of these four dreams are the most common. Find out which other dreams you all have. For example, do you dream of being lost in a tunnel, or being able to fly? What meaning, if any, do you give to these dreams?

2 As a class, discuss or debate whether it would be a good idea to be able to control your dreams.

Listening comprehension

Dream on

Listen to the extract from a weekly radio science show, in which reporter Grace Miller discusses a new scientific innovation which may change the way we think about dreaming. Listen to the recording and then answer the questions below.

Choose the correct answer from A, B, C, or D. Write the letter in the box provided.

1. According to the reporter, the show discusses an invention that can …

A. create dreams.
B. interpret dreams.
C. influence dreams.
D. investigate dreams.

2. The invention will also be able to …

A. improve the experience.
B. erase the experience.
C. lengthen the experience.
D. intensify the experience.

3. The inventor, Professor Wiseman, is an expert in …

A. psychiatry.
B. philosophy.
C. psychology.
D. technology.

4. So far the app has been tested by volunteers who want to …

A. understand their dreams better.
B. understand themselves better.
C. download their dreams.
D. have better dreams.

5. ***Identify the four statements made by the radio presenter during the segment.***

A. The kind of dream is selected for you from an app.
B. The app can monitor the dreamer's sleep patterns.
C. The app then creates rapid eye movement for the sleeper.
D. The dreamer then follows a sequence of musical stimuli.
E. The dreamers select which "soundscape" they wish to follow.
F. Each soundscape stimulus suggests a different type of dream.
G. The app turns itself off after the selected dream has finished.
H. The app collects and records each dreamer's experiences.
I. Professor Wiseman is creating a data bank of descriptions of his volunteers' dreams.
J. One day dreamers will be able to upload their dreams to social media sites.

HL extension (HL)

Listen to recording again. Write a clear set of step-by-step guidelines which explain to the reader how to use the app. A good answer will explain the purpose of the innovation and how to use it. The best answers will also convince the reader to download and use the app by describing its potential benefits to the user.

Complete the sentence below with information from the recording.

6. In a recent survey 15% of respondents …

7. People's ability to work well can be improved by pleasant dreams and …

8. The presenter admits there is still not much understanding about …

9. The presenter has not used DreamOn technology herself but she may …

Oral activity: Discussion

Read the following extract from a recent magazine article, then undertake the activities that follow.

Visions of the future: 5 hi-tech inventions we'll hopefully be using in 2030

Alun Palmer

Futurologist Ian Pearson has a list of 5 hi-tech innovations that he claims will be sure-fire hits by 2030.

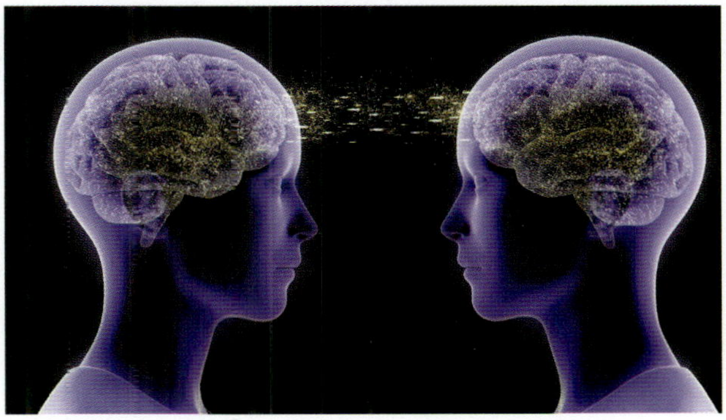

1. **Dream linking**

   It will be possible for two people to share dreams, and they may even be able to interact in them.

2. **Shared consciousness**

   Many people believe we will one day have full links between our brains and an external computer.

   We will be able to directly access more information outside the brain, making us much smarter, with thought access to most of human knowledge.

3. **Active contact lenses**

   These contact lenses will deliver a full 3D experience. They will even let you watch movies or read your messages without opening your eyes.

4. **Immortality and body sharing**

   When your body dies, most of your computer-based mind will carry on.

   You'll buy an android body and carry on. Life really begins after death.

5. **Exoskeletons**

   Polymer gel muscles will be five times stronger than natural ones, so you could buy clothing that gives you superhuman strength.

   Imagine free-running and leaping between buildings like a superhero, and having built-in reactive armour to make you bulletproof too, with extra super-senses also built in.

   Exoskeletons might become very popular leisure and sports wear, as well as the obvious military and emergency service uses.

Adapted from http://www.mirror.co.uk/news/technology-science/technology/10-hi-tech-inventions-well-using-1451863

Imagine it is the year 2040. All of the ideas mentioned in the article, "Visions of the future", have become reality. Your group has been selected to undergo one of the enhancements mentioned in the text. Which one would you choose?

Brainstorming

In a group discuss the potential benefits and drawbacks of each innovation.

Start by giving each of the five innovations a rating of 1 to 5, in which 1 is the highest score. Decide which enhancement your group would most like to undergo. Use your negotiating skills to reach a decision you can all agree on.

Presenting

Present your choice to the rest of your class explaining in detail what benefits your innovation will have for yourself and your group in the future.

Peer assessment

In small groups, assess the discussion or the final presentation given by your classmates. You may use the rubrics on page 302 as a basis for your comments.

Internal assessment (SL)

Take a look at the visual stimuli below. The images relate to the theme of "Human ingenuity".

Brainstorming

In pairs, choose one of the images above then discuss and answer the following questions.

- What is the main idea in the image? How does it relate to the title of this section of the chapter, "The future of humanity"?
- What do you see in background of the photograph? What does the background tell you about the location and context of the photograph?
- Look at the foreground of the photograph. Describe the person or people you can see.
- What scientific and technological ideas are being demonstrated in the photograph? How does the action relate to the title of the chapter, "Scientific and technological innovation" and an Anglophone culture?
- How would you feel if you had access to the innovation shown in the photograph? Give your reasons.

Presenting

Based on your answers to the questions above, prepare a four-minute presentation on the photograph.

Remember that the presentation should not only include a description of the photograph, but should also connect it to the topic of human ingenuity in an English-speaking society. Present your photograph and topic to your classmates. Remember that in the actual examination you will have 15 minutes to prepare your presentation.

Peer assessment

Assess the presentations given by your classmates. Use the SL IA criteria to guide your assessment:

	IA (SL)
Criterion A	Language
Criterion B	1. Message: visual stimulus 2. Message: conversation
Criterion C	Interactive skills: communication

Suggest ways in which your classmates can improve their presentation techniques.

Internal assessment (HL)

The Birth of Bionic Man

Context

Astronaut Steve Austin is severely injured in an aeroplane crash. Scientists rebuild his body in an operation that costs six million dollars. His right arm, both legs and the left eye are replaced with 'bionic' materials that enhance his strength, speed and vision far above normal human capabilities. He can run at speeds of 100 km/h, and his eye has a 20:1 zoom lens and infrared capabilities, while his bionic limbs have the strength of a fork lift truck.

The passage here describes the process of creating the bionic man.

His heart valves were damaged? Replace them with the Hufnagel valve and supporting internal apparatus. His skull was crushed? Replace the bone with cesium and with new alloys where needed. Design a spongy center layer and another outer layer to protect the brain case inside. He could then endure a direct blow ten times greater – without suffering injury – than the sledgehammer thuds that cracked his skull in the first place.

Replace ribs. Install – and install was the proper word – added tendons, plastic valves, arteries and veins where needed. Blinded in his left eye? Well, they weren't that good because the human eye is a miracle of jelly and water and light-sensitive elements and rods and electrical impulses trickling their way through bundles of nerves to a gray convoluted mass of three pounds encased within the skull – no, they couldn't 'yet restore vision when the optic nerve was mangled, and Austin's optical nerve was so much biological garbage.

But they could make use of the area where there had been an eyeball to build a marvelously small and efficient camera into where his living camera system had been. Steve Austin became a man with one living eye and one extraordinary camera that recorded on tiny supersensitive film what its human carrier saw with the living eye. None of these could compare with the miracle of the recreated living limbs – the arm with its bionic bones, and the legs with their computer-directed systems.

It was one thing to construct the limbs that were to receive the nerve impulses flowing to and from the brain. It was another to mimic the nerve fibers and systems for transmitting the impulses from the brain into the spinal cord and on down the message networks. To Steve Austin's arm stump they double-engaged the bionics and the natural bone to exceed by far the original level of strength and resistance.

...

If the bionics arm was not quite the same as the original arm, it was in many ways superior. Steve Austin's arm was more than a human arm; it was also capable of performing as a battering ram, a vise, a bludgeon – a tool and a weapon. His legs were also tremendous pistons. His heart and circulatory systems served a body without the need of supporting two legs and an arm. The bionics systems with their nuclear amplifiers attended to all energy needs, and so Austin's endurance increased dramatically. He was dependent as ever on his heart and lungs and other systems. But he could run a day and a night because there was no energy drain from the legs hammering against the earth.

Cyborg a.k.a. The Six Million Dollar Man by Martin Caidin

Brainstorming

In small groups, discuss the following questions then summarize your discussion in point form.

1. What injuries has Steve Austin suffered?
2. What enhancements have been made to his body?
3. Describe the ways in which the 'bionic man' has superior physical powers to an ordinary human being.
4. Describe the psychological and emotional impact of the accident and the subsequent operations on Steve Austin.
5. Do you agree that we should use science and technology to improve on nature to create superhumans?

Presenting

Based on your answers to the questions above, prepare a four-minute presentation on the photograph.

Make your presentation to your classmates. Remember that in the actual examination you will have 20 minutes to prepare your presentation.

Students listening to the presentation should prepare individual questions about the text. They can put these questions to you at the end of your presentation.

Note

In your internal assessment, the literary extract will not exceed 300 words. You will be shown two, one from each of the works of literature studied in class.

Peer assessment

Assess the presentations given by your classmates. Use the HL IA criteria to guide your assessment:

	IA (HL)
Criterion A	Language
Criterion B	1. Message: literary extract 2. Message: conversation
Criterion C	Interactive skills: communication

Suggest ways in which your classmates can improve their presentation techniques.

Paper 1 practice

Exam tip

At Standard Level you should write between 250 and 400 words.

At Higher Level you should write between 450 and 600 words.

1. As an intern working for a telecommunications company, you have been asked to create a short text to convince the general public to use the company's services. Your text should describe the main services your company is offering, and persuade the audience that these services are superior to those of other rival business operations. Choose one of these three text types to express your ideas.

A set of guidelines	**A leaflet**	**A proposal**

2. As part of its Information Technology policies, your school is about to adopt an important innovation regarding the classroom use of laptops, smartphones, or other communications device. Create a text to be addressed to parents which explains the reasoning behind this decision and the expected benefits for students. Choose one of these three text types with which to communicate your message.

A news report	**An advertisement**	**A pamphlet**

3. A biotech company is looking for volunteers to undergo a scientific enhancement to a normal human capacity. On behalf of the company write a suitable text which explains the nature of the enhancement, the nature of the medical procedures to be carried out, as well as the benefits for the individuals concerned. Choose one of these three text types to communicate the company's objectives.

An advertisement	**A newsletter**	**A formal letter**

Brainstorming

1. Reflect on everything you will you need

2.
- Generate ideas to be used in your text.
- If necessary, research additional material to support your opinions.

3. Sort ideas
- Put the ideas in order.
- Find good examples or evidence to support each idea.

4. Establish what else you need to think about, e.g.
- language and level of formality
- audience for the text
- context and text type .

Planning

You may wish to think about the concepts below to help you plan your written text. Think about what measures you will take to make sure your text communicates its message clearly and effectively. Reflect on the:

- context
- audience
- purpose.

Once you have planned your text, write a first draft.

Remember to include any special features of the text type, such as headlines, by-lines or layout.

Self-management skills ATLs

As you develop new language skills, learn to reflect on what you are learning.

Ask yourself these questions:

- What can I already do?
- What will I work on next?
- What can I do to become a more efficient and effective learner?
- How can I become more flexible in my choice of learning strategies?
- What factors are important for helping me learn well?
- Consider keeping a journal to record such reflections.

Drafting

Reread the completed draft of your text.

Remember you will be assessed on three criteria: **Criterion A:** Language, **Criterion B:** Message, **Criterion C:** Conceptual understanding (including audience, context and purpose).

Make any necessary changes.

Conclusion to research question C

How might future scientific and technological innovation change the human species?

- Now that you have completed the section, what do you now think is the answer?
- To what extent have your opinions on the subject changed since the beginning of this chapter? To what extent have your opinions remained the same?
- What conclusions about scientific and technological innovation and the human body have you come to in this section?
- Justify your answers.

Conclusion to the chapter

How do developments in science and technology influence our lives?

When we began the chapter, you debated this research question: How do developments in science and technology influence our lives? Now that you have completed the chapter, answer the following questions.

- Now that you have completed the chapter, what are your conclusions about the research question?
- In particular, you may want to consider this issue: What will be the role of scientific and technological innovation in the transformation of society now and in the future?
- To what extent have your opinions on the subject changed since the beginning of this chapter? Justify your answers. Which innovations do you find really interesting?
- How do you think scientific and technological innovation will affect your life?
- What more would you like to know about the subject?

Beyond the classroom

CAS

1. Creativity and activity: Using text types

In this chapter you have learned how to write a variety of publicity materials: advertisements, newsletters, flyers and leaflets.

Now use these skills to advertise a CAS project of your choosing. What aspects of the activity do you want to promote? Think about the language you will use to make sure that the material addresses the intended audience using the same level of formality as if you were talking to your customers in person. Remember that effective advertising and publicity must make the readers want to read it.

- Always visualize the members of the school community you want to reach.
- Keep in mind the needs and requirements of this target group.
- Write down what you know about the person and think about how to market your chosen project to them.
- Which persuasive techniques could you use to communicate your message?

2. Ideas for service

Research a CAS project supported by your school or another project in which you have a personal interest. The project should reflect an issue of global significance and which can be publicized from a local perspective.

For example, you could choose to explore an agency or organization that works in one of the following areas of global concerns:

- Science, technology and social equality and inequality
- Conflict, peace and security
- Economic and/or environmental sustainability
- Health and development

How can you interest local people in the project? Think about ways you can encourage students to help those in need. Use your creativity to create a publicity campaign for the project of your choice using a range of materials, such as advertisements, newsletters, flyers and leaflets.

Suggested reading

Young adult science fiction is frequently action packed. Contrary to popular belief, these books are not simply popcorn. Almost all science fiction leads the readers to new worlds. Sometimes it is to a dystopian vision of our world; sometimes readers travel to distant planets such as Kurt Vonnegut's Tralfamadore. Many of them tackle surprisingly deep moral issues. Here are just a few:

Flowers for Algernon	Daniel Keyes
Slaughterhouse 5	Kurt Vonnegut
Brave New World	Aldous Huxley
I, Robot	Isaac Asimov
The Chrysalids	John Wyndham
The Stars My Destination	Alfred Bester
The Hitchhiker's Guide to the Galaxy	Douglas Adams

9 SOCIAL ORGANIZATION
21ST-CENTURY LEARNING

Chapter summary

Theme
Social organization

Topics
Education; The working world; Higher education

Conceptual understanding
Variation

Research question for the chapter
What opportunities and challenges does the 21st century bring to education and work?

Additional research questions for each text
A What skills will I need to enter the job market?
B How can I make a really effective college application?
C Why do you need to be a really effective 21st-century learner?

TOK questions
- How do we will know whether to use text speak?
- What ways of knowing can we use to predict the future of communication?

Communication skills

Listening skills
- Receptive
- Productive

Oral and interactive skills
Role-play and drama

Written text type(s)
Formal correspondence/Supporting letters

Research question for the chapter:

What opportunities and challenges does the 21st century bring to education and work?

1. What are your first thoughts and reactions to the question above?
2. What justifications would you give for your answer?
3. What more would you need to know before you can come to a definitive conclusion about the question?

Read the following newspaper article. In groups first list and then discuss how the ideas contained might affect you in your working lives. Make a list of your conclusions.

Education for the 21st century

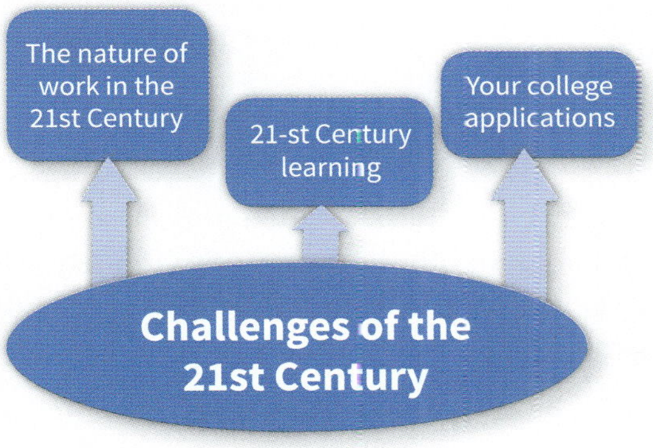

According to the World Economic Forum the gap between the skills people learn in school and the skills they need for work is becoming ever greater.
In the 19th and 20th centuries national education systems developed hand in hand with industrialized societies. Nations needed to educate entire populations to perform useful roles within factories, commercial organisations and government administration.
In this system, teachers instructed basic knowledge: maths, science, history geography, first and maybe second languages. Students absorbed that information and were tested on it. In this way children developed the basic skills of numeracy and literacy and were made ready for work.
However, the social and economic contexts in which schools are now operating are so very different from previous centuries. The twin forces of technology and globalization are driving 21st-century learning.
These twin forces are creating a world of constant and rapid change. Technological innovation means knowledge is instantly obtainable. Because of globalization, national boundaries are dissolving and work connections are becoming increasingly internationalized. As a result, teaching methodologies with regard to knowledge and skills has got to meet these challenges. The modern world will need workers who have more sophisticated ways of processing information.
There is already less demand for skilled workers who can simply follow instructions. Increasingly, workers will have to problem solve and think critically.
According to the WEF report today's school leavers must know how to use technology in order to collaborate, think critically, communicate and solve problems. Only with these skills will they be relevant to the job market of the future.

Section A: The working world

Research question A:

What skills will I need to enter the job market after I finish my studies?

1. What are your first thoughts and reactions to the question above? Make a list of points.
2. What reasons would you give for your answers?
3. What more would you need to know and what would you need to do before you could come to a definitive conclusion about the question?

Research skills ATLs

This chapter concerns 21st-century skills, so use your media literacy skills to research information about the nature of work in the 21st century.

To complete this task, interact with media to use and create ideas

- Locate, organize, analyze, evaluate, synthesize and ethically use information from a variety of sources and media.
- Demonstrate awareness of media interpretations of events and ideas.
- Make informed choices about personal viewing experiences.
- Seek a range of perspectives from multiple and varied sources.
- Compare, contrast and draw connections among (multi)media resources.

Before you read

To help you think about the research question, you might first like to discuss the meaning of the word "work". How is the concept of "work" different to the concept of "employment"?

In pairs or groups study the photograph here. What is the photograph suggesting about the nature of work in the future?

Conduct an Internet search to research the types of jobs that will be available to future generations. You may want to hold a class discussion about the kind of jobs that will be available to you and the way work will be organized by the time you have finished college or university.

Make a list of your conclusions. Now read the text.

What Work Will Look Like In The 21st Century

Dave Carvajal

The three tech trends that are shaping how you'll live and work in the century ahead

I spend plenty of time at Dave Partners talking about work in the tech world. In this week's post I am going to look at how the best minds out there are thinking about how tech is changing work itself – for all of us, whether we work in tech or not. Recently I have written about how we have so many new tools now that have changed the nature of what we can do at work. Here are some of the most exciting qualities of tech-enabled work in the 21st century.

1 ____________________

In the age of crowd-sourcing, crowd-funding and the massive cooperative projects that create open-source software, traditional business hierarchies feel rather out of date. More and more business leaders are switching to structures that allow employees to switch teams, communicate and work together across traditional boundaries. Workers can get things done without worrying about anyone's precise job description.

2 ____________________

Mark Cuban, on his Twitter, says that "jobs" are on the way out. Instead of reporting to a single employer for a set number of hours a day, 21st-century workers will operate in a perpetually open marketplace, selling chunks of time and skills to whomever can benefit from them. As more and more industries switch to a freelance model, and more and more workers rack up second jobs and freelance gigs in their spare time, it's not hard to imagine that we'll see ourselves — not as people with "jobs" – but as professionals with varied client bases that can make use of all our different talents.

3 ____________________

The Internet with all the cloud services, communication tools, and collaborative mechanisms means that almost no-one honestly needs to work in an office any longer. Almost any work you can imagine can be done from a laptop in your living room, or even from your phone.

Flexibility means that you have more options and contexts than ever before in which to get your work done — that a snowy day or a delayed train doesn't mean you can't get to work on time. It just means you can't get to your chair on time. When work becomes free, we all become free to move, which is one of the most heartening developments of all.

4 ____________________

Granted, all this sounds drastic. We should remember there's a lot to be said for stability and experience. For example, a permanent employee who's been working on your team for five years can contribute more than someone who's been brought in for an hour, simply because they know the business and you on a deeper level that only experience can buy. Moreover none of this renders offices obsolete. The kind of complex information transfer, collaboration, training and social cohesion that a truly great company needs is much easier to communicate face to face.

Match the headings with the paragraphs in the text.

- **A** Using technology in the 21st century
- **B** A word of caution
- **C** A generation of transformation
- **D** The danger of long-term employment
- **E** Collaborative working
- **F** The 21st-century office
- **G** Traditional working practices
- **H** Mobility
- **I** Fixed-term contracts
- **J** Employment in a free market

Choose the correct answer from A, B, C, or D. Write the letter in the answer box provided.

5 The text is:

A. an official report
B. an article from a lifestyle magazine
C. a technology blog
D. a news story

6 The text seems to be addressed to:

A. an audience of computer scientists
B. students and work seekers
C. a public with an interest in the subject
D. the general public.

7 The writer seems to be:

A. an entrepreneur
B. a journalist
C. a technology specialist
D. a politician.

Answer the following questions.

8 What is causing such a massive transformation in the ways we work?

9 Why is flexible working more productive for employers and employees?

10 Which word in paragraph 3 describes independent working?

11 According to paragraph 4, which word best describes the advantages of this new way of working?

12 In the final paragraph, identify the phrase which explains why long-term employees are often so valuable to a company.

Self-management skills ATLs

Consider the process of learning; choosing and using learning skills

Think about your own personal academic and professional goals.

As a future potential job seeker, make a list of all the skills and qualities mentioned in the article on page 341 that you will want to acquire by the time you enter the world of work.

Make a list of the relevant skills you already possess.

Draw up a plan of action to make sure that you able to acquire these skills when the time comes.

- Identify skills relevant to your personal academic and professional goals.
- Develop new skills, techniques and strategies for effective learning.

HL extension HL

Having read the text, *What Work Will Look Like In The 21st Century*, and having answered the comprehension questions, what more have you learned about the future of work?

Use your insights to draw up a set of guidelines for your fellow DP students explaining how they can best prepare for their future career. The best responses will give clear advice using examples and evidence from the text.

Oral activity: Role-play

As we have seen in earlier chapters, one primary purpose of role-playing exercises is to allow us to explore new ideas and look at the concepts we are learning from new perspectives. As a result, role-playing exercises can force us to adopt opinions and positions that we might not normally have. For instance, a role play can show us how to see matters from other people's perspectives, and to resolve conflicts and make compromises.

By acting out a role in an empathetic manner we may come to see other people's perspectives in a new light. We can also learn that the world is a complex place with complicated problems that need more thought than a quick "knee-jerk" answer can provide.

Internship interview

A technology and communications company, such as the one described in the text on page 341, is advertising a summer internship to DP students. Having made an application, you are invited to an interview. Role-play the interview, in which one person plays the interviewer and one the applicant.

Brainstorming

Agree on the purpose of the role-play and assign roles. Decide what questions an employer might ask. Look at your answers to the HL text handling extension task. You might be able to use some of them to stimulate the questions for the interview.

The person playing the interviewee should take time to prepare answers to the interviewer's questions.

Create back-stories for the characters. What company is the interviewer representing? What goods do they produce? Or what services do they offer?

What do you know about the interviewee? What will be the person's educational background? What useful work experience will the person have? What skills does the person possess? Produce suitable cue cards such as the one below.

Employer's cue card
Name:
Character description:
Relationship to other character in the role-play
The issue the character is facing:
The character's purpose:
The character's questions:
A
B
C
etc.

Social skills ATLs

A role play requires a great deal of cooperative interaction. At the same time you must be able to successfully argue a point of view. Use your social skills to ensure that the activity comes to a successful conclusion.

On the on hand you need to:

- listen actively to other perspectives and ideas
- encourage others to contribute.

On the other hand you must:

- exercise leadership
- advocate for your own rights and needs
- negotiate effectively.

The final outcome must be to:

- manage and resolve conflict
- work collaboratively in teams.

Interviewee's cue card

Name:

Character description:

Relationship to other character in the role-play

The character's purpose:

The character's supporting points :

A

B

C

etc.

Presenting

Conduct the role-play, giving feedback at the end of the presentation to your audience to explain what lessons you have learned from the experience.

Oral communication skills

	Good	Improvement possible	Needs some improvement	Needs a lot of improvement
Eye contact	Has good eye contact with audience.	Has eye contact with the audience most of the time.	Sometimes has eye contact with the audience.	Does not have eye contact with the audience.
Enthusiasm	Shows great enthusiasm for the topic.	Shows enthusiasm for the topic.	Shows some enthusiasm for the topic.	Shows little enthusiasm for the topic.
Preparation and organization	Very prepared and well organized.	Mostly prepared and well organized.	Somewhat prepared and organized.	Not very prepared or organized.
Clear speech	Speaks very clearly and is very easy to understand.	Speaks clearly most of the time and is fairly easy to understand.	Sometimes speaks clearly and is sometimes easy to understand.	Does not speak clearly and is quite difficult to understand.
Knowledge of topic	Shows excellent understanding of the topic.	Shows good understanding of the topic.	Shows some understanding of the topic.	Shows little understanding of the topic.

Listening comprehension

Click the icon to practice the listening section of Paper 2. After you have listened to an audio track you will complete a set of accompanying activities.

Internal assessment (SL)

Take a look at the visual stimulus below. The image relates to the theme of "Social organization".

Brainstorming

In pairs, discuss and answer the following questions.

- What is the main idea in the visual stimulus? How does it relate to the till of the section, The working world, in an Anglophone culture?
- Look at the foreground of the photograph. Describe the people and objects you can see.

What are they doing?

- What do we learn about the way the people in the picture are working?
- Do you think you would like to work in such an environment? Explain your answers.
- What skills do people need to be able to work in this way?

Preparation and presentation

Based on your answers to the questions above, prepare a four-minute presentation on the photograph.

Remember that the presentation should not only include a description of the photograph, but should also connect it to the topic of 21st-century learning and the theme of "Social organization" in an English-speaking community. Present your photograph and topic to your classmates. Remember that in the actual examination you will have 15 minutes to prepare your presentation.

Peer assessment

Assess the presentations given by your classmates. Use the SL IA criteria to guide your assessment:

	Internal assessment (SL)
Criterion A	Language
Criterion B	1. Message: visual stimulus 2. Message: conversation
Criterion C	Interactive skills: communication

Suggest ways in which your classmates can improve their presentation techniques.

Internal assessment (HL)

Read the following passage, then answer the questions that follow.

The Stars My Destination

This award-winning science fiction novel is set in the 24th century. Gully Foyle is an uneducated, unambitious worker whose life is at a dead end. At the start of the book he finds himself drifting in space after space pirates attacked his spaceship. He is the only survivor. After six months waiting for rescue, a passing spaceship, the Vorga, ignores his signal and abandons him. Foyle is enraged and wants revenge. He now has a reason to live, so he educates himself in order to restart the spaceship.

He did what [his former self] could not do; he rescued himself.

For two days he combed the wreckage in five-minute forays, and devised a harness for his shoulders. He attached an air tank to the harness and connecting the tank to his spacesuit helmet with an improvised hose. He wriggled through space like an ant dragging a log, but he had the freedom of the Nomad for all time.

He thought.

In the control bridge he taught himself to use the few navigation instruments that were still unbroken, studying the standard manuals that littered the wrecked navigation room. In the ten years of his service in space he had never dreamt of attempting such a thing, despite the rewards of promotion and the pay; but now he had *Vorga-T:1339* to reward him.

He took sights. The Nomad was drifting in space on the ecliptic, three hundred million miles from the sun. Before him were spread the constellations Perseus, Andromeda, and Pisces. Hanging almost in the foreground was a dusty orange spot that was Jupiter, distinctly a planetary disc to the naked eye. With any luck he could make a course for Jupiter and rescue.

Jupiter was not, could never be habitable. Like all the outer planets beyond the asteroid orbits, it was a frozen mass of methane and ammonia; but its four largest satellites swarmed with cities and the populations now at war with the Inner Planets. He would be a war prisoner, but he had to stay alive to settle accounts with *Vorga-T:1339*.

Foyle inspected the engine room of the nomad. There was Hi-thrust fuel remaining in the tanks and one of the four tail jets was still in operative condition. Foyle found the engine room manuals and studied them. He repaired the connection between the fuel tanks and the one jet chamber. The tanks were on the sunside of the wreck and warmed above freezing point. The Hi-thrust was still liquid, but it would not flow. In freefall there was no gravity to draw the fuel down the pipes.

Foyle studied a space manual and learned something about theoretical gravity. If he could put the Nomad into a spin, centrifugal force would impart enough gravitation to the ship to draw fuel down into the combustion chamber of the jet. If he could fire the combustion chamber, the unequal thrust of the one jet would impart a spin to the Nomad.

But he couldn't fire the jet without first having the spin; and he couldn't get the spin without first firing the jet.

He thought his way out of the deadlock; he was inspired by *Vorga*.

Foyle opened the drainage petcock[1] in the combustion chamber of the jet and tortuously filled the chamber with fuel by hand. He primed the pump. Now, if he ignited the fuel, it would fire long enough to impart the spin and start gravity. Then the flow from the tanks would commence and the rocketing would continue.

Foyle brought ice from the frozen galley tanks, melted it with his own body heat, and added water to the jet combustion chamber. The fuel and the water were non-miscible, they did not mix. The water floated in a thin layer above the fuel.

From the chemical stores Foyle brought a silvery bit of wire, pure sodium metal. He poked the wire through the open petcock. The sodium ignited when it touched the water and flared with high heat. The heat touched off the Hi-thrust which burst in a needle flame from the petcock. Foyle closed the petcock with a wrench. The ignition held in the chamber and the lone aft jet slammed out flame with a soundless vibration that shook the ship.

[1]petlock = valve used to control the flow of liquid or gas.

The Stars My Destination, by Alfred Bester

Note

In your internal assessment, the literary extract will not exceed 300 words. You will be shown two, one from each of the works of literature studied in class.

Self-management skills ATLs

When you undertake your Internal Assessment make sure that yon are in command of the situation and yourself.

Presenting is stressful, so remember to follow these guidelines to manage your own state of mind:

- Practice focus and concentration.
- Practice strategies to overcome distractions.
- Persevere with the task – don't give up easily.
- Practice strategies to reduce stress and anxiety.
- Practice "bouncing back" after mistakes and failures.

Brainstorming

In small groups, discuss the following questions then summarize your discussion in point form.

- What are the first steps Gully Foyle takes to rescue himself?
- Why does Gully Foyle intend to steer the spaceship towards the moons of Jupiter once he has started the engines?
- Describe and explain the different topics Gully must learn in order to get the spaceship's engines started.
- In your opinion, what learning skills does Gully demonstrate in the passage?
- How would you react if you found yourself in a similar situation? What skills do you possess that would help you to escape from the situation?

Preparation and presentation

Based on your answers to the questions above, prepare a four-minute presentation on the photograph.

Make your presentation to your classmates. Remember that in the actual examination you will have 20 minutes to prepare your presentation.

Students listening to the presentation should prepare individual questions about the text. They can put these questions to you at the end of your presentation.

Peer assessment

Assess the presentations given by your classmates. Use the HL IA criteria to guide your assessment:

	Internal assessment (HL)
Criterion A	Language
Criterion B	1. Message: literary extract 2. Message: conversation
Criterion C	Interactive skills: communication

Suggest ways in which your classmates can improve their presentation techniques.

Paper 1: Formal Written Correspondence

When you write a formal letter you will have a specific role, such as a customer, job applicant or college applicant. Your correspondent will probably be a specific individual or small group with a specific professional role within an organization: admissions officer, editor, or human resources manager.

Even though it is becoming less necessary to handwrite letters, you may need to compose electronic letters to a number of recipients for a number of reasons. Here are some of them.

- An application for a job or internship to a company's human resources officer.
- An enquiry to an academic office about a course of study and/or the facilities available at a specific college.
- A letter of complaint to a customer relations officer or a local government official.
- A letter of apology to an individual for any inconvenience/embarrassment/damage/offense caused.

You will want to influence your reader; therefore, you will want to communicate your ideas in a clear, organized manner.

There are many other reasons to write professional correspondence. The table below details four of the most important.

Three examples of professional correspondence

	The letter of enquiry	The letter of application	The letter of complaint
Structure and contents	A letter written when writing to an organization or individual speculatively.	A letter written when applying for an advertised position.	A letter written to complain about goods or services received.
Opening paragraph	Introduce yourself briefly and give your reason for writing.	Briefly identify yourself and the position you are applying for.	Introduce yourself briefly and explain the exact nature of your complaint.
Middle paragraphs	Make your points; for example, your reasons for inviting someone to an event or reasons for enquiring about / applying for a position	**1.** The reasons why you are interested in working for the company. **2.** Relevant qualifications and experience. **3.** Skills you have developed. **4.** Personal qualities.	Set out the exact narrative sequence of events that led to you receiving a faulty product or poor service. Explain what outcome or action you want.
Closing paragraph	Words of thanks.	Give your availability for interview, thank them for their consideration, and restate your interest.	Explain what action you will take if you do not receive satisfaction. Explain what specific action you want the addressee to take to resolve the problem.

Style tips

It has been said that formal letter writing is like a wedding; there are certain conventions that have to be followed. One set of conventions relate to form and layout. The other conventions relate to language and register.

	Required	Not acceptable
Language and register	• Correct punctuation • Paragraphing • Formal vocabulary and phrasing	• Contractions • Smileys, emoticons and emojis • Idiomatic language • SMS words • Deliberate misspellings/slang, for example, "gonna" • Swear words

This will need much planning. In order to achieve this, the formal letter should be free of grammatical and spelling mistakes. Keep in mind that you need to be polite and formal at all times.

Sample letter of enquiry

Name of organization

Dear ____________________,

I am currently an International Baccalaureate Diploma Student student in (name of school/ college), and I am writing to inquire about the possibility of a volunteer position in your organization. I plan on graduating in June, 20XX and I would be interested in beginning between June and September of the same year. I am hoping to volunteer for a period of approximately nine months.

As part of my International Baccalaureate Diploma, I have taken X Y and Z as higher subjects. As a result I have some knowledge of A B and C. Therefore, I feel I would be able to contribute to ____

For social service I have volunteered at ...As a result, I have experience of __________ ____________________ This will enable me to ______________________________

In addition I am a keen (hobby/interest/skill). Therefore, I would be willing to ____________________

Throughout the course of my senior school, I have become very interested in working for a not-for-profit organization in developing countries. I have been especially intrigued by (name of organization) and its work in the area of ______________________________

I am planning a visit to (name of the city /state/country) sometime early this summer. If possible, I would like to visit (name of the organization) at that time. I would be happy to discuss my application with you, either in person or via a video call.

Enclosed is a copy of my CV. I have asked two of my teachers to write references on my behalf. I look forward to hearing from you.

Sincerely yours,

James Wu

Discussion: Analysis of a formal letter

How many of the techniques listed below does the writer use in his formal letter?

Elements of a formal letter	Used correctly? Yes / No / Unsure
A. The writer addresses the reader correctly.	
B. The writer introduces himself clearly.	
C. The writer explains the purpose of the letter clearly.	
D. The writer makes a series of supporting points / explanations.	
E. The writer gives evidence to support any points / explanations.	
F. The writer uses paragraphing appropriately.	
G. The writer closes the letter appropriately.	
H. The writer uses a formal register at all times.	
I. The writer includes all the necessary information for the reader.	

What suggestions could you make help the writer to improve his letter of enquiry?

Writing activity: Formal correspondence

Here are three opportunities to practice writing up professional correspondence.

Note

At Standard Level you should write between 250 and 400 words.

At Higher Level you should write between 450 and 600 words.

1. Using ideas from the model letter on the previous page write a letter to the NGO of your choice volunteering your services either over the summer or for a gap year.
2. What company or organization would you most like to work for? What department would you most like to find out about? What relevant skills do you possess? Imagine applying for an internship with that company. Write a letter of enquiry asking about possible internships or paid work for the summer holiday with the employer of your dreams.
3. Re-read text A: *What Work Will Look Like In The 21st Century*. Write a letter to the author offering your opinion on the article and asking advice about how best to develop your own skills set to meet the demands of a future employer. You should state which profession or vocation you are contemplating.

Brainstorming

During the first stage write down as many ideas as you can about the letter you wish to write. What are the important points you wish to mention?

Consider the context in which you are writing. Who is the audience? What level of formality will you use to address your audience?

1. Reflect on everything you have learned in this section
   - Choose your focal point and your point of view. What information would you like to mention?

→

2.
   - Generate ideas to be used in your text.
   - If necessary, research additional material to support your letter.

Drafting

Write a first draft of the body of your letter. When you have finished, check it against the rubric below.

Elements of a formal letter	Yes / No / Not sure
A. I have addressed the reader correctly.	
B. I have introduced myself clearly.	
C. I have explained the purpose of the letter clearly.	
D. I have made a series of supporting points / explanations.	
E. I have given evidence to support my points / explanations.	
F. I have used paragraphing appropriately.	
G. I have closed the letter appropriately.	
H. I have used a formal register at all times.	
I. I have included all the necessary information for the recipient.	

Now complete a second draft of your letter, taking into account the improvements you have suggested to yourself.

Remember you will be assessed on three criteria: **Criterion A:** Language, **Criterion B:** Message, **Criterion C:** Conceptual understanding (including audience, context and purpose).

Conclusion to research question A

What skills will I need to enter the job market?

Now that you have completed the section, what do you think is the answer?

- To what extent have your opinions changes since the beginning of this chapter? To what extent have you opinions remained the same?
- What big ideas have you learned about 21st-century skills in this section? Explain your answers.

Conceptual understanding: Variation

21st-century skills

Look at the infographic.

Discuss the skills and competences the poster lists. In groups consider whether all these skills are equally important.

Alternatively, rank these skills from most important to least important.

Conduct a self-assessment survey. Which skills have you already mastered? Which skills do you need to develop further?

Share your findings with your group, decide what steps you can take to improve those skills.

Now consider the ways in which the infographic communicates information.

Answer these questions.

- What was the writer's purpose in creating the text?
- Who is the intended audience for the text?
- What is the overall (and unstated) message of the text?

Now identify the variety of language used by the writers.

- Why have they used this specific variety of language?
- What are the features of this variety of English?

Make a list of the features of this variety of English.

Conceptual understanding: Variation

Variation is a characteristic of **language**: there is more than one way of saying the same thing. For example, speakers of English may vary pronunciation (accent), and word choice (lexicon). This is often due to geography, so speakers of British English sound different and sometimes use different vocabulary to, say, the Irish, Canadians, South Africans or New Zealanders. As a research project, look at the variations in vocabulary that exist in the USA and the UK, or UK and Australia. Alternatively find out about the varieties of English that exist in Sierra Leone, Papua New Guinea. Jamaica or Hawaii.

Other variations occur on a more local level. Most Anglophone countries have regional accents. So, for example, within England there are big differences between the way English is spoken in London (South East), Birmingham (Midlands) and Manchester (North West) and the other English regions. Other variations are due to **social class**. There can be huge differences between the English of the working classes and middle classes. Other variations are related to factors such as gender, community and age.

Study the poster on the previous page, *The Top 10 Skills employers are looking for.*

- What variety of English have the authors used to communicate their message?
- How do audience and purpose influence the author's choice of language?

How would you have to vary the language and the images of the poster on page 353 to make them relevant to an audience of 11-year-olds? How would you vary your language to explain these ideas to a much younger audience?

How would you change the vocabulary of the text? What changes would you make to the sentence structures? In what other ways could you vary your poster to communicate the same message to a group of 11 year olds?

When you have completed your discussions, create a new poster explaining the need for 21st century skills targeted at this much younger audience.

Present your poster to your class explaining how you have varied your use of English to communicate the same ideas to a different audience.

Section B: Higher education

Research question B:

How can I make a really effective college application?

1. What are your first thoughts and reactions to research question B? Make a list of points.
2. What reasons would you give for your answers?
3. What more would you need to know and what would you need to research before you could come to a definitive conclusion about the question?

Before you listen

Soon you may be heading off to college. What do you think it will be like?

How can you make sure that you will be successful? To answer these questions, you may need to analyze the idea of "a successful college life".

To help you with the task, here is some advice offered to first year students by a group of college counselors. Read through the list and categorize the ideas into different aspects of college life

1. Be organized.
2. Be prepared to feel stressed.
3. Cope with homesickness.
4. Don't cut corners when revising.
5. Don't keep going home.
6. Don't make hasty decisions about a future career.
7. Develop learning skills.
8. Don't procrastinate.
9. Find the best place to study.
10. Use the Careers Services.
11. Get involved on campus.
12. Get to know your academic adviser.
13. Get to know your roommate and others in your residence.
14. Get to know your teachers.
15. Go to classes.
16. Go to the orientations.
17. Know the course requirements and due dates.
18. Make connections with students in your classes.
19. Manage your money.
20. Seek a college / social life balance.
21. Seek help whenever you need it.
22. Stay healthy.
23. Strive for good grades.
24. Take responsibility for your actions.
25. Use all available study resources.

Working in groups, look at the diagram opposite. Use it to categorize the advice above into different aspects of college life so that you can say, "Here are the four most important things I need to think about in my first year at college".

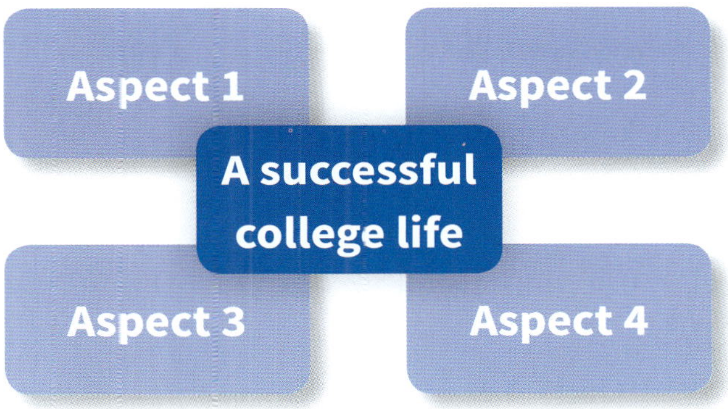

Listening comprehension

How to integrate during your first year at college

You are going to listen to a recording of a college adviser explaining how students can make a success of their first year at college. Listen to the extract, then answer the questions that follow.

Answer the following questions.

1. At what point in the college year is the counselor addressing her audience?
2. Which specific group of students does the speaker appear to be addressing?
3. According to the speaker how can her talk help students integrate?
4. List three ways the speaker believes members of the audience can improve their appearance.
5. ***Choose the three true statements made by the speaker in the broadcast.***

   A. The speaker believes it is necessary to overcome shyness.
   B. It is best not to make unfunny jokes.
   C. It is best to avoid uncomfortable conversations.
   D. People do not like being asked questions about their appearance.
   E. We should plan what to say when meeting new people.
   F. Saying nothing can make you seem mysterious and attractive.
   G. The speaker believes people enjoy being asked about themselves.

Complete the sentences below with information from the recording.

6. You can make your views known by…
7. Publicizing your opinions…
8. People will never dislike you if you prove to be …
9. The speaker thinks the advice will help the audience…

HL extension HL

Look back at the "Before you listen" exercise you have already completed, and compare it to the address you have just heard. Listen to the address again and make notes on these questions.

- Which topic did the speaker address?
- Which specific points did she make?
- Do you think that the speaker's advice is really essential for the audience?
- Which additional, and possibly more important, topics could she have mentioned?

Write an email to a friend of 100 to 150 words evaluating the speaker address and explaining what additional information you would like to have heard about.

Oral activity: Role-play College interviews

Divide into pairs. One person should play the interviewer and one the interviewee.

Imagine you have to attend an interview to get into the college of your choice.

Clearly you will need to be really well prepared for a fifteen minutes that could change your future. Use this opportunity to practice your interview skills.

Brainstorming

Here a 16 more common college interview questions.

What questions do you think a college admissions officer might ask you?

- **A.** Tell me about any community service you have undertaken.
- **B.** Tell me about yourself
- **C.** What are your academic strengths?
- **D.** What can you contribute to the college?
- **E.** What cross-curricular skills do you possess?
- **F.** What do you expect to be doing ten years from now?
- **G.** What do you like to do for fun?
- **H.** What is your favourite book?
- **I.** How have you addressed your academic weaknesses?
- **J.** What makes you unique?
- **K.** What are your best problem-solving strategies?
- **L.** What would you most like to change at your high school?
- **M.** Who is the person you admire most?
- **N.** Why do you want to come to this college?
- **O.** Why do you want to go to college?
- **P.** Why do you want to study [subject]?

Make a list of any additional questions that a university admissions officer might ask.

Planning

Each person should choose 10 college interview questions from the list above. Do not reveal the questions to your partner. Put the questions in the most logical order.

Produce a cue card with all the questions.

At the same time use your research skills to develop suitable answers to all the potential questions.

Create answer cards containing the question and key words to help you remember your responses.

Use your time-management skills to make sure that you are well prepared for the task.

Presenting

Conduct the role-play, taking turns to play the interviewer and interviewee. Ask another group to give feedback, both on the quality of the questions and answers and the performance of the role-play.

You can use the "oral communication skills" table on page 344 for this purpose.

Internal assessment (SL)

Take a look at one of the visual stimuli below. The images relate to the theme of "Social organization".

Brainstorming

In pairs, choose one photograph then discuss and answer the following questions.

- How does the image relate to the theme of the section, "College applications" in an English-speaking country?
- What does the image tell you about the location and context of the picture?
- Look at the foreground of the picture. Describe the people you can see.
- What is the story behind the photograph?
- How would you feel if you were the young person in the picture?
- How does the picture relate to the theme of the chapter: "21st-century learning?"

Presenting

Based on your answers to the questions above, prepare a four-minute presentation on the photograph.

Remember that the presentation should not only include a description of the photograph, but should also connect it to the topic of 21st century learning in an Anglophone culture. Present your photograph and topic to your classmates. Remember that in the actual examination you will have 15 minutes to prepare your presentation.

Peer assessment

In small groups, assess the presentations given by your classmates. You may use the rubrics on page 344 as a basis for your comments.

Communication skills ATLs

When you interpret your photograph for your Internal Assessment, use these valuable communication skills:

- Take effective notes in the preparation time.
- Make effective summary notes for your presentation.
- Use a suitable organizer for preparing your presentation.
- Organize and depict information logically so you can refer to your notes during your presentation.
- Express your ideas accurately and concisely.

Internal assessment (HL)

Read the following passage, then answer the questions that follow.

A college interview

LaVaughn is attempting to achieve her life's ambition: to become the first in her family to attend college. She has applied for a special program called WIMS – Women in Medical Science. In this scene, LaVaughn is interviewed for a place on the course.

Someone calls my name, I go through the open door,
the interviewer puts out her hand to shake
and I put mine out and I look her in the eye
and don't look away
till we are finished and she lets my hand go.
"Please sit down. That's a good handshake," she says.
I send mental message to the Guidance Man
and listen hard for her questions.

She wants to know why I want to be in WIMS.
She wants to know if I do science in my spare time.
I say I'm going to Summer Science for two summers
and not missed a day.
I can't tell if that's a good answer or not,
I sit upright on the chair and hope.

"Your test score is quite nice.
Have you had experience in memorizing scientific data?"
I hear "Lithium 3, beryllium 4, boron 5, carbon 6, nitrogen 7, oxygen 8…"
coming out of my mouth
before I noticed it is foolish and ridiculous.
I stop. She looks at me. She smiles. I don't know why.
She would not let me into the class if she knew
how many hours my mom had quizzed me
on the periodic table,
saying, "It's like I know this myself, LaVaughn
and I don't get any of it –
The numbers look like they *should* add up –"
and how I have lain in a hot bath and cried with the effort.
Then the interviewer asks, "What is it about science
that compels your interest?"
I think about Mendel and his pea plants
how he thought up dominant and recessive genes
and got ignored till after he was dead,

but he might not be unusual enough.
I think about the little kids and the frogs and the swamp
none of it seems right to bring up. "I like the labs..."
I say, and I know I should walk out of the room
right now
because I have failed.

I don't know why I began blurting:
"And an adult human eyeball
is 2.5 centimeters in diameter,
and the blue whale's is 15 centimeters
and the giant squid has an eyeball that's 25 centimeters.
25 centimeters! An eyeball!"

The interviewer looked at me and nodded her head.
"Yes," she said, and then she said "Yes," again.
She did not look away from me
and I blurted again,
"Somebody goes blind every five seconds in the world.
Isn't that terrible? And once every minute a child does.
Isn't that the saddest thing?"
This was wrong, all wrong.

She said, "Your application says you want to be a nurse,
LaVern. What makes you think
you would be a good one?"
She has my name wrong.
"Uh, I've worked in the hospital for more than two years,
the Children's
folding laundry – I mean it's only laundry, but –
uh, I've seen many little kids being sick,
with cancer, leukaemia, terminal diseases–
I want – Uh, I want to help in some little way –"
I rub my right hand on my skirt,
my hand is sweaty and cold,
and the interviewer says, "Thank you, LaVern."
And even with the shakes and quivers all through me,
I tell her, "My name is LaVaughn. Please? It's LaVaughn."
Why did I put "please?" in there?
She looks quickly down at the paper
and says,' Oh – Well, thank you, LaVaughn."
She stands up, I stand up,
she shakes my hand, looking at me with a straight mouth
and I looked in a straight line between her eyes
and shake back.

I walked out of the office,

Note

In your internal assessment, the literary extract will not exceed 300 words. You will be shown two, one from each of the works of literature studied in class.

Through the hall to the elevator,
out of the elevator to the bus stop.
I should not have said
all those disjointed things –
a giant squid's eyeballs –
Why in the world did I tell her I folded laundry?
Laundry does not take any skill.

This Full House, by Virginia Euwer Wolff

Brainstorming

In small groups, discuss the following questions then summarize your discussion in point form.

1. What are the signs that LaVaughn is nervous throughout the interview?
2. What skills, attitudes and aptitudes is the interviewer assessing through her questions to LaVaughn?
3. Why does LaVaughn think she has answered certain questions very badly?
4. What is your overall assessment of LaVaughn's interview? How well or how badly has she performed?
5. On the basis of this interview, would you offer her a place on the nursing course? Justify your answers.

Presenting

Based on your answers to the questions above, prepare a four-minute presentation on the contents of the text.

Make your presentation to your classmates. Remember that in the actual examination you will have 20 minutes to prepare your presentation.

Peer assessment (IA)

In small groups, assess the presentations given by your classmates. You may use the HL IA assessment criteria in the Language B guide as a basis for your comments.

Paper 1: Letters of application

Read the following guidelines. As you read, make a list of the 10 most important lessons you have learned from the text.

How to write a college interest letter

Step 1: Laying the groundwork

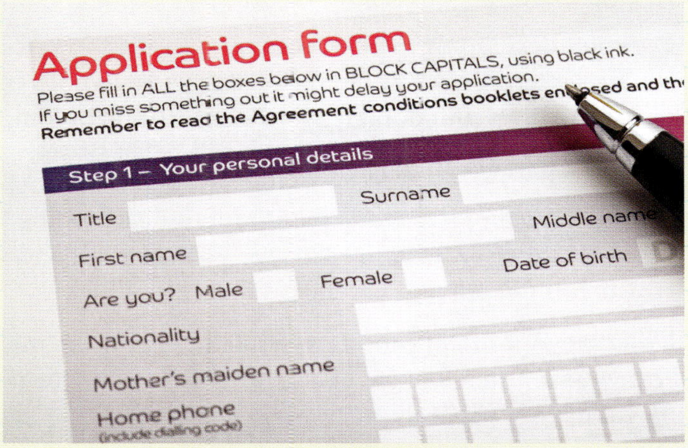

Research the college or educational program thoroughly.

Take note of the exact name of the college or program you are applying to. You don't want to mention 'X University Law School' if the name is actually 'X University School of Law.'

Read the mission statement, program description, and program requirements to ensure that it is the right fit for you.

Take note of specific courses that appeal to you. You might want to refer to some of these in your letter.

Read all of the application directions thoroughly.

Ensure that you understand all of the instructions and that you know what documents to prepare. For example, many colleges request both a completed application form and a personal essay.

Examine your own accomplishments.

You may find it helpful to create a list of accomplishments, skills, and achievements.

Reflect on your achievements. Academic, employment, volunteering and extracurricular activities are all relevant.

Define your goals.

You will likely have two sets of goals in your letter: your goals while you are in the program and your future career goals. Ask yourself: How will this particular course of study help my personal and academic development? Decide what your career goals are.

Step 2: Organizing your ideas

Write your thesis statement. Like all other academic essays, your letter of interest needs to have a central focus. In this case, this focus will be you: your reasons for applying: your plans for the college or program you're attending, your future goals, and how you are a good fit for the program or school. What would be your thesis for your letter of interest?

Outline your academic journey so far.

Why are you applying for this particular program? Answer these questions:

When did you realize that you wanted to pursue this field?

What challenges have you faced and overcome?

Step 3: Organizing your writing

Plan your introduction. Your introduction should introduce the program to which you're applying and your personal goals. It should give your readers some idea of who you are, why you have chosen your field, and why you are applying to this particular program.

Formulate a few clear and concise introductory statements about your interest in the program and its alignment with your goals.

Consider developing a 'hook' for your introduction. You could begin with a statement that grabs the reader's interest, such as 'I haven't always known I wanted to do X. In fact, I thought for a long time I wanted to do Y.' But don't let your introduction become your life story.

Devote a paragraph to each main idea.

In general, plan at least one paragraph for each of the following: your personal qualifications and previous experience, your plans for your studies, and your future goals and why the program to which you're applying will help you achieve them.

Describe your qualifications in terms of your academic experiences, your personal traits and skills, and your recent and current activities. Relate any responsibilities or experience to skills that will be useful in your program.

Discuss your area(s) of interest. Don't simply say you want to study 'History', for example. Instead, state which specific aspects or areas of 'History' you are interested in.

Describe your future goals, where possible. What do you want to become? Then, demonstrate how the skills you expect to develop in your program will contribute to your achieving these goals.

Provide evidence for each main idea. Examples of evidence include experiences, skills, and personal traits. For each claim that you make, you should have at least one piece of evidence to support it.

Develop the conclusion. An effective college interest letter leaves the admissions committee with a clear understanding of who you are and what you hope to accomplish. Close your letter by conveying that you are highly motivated, dedicated to excelling in the program, and focused on achieving your academic and/or professional goals.

Step 4: Proofread carefully

Your letter is your first chance to make an impression on the admissions committee. Careless proofreading and grammar errors can seriously damage a reader's opinion of your preparation or seriousness, so read over your letter at least twice.

Read your letter aloud. This will help you catch awkward phrases and any missing or incorrect words. Rewrite as necessary.

When you have finished reading, compare your "10 most important lessons about writing college applications" with other students in your class. What conclusions do you come to?

Writing activity: college letters

Write a response to one of these prompts.

1. Use this opportunity to practice writing your letter of application or accompanying letter to the college of your choice. Make the best use of the advice given in this section.
2. An overseas educational foundation is offering 50 students from around the world the opportunity to spend a 'semester at sea' on board a cruise ship which travels around the world. The successful applicants will visit 20 countries and while at sea study university foundation courses. Write your letter of application.
3. You have already been accepted at the college of your choice but have now decided to spend a gap year working abroad for an NGO. Write a letter to the college admissions office explaining why you wish to take this course of action, and listing the skills and benefits you will gain from the experience. In your letter you must ask for a deferment, so that you can start your studies a year later than anticipated.

Reread the completed draft of your letter and revise as necessary.

Remember you will be assessed on three criteria: **Criterion A:** Language, **Criterion B:** Message, **Criterion C:** Conceptual understanding (including audience, context and purpose).

Note

Normally at Standard Level you should write between 250 and 400 words and at Higher Level you should write between 450 and 600 words. However, in this instance, you are practicing life skills, so you may want to write responses that are longer than the usual assessment guidelines.

Communication skills ATLs

Make sure to use all the conventions and formatting associated with formal correspondence.

Consider the context in which you are writing.

- Who is the audience?
- What is its purpose?
- What level of formality will you use to address your audience?

Conclusion to research question B

How can I make a really effective college application?

1. What have you learned about writing effective college application letter and being interviewed for a college place in this section?
2. What reasons would you give for your answers?
3. Now that you have completed this section what general advice on this topic would you give to younger students applying to college next year?

A TOK moment

TOK

In this extract from the comic play *Pygmalion,* the flower girl, Elisa Doolittle, has decided that she wants to take lessons in order to speak middle class English. She chose Professor Henry Higgins to be her teacher as she had met him by chance the night before, without knowing that he is the most distinguished Linguistics teachers in Victorian England. She arrives unannounced at the Professor's grand London residence where she is met by Mrs Pearce, the housekeeper, and Colonel Pickering, Higgins' houseguest. The subsequent informal interview goes very badly. Read the extract and think about the varieties of English that you can observe. Is the language of the speakers appropriate to the situation? Make a list of your observations.

The flower girl enters in state. She has a hat with three ostrich feathers, orange, sky-blue, and red. She has a nearly clean apron, and the shoddy coat has been tidied a little.

HIGGINS [*brusquely, recognizing her with unconcealed disappointment, and at once, baby-like, making an intolerable grievance of it*] Why, this is the girl I jotted down last night. She's no use: I've got all the records I want of the Lisson Grove lingo; and I'm not going to waste another cylinder on it. [*To the girl*] Be off with you: I don't want you.

THE FLOWER GIRL. Don't you be so saucy. You ain't heard what I come for yet. [*To Mrs. Pearce, who is waiting at the door for further instruction*] Did you tell him I come in a taxi?

MRS. PEARCE. Nonsense, girl! what do you think a gentleman like Mr. Higgins cares what you came in?

THE FLOWER GIRL. Oh, we are proud! He ain't above giving lessons, not him: I heard him say so. Well, I ain't come here to ask for any compliment; and if my money's not good enough I can go elsewhere.

HIGGINS. Good enough for what?

THE FLOWER GIRL. Good enough for ye-oo. Now you know, don't you? I'm come to have lessons, I am. And to pay for em too: make no mistake.

HIGGINS [*stupent*] WELL! ! ! [*Recovering his breath with a gasp*] What do you expect me to say to you?

THE FLOWER GIRL. Well, if you was a gentleman, you might ask me to sit down, I think. Don't I tell you I'm bringing you business?

HIGGINS. Pickering: shall we ask this baggage to sit down or shall we throw her out of the window?

THE FLOWER GIRL [*running away in terror to the piano, where she turns at bay*] Ah-ah-ah-ow-ow-ow-oo! [*Wounded and whimpering*] I won't be called a baggage when I've offered to pay like any lady.

Motionless, the two men stare at her from the other side of the room, amazed.

PICKERING [*gently*] What is it you want, my girl?

THE FLOWER GIRL. I want to be a lady in a flower shop stead of selling at the corner of Tottenham Court Road. But they won't take me unless I can talk more genteel. He said he could teach me. Well, here I am ready to pay him—not asking any favor—and he treats me as if I was dirt.

As a TOK exercise now consider these questions.

- In what way is the flower girl's behaviour inappropriate as an interviewee?
- In what way is Professor Higgins' behaviour inappropriate as an interviewer?
- In what way is Professor Higgins' language inappropriate to the situation?
- Given her circumstances, is the flower girl's language inappropriate in the context?
- How do we know what is the correct variety of language to use in a specific context?
- Which TOK ways of knowing can best help us make the correct choices?

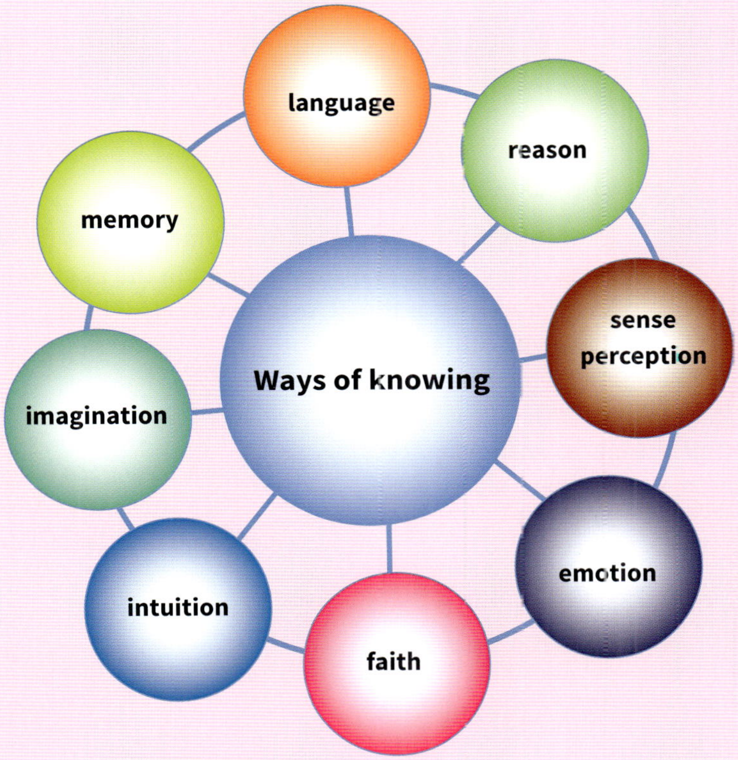

Why is it so important to know what variety of English to use:

a. in your social life
b. in your academic life
c. in your future professional life?

Section C: Education

Thinking skills ATLs

The poster below creates a relationship between the ATL skills you have developed in this course and 21st-century learning skills.

The International Baccalaureate promotes a number of Approaches to Learning which you have developed in this book.

How important are all these skills to you above and beyond their use in the classroom?

When you have come to a conclusion, think about how you could use a media platform to convey this message to primary students aged 10 or 11.

Research question C:

Why do you need to be a really effective 21st-century learner?

1. What are your first thoughts and reactions to research question C? Make a list of points.
2. What reasons would you give for your answers?
3. What more would you need to know and what would you need to do before you could come to a definitive conclusion about the statement?

Before you read

In groups study the poster. What messages is the poster communicating? How many of the skills mentioned in the poster do you already possess? Make two lists of the 21st-century skills which you already master and those you still need to improve.

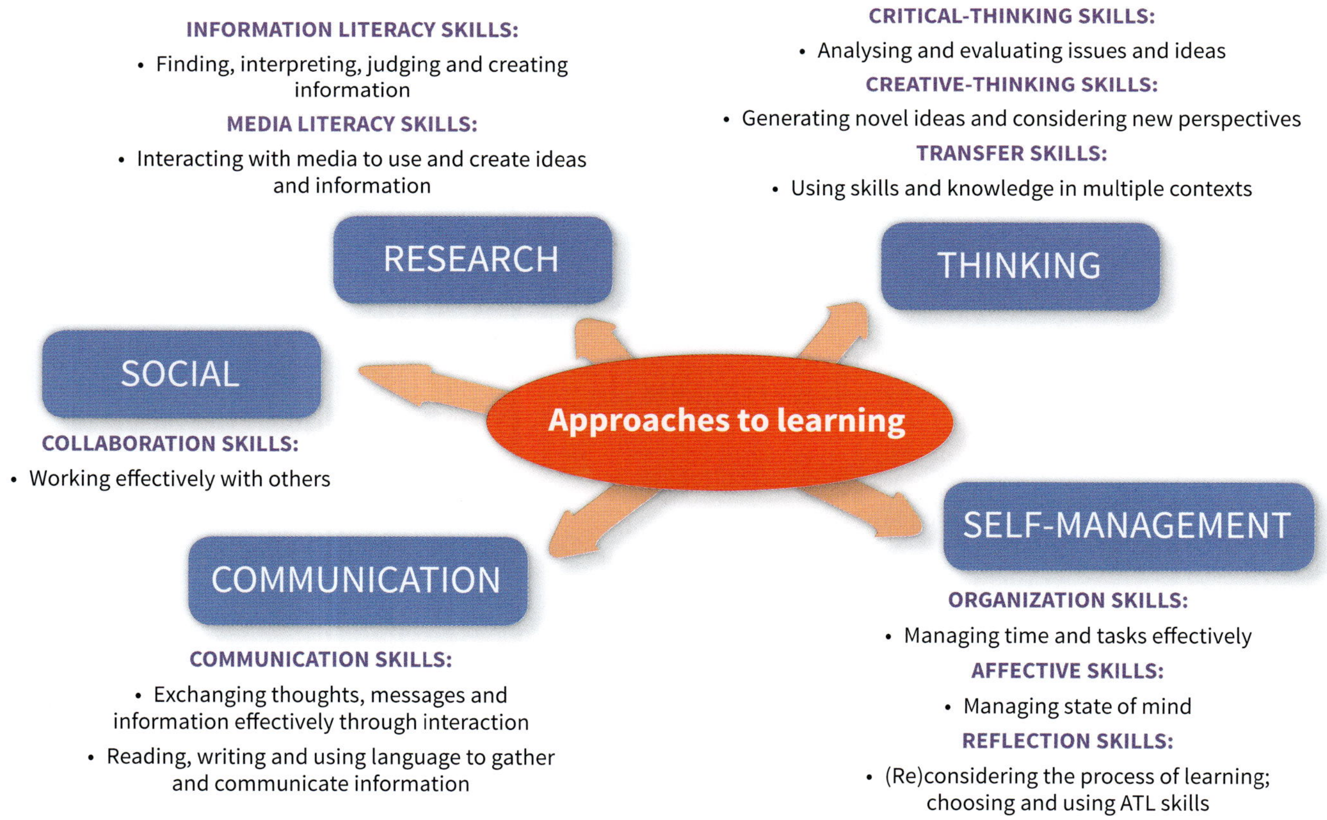

Judging by your findings, how employable do you think you are at the moment? What practical skills can you offer an employer?

What does it mean to be a 21st-century learner?

Eric Mthembu

The classroom we knew years back doesn't exist anymore. Desks lined up in rows, chalkboards, and independent work has been exchanged for interactive technologies, movable desks and unconventional learning spaces.

Today's learners enjoy collaborating with each other and sharing knowledge and resources. Passionate educators also share their experiences and learn from peers. They're always on the lookout for learning strategies and pedagogically sound practices to best help their students succeed.

Technology has been central to successful learning strategies. It can foster collaboration – so that groups of students can share a mutual understanding of the learning processes; negotiate new ideas through social interactions; co-construct answers to problems; and engage in active participation.

Twenty-first-century learning means that students still have to master content. But now they also produce it. They learn to synthesize, and evaluate information from a wide variety of subjects and sources while understanding and respecting diverse cultures. Students demonstrate the 3 Rs: reading, 'riting and 'rithmetic, but also the 6Cs: collaboration, critical thinking, creativity, computational thinking, contribution and communication.

Using technology, pupils in classrooms all around the world are connecting to their local communities, to the workforce, and to other schools and organizations around the world. Students must therefore develop the intercultural understanding necessary to share and work on ideas with people from different cultures while adding input and making suggestions in a respectful and responsible way.

'Success in the 21st century requires knowing how to learn. Students today are likely to have several different careers in their lifetime. They must develop strong critical thinking and interpersonal communication skills in order to be successful in an increasingly fluid, interconnected, and complex world', says Candice DuPreez, Chief Operations Officer at Vastratech.

All children are creative and the goal of schools should be to preserve this creativity instead of hindering it, which has too often been the case in the schooling process. By allowing students multiple outlets for their creativity, to add to ideas and projects, and to create input, students can express their ideas and creativity not just in art classes but for the rest of their lives.

It may take some time before all teachers are properly equipped to educate in the 21st century. Once more are trained, the results will be dramatic. Children will be engaged and eager to learn. In fact, they will carry on learning at home and over holidays, and they will have the resources they need to keep learning no matter where they are. This ability to foster a love of learning is truly the role of education in the 21st century.

https://southafricatoday.net/press-release/what-does-it-mean-to-be-a-21st-century-learner/

Reading comprehension

The sentences below are either true or false. Tick [√] the correct response then justify it with a relevant brief quotation from the text.

		True	False
1.	According to the writer there has been little change in classrooms in South Africa.		
Justification:			
2.	Children like group learning and teamwork.		
Justification:			
3.	Technology has had only a limited impact on learning.		
Justification:			
4.	Students no longer need to learn information.		
Justification:			
5.	Children in schools are increasingly going outside their classrooms to learn about the world.		
Justification:			
6.	The way students learn is now at least as important as what they learn.		
Justification:			
7.	A good school will help children to develop their imagination.		
Justification:			
8.	The majority of teachers can already make use of these new teaching techniques.		
Justification:			

Answer the following questions

9. Name three characteristics of the 21st-century classroom.

   a. ____________________ b. ____________________ c. ____________________

10. According to the writer, in what ways are 21st-century teachers very similar to their students?

    ____

11. According to the text, what do today's students need to develop in order to work with members of communities different to our own?

    ____

12. According to Candice DuPreez, why will students need 21st-century skills in their adult lives?

    ____

Answer the questions by writing the correct answer in the box

13. The greatest benefit of 21st-century learning will be to:

A. educate teachers better
B. improve the status of education
C. create lifelong learners
D. encourage learning in the holidays.

14. The text seems to be addressed to:

A. parents
B. students
C. teachers
D. the general public.

15. The text is:

A. an official report
B. a magazine article
C. a proposal
D. a news report.

Listening comprehension

Click the icon to practice the listening section of Paper 2. After you have listened to an audio track you will complete a set of accompanying activities.

HL extension

HL

Make a list of all the features of 21st-century learning mentioned in the text. Categorize them into the table below.

Necessary equipment	Teaching methodologies	Student activities

How many of these features are already available to you in your present school? What additional facilities would students need in your school to become better 21st-century learners? Write a proposal of 100 to 150 words to your principal suggesting ways to improve learning in your school.

Oral activity: Discussion

Consider what you have learned from the text *What does it mean to be a 21st-century learner?* With your teacher discuss and debate answers to the following questions.

- Do you think this English B Course Companion is suitable for the needs of 21st-century learners?
- What suggestions would you make to the authors to make the English B Course Companion even more compatible with the aims of 21st-century learning?

In class make lists of the positive features of the book and the methodologies within it, and your suggestions to the authors.

Decide what action to take with the conclusions you have come to.

Oral activity: Role-play

Your school is reviewing its approach to teaching and learning. There is a large group of students, parents and other members of the community who are worried about exam results and who would welcome a return to traditional teaching methods. There is another group who argue in favour of introducing more, not less, inquiry-based learning into the curriculum.

https://www.edutopia.org/discussion/10-signs-21st-century-classroom

Document A: Ten signs of a 21st century classroom

1. Integration of technology

Students using technology to seek, evaluate, synthesize and communicate in a different ways than was possible before.

2. A collaborative learning environment

Collaboration fosters the development of new ideas and exposes students to opposing viewpoints. It develops social and thinking skills

3. Opportunities for creativity

Creative opportunities, such as brainstorming, not only help understanding, but also build students' confidence as they learn to think independently and find solutions to difficult problems.

4. Inquiry-based learning

The core idea is that students approach a new topic by looking to answer a research question. Learning is organized in such a way that they can find answers, come to conclusions and then apply what they have learned to the world beyond the classroom. It is a cornerstone of current teaching methods.

5. Justification for answers

In the past students were only asked to find answers. By developing critical thinking we can encourage students to approach a problem from a number of angles and discover what they truly believe.

6. Writing for reflection

Self-reflection reinforces metacognitive learning (learning about learning). If students use a blog for reflection, they may even be surprised to learn that others are interested in their thoughts.

7. Use of problem solving methodologies

Problem solving goes well beyond science classrooms. Having a problem solving approach can aid students in many other areas such as composing a short story or solving an economics problem.

8. Hands-on learning

Students learn best by doing rather than listening.

9. Teacher as facilitator

The teacher is no longer an authoritarian figure standing in the front of the room scrawling on a chalkboard. As educators, our role is to work beside students providing support and encouragement for their inquiries.

10. Transparent assessment

Students perform better and form stronger connections with material if they are able to understand how they are assessed and how that assessment is measured. Students need to see and understand the formative and summative assessments rubrics used to measure their development and exam performance.

https://www.edutopia.org/discussion/10-signs-21st-century-classroom

Create a role-play in which representatives of both sides come together to discuss the way forward.

Study the following documents.

DOCUMENT B: TWELVE PRINCIPLES OF TRADITIONAL EDUCATIONAL METHODS

1. The school takes responsibility for supplying all learning facilities and resources.

2. Students work from textbooks and workbooks using pen and paper to record answers

3. Teachers have subject knowledge and share it with students

4. The teacher is in charge and will often lecture

5. Students take notes, and master the skills of the subject

6. Teacher stands at the front of the class

7. Students sit at quiet rows of desks

8. Learning is achieved by memorization and homework.

9. Teachers give frequent tests and exam practice to test knowledge and understanding

10. Students are motivated to achieve excellent grades

11. There are clear and distinct classroom rules

12. The school promises to prepare students for the 'real-world'

Thinking skills ATLs

This exercise allows you to practice meta-cognition or "thinking about thinking".

Here are some questions to think about:

- What are the best ways to learn?
- Are there differences in the ways we learn facts and the ways we learn skills?
- What are the most effective ways of learning?
- Do we all learn equally well using the same methods?

Brainstorming

Create the characters' backstories, personalities and their opinions; use the information you have been given to produce cue cards. You may want to add information and ideas of your own.

Name:

Description of the group:

The group's point of view:

The group's arguments and evidence:

A

B

C

etc.

You may wish to modify the cue card to meet your exact purpose in this particular role-play, that is, to present a coherent point of view either supporting or opposing traditional forms of teaching and learning.

Peer assessment

In small groups, assess the role-plays undertaken by your classmates. You may use the criteria "Oral communication skills" rubrics on page 344 as a basis for your comments.

Presenting

Conduct the role-play. When you have finished, explain to your audience what you have concluded about which forms of learning are the most suitable for your school in the face of: (a) the short-term need to do as well as possible in exams, (b) the long-term employment challenges of the 21st century.

Internal assessment (SL)

Take a look at one of the visual stimuli below. The images relate to the theme of the chapter, "Social organization".

Brainstorming

In pairs, choose one of the pictures then discuss and answer the following questions.

- Explain how the picture relates to the theme of the section, "21st-century learning" in an Anglophone community.
- What do you see in background of the picture? What does the background tell you about the location and context of the picture?
- Look at the foreground of the picture. Describe the people you can see.
- Explain what is happening in your chosen picture.
- What is the main idea in the picture? How does it relate to the theme of the chapter: "Education"?

Presenting

Based on your answers to the questions above, prepare a four-minute presentation on the photograph.

Remember that the presentation should not only include a description of the photograph, but should also connect it to the topic of 21st-century learning in an English-speaking society. Present your photograph and topic to your classmates. Remember that in the actual examination you will have 15 minutes to prepare your presentation.

Peer assessment

In small groups, assess the presentations given by your classmates. You may use the SL IA assessment criteria in the Language B guide as a basis for your comments.

Internal assessment (HL)

Read the extract from the novel Mister Pip and then answer the questions that follow.

Meeting Mr Dickens

The novel is set on the island of Bougainville, today part of Papua New Guinea. The book follows the fortunes of the teenage narrator, Matilda, who is growing up in a distant and neglected rural community, which is now being blockaded by one of the warring factions in a violent civil war. The novel opens with the arrival of Mr Watts who is married to Grace, a native of Bougainville. This fact explains why he has remained after all the other Europeans abandoned the island. Watts decides to take on the task of educating the local children at the abandoned school. With very few other resources available, he decides to introduce his students to one of the only books he possesses, Great Expectations, by the great nineteenth-century writer, Charles Dickens.

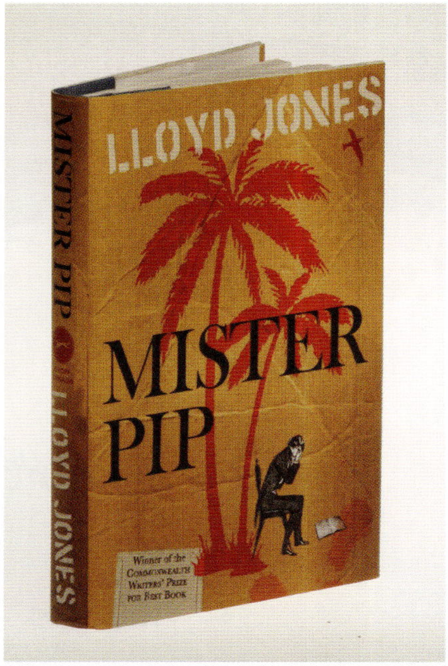

I had never been read to in English before. Neither had the others. We didn't have books in our homes, and before the blockade our only books had come from Moresby, and those were written in pidgin. When Mr Watts read to us we all fell quiet. It was a new sound in the world. He read slowly so we heard the shape of each word.

(...)

He kept reading and we kept listening. It was sometime before he stopped, but when he looked up we sat stunned by the silence. The flow of the words had ended. Slowly we stirred back into our bodies and our lives.

Mr Watts closed the book and held the paperback up in one hand like a church minister. We saw him smile from one corner of the room to the other. 'That was chapter one of *Great Expectations*, which, incidentally, is the greatest novel by the greatest English writer of the nineteenth century, Charles Dickens.'

Now we all felt silly as bats for thinking we were going to be introduced to someone by the name of Mr Dickens. Perhaps Mr Watts had an idea what was going on in our heads, though. 'When you read the work of a great writer,' he told us, 'you are making the acquaintance of that person. So you can say you have met Mr Dickens on the page, so to speak. But you don't know him yet.'

One of the younger kids, Mabel, put up with her hand to ask a question. At first we thought Mr Watts hadn't seen her because he carried on over the top of Mabel's waving hand. 'I welcome questions. I won't always be able to answer them. Remember that,' he said. 'Also, when you raise your hand to ask me something, would you be so kind as to give your name?'

He nodded in Mabel's direction.

'...

'Mabel, Mr Watts,' she said.

'Good I'm very pleased to meet you, Mabel. That is a very pretty name,' he said.

Mabel shone. She wriggled into her desk. Then she spoke.

'When can we say we know Mr Dickens?'

Mr Watts brought up two fingers to his chin. We watched him think for a moment.

'That is a very good question, Mabel. In fact, my first response is that you have asked me something to which there is no answer. But I will give it my best shot. Some of you will know Mr Dickens when we finish the book. The book is fifty-nine chapters long. If we read a chapter a day, that's fifty-nine days.'

This was difficult information to bring home. We had met Mr Dickens but we did not know him yet, and would not know him for another 58 days. It was 10 December 1991. I quickly calculated–we might not know Mr Dickens until 6 February 1992.

From* Mister Pip – *Lloyd Jones

Brainstorming

In small groups, discuss the following questions then summarize your discussion in point form.

1) How do we know that the narrator and her school friends have had little formal schooling?
2) How do we know that the class has enjoyed the reading of *Great Expectations*?
3) Explain the confusion in the class after Mr Watts told the children they were going to meet Mr Dickens?
4) Comment on and evaluate Mr Watts' teaching methods. Would you say he was a successful teacher?
5) Do you think Mr Watts would succeed as a teacher in a 21st-century teaching environment?

Presenting

Based on your answers to the questions above, prepare a four-minute presentation on the contents of the text.

Make your presentation to your classmates. Remember that in the actual examination you will have 20 minutes to prepare your presentation.

Students listening to the presentation should prepare individual questions about the text. They can put these questions to you at the end of your presentation.

Peer assessment (IA)

In small groups, assess the presentations given by your classmates. You may use HL IA assessment criteria in the Language B guide as a basis for your comments.

Note

In your internal assessment, the literary extract will not exceed 300 words. You will be shown two, one from each of the works of literature studied in class.

Oral activity: Discussion

There are many students around the world who are learning in very similar conditions to the children in this picture. What can be done to make sure that they are better equipped for learning and for life in the 21st century?

Are we creating a two-tier education system in which students with access to excellent educational facilities leave the less well-off further and further behind?

Discuss these issues with your peers. What practical, positive conclusions and solutions can you find?

Paper 1 (HL/SL) practice

Choose one of the tasks below and write between 250 and 400 words (SL)/ 450 and 600 words (HL).

1. A local company is offering a summer internship programme which is offering the opportunity to gain valuable work experience in a professional environment in exchange for carrying out routine office tasks. Write a text in which you outline your suitability for the post on offer and explain what skills you can offer the company.

A formal letter	A proposal	An essay

2. You attended a music concert at which a major star was scheduled to perform. Although the concert lasted over three hours the headline performer was only on stage for 30 minutes, or less. You feel that this was very unsatisfactory. Write a text to the organizers of the event explaining why you are so dissatisfied and demanding some form of compensation.

A report	A formal letter	A personal letter

3. A university near you is proposing an open day for a limited number of potential students. The open day will feature both a tour of the campus and an opportunity to meet current undergraduate students. The afternoon participants will take part in a forum entitled '*The future of education in the 21st century*'. You are interested both opportunities: to visit the university and to take part in the forum. Write a text in which you outline your reasons for wanting to visit the university and explain why you would be a suitable contributor to the forum.

An essay	A letter of application	A letter of inquiry

Planning

You must think about the concepts below to help you plan your written text. Think about what measures you will take to make sure your text communicates its message clearly and effectively:

- context
- audience
- purpose

Write a draft of your text. Remember to include any special features of the text type you have chosen.

Drafting

Re-read the completed draft of your text. Remember you will be assessed on three criteria: criterion A, language; criterion B, message; criterion C, conceptual understanding (including audience, context and purpose). Make any final changes.

Conclusion to research question C

Why do you need to be a really effective 21st-century learner?

Now that you have completed this section what are your thoughts about the question above?

1. What justifications would you give for your answers?
2. What big ideas have you learned about the need for 21st skills in this section?
3. Which skills will you need to develop further when you continue with your studies after completing IB?

Conclusion to the chapter

What opportunities and challenges does the 21st century bring to education and work?

When we began the chapter, you debated this research question. Now that you have completed the chapter, answer the following questions:

- Now that you have completed the chapter, what are your conclusions about the research question?
- To what extent have your opinions on the subject changed since the beginning of this chapter?

Justify your answers.

In particular, you may want to consider this issue: What opportunities and challenges will the 21st century bring you?

What else would you like to know about the subject?

Beyond the classroom

CAS

Experience 1: Creativity and activity: Using formal letters

In the course of your last two years of school there will be many occasions on which you will need to write a variety of such letters. You may need to write letters of application to colleges or to potential employers. You may wish to write letters of enquiry to universities, gap year providers or other organizations in which you are interested. Use the advice you have been given in this chapter to help you to compose, draft and redraft your correspondence. Use this checklist.

Elements of a formal letter	Used correctly? Yes / No / Unsure
A. I have addressed the reader correctly.	
B. I have introduced myself clearly.	
C. I have explained the purpose of the letter clearly.	
D. I have made a series of supporting points / explanations.	
E. I have given evidence to support my points / explanations.	
F. I have used paragraphing appropriately.	
G. I have closed the letter appropriately.	
H. I have used a formal register at all times.	
I. I have included all the necessary information for the recipient.	

Experience 2: Ideas for service

In this chapter we have looked at the benefits and some of the problems associated with the theme of 21st-century learning. This is a subject which will affect all students as they prepare to enter the workforce of the future. Here are two ways in which you can contribute to the discussion and make sure that other, younger students are aware of the issues.

1. Create presentations on 21st-century skills and on employment in the future. Think of ways in which to communicate the information. This could be through face-to-face meetings and assemblies. Alternatively, you may wish to use social media as a platform for disseminating your ideas.
2. If you feel that your school could do more to promote the 21st-century learning, why not write a formal letter to your school management outlining your ideas and putting forward a set of practical proposals?

Suggested reading

Teacher Man, by Frank McCourt

Goodbye, Mr Chips, by James Hilton

The Prime of Miss Jean Brodie, by Muriel Spark

The Make Lemonade Trilogy, by Virginia Euwer Wolff

Academy X, by Andrew Trees

Mister Pip, by Lloyd Jones

10 SHARING THE PLANET: OUR RIGHTS!

Chapter summary

Theme
Sharing the planet

Topics
Human rights, equality and ethics

Conceptual understandings
Audience

Research question for the chapter
What ethical issues arise from living in the modern world and how do we resolve them?

Additional research questions for each text

A Does the definition of human rights differ in different Anglophone cultures?
B How is the problem of trafficking in persons addressed by the media?
C How can we go beyond the narrow categorizations of gender roles?

TOK question

- What role does language play in determining human rights?
- Are human rights ethically binding?

Communication skills

Listening skills

- Receptive
- Interactive

Oral and interactive skills

- Receptive: listening to a report
- Productive: presenting to classmates
- Interactive: discussions

Written text type(s)

- Newspaper article
- Opinion column
- Pamphlet

Research question for the chapter:

What ethical issues arise from living in the modern world and how do we resolve them?

1. What are your first thoughts and reactions to the question above?
2. What justifications would you give for your answer?
3. What more would you need to know before you can come to a definitive conclusion about the question?

Thinking and communication skills (ATLs)

The activity below involves reflection, higher-order thinking in the form of creation, and the ability to express yourself in writing in a coherent and persuasive manner.

What, in your opinion, do these images represent?

Get into four groups. Each group chooses one of the images above.

→ Write a newspaper headline for the topic or issue represented in your chosen image. Your headline should capture the most important aspect of the image that should be remembered.

→ Share your headline with the other groups.

Section A: Human rights

Research question A:

Does the definition of human rights differ in different Anglophone cultures?

Before you read

List some of the issues that you think fall under the category "human rights".

Come up with at least 12 questions about those issues. Use these question-starts below to help you think of interesting questions:

- What …?
- Why …?
- How different would it be if …?
- What are the reasons …?
- Suppose that …
- What if …?
- What if we knew …?
- What is the purpose of …?
- What would change if …?

In groups, review the questions and highlight those that seem most interesting. Then, select one or more of your questions to discuss for a few moments.

What new ideas do you have about the topic that you didn't have before?

Did you have police brutality or violence against women on your list? Do you think the intensity of human rights violations differs from one country to another? Discuss your answers to these questions and then read the report below to learn more about human rights in Jamaica.

HUMAN RIGHTS in Jamaica, 2015/2016 report

Excessive use of force by the police and extrajudicial executions continued. A Commission of Enquiry into alleged human rights violations during the 2010 state of emergency was under way.

[...17...]

Jamaica continued to have one of the highest homicide rates per capita in the world. Violent crime remained a key concern for the public. Between January and June, police recorded 1,486 reports of serious and violent crimes, classified as murders, shootings, rapes and aggravated assaults. According to media reports, there were more than 1,100 murders during the year, an increase of approximately 20% compared with 2014.

The Dangerous Drugs (Amendment) Act 2015 came into force in April, removing powers of arrest and detention for possession or use of small quantities of cannabis and allowing members of the Rastafarian faith to use the drug for religious purposes.

In May, Jamaica was examined under the UPR[1]. Jamaica accepted 23 of the 177 recommendations made.

The government took steps to establish a National Human Rights Institution.

[...18...]

Human rights organizations continued to highlight concerns around arbitrary arrests and ill-treatment in police custody.

After years of rising numbers of police killings (over 200 per year from 2011 to 2013), the numbers began to decline in 2014 and 2015. The Independent Commission of Investigation (INDECOM), an independent police oversight agency, reported 50 killings involving the police in the first half of 2015, fewer than for the same period of 2014.

A long-overdue Commission of Enquiry into human rights violations committed during the 2010 state of emergency began in December 2014 and was scheduled to be completed in early 2016. During the state of emergency, 76 civilians were killed by security forces, including 44 who were alleged to have been extrajudicially executed.

[...19...]

Major backlogs in the judiciary led to continued delays and hampered access to justice. In particular, investigations into police killings remained slow. With a high number of new cases and few resources, the capacity of the Coroner's Court to help resolve the backlog also remained limited.

[...20...]

According to the Jamaica Constabulary Force, 29 children were murdered between January and June, suggesting a failure by the state to protect children from extreme violence and abuse. Conditions of detention and treatment of juvenile offenders were poor. The NGO Jamaicans for Justice (JFJ) documented high levels of attempted suicide among children and young people in juvenile prisons, raising serious concerns about the psychosocial health and well-being of juveniles in state institutions. JFJ also reported that juvenile offenders were not presented promptly before a judge, exceeding the constitutional period to assess the legality of detention and contravening the UN Convention on the Rights of the Child.

[...21...]

High levels of gender-based violence and domestic violence continued with high numbers of women killed by their spouse or partner. Some women were at risk of sexual violence due to their real or perceived gender expression.

The government was finalizing a National Strategic Plan of Action to Eliminate Gender-based Violence in Jamaica. A Joint Select Committee of Parliament was under way to review the Sexual Offences Act 2009. Civil society organizations made recommendations during the review, which included widening the definition of rape, decriminalizing sex work, and using gender-neutral language throughout the Act.

– Amnesty International Report, 2015/16

Reading comprehension

1. Skim through the text quickly to get a feeling of what it is about. What is the text's overarching idea?

Find the words or phrases in the text which mean the following.

2. accumulation of uncompleted work
3. minor
4. severe
5. disregarding/disobeying
6. outside the course of legal proceedings
7. supervision
8. grouped
9. presumed
10. uninformed/erratic
11. hindered/obstructed
12. sanctioning/legalizing
13. unnecessary/extreme
14. late
15. sensed
16. without delay

In Text A above the paragraph headings 17 to 21 are missing. Choose the correct heading for each paragraph.

17. ◯
18. ◯
19. ◯
20. ◯
21. ◯

A. Violence against women and girls
B. Introduction
C. Juvenile detention
D. Justice system
E. Police and security forces
F. Lack of justice
G. Violence against female partners
H. Background
I. Children's rights
J. Police arbitrary actions

22. ***Read statements A to F. Identify the three statements that are correct.***

A. The rate of homicide in Jamaica decreased between 2010 and 2014.
B. People of certain faiths in Jamaica can use drugs for spiritual reasons.
C. People in Jamaica may be arrested at random.
D. Some civilians may have been put to death without being sent for trial.
E. Child psychologists take care of juveniles' psychosocial health in Jamaican prisons.
F. Actual gender expression is the main reason why women in Jamaica are abused.

◯ ◯ ◯

To whom or to what do the following words or phrases refer?

23. the drug (line 11)
24. the same period (lines 19 and 20)
25. who (line 23)
26. the state (line 31)
27. their (line 39)
28. the Act (line 44)

Choose the correct phrases from the text to complete the following sentences.

29. One of the Jamaican public's main worries is …
30. The use of small quantities of certain drugs was permitted in …
31. The numbers of police killings in Jamaica …
32. The Coroner's Court in Jamaica finds it difficult to resolve the build-ups of past police killings because of the …
33. A number of children were killed in Jamaican prisons because of …
34. The recommendations made by civil society organizations regarding gender-based violence in Jamaica include …

Communication and social skills ATLs

The focus here is on developing the ability to communicate orally in a coherent and effective manner, coupled with cooperating with others to solve problems through exploration.

Oral activity: Discussion

Having read Amnesty International's report on Jamaica, individually list the human rights problems that Jamaica is currently facing. Be as specific as possible.

In groups, share your ideas, and then suggest solutions to those problems.

Sort the list into actions that relate to solving the problem in the near or the distant future.

Pick one idea from the list that you think has the most merit and explain it to the other groups.

Listening comprehension

Click the icon to practice the listening section of Paper 2. In this gap-filling exercise, there are a number of statements with blank spaces. Identify the correct phrase from the text to fill each space.

Internal assessment (SL)

Take a look at the visual stimulus below. The image relates to the theme of the chapter: "Sharing the planet".

Brainstorming

In pairs, answer the following questions.

- What is the main idea in the photograph?
- What do you see in the photograph?
- Which direction of thought is the photograph inviting you to take? Do you agree with that direction?
- How does the photograph relate to the text on human rights in Jamaica that you read earlier?
- How does the photograph relate to human rights in Anglophone countries in general? Think of specific examples.

Presenting

Based on your answers to the questions above, prepare a four-minute presentation on the photograph.

Remember that the presentation should not only include description of the photograph, but should also connect it to the topic of human rights and an Anglophone culture. Present your photograph and topic to your classmates.

Peer assessment

In small groups, assess the presentations given by your classmates. You may use the aspects below as a basis for your comments.

	Good	Improvement possible	Needs some improvement	Needs a lot of improvement
Eye contact	Makes good eye contact with audience.	Makes eye contact with the audience most of the time.	Sometimes makes eye contact with the audience.	Does not make eye contact with the audience.
Enthusiasm	Shows great enthusiasm for the topic.	Shows enthusiasm for the topic.	Shows some enthusiasm for the topic.	Shows little enthusiasm for the topic.
Preparation and organization	Very prepared and well organized.	Mostly prepared and well organized.	Somewhat prepared and organized.	Not very prepared or organized.
Clear speech	Speaks very clearly and is very easy to understand.	Speaks clearly most of the time and is fairly easy to understand.	Sometimes speaks clearly and is sometimes easy to understand.	Does not speak clearly and is quite difficult to understand.
Knowledge of topic	Shows excellent understanding of the topic.	Shows good understanding of the topic.	Shows some understanding of the topic.	Shows little understanding of the topic.

Using these aspects, suggest ways in your classmates can further improve their presentation skills.

Self-assessment ATLs

This is an effective formative assessment tool that helps you to reflect on your performance in order to improve it. Although not explicitly practiced here, the purpose of peer assessment is to help you to reflect on the feedback given from your peers and use it to improve your presentation skills.

Internal assessment (HL)

Blink by Matt Blackwood

Adam didn't blink from the high pitched screams.

His eye simply pressed harder against the viewfinder, making sure the pandemonium was in focus. With a flick of his wrist, he quickly re-framed the woman sobbing in a prenatal position in the dirt. Her body still convulsing from the shock of being dragged head-first by three police officers. Adam zoomed in to get the trickle of blood that ran from her nose, but strands of her hair were in the way.

As back up, he still had that shot of the Goth being pulled across the square, and some decent close-ups of police diving in and wrenching protesters from their line of defiance.

"Do you know how much longer this will take?"

Michelle and her Sunsilked hair had already aimed shotgun mics at young kids with placards and spruiked an impassioned piece to camera, and had since moved on to her mobile, no doubt organising dinner with friends. Adam and Michelle had been at the City Square since 7am, because word had spread that the Mayor had placed a time limit on freedom of speech. The result was cutaways of sincere faces, manifestos on walls, and milk crates stuffed with free clothes.

In the hours spent framing and re-framing and weaving between protesters, not once did Adam share more than a nod with those around him. After all, it wasn't Adam's job to mention that he also liked growing organic food, or that Oxfam was one of his Twitter friends, or that he bought local whenever he could. It wasn't his job to say that he also once used milk crates for clothes. He stole six of them from the back of Franklins, and had one cube for shirts, another for pants, and one reserved for jocks and socks. But after scoring a camera op job, he moved to Southbank, and the crates were the first things to be Ikeasized. Now his bedroom wall was faux oak with sliding glass doors. It cost him two weeks' pay, and despite all the drawers, there never seemed enough room for underpants.

"If you squeeze us in at six I promise to be out by quarter to seven."

Michelle put on her baby voice. It came out whenever unlikely favours were required.

Adam loosened the tilt handle and panned for something lead worthy.

The frame landed on the cute student they had interviewed earlier. She was the one doing honours in politics and spruiked the virtues of tutoring refugees. Two hours ago her bluey green eyes were brimming with optimism. Now they were grey with fear.

The whole reason why Adam went into journalism was to make a difference. He studied hard and got top marks to score work experience at 3AW. There he made coffees for Neil Mitchell. He then covered bushfires and car crashes, heatwaves and Chimpanzee births, and now as Adam gazed deeper into the eyes of a girl he hardly knew, he found himself questioning the difference he was actually making.

A flash of blue and white paused in front of the girl. Her mouth primed for a scream.

The police officer leapt at the girl, pulling her shoulders and ripping the vintage lace dress that Adam had silently admired. Hands pulled at her hair, and when she wouldn't yield, they grabbed her slender neck.

The camera began a slow tilt forwards with no-one to hold it upright.

Adam had fled its side, dashing between the wire fence, and with a running jump, he hip-and-shouldered the officer to the ground.

"Sorry mate," came the apology for the bump back to reality.

Another camera op was trying to squeeze in the space between elm trees and wire fence.

"No worries, I'm done anyway," and pulling away from the eyepiece, Adam flicked a switch, and the wailing pain of the university girl blinked to something nearing black.

Note

In your internal assessment, the literary extract will not exceed 300 words. You will be shown two, one from each of the works of literature studied in class.

Brainstorming

In groups of four, discuss the following then summarize your discussion in point form:

- What is the main idea in the text?
- How does the author illustrate that Adam and Michelle were not emotionally involved in the events taking place in the square?
- How is the brutality of the police described in the short story? What do you notice about the language used to describe the situation?
- How is the situation described? And the protestors?

Planning

Re-read the text and identify the words and phrases the author uses to describe the reporters and the protestors. You could list them in a table like the one below.

Reporters	Protestors

What are the similarities between these groups of words? What are the differences?

How and why does the author minimize the similarities and emphasize the differences?

How, in your opinion, does the short story highlight violation of human rights?

Self-management ATLs

This type of assessment is directly connected to metacognition as it helps you to reflect on the benchmarks used in the internal assessment, develop your understanding of the assessment criteria, reflect on your performance and aim to improve it.

Presenting

Prepare a four-minute presentation about the short story in which you highlight the similarities and differences between the protestors and the reporters who are covering a news items that is connected to violation of human rights.

Peer assessment

In groups of four, assess the presentations given by your classmates. Use the HL IA assessment criteria in the Language B guide to direct your assessment.

Suggest ways your classmates can improve their presentation techniques.

Writing skills: Paper 1 Magazine/newspaper article

Magazine or newspaper articles, also known as feature articles, are designed to encapsulate more than news reports do. They are not just concerned with reporting facts with evidence; they investigate a range of issues, ideas, opinions and experiences. As a mass media text type, a magazine article is designed to inform, entertain and/or persuade.

As with all text types, when you write a magazine article, you need to think about your audience. For example, an article in a scientific magazine is expected to include the scientific jargon appropriate to the topic and to the audience of that magazine. An article discussing the same issue in a magazine for teenagers would not be very appealing if the same scientific jargon were used.

In comparison to news reports, articles provide more background information and analysis on their focal topics. Some examples of articles that you may be asked to write are:

- an analysis and opinion on an issue or topic
- a profile of, or an interview with, a well-known person
- a personal experience or anecdote related to one of the English B themes: identities, experiences, human ingenuity, social organization and sharing the planet
- some background information on a local, national or international event
- a human interest story about a unique or unusual event.

How is an article structured? Look at the following example.

Mass media texts

Mass media texts are created for distribution to a large audience that is targeted because of an interest that, at least initially, lies primarily with the producer of the text, since the person or entity responsible for a mass media text has no way of knowing exactly who will take the time and interest to understand the message or possibly ignore it. Mass media texts tend to be characterized by the need of the producer of the text to project authority, desirability or exclusivity, and the conscious choice of a particular medium or technology that is appropriate to reach the targeted audience. The level of formality in the register of these texts will vary according to linguistic and socio-cultural norms of the target language.

Language B guide for first exams in 2020

Damning report on exploitation in the Australian fashion industry

Beau Donnelly — Published April 16, 2015, 6.53PM

Nine out of 10 companies supplying clothes to Australian consumers do not know where their cotton is sourced and most fail to pay overseas workers enough to meet their basic needs, an investigation into the fashion industry shows.

Next week marks the two-year anniversary since Bangladesh's Rana Plaza factory collapse in which more than 1100 workers died, but a report card on the industry notorious for poverty-level wages has revealed many brands still exploit their workers.

An article needs an eye-catching title. If the title is not interesting, readers will not be interested in reading it. Note the use of the word 'damning' in this title. Why, do you think the writer chose it?

This is the by-line. The by-line usually features the name of the author, publication or location, and the date the article was published.

Most newspaper articles include a short paragraph at the beginning that aims to summarize the focal issue in an article and grab the audience's attention. What purpose, in your opinion, do the statistics "nine out of ten companies" in this paragraph serve?

The introduction, or lead, in a feature article is an attention grabber. It aims to interest readers to read further. Generally, you can do the following when writing your introduction: ask a provocative question; make a provocative thesis statement; relate an experience, personal or otherwise. Which of those has the writer of this article used?

The main body of the article is devoted to the focal issue the writer plans to discuss. In other words, it is the "meaty" part. It consists of several paragraphs that provide further detail and expand the main topic of the article into subtopics. Read the main body paragraphs in the article and note the subtopics chosen by the writer of the article.

- How do those subtopics support the main topic of the article?
- How does the writer present detail?
- What approach has the writer chosen: the one-sided approach in which only the writer's viewpoint is presented? Or the "balanced but undecided" approach in which more than one viewpoint is outlined?
- Which tone and style has the writer adopted: the personal that uses the first-person narrative and informal language or the impersonal that focuses more on the topic and deploys the passive voice? Why do you think the writer of this article chose this style?

The conclusion should tie everything together while leaving a lasting impression. This can be achieved by:

- reminding the reader of the article's main idea
- suggesting an appropriate course of action or make a recommendation
- explaining a person's future plans if you are writing about a person
- saving an unexpected piece of information until the last paragraph.

Which of the techniques above has the writer of the article adopted? Why?

The Australian Fashion Report, to be released on Friday by Baptist World Aid, points to the increased risk of child and forced labour in the garment industry because most local companies are unable to trace or fail to monitor their supply chains.

Co-author Gershon Nimbalker said while there had been improvements at the final stages of production in the two years since the organisation's first audit of the fashion industry, very little had been done to address working conditions earlier in the supply chain, where some of the worst abuses often occur.

"Most of us are at risk of being connected to slavery in the cotton fields because companies who we're buying from haven't traced their cotton to make sure that there is no forced labour and child labour," he said. "We don't want to see another Rana Plaza equivalent deeper in the supply chain before fashion companies start taking action."

Researchers examined 59 apparel companies collectively supplying more than 200 clothing brands in Australia and graded them on their policies, transparency, supply chain traceability and worker rights. About 75 per cent of companies responded to a survey about their business practices, with the remaining businesses graded solely on publicly available information.

The report said 91 per cent of companies did not know where all their cotton comes from and 75 per cent did not know the source of all their fabrics. Most companies do not carry out regular random inspections or have a system in place for workers to raise complaints. And while eight companies had taken steps to improve low wages for overseas workers only two proved they paid a full living wage.

According to the report, the production cost of a T-shirt in Bangladesh would increase from about 50c to 80c if workers were paid a living wage. The minimum wage in Bangladesh is currently US$68 ($88) a month.

Carolyn Kitto, spokeswoman for anti-slavery group Stop the Traffik, said the cost of paying workers enough to live on would make little difference to the end cost to Australian consumers because they were being paid so little.

Ms Kitto said she had met women in India who had been coerced into working in spinning, weaving and dyeing mills and forced to labour under appalling conditions.

"I've seen photos of rooms that would be about the size of my bedroom where 50 girls have lived," she said. "They don't have any safety equipment so they inhale and ingest cotton fibre. Their food is sometimes laced with hormones to stop them menstruating because they're regarded as less productive when they're menstruating."

Two thirds of companies graded in the 2013 report have improved their practices and more than a dozen have now signed the Accord on Fire and Building Safety in Bangladesh, pledging a safe work environment in the ready-made garment industry.

Writing activity

Refer to the HL literary extract on pages 388 and 389, then change it into a newspaper article.

Brainstorming

In pairs:

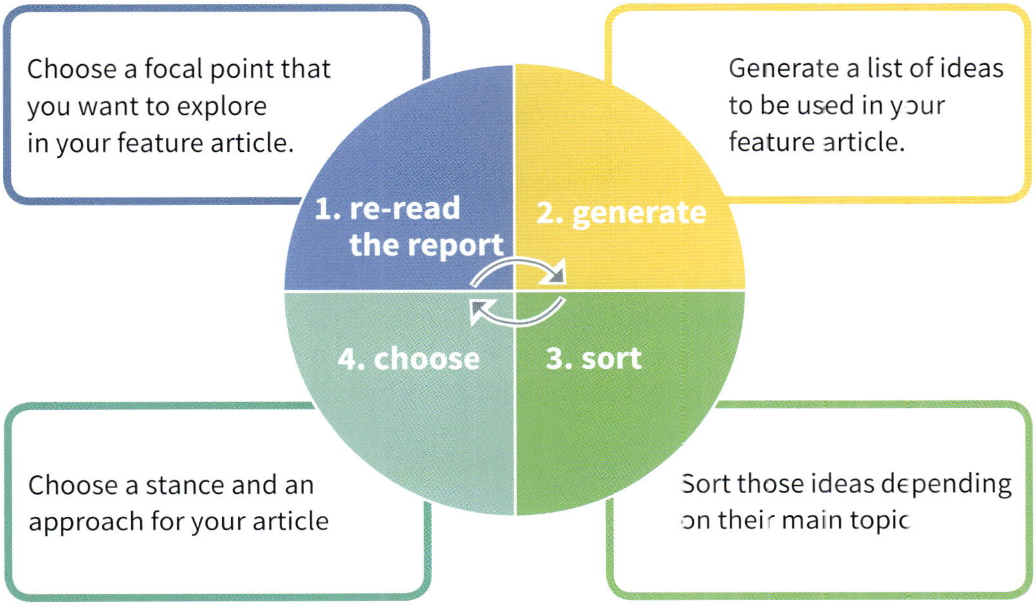

Planning

In pairs decide how you will grab your audience's attention. What should appear in your introduction? What is your conclusion? Connect these to the stance and approach you have chosen to take.

Decide the tone and style of your article. Do you know who your audience is? What is the best way to address this audience? Now choose the best tone and style for your article.

Decide how you are going to order your subtopics. Which should go first? Which should appear last? What should appear in the middle? Does your chosen order ensure that your ideas will be coherent and your writing will flow smoothly?

Drafting

Individually, write a draft of the body of your article. When you are done, revise this draft to make sure it makes sense.

Add an introduction and conclusion to the body. Re-read what you have written. Do the transitions make sense? Are your paragraphs well connected? How interesting is your article?

Write an eye-catching title and do not forget the by-line.

Re-read the revised draft of your article for one last time. Make any final changes.

Paper 1 (HL/SL) practice

Choose one of the tasks below and write between 250 and 400 words for SL or 450 and 600 words for HL.

Task 1

A recent debate focusing on the importance of education was shown on your national TV. You would like to clarify to your fellow classmates, teachers and the school community how important it is to educate every child in your country. Write a text in which you define education, clarify its importance, and suggest ways in which educating every child can be achieved.

Letter | Newspaper article | Speech

Task 2

Your town council would like you to help in spreading awareness of human rights issues in your town and show what the community has already done to ensure that civil rights are protected. Write your text.

Newspaper article | Brochure | Email

Conclusion to research question A

Does the definition of human rights differ in different Anglophone cultures?

1. Now that you have completed this section what are your thoughts and reactions to the question above?
2. What justifications would you give for your answers?
3. What more would you need to know before you can come to a definitive conclusion about the statement?

A TOK moment

TOK

In his essay "The Language of Ethics" (2010), David Schmidtz discusses how language affects our perception of "right" and "good". Collette Phair references Schmidtz in her article "Does Language Affect Our Culture and Personal Ethics?" and asserts that "The field of ethics uses specific terms to designate subfields, values, and areas of inquiry, i.e. 'good' (what we should want) versus 'right' (what we should do). Professor David Schmidtz sees ethics as a concrete system with rules to learn, in some ways similar to mathematics. Thus the terminology of the ethics field defines how students of ethics come to think and develop new theories." ("Does Language Affect Our Culture & Personal Ethics", 2016)

Access the two articles mentioned above. Both are available online.

Skim through the articles and reflect on your understanding of good and right.

In groups of four, discuss the following questions:

- How would you define "good" in relation to human rights?
- How would you define "right" in relation to human rights?
- How does our notion of "good" and "right" affect our understanding of human rights? What role does language play in this understanding?

Section B: Ethics

Research question B:

How is the problem of people trafficking addressed by the media?

Before you read

Individually, think...

- what do you know about the topic of trafficking in persons in any Anglophone culture?

In pairs, discuss...

- any questions or elements that puzzle you about this topic.

In groups, decide...

- how you can best explore this topic to find answers to your questions.

Human Trafficking AND Moral Imperatives

A recent article in the *New York Times* shows how human trafficking has become a global problem. If 200 years ago slavery showed a ruthless side of humanity, it seems that today the problem returns, only now, the trade is not in the open, but hidden, fed by drugs, deception, even kidnapping. How could anyone deceive a young girl knowing she will end up in a brothel in a European capital with no passport, beaten, drugged & exploited?

Today, millions of people move away from home to work for little or no money, often under abusive conditions. Confronting issues like illegal mining in South America and the forced prostitution of women from the former Yugoslavia, the former Soviet Union and North Africa, the International Organization for Migration has conceived awareness campaigns tailored to particular countries and cultures. Here are just three examples amongst many:

Vietnam: Many Vietnamese women and girls are trafficked through Dong Tham, An Giang, and Kien Giang to Cambodia for sexual exploitation. In 2004, Cambodian police estimated that more than 50,000 girls were in brothels throughout Cambodia, many of whom were Vietnamese.

Philippines: Philippine men, women, and girls were trafficked for labor and exploitation to Saudi Arabia, Kuwait, the United Arab Emirates, Qatar, Bahrain, Malaysia, Hong Kong, Singapore, Japan, South Africa, North America, and Europe. The government and NGO estimates on the number of women trafficked range from 300,000 to 400,000 and the number of children trafficked range from 60,000 to 100,000.

China: Chinese women and children are trafficked for exploitation in Malaysia, Thailand, the United Kingdom, the United States, Australia, Europe, Canada, Japan, Italy, Burma, Singapore, South Africa, and Taiwan. Many Chinese are recruited by false promises of employment and are later coerced into prostitution or forced labor. Children are sometimes recruited by traffickers who promise their parents that their children can send remittances back home.

The common denominator of human trafficking is that people are lured into this trap by the promise of a better future.

The issue has ramifications for our own backyard. This article in the *New York Times* exposes how a 15-year-old girl is abducted to work as a prostitute in Miami (check out the list of 9 individuals arrested who were involved in the ring). A former Miami Beach police officer and his friend arrested for drugging women and then filming them in sex acts.

In light of the theories we've studied in Chapter 2, which is in your opinion the best moral theory that can deal with this problem? Egoism, Utilitarianism or Kant's Categorical Imperative?

Comments

By: J. V. (September 6, 2011 at 7:48 PM)

Human trafficking is **[5]**, in my opinion at least. As far as I am concerned, women, children, and men should not be **[6]** in such a way because they have moral rights. The moral theory that would best deal with this problem, in my opinion, is Kant's Categorical Imperative (Kant, 70). Human trafficking should be **[7]** immoral. In Utilitarianism, if the majority **[8]** human trafficking because there is pleasure and happiness so be it. Meanwhile, an egoist would accept human trafficking if and only if it **[9]** their well-being in the long run (Triff). Kant's Categorical Imperative states that we should act in a way in which we can **[10]** the maxim of our actions to become a universal law. I can only embrace something as a moral law only if all other rational beings can also embrace it. For instance, suppose a kidnapper rapes a little girl, applying the universal acceptability, the man would have to be willing to accept it if he were being raped, something he would **[11]** be unwilling to do. I believe that Kant's Categorical Imperative would be the best theory for dealing with human trafficking.

By: K.M (September 7, 2011 at 1:59 PM)

Human trafficking is a huge global issue. Each moral theory relates to this problem.

Obviously the people behind these operations are Egoists because they are solely thinking about their well-being in the long run. The Egoists are making a huge profit and will continue to contribute to human trafficking unless at some point it becomes detrimental to their well-being.

Utilitarianism believes that so long as majority of the people are satisfied then the act is morally correct. In a situation like human trafficking the majority is happy with the situation. The heads of the organizations and the men and women paying for these services are pleased with what is going on. However, the people involved and actually being sold for sex may not be so happy but in this case they are the minority.

The moral theory that would be best used to rule human trafficking as immoral would be Kant's Categorical Imperative. This is because this theory says that an act is moral if people can will the maxim to become a universal law. Meaning if it is something that everyone would not be comfortable with, no exceptions, it would be immoral. In the case of human trafficking everyone would have to consider if they would like being sold for sex, or if it were their kids or family members, if it would still be acceptable. The people paying for these services would have to consider if they were the ones performing these acts or if it were their own children. Of course you will get an occasional pervert who would not mind either way, but the majority would not be okay with it and would rule human trafficking immoral.

By: R. B. (September 8, 2011 at 11:38 AM)

This has to be one of the most immoral acts that is going on in the world today. I do not understand how people can even put a price on young girls for sex or labor. In my opinion it is a serious problem and I cannot believe how fast this business is growing according to the statistics in the art cles.

I do indeed agree to the fact that it is an egoistic act. For those who are unsure of what egoism is; egoism is basically being motivated only for self-interest. Kidnapping and exploiting girls against their will just to make a few dollars has egoistic written all over it. The traffickers are only concerned about how this young girl or this person that they kidnapped will better their self-interest, whether it is with money, sex, labor, etc. However, I disagree that human trafficking is an example of Kant's Categorical Imperative. Kant's theory says that an action is right only if that action is right with everyone else. This is the only minor fault that Kant's theory has. There are always going to be a group of people or a minority that have a different opinion on an action.

The Utilitarianism theory says that the proper course of action is good only if it maximizes the well-being of the majority of the society. I believe we all can agree that if human trafficking comes to an end, it can and will better our society as a whole. Then again there are arguments to counter that which means the Utilitarianism theory also has faults. Human trafficking is wrong and immoral and in my opinion is growing because authorities have ignored the fact that it is going on in their own society.

This should start to be taken more seriously.

Reading comprehension

Answer the following questions.

1. How has slavery changed in the past 200 years?
2. Which word between lines 1 and 11 is closest in meaning to "customized"?
3. Why would Chinese parents send their children with traffickers to foreign countries?
4. What do all human trafficking practices have in common?

Which words go in the gaps numbered 5 to 11? Choose the words from the list below.

accepts	agrees	broken	choose	corrupt
exploits	immoral	locally	maximizes	presumably
universally	unlikely	violated	will	

12. ***From statements A to F, identify the three that correspond to K.M's ideas as they appear in his/her comment.***

A. Human traffickers believe in Kant's Categorical Imperative as their moral theory.

B. Traffickers will only quit practising trafficking if it negatively affects their welfare.

C. In one moral theory, a practice is acceptable if most people find it pleasurable.

D. In Utilitarianism, the opinion of trafficked people is important.
E. Egoism is a theory that considers trafficking in persons immoral.
F. According to Kant, trafficking in persons can only become moral if those benefiting from it do not mind being violated.

Identify whether the sentences below are true or false. Provide a quotation to support your answer.

		True	False
13.	Human trafficking is a dying occupation.		
Justification:			
14.	Selfishness underpins Egoism.		
Justification:			
15.	The act of human trafficking represents Kant's theory.		
Justification:			
16.	Society will benefit from putting a stop to trafficking in persons.		
Justification:			
17.	Trafficking in persons is prospering because governments turn a blind eye to it.		

HL extension HL

18. Of the people who responded to the blog, who expresses the following opinions? You can choose one, two or all three.

A. Determining the monetary worth of a human being is unfathomable.
B. The opinion of minorities does not count.
C. Trafficking in persons is an evil practice.
D. People have rights; therefore, they should not be exploited.
E. Traffickers are Egoists.

Answer the following questions.

19. To whom does "whom" (line 14) refer?

20. Which word between lines 20 and 30 shows that Chinese women and children do not choose prostitution willingly?

21. Whose friend is being referred to in line 29?

22. What does the phrase "in light of the theories we've studied in Chapter 2" (line 31) tell us about the profession of the writer?

23. From your reading of the original blog entry, which moral theory would the writer choose to explain trafficking in persons? Which theory would he choose to condemn it? Justify your answers.

Listening comprehension

Radio report on people trafficking in the US

Listen to the report on trafficking in persons in the United States of America, then answer the questions that follow.

1. What was the name of the organization to return trafficked African girls to their homes?
2. How many girls are still missing since the previous October?
3. What are trafficked girls likely to face?
4. Where does the human rights activist work?
5. What are American children in danger of?
6. ***From statements A to F, identify the three that are true according to the interview.***

   A. According to the report, approximately 250 girls have been recently kidnapped.
   B. According to the report, a number of girls recently escaped their kidnappers.
   C. The rescuing of more than 150 trafficked children into the US is considered a great success.
   D. Approximately more than a quarter of a million children have been trafficked into the US.
   E. American children are in danger of being exploited on American soil.
   F. Trafficking increases in occasions like sporting events.

Choose the correct answer from A, B, C or D.

7. According to Jamina, the law in the United States …

   A. sympathizes with traffickers
   B. does not condemn buyers
   C. considers the trafficked children criminals
   D. allows traffickers to exploit American children.

8. Jamina insists that changing the crime and punishment culture regarding trafficking in persons starts with …

   A. arresting all traffickers
   B. arresting all those involved in trafficking
   C. realizing that trafficked children are victims
   D. rehabilitating traffickers and buyers.

9. Jamina believes that one of the reasons why buyers are not punished is that …

   A. they are black or brown
   B. they are not blamed
   C. they are middle class, white men who are married
   D. they do not fit the stereotype of a criminal.

HL extension

HL

Monica listened to the report and is excited about telling her friend Rachel about it, so she emails her. Listen to the report again and complete the spaces in the email with words or phrases from the list below.

approval of	not tolerated	sports games
big events	particularly girls	take their civic duty
do not apprehend	passed	take those criminals
do not approve of	perpetrators	taking part in the event
mostly underage	rejected	
not liable to penalty	resistance to	

From : monica.boris@email

To : rachelblue@email

Subject : An interesting report on trafficking in persons.

Date : 16/09/2016

Hi Rachel

Hey, remember our recent English B lesson about human trafficking? I was browsing the Internet looking for resources and came across an interesting report about trafficking in the United States on MSNBC.

The reporter interviews a lady who works with such issues, and she claims that American children, [10], are being exploited, especially during [11]. The lady claims that such things happen on those occasions because the perpetrators are [12] by law. The reporter insists on knowing how that is possible, and the lady claims that law enforcement agencies [13] buyers, only traffickers. She believes that that is the case because those trafficked children are labelled in a way that denotes [14] the crimes being committed against them. Can you believe this? Thank God the lady mentioned that there is a legislation that considers buyers [15]! I sincerely hope it had been [16] by the Senate, especially that the reporter encouraged the public to [17] seriously and vote in favour of the legislation.

So, what do you think? Should we show this to Mrs. Bremman tomorrow and use it as a source in our upcoming research paper?

XOXO
Mon.

Research skills

ATLs

The activity promotes good research practices such as comparing, contrasting and validating information, which in turn improve higher-order thinking.

Oral activity: Discussion

From what you have read in this section, how big a problem is trafficking in persons? Peruse some sources, online or otherwise, to get an idea of how big the problem is in Anglophone cultures of your choice and what different governments are doing to address it.

In groups:

- list the actions taken by governments into feasible and unfeasible
- examine the unfeasible actions and come up with ideas that may turn them into feasible ones
- list those modified actions in order of importance
- pick one action from the list that you think has the most merit and explain it to the other groups.

Internal assessment (SL)

Take a look at the visual stimulus here. The image relates to the theme of the chapter: "Sharing the planet".

Brainstorming

In groups of three, discuss the following questions.

- What message is the picture communicating to you? How does it relate to an English-speaking community?
- Which viewpoints are missing from the picture?
- How does the picture relate to the text on people trafficking that you read earlier?

Presenting

Based on your answers to the questions above, prepare a four-minute group presentation.

Use your answers to the questions above to map out your presentation. The following should help you:

1. Address the focus of the picture.
2. Describe the picture in no more than 30 seconds.
3. Connect the picture to the topic and mention the stance it invites you to take.
4. Address the topic: define it, mention how it is affecting Anglophone cultures, highlight its issues, and/ or suggest ways in which it can be terminated. Make sure your presentation is precise and concise; you have only 4 minutes.
5. Decide on who will say what: this is a group presentation and all participants should get the chance to speak.

Remember that the presentation should not only include description of the picture, but should also connect it to the theme "Sharing the planet" and the topic of human trafficking in an Anglophone culture.

Conceptual understanding: Audience

Imagine that your teacher invited you to present the picture to a group of first graders. How would you change your presentation to make it appealing to your audience? How would the language (register) and the style of the presentation change? Why?

Present to your classmates.

Peer assessment

When you and your classmates engage in assessing each other, you are developing your understanding of the course requirements and the assessment criteria. Peer assessment empowers your to determine your own learning and develop life-long learning skills.

Peer assessment

In groups of three, assess the presentations given by your classmates. Use the following to guide your assessment:

A. clarity of presentation and wording.

B. clarity of description of the picture: were you able to understand the focus of the photograph?

C. connection between picture and the theme/ topic (Sharing the planet/ people trafficking).

D. Flow of ideas: is the flow of ideas smooth? Do presenters use appropriate cohesive devices and linking words?

E. Complexity of ideas: are ideas exemplified, justified and/or explained?

Suggest ways in which your classmates can improve their presentation techniques.

Note

In your internal assessment, the literary extract will not exceed 300 words. You will be shown two, one from each of the works of literature studied in class.

Internal assessment (HL)

Before you discuss the short story below, consider the following:

- What is your definition of freedom?
- Is freedom an absolute concept? Or is it contextual, i.e. does it depend on the period in history and the society in which we live?
- Are there rights that you take for granted? Can you imagine what your life would be like if those rights that you enjoy were not a given?

THE DIARY OF A SLAVE

By AshTree, Clarksville, TN

If a slave had been able to write, what would they say? If they were on the ship, no idea where they are going, how would they express this confusion and mix of emotions? In this story, I take on the persona of Asha Larai, a young twelve-year-old girl on a slave ship during 1624. Just five years ago, her parents were taken to become some of the first slaves, and now it is her turn. I give her a voice and let her speak with my knowledge. She bleeds through the paper.

Dear Diary,

I sit, surrounded by people not six inches away, underneath the deck of a boat. I stare at the bodies-rows and rows of bodies. Some left us because of disease, others old age. Holding my breath is pointless, the acrid smell never goes away and even when I do get off this ship, I will still remember that distinctive scent. The groans grow so loud that I cover my ears and try to muffle the sounds with my own singing. Last night I sang until my body passed out from exhaustion and I could only hope that I would make it until the next day. I've become so accustomed to tears constantly wetting my face that it would feel odd not to cry. The cycle makes this seem normal. Maybe that is why I continue to cry - stopping would break the cycle and I would have no daily ritual to follow.

Some days I wonder why I'm kept down here. I am so young compared to the rest of us. Yet the others and I are still hidden as the white men's dirty secret. When they feel the need to be entertained, the secret is divulged. They force us onto the deck, group by group, to dance. The winter air is refreshing at first, but then I cannot stop shivering and I don't want to move. It is so cold and my fingers hurt from frostbite. We are humiliated while at our lowest points. Our hope and dignity disappears behind the crack of a whip. The red marks are everlasting mementos of our masters' cruelty. I used to dream of mutiny, revolting against the people who kept us aboard. Then I wonder, what about the ones who die, are thrown overboard, or executed? Who shall act as our providence and save us from such a death? Only those who have endured this would side with us and surely we would lose. Why had this happened? Were they simply punishing us for our race?

Today, I looked at skin in a way I never did before. It disgusted me. I stared down at my arms and legs. They were the tint of mud, stained like dirt, the color of a moth or rotting potatoes. It was the cause of my pain. I was angry- not only at skin, but also at my parents, the white men that control this world, and everything else I could think of. If I weren't black I wouldn't be sitting in this dark abyss, sweating from the others' body heat in the middle of winter. I wouldn't be fed this slop, using an overflowing bucket for a restroom, or dying slowly at such a young age. I wouldn't have been separated from my parents. I wouldn't be here now - afraid, lonely, and waiting to arrive at a destination I'm unsure of. The loneliness makes me miss everyone - even the people I despised. I just want to feel safe. I miss my family and friends and I cannot bear to think that they are going through the same things I am right now.

I have never loved my brother more than I do now. Abdu, I pray to see you again one day. Grandmother Etana, I wish with all my tears to be in that little hut with you again. You all were my security blanket. Here I have none and everything is so overwhelming. I am not sure I can take it any longer. I have awful nightmares and I always wake up with sweat and tears dripping off my body. At least I had one good dream while I was here. I dreamt of Africa, and it was beautiful! I saw everyone again. I could no longer taste blood on my tongue, hear the screaming and groaning of insane elders, or reach out to touch a dead person's cold and rigid skin on any side of my body. For once, there was grass instead of water licking a boat and tossing it around. I kissed the ground. I kissed brother, mom, dad, and grandmother. It was a perfect world. My life had gone right and I'd long since forgotten of these scaring memories. Yet then, I awoke that night to see an old man dying of a heart attack. His sparkling blue eyes turned grey as his spasms came to a cessation.

Would I have been better off shot by one of the white men? Would I rather stay here and wilt like a dying rose? Right now I do not know why I make myself endure this torture. My life will never be the same after living this way, so why even try to live? I cannot live a life wanting to kill myself, too cowardly to perform the deed. Yet, isn't it cowardly in itself to hang oneself or fast until your body gives up. Maybe it is braver to undergo the suffering, but my body can't take much more. All I know is someday I'll be free - even if it is among the dead I wander, I won't be here.

Asha Larai died on December 13th 1624, her hopes still high.

Conceptual understanding: Variation

The use of register and language in general varies depending on certain other concepts. Two important concepts are perspective and context. When the perspective changes, the kind of language used changes and so does register. For example, the observer in this activity is not expected to use the same kind of emotive language that the slave uses. The same applies to context.

How does the above affect the audience of the literary work? How will the language used change if, instead of assuming the role of your audience was the buyer, the seller, the slave or an observer? How is that linked to perspectives and context?

Presenting

Divide into four groups. Each group should assume one of the following roles: buyer, seller, slave, observer.

In your group, prepare a four-minute presentation, addressing the guiding questions below for your assumed role.

Buyer	Seller
1. Asha has yet to arrive at her destination. Based on what you have read, how do you think her buyer will treat her? 2. Asha says, "Why had this happened? Were they simply punishing us for our race?" What does this tell you about those who will buy her?	1. How, in your opinion, does the slave seller perceive the number of slaves on the ship? 2. Asha says "Would I have been better off shot by one of the white men?" What does this tell you about the sellers and how they treat those slaves?
Slave	**Observer**
1. Can you identify with Asha's plight? Why? Why not? 2. Asha says, "All I know is someday I'll be free - even if it is among the dead I wander, I won't be here." In your opinion, how will Asha be free?	1. Asha says, "I just want to feel safe." What other concepts are related to safety as shown in the short story? How important are those concepts in your opinion? 2. What does the short story tell you about how slaves perceive themselves?

Present to your classmates.

Peer assessment

After each presentation, hold a short, whole-class discussion in which you address the following:

- How clear was the perspective of the group's chosen role?
- How has the presentation improved your understanding of slavery and the issues related to it?

Suggest ways in which the group can improve their focus on perspective and their presentation techniques.

Conceptual understanding: Audience

Reflect on everything you have learned in this section about trafficking in persons. In groups of four, change the short story to reflect the suffering of a trafficked girl. Your audience is law-makers who aim to pass a law prohibiting trafficking in persons in their country. How would your story differ from the original? What role has the specific audience played in how your story changed?

Paper 1: Opinion column

As their name denotes, opinion columns give strong opinions regarding a certain topic. However, although they are all about the opinion of the writer, good opinion columns contain facts that show that the writer is knowledgeable about the topic and should be believed

As with all written pieces, the audience of the opinion column is very important. You are writing to convince the audience of your opinion, and knowledge of this audience determines the tone and register that you use.

Here are a few cardinal rules that should be taken into consideration when writing an opinion column:

- Have a clear opinion and be opinionated about it.
- Do not ignore the opinions of others. The best opinion articles refer to other viewpoints and refute them.
- Adapt your language to your audience and the context.
- Use conversational, emotive and persuasive language.
- Present yourself as an expert on the subject.
- Include facts, especially unknown ones, to support your argument.

Look at the example below to see how an opinion column is structured.

https://midwiferytoday.com/

Birth
Is A Human Rights Issue

by Jan Tritten

"We hold these truths to be self-evident, that all men [and women] are created equal, that they are endowed by their Creator with certain unalienable Rights, that among these are Life, Liberty and the pursuit of Happiness." (US Declaration of Independence)

Every mother and baby has the right to be treated with reverence and respect during the birth process, including pregnancy and beyond.

> An opinion column needs an eye-catching title that clarifies and emphasizes the opinion of the writer. The title is usually followed by the writer's name and the kind of publication in which the column appeared.

> Writer uses a powerful quote from the Declaration of Independence to emphasize her position and set the tone of her column.

When a woman becomes pregnant, she and her baby have unalienable rights. First, the right to life: In June of this year, the United Nations Human Rights Council adopted a landmark resolution acknowledging maternal mortality and morbidity as a human rights issue [1]. The adoption of this resolution prods governments to "change the way they view maternal death—that is, as a human rights issue no less serious than executions, arbitrary detentions, or torture" [2].

> Writer follows up on the topic of rights, linking pregnancy and birth to the Declaration of Independence, and using quotations to strengthen argument.

Next, the right to liberty: The word "liberty" contains aspects of freedom, independence, autonomy, emancipation. These concepts are not usually considered in relation to the childbearing year. It is time to declare that mothers and babies have the right to liberty in pregnancy and birth.

> Emphasis of opinion.

Finally, the pursuit of happiness is of utmost importance to those of us who care for mothers and babies. Most births around the world lead to some varying degree of preventable trauma for the mother and baby. I say it is preventable because much of it is iatrogenic, caused by the doctor or midwife. In many cases, if the mother, baby and birthing process had been treated with respect, the trauma would possibly have never taken place. Instead, the mother likely would have had the most miraculous experience of her life. At the very least, she would have felt a part of the decision-making process if things still did not go as planned. Birth today is a doctor dictatorship in many practices and in many hospitals. Mothers and babies are missing the healthiest possible beginning, both physically and emotionally. Their human rights are being violated.

> Position of the writer is clear. Note the persuasive and emotive use of the underlined phrases and sentences, and their effect on the reader.

Pregnancy and birth are usually the most crucial and powerful passages in a woman's life. This can be perceived by the mother as either a powerfully great experience or a traumatic ordeal. Mom will generally have one of these reactions and those feelings will last her entire life, even if they are buried in the busy job of mothering. She will either soar at the thought of her birth or be driven to the depths of sorrow, especially in this age of the cesarean cut. The same is true of the way the birth experience imprints on the baby. Though he or she may not consciously remember it, the experience will have many life-long effects on the child.

> Reasons for opinion, with examples. Note the use of the underlined emotive words.

In most of the world, birth practices almost always lead to the traumatic side of birth. This is so unnecessary because women have within them the ability and the instinct to have a great childbearing experience. The importance of breastfeeding has finally been proven, yet traumatic birth experiences often add up to the inability to breastfeed long-term. A mother who has had the natural oxytocin high from her birth is much more likely to be successful in breastfeeding her child. I wonder if this oxytocin effect can last longer than we are able to record now. Midwives and doulas are key, because they spend the time making a crucial relationship with the family. Their nurturance is key to any system of health.

> Use of facts to emphasize importance of opinion.

...

We have caused incredible trauma in the birth room and in nearly every pregnancy. When I first started practicing homebirth 33 years ago we had not invaded the uterus. Moms at least made it through pregnancy without too much worry and trauma. Even our words now cause trauma and worry. A woman should come out of every prenatal visit with a renewed sense of well-being and confidence. Instead, our words are often swords that cut her down long before the cesarean knife, which will cut open one in three bellies. These are huge human rights violations.

The use of "we" implies that all human beings should share the writer's opinion. Technique is used to grab the reader's attention.

At our conference in Strasbourg, France, which is the seat of the European Court of Human Rights as well as the European Parliament, we plan to take this issue apart and make plans for changing birth practices. The theme is "Birth Is a Human Rights Issue," which is also the theme of our Summer 2010 magazine. I truly hope you can join us there for this pioneering event. It is time to start a revolution in birth. You are part of that revolution.

The writer establishes herself as an authority of the topic.

Jan Tritten is the founder and editor-in-chief of *Midwifery Today* magazine and a midwife who was in active practice from 1977 to 1989. She became a midwife in 1977 after the powerful homebirth of one of her daughters. Her mission is to make loving midwifery care the norm for birthing women and their babies throughout the world. Meet Jan at our conferences around the world!

A brief biodata and references to ensure that the audience remember that the writer is knowledgeable and that her argument has been supported by research.

1. United Nations General Assembly; Human Rights Council. 2009. "Preventable maternal mortality and morbidity and human rights." http://www.who.int/pmnch/topics/maternal/20090617_hrcresolution.pdf. Accessed 26 Oct 2009.
2. Stoffregen, Morgan. 2009. "UN Resolution Recognizes Maternal Mortality as a Human Rights Issue." International Budget Partnership e-newsletter, No. 49, Jul-Aug.http://www.internationalbudget.org/resources/newsletter49.htm#IIMMHR. Accessed 3 Nov 2009.

Writing activity

Write an opinion column to be published in your school magazine about human trafficking in an Anglophone country you are familiar with.

Brainstorming

In pairs:

- Determine how you will establish yourself as an authority on the subject.
- Research some facts to support your opinion.
- Reflect on everything you have learned in this section. Choose your focal point and your stance. What main idea would you like to emphasize in your opinion column?
- Generate a list of ideas to use in your opinion column.
- Sort these ideas into key supporting points and paragraphs. Decide which examples to use.
- Choose any counterarguments you will refute.

Planning

In pairs decide how you will grab your audience's attention. What should appear in your introduction? What is your conclusion? Connect those to the stance and approach you have chosen.

Decide the tone and style of your opinion column. Do you know who your audience is? What is the best way to address this audience? What emotive and persuasive words and phrases will help you to support your opinion?

Decide how you are going to order your subtopics. Which should go first? Which should appear last? What should appear in the middle? Does your chosen order ensure that your ideas will be coherent and your writing will flow smoothly?

Decide how you will incorporate the facts that will support your argument and how best to refute the counterargument: will you allude to it or clearly mention it?

Think of where you will establish yourself as knowledgeable in the field. Will you incorporate that in the body of the column or will you add a brief biodata at the end?

Drafting

Individually, write a draft of the body of your opinion column. When you are done, read it through carefully and ask yourself whether it makes sense. Make any necessary revisions.

Add your introduction and your conclusion to the body. Re-read what you have written. Do the transitions make sense? Are your paragraphs well connected? How interesting is your opinion column?

Write an eye-catching title and do not forget your name and the publication.

Re-read the new draft of your opinion column one last time. Make any final changes.

Paper 1 (HL/SL) practice

Choose one of the tasks below and write between 250 and 400 words for SL or 450 and 600 words for HL.

You were given this visual stimulus and asked to explore its topic in a writing piece aimed at teenagers in the 21st century. You would like to explain to teenagers the dangers of trafficking in persons and suggest ways in which it can be fought using one of the following text types:

Pamphlet | Opinion column | Email

Conclusion to research question B

How is the problem of people trafficking addressed by the media?

1. Now that you have completed this section, what are your thoughts and reactions to the question above?
2. What justifications would you give for your answers?
3. What more would you need to know before you can come to a definitive conclusion about the statement?

Thinking skills ATLs

Reflection in this exercise helps you develop your critical thinking abilities by assessing how what you have learned led to more questions and areas that need to be answered and explored.

A TOK moment

TOK

Can human trafficking ever be justified on either moral or ethical grounds?

Dan Robb, Spec agent DHS Retired, PhD (CJ), Adj Professor (6 yrs), Grad Cert Forensic Psych

596 Views • Dan has 120+ answers in Ethics

In most cases, there is a continuum. IMO, in human trafficking, kidnapping and slavery is one extreme, and the other is helping people escape a desperate situation (even if for profit). One example of an illegal but ethical exploit in human trafficking: Underground Railroad - Black History - HISTORY.com

Written Oct 14, 2015

Annika Schauer, Once loaned Jimmy Carter an alarm clock

490 Views

There are instances in which human smuggling is morally justified, but there are no circumstances in which human trafficking is OK. Refer to Miguel Valdespino's answer for the UN definition of human trafficking.

Written Oct 18, 2015

Andre Farhat, Am I right, guys?

389 Views

Why in the world would you ask that?
Considering that people trafficking implies their unwillingness, and considering that morality is regarded by a vast majority as dependant on the freedom of choice under the condition that your actions do not hurt others, then it is not compatible with moral actions as defined thus. If morality is defined otherwise, then everything is up for debate.

Written Oct 15, 2015

Skim through the responses to the question "Can human trafficking ever be justified on moral and ethical grounds?" Reflect on your understanding of the words "moral" and "ethical".

Look up the definitions of morals and ethics in a dictionary and compare them to the responses above. Do the writers seem to have a strong understanding of the difference between morality and ethics?

In groups of four, discuss the following questions:

- How would you define "morality" in relation to human trafficking?
- How would you define "ethics" in relation to human trafficking?
- How does our notion of "moral" and "ethical" behaviour affect our understanding of trafficking in persons? Can a moral action, in that case, be considered unethical and vice versa?

David D'Esposito, ethical conundrum

473 Views

If it can, I certainly don't see how.

One of the primary tenets of societal morality and ethics is the freedom of individuals to make their own choices, to the degree that it does not impinge on the freedoms of others.

Human trafficking directly oppresses the freedom of the trafficked individual, by making them property of another.

Morality is decided by what is best for society, as a whole, as well as the individuals, therin.
Slavery simply cannot be said to be good for either.
(Ignoring the direct benefit to the individuals holding slaves, or the limited societies that implement them, as those benefits are at odds with the general welfare of the greater society, be it national or global, and specifically to the society from which the slaves are acquired.)

So, while I can't entirely rule out some unforeseen circumstance in which it could be considered moral or ethical, that hypothetical circumstance remains out of my ability to imagine.

Written Oct 14, 2015

Miguel Valdespino, Eclectic interests, deep thoughts

315 Views • Miguel has 150+ answers in Ethics

Never. Let's look at a definition. The UN definition is:

Article 3, paragraph (a) of the Protocol to Prevent, Suppress and Punish Trafficking in Persons defines Trafficking in Persons as the recruitment, transportation, transfer, harbouring or receipt of persons, by means of the threat or use of force or other forms of coercion, of abduction, of fraud, of deception, of the abuse of power or of a position of vulnerability or of the giving or receiving of payments or benefits to achieve the consent of a person having control over another person, for the purpose of exploitation. Exploitation shall include, at a minimum, the exploitation of the prostitution of others or other forms of sexual exploitation, forced labour or services, slavery or practices similar to slavery, servitude or the removal of organs.

This is immoral in that it uses immoral means and it has an immoral end.

Written Oct 14, 2015

Section C: Equality

Research question C:

How can we go beyond the narrow categorizations of gender roles?

Before you read

In groups of four, reflect on gender issues in your country or those you have learned about while studying social sciences and answer the following questions:

- List as many gender issues as you can. How have those issues affected the way women are treated and perceived nowadays?
- Reflect on the issues you have identified and their consequences. What could you do to make the situation for women fairer?
- Sort your ideas into actions that are related to making the situation fairer in the past, the present and the future.
- Pick the most powerful idea from your list, the one that featured in all three categories, expand on it and present it to your classmates.

Gender Equality

NOV. 30, 2012

In each issue, the editors of Global Agenda invite contributors to explore one of the big questions of the year. In this issue we asked: What does Gender Equality mean? Is it achievable? Below are responses from Naomi Wolf, Ronan Farrow, and Naina Lal Kidwai.

NAOMI WOLF- Author of "The Beauty Myth"

When I hear the words "gender equality," or "feminism," I am always baffled as to why these concepts could ever be contentious. To me, these ideas are so mainstream, so much a part of our basic cultural heritage.

What "gender equality" or "feminism" should mean — I suppose if gender equality is the goal, feminism is the process of how we get there — is the logical extension of the core idea of democracy.

I date my feminism to the Enlightenment — to Mary Wollstonecraft, who wrote, at the end of the 18th century, "A Vindication of the Rights of Woman." Her essay was squarely aligned with other Enlightenment thinkers' appeals to reason, to the rights of man, and to the notion of equality of dignity among all people. This Enlightenment vision is so powerful, and so right, that it has spread around the world, from the "one person, one vote" advocates in Sierra Leone, to the Tahrir Square protesters in Egypt, to the furious parents in Sichuan Province in China, who fought the regional Communist Party's refusal to release information about how their children died in a poorly-built school during an earthquake. Underlying all of these movements is the democratic ideal from the 1790s that asserts: No one person has the natural right to suppress, silence or dominate any other person, simply because of where both are situated in society.

But what that set of beliefs isn't is as important as what it is. Feminism, in my view, should always have kept that original precept in sight as it pursued its aims from one generation to the next. It doesn't prescribe lifestyle choices. It doesn't dictate sexual decisions. It doesn't define itself in terms of cultural battles. True feminism empowers anyone to be free and to have equal opportunity and access to equal legal rights and the rule of law. But it doesn't dictate what that free person should be doing with her or his freedom.

Unfortunately, Western feminism is too often bogged down in cultural battles, in asserting a checklist of political policies. For two decades, I have been insisting that there can certainly be a right-wing, a libertarian, and a left-wing feminist agenda — because what makes a "feminist" is not the policy outcome. Democracy is a concatenation of voices arising out of many individual free lives.

I think we need to [21] in the fight for gender justice in the West. The feminists of Africa, Asia and the Middle East have now outstripped Western feminists as pioneers for gender justice — partly because they do not see women's fight for justice as pitting them against men, against family life or even against faith. They draw on the Wollstonecraftian heritage of democracy and human rights, which is [22] or dismiss.

RONAN FARROW- Writer and diplomat, most recently special adviser to Hillary Clinton

I grew up with seven sisters. I tolerated boy bands. I learned to put the seat down. I also [23] of women's leadership. My childhood dinner-table fights would still be raging without steely negotiation from girls. Years later, watching an argument rage in a dusty classroom in Dhaka, Bangladesh, I remember seeing that same power. At first, only the men talked. But finally, Nipa Masud, seated in the back with a dangerous glint in her eye, leapt to her feet, unleashed a torrent of critiques. The floodgates open, every girl spoke up, swiftly ending the debate. The girls didn't speak first, but they spoke loudest. There can be no confronting our challenges without those voices. Countries with more women in their governments are less likely to suffer internal armed conflicts. Goldman Sachs projected that leveling women's and men's employment rates would add 9 percent to the United States' G.D.P., 13 percent to Europe's, and 16 percent to Japan's. In some ways, we are closer to securing equal space for women to participate than ever. Gender gaps in primary and secondary education rates are closing. More than half a billion women joined the work force over the last 30 years. But women everywhere still face senseless obstacles. In October, militants in Pakistan gunned down 15-year-old Malala Yousafzai for her activism supporting girls' education. Countless stories like hers never reach the world. It is up to all of us to protect women, their rights and their opportunities. In a recent McKinsey survey of successful female businesswomen, an overwhelming majority said they don't aspire to top positions. Women who have made it to the top need to stay there and fight for a world where Nipa, Malala, and countless girls like them are not just able, but expected, to lead.

NAINA LAL KIDWAI- Head of HSBC India

The reality of gender equality is complex and diverse, even more so in India. What is theoretically simple — that men and women have the same rights and opportunities in every walk of life — is more difficult to implement and measure. An increasing number of companies recognize that a healthier gender mix makes for good business, helping talent retention and enhanced innovation. What must also be recognized is the revolution in the smaller towns and villages that is even more important, as it will impact a larger number of women. HSBC has given me opportunities to interact with rural women in India and I have seen their contributions and progress — albeit at a slow pace — at close hand. Once a woman steps out to earn her livelihood, she becomes independent, not just economically but psychologically. She gains better control over the family's finances and acquires stronger decision-making powers. With a rise in the number of schools and vocational training centers, women everywhere now [24] to gain knowledge and acquire skills. As a result, we see women from smaller regions in India becoming engineers, doctors and even astronauts, [25] a few decades ago. I remain optimistic on the ever-greater participation of women in public, corporate and political decision-making.

Reading comprehension

Answer the following questions.

1. Why is Naomi puzzled by people who find the concepts of feminism controversial?
2. How, according to Naomi, will gender equality be achieved?
3. How is Wollstonecraft's work similar to that of other thinkers of her time?
4. How did the people of Sichuan demonstrate their understanding of the vision of Wollstonecraft and other thinkers?
5. Which word between lines 9 and 17 is similar in meaning to "principle"?

Find the word in the right-hand column that could meaningfully replace one of the words on the left.

6. precept (line 19)
7. pursued (line 19)
8. prescribe (line 19)
9. dictate (line 20)
10. bogged down (line 23)
11. concatenation (line 26)

A. argued
B. communicate
C. direct
D. guideline
E. helped
F. impose
G. invalidate
H. principle
I. release
J. series
K. sought
L. stuck

Match the first part of the sentence with the appropriate ending on the right. Write the appropriate letter in the boxes provided.

12. Western feminists...
13. Females in debates…
14. When females outnumber males in a society, people are…
15. When the same number of men and women work, the country's economy is…
16. More girls nowadays are…

A. prone to engage in wars.
B. speak loudly and quickly to silence their male colleagues.
C. expected to improve to an extent.
D. are on a par with their African counterparts in their struggle for equality.
E. denied equal participation in the work field.
F. use valid arguments to win.
G. entitled to school education.
H. have fallen behind their Asian counterparts in their fight for equality.
I. expected to live peacefully.
J. expected to improve marginally.

17. *From statements A to H, select the four that are true according to Farrow and Kidawi (lines 40–53). Write the appropriate letters in the boxes provided.*

A. The problems facing women in their work are understandable.

B. Malala was shot because she stood up for the rights of women to work.

C. We do not know much about the perils facing women who fight for their rights.

D. A good number of women do not want to be leaders in their field.

E. Female leaders can relax once they reach the top of the professional ladder.

F. Women executives are expected to fight for women's rights.

G. Executing gender equality in India is simple and achievable.

H. Companies in India are developing an understanding of the importance of a mixed-gender workforce.

To whom or to what do the following words or phrases refer?

18. it (line 54): ....

19. their (line 55): ....

20. she (line 57): ....

HL extension HL

Which phrases go in the gaps between lines 27 and 62? Choose the phrases from the list and write them in the spaces below.

abused the power	reinvent our Enlightenment heritage
have the desire	very hard to mock
have the opportunity	which was conceivable
quite easy to mock	which was unimaginable
reassert our Enlightenment heritage	witnessed the power

21. ....

22. ....

23. ....

24. ....

25. ....

The sentences below are either true or false. Tick [✓] the correct response then justify it with a relevant brief quotation from the text.

		True	False
26.	The Enlightenment democracy ideal is not given the importance it deserves.		
Justification:			
27.	Feminism has a fixed set of gender pronouncements.		
Justification:			
28.	Watching an argument reminded Farrow of his sisters' strength.		
Justification:			
29.	The Bengali girls did not engage in a debate at the beginning.		
Justification:			
30.	We cannot address our difficulties without the participation of women.		

Choose the correct answer from A, B, C, or D. Write the letter in the box provided.

31. The word "senseless" (line 43) suggests that...
- **A.** the problems women face are real.
- **B.** the problems women face are more fictitious than real.
- **C.** women still face absurd problems.
- **D.** women find the problems that face them absurd.

32. Farrow believes that...
- **A.** women should protect other women's rights.
- **B.** women's rights are everybody's responsibility.
- **C.** Malala does not have the aptitude to become a leader.
- **D.** Nepa resembles his sisters.

33. According to Kidwai, a gender mix in a company...
- **A.** decreases retention of employees in general.
- **B.** should be the norm in urban communities.
- **C.** improves business prospects for women.
- **D.** retains talents.

34. Individualism occurs when women...
- **A.** earn their living.
- **B.** become economically dependent.
- **C.** become psychologically independent.
- **D.** deserve their keep.

Oral activity: Discussion

The United Nations' Universal Declaration of Human Rights stipulates that all humans, irrespective of their gender, ethnicity or race, have a right to freedom, justice and peace. Why, then, is it important to discuss women's rights?

In groups, make a list of different perspectives and then use the following script skeleton to explore each one:

- I am thinking of women's rights from the point of view of [the viewpoint you've chosen, for example, abusive men, other women, enlightened men, feminists]
- I think [describe the topic from your viewpoint; be an actor, take on the character of your viewpoint]
- A question I have from this viewpoint is [ask a question from this viewpoint]

What new ideas do you have about the topic that you didn't have before? What new questions do you have?

Research and thinking skills ATLs

In our modern world, research involves more than comparing and contrasting data. A huge importance is placed on validating this data, especially in a world in which information is available at the click of a button. These research skills also help you to improve your metacognition and higher-order thinking through the use of synthesis and evaluation.

Internal assessment (SL)

Take a look at this visual stimulus. The image relates to the theme of the chapter: "Sharing the planet".

You have been given this visual stimulus and asked to prepare a four-minute presentation on the topic the stimulus highlights. In groups of four, prepare your presentation and present it to your classmates. The mind map below should remind you of the ground rules that you have to observe when preparing a presentation.

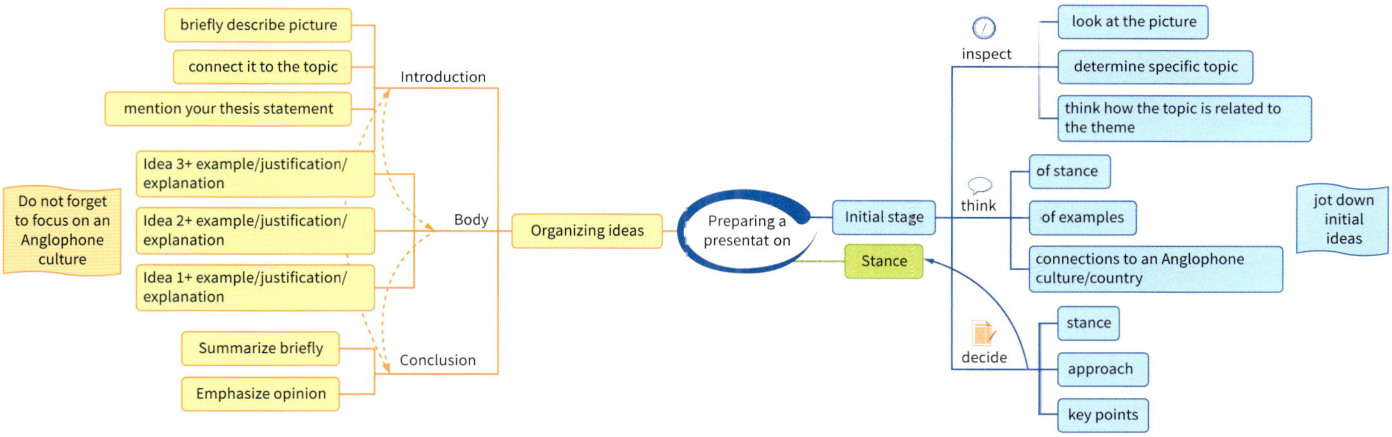

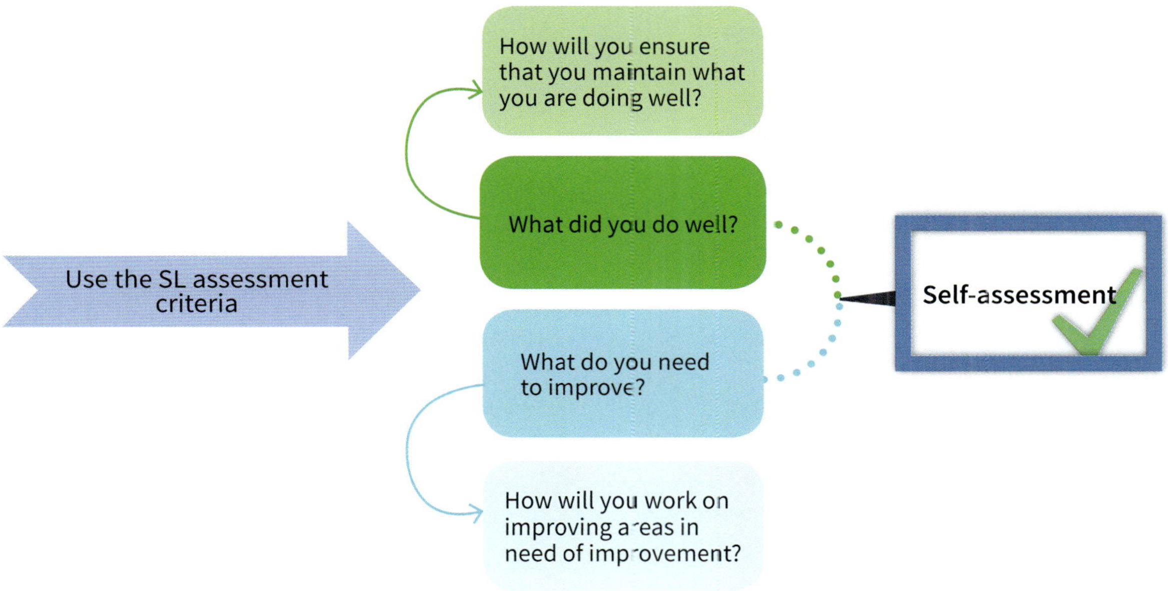

Internal assessment (HL)

Divide into three groups. Each group should read the story below from the perspective of one of the following: the flight attendant, the little girl or the couple sitting next to the girl.

Note

In your internal assessment, the literary extract will not exceed 300 words. You will be shown two, one from each of the works of literature studied in class.

So what are you, ANYWAY?

by Lawrence Hill

Carole settles in Seat 12A, beside the window, puts her doll on a vacant seat and snaps open her purse. She holds up a mirror. She looks into her own dark eyes. She examines her handful of freckles, which are tiny ink spots dotting her cheeks. She checks for pimples, but finds none. Only the clear complexion that her father sometimes calls "milk milk milk milk chocolate" as he burrows into her neck with kisses.

"This is yours, I believe." A big man with a sunburnt face is holding her doll upside down.

"May I have her please?" Carole says.

He turns the doll right side up. "A black doll! I never saw such a thing!"

"Her name's Amy. May I have her please?"

"Henry Norton!" cries the man's wife. "Give that doll back this instant!"

Carole tucks the doll close to the window.

The man sits beside Carole. The woman takes the aisle seat. "Don't mind him," the woman says, leaning towards Carole. "By the way, I'm Betty Norton, and he's my husband, Henry."

The man next to Carole hogs the armrest. His feet sprawl onto her side. And he keeps looking at her.

The stewardess passes by, checking seat belts. "Everything okay?" "May I go to the bathroom?" Carole asks.

"Do you think you could wait? We're about to take off." "Okay."

Carole looks out the window, sees the Toronto airport buildings fall behind and wonders if her parents are watching. Say goodbye, she instructs Amy, waving the doll's hand, say goodbye to Mom and Dad. The engines charge to life. Her seat hums. They taxi down the runway. "She feels a hollowness in her stomach when they lift into the air. Her ears plug and stay that way until the plane levels out over pillows of cotton. They burn as bright as the sun. So that is what the other side of the clouds look like!

"Excuse me. Excuse me!" The man is talking to her. "You can go to the bathroom now, you know."

"No, that's all right," Carole says.

"Traveling all alone, are you?" Carole swallows with difficulty.

"Where do you live?" he asks. "Don Mills."

"Oh, really?" he says. "Were you born there?"

"Yes."

"And your parents?"

"My mother was born in Chicago and my father was born in Tuscan."

"And you're going to visit your grandparents?"

She nods.

"And your parents let you travel alone!"

"It's only an airplane ride! And I'm a big girl."

The man lowers the back of his seat, chuckling. He whispers to his wife. "No!" Carole hears her whisper back, "You ask her!"

Carole yawns, holds Amy's hand and goes to sleep. The clinking of silverware wakens her, but she hears the man and woman talking about her, so she keeps her eyes shut.

"I don't know, Henry," says the woman. "Don't ask me. Ask her."

"I'm kind of curious," he says. "Aren't you?"

Carole can't make out the woman's answer. But then she hears her say: "I just can't see. It's not fair to children. I don't mind them mixed, but the world isn't ready for it. They're neither one thing nor the other, Henry, wake that child and see if she wants to eat."

When the man taps her shoulder, Carole opens her eyes. "I have to go to the bathroom," she says.

"But they're going to serve the meal," the man says. "Henry! If she wants out, let her out. She's only a child."

Carole grimaces. She is definitely not a child. She is a young lady! She can identify Drambuie, Kahlua, and Grand Marnier by smell!

Once in the aisle, Carole realizes she has forgotten Amy.

Henry Norton hands her the doll. “There you go. And don’t fall out of the plane, now. There’s a big hole down by the toilet.”

“There is not!” Carole says. “There isn’t any such thing!” She heads down the aisle with an eye out just in case there is a hole, after all.

Coming out of the toilet, Carole fins the stewardess. “Excuse me, miss. Could I sit somewhere else?”

“The woman frowns, “Why?”

“I don’t like the window.”

“Is that it? Is that the only reason?” “Well…yes.”

“I’m sorry, but we don’t have time to move you now. We’re serving a meal. Ask me later, if you like.”

After Carole has eaten and had her tray taken and had been served a hot face towel, the man says: “What are you, anyway? My wife and I were wondering.”

Carole blinks, sees the man’s clear blue eyes and drops her head. “What do you mean?” she says.

“You know, what are you? What race?”

Carole’s mouth drops. Race? What is that? She doesn’t understand. Yet she senses that the man is asking a bad question. It is as if he is asking her something dirty, or touching her in a bad place. She wishes her Mom and Dad were there. They could tell what “race” meant.

“That doll of yours is black,” Henry Norton says. “That’s a Negro doll. That’s race. Negro. What’s your race?”

The question still confuses her.

“Put it this way,” the man says. “What is your father?”

The question baffles her. What is her father? He is her Dad! He is her Dad and every Sunday morning he makes pancakes for the whole family and lets Carole pour hot syrup on them and afterwards he sits her on his lap and tells stories.

Mrs. Norton leans towards Carole. “Say you had a colouring book. What colour would you make your Dad?” “I never use just one colour.”

“Okay. What colour would you make his face?”

“Brown.”

“And your mother?”

Carole imagines a blank page. What would she put in her mother’s face? She has to put something in there. She can’t leave it blank.

“I don’t know.”

“Sure you do,” Mrs. Norton says. "How would you colour your mother’s face?”

“Yellow.”

Carole sees Mr. and Mrs. Norton look at each other.

“Is your mother Chinese?” Mrs. Norton asks.

“No.”

“Are you sure you’d colour her yellow?” “No.”

“What else might you colour her?”

What else? Carole feels ashamed at her stupidity. A tear races down her cheek. “Red,” she says finally.

“Red! You can’t colour a face red! Is your mother white? Is she like me? Her face! Is it the same colour as mine?”

“Yes.”

“And your father’s brown?” Carole nods.

“When you say brown, do you mean he is a Negro?”

“Yes.” Of course her father is a Negro. If Mrs. Norton wanted to know all along if her Dad was a Negro, why didn’t she just ask?

“So you’re mixed?” Mrs. Norton says. “You’re a mulatto!”

Carole’s lip quivers. What is a mulatto? Why do they keep asking her what she is? She isn’t anything!

“So is that it? You’re a mulatto? You know what a mulatto is, don’t you? Haven’t your parents taught you that word?”

Approaching with a cart of juice, the stewardess looks up and smiles at Carole. That gives her a rush of courage.

“Leave me alone!” she screams at Mrs. Norton. Passengers stare. The stewardess spills a drink. Mrs. Norton sits back hard in her seat, her hands raised, fingers spread. Carole sees people watching.

"Why do you keep asking me if my Dad is Negro? Yes, he's Negro! Okay? OKAY? Negro Negro Negro!"

"Calm down," Mrs. Norton says, reaching over.

"Don't touch her," the stewardess says.

"Who are these people?" someone says from across the aisle. "Imagine, talking to a child like that, and in 1970!"

One woman sitting in front of Carole stands up and turns around. "Would you like to come and sit with me, little girl?"

"No!" Carole shouts. "I don't like all these questions. She keeps asking me how I would colour my parents in a colouring book! Why do you keep asking me that?"

Mrs. Norton pleads with Carole to stop.

"How would you like it if that happened to you?" Carole says. "So what are you, anyway? What are your parents? How would you colour them? Well, I don't care! I don't even care!"

"How would you like to come and sit with me?" the stewardess says smiling. "I'll make you a special drink. Have you ever had a Shirley Temple?"

Carole nods enthusiastically. Already she feels better. Clutching Amy, she passes by the Nortons, who swing their legs to let her out.

"My God," Carole hears Mrs. Norton tell her husband, "talk about sensitive."

In your groups, prepare a four-minute presentation based on your reading. Take into consideration the questions below.

Describe the flight attendant. Which words or phrases prove that your image is correct?

What would you do if you were this flight attendant?

Describe the couple sitting next to the little girl. Which words or phrases prove that your image is correct?

What would you do if you to make this couple more tolerant of other ethnicities?

Describe the little girl. Which words or phrases prove that your image is correct?

What would you do if you were in this girl's shoes? How would the incident affect you?

Present to your classmates.

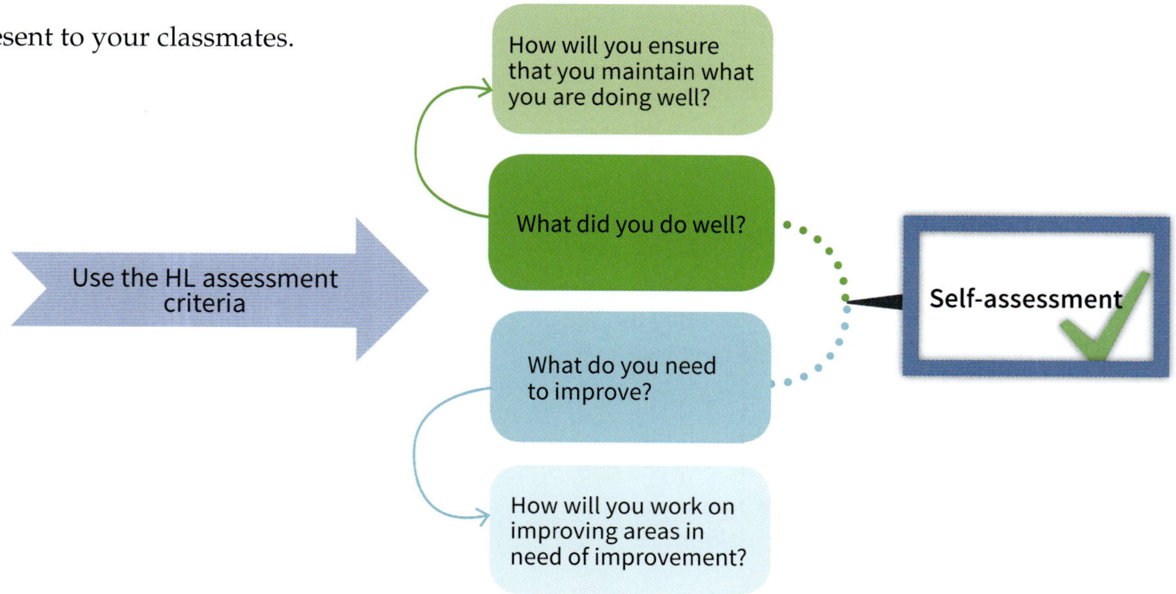

Paper 1: Pamphlets

Pamphlets are essentially mass media pieces of writing that aim to communicate something to readers and sometimes persuade them to take a certain action, for example, to buy a product, sign a petition or assemble a device.

The figure below shows us what to take into consideration when writing pamphlets.

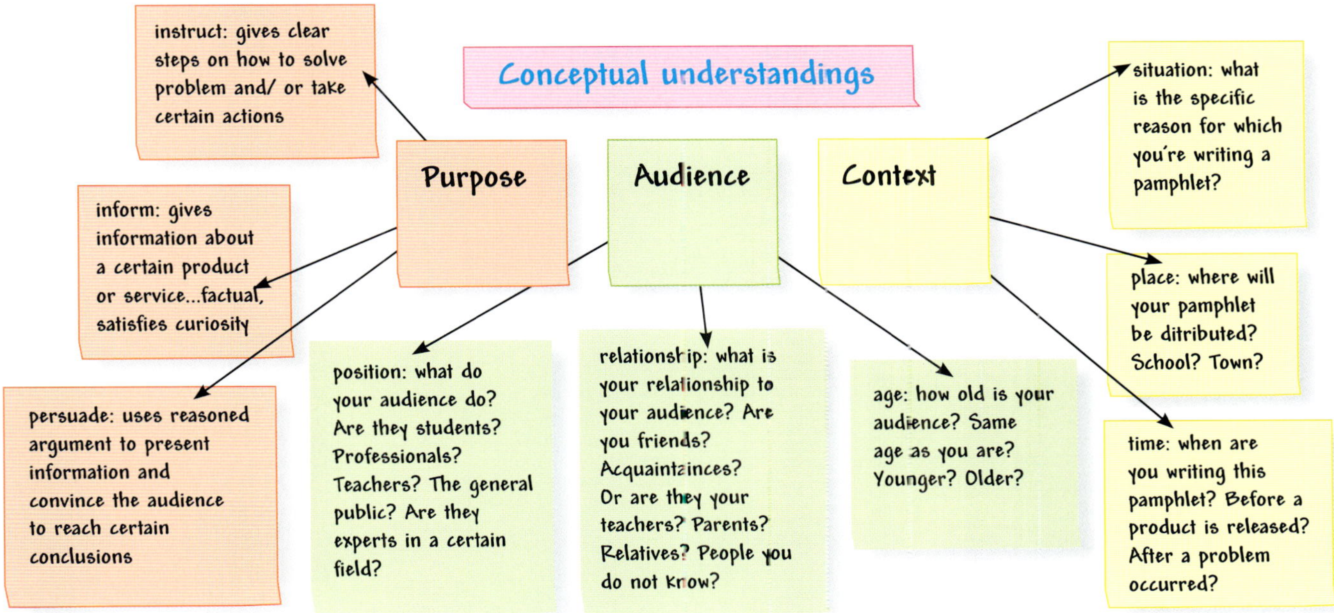

Structure

Irrespective of their purpose, audience and context, all pamphlets share the following features.

Heading/title and opening: The title should be brief, summarizing the point. Try to use a short, memorable phrase. To ensure that your readers read further than the title:

- give the name of the organization or company that has produced the text
- write a clear focused heading/title
- state the purpose of the leaflet
- state your message.

Subheadings: Subheadings are used to give further explanation. You can also use headings to separate your ideas. Sometimes the subheadings are questions.

Body text:

- Use short paragraphs and mark them with headings.
- Make sure your first sentences contain the point of the message.
- Begin with the benefits of your message.
- Organize your paragraphs from most important to least important.

Close: Make sure your readers know what to do next. Include an email address, telephone number, website, or some other form of response mechanism such as a reply coupon.

Inviting the audience to act, complete with address, telephone number & email address

If you would like to find out more about these issues, we have a free booklet that explores them in more detail, as well as resources to find out more. Contact:

Women's Policy Office
P.O. Box xxxx
4th Floor
West Building
St. John's, NL
AIB xxx

Telephone: (709) 729-xxxx
E-mail: WPO@xxx

The Effects of Stereotyping

Stereotypes are always less than the whole picture. They allow people to be treated based on only certain aspects of who they are. Stereotypes IGNORE HUMAN DIVERSITY and individual abilities and talents.

Stereotypes LEAD TO UNFAIR TREATMENT of people through decisions based on prejudice and actions that discriminate. Many kinds of discrimination are not only unfair, but illegal.

Stereotypes can LEAD TO VIOLENCE AND ABUSE. It is easier to abuse people when we believe they are not like use and are not equal to us.

Stereotypes INVOLVE LIES AND MYTHS about people. When we believe lies about ourselves, we feel oppressed. When we believe them about others and act according to these lies, we oppress others. Oppression occurs when one group has power over another. We have to see ourselves as "groups" first – as "us" versus "them".

What Can We Do?

Oppression is not any one person's problem, yet the solution lies with all of us. We need to see that what we want is personal power – the power to make decisions and choices for ourselves – not power over others.

Stereotypes grow and spread in our families, our communities, out cultures, out organizations and media. If we want to think of how big sterotyping is, we can think of the images of women shown on television screens all over the world. But even though sexism is global, we can all work against it and other stereotypes.

We are capable of change. Only a generation ago, stereotyping, prejudice and discrimination based on religion were common in this province. We have come far, and can go much farther.

We can…

- think about the issues
- talk about the issues
- approach each new person we meet with openness
- treat each other with respect
- find out more.

Celebrating diversity

Respecting Differences

Women's Policy Office

The name of the organization

Simple, direct style with bullet points

Subheadings

Definitions to clarify message

Have you or someone you know…

- felt you were treated unfairly because of your age?
- been shut out of a program, activity or chance of a job because of a disability?
- felt people were assuming things about you based on race before they even knew you?
- gotten unequal treatment because you are a women?
- felt uncomfortable or in danger in a situation because you are lesbian or gay?
- been denied a service or treated unfairly because you are poor?

• • • • •

If so, you or the person you know has faced discrimination. Discrimination is unfair treatment. It is against our rights as human beings.

The examples above show six kinds of discrimination: ageism, ableism, racism, sexism, heterosexism and classism.

Discrimination is

Sometimes, we think: "That kind of thing has never happened to me."

Yet many people in this province have felt the sting of comments about Newfoundlanders.

Are we really lazy good-for-nothings addicted to government handouts? Of course not.

This is a stereotype. Ageism, ableism, racism, sexism, heterosexism and classism are also based on steretypes.

unfair treatment

People Experience Discrimination and Stereotyping Every Day…

The bank wouldn't cash my check, They wanted a driver's license. Of course I don't have one. Where would someone on my income get a car? ***-- Classism***

The doctor didn't really listen. He said I should expect discomfort at my age. But this pain was new. I kept saying that. ***– Ageism***

The minister in my home town just comes right out and says he is praying for homosexuals to give up their evil ways and avoid the flames of hell. ***– Heterosexism***

He said, "You must find it really cold here." He said it just because I'm a woman of colour. I said, "Oh no., I was born in Winnipeg." ***-- Racism***

My employer was going to let me go. He saw that as the way to solve the problems of my hearing loss. But all we needed were a few changes around the office. ***-- Ableism***

The supervisor said the first shot at the jobs would go to family men, breadwinners. I said nothing. Now I wish I'd said, "I win the bread and make it too." ***-- Sexism***

We all live with stereotypes. We all carry some of them with us.

A stereotype is a general idea about a group of people. It is always too narrow to be accurate.

Stereotypes lead to prejudice and discrimination.

SEXISM is prejudice or discrimination based on gender.

RACISIM is prejudice or discrimination based on race or cultural background.

HETEROSEXISM is prejudice or discrimination based on sexual orientation.

ABLEISM is prejudice or discrimination based on ideas of ability and disability.

CLASSISM is prejudice or discrimination based on class, income, status and/or source of income.

AGEISM is prejudice and discrimination based on age.

Together, these ISMs affect the everyday lives of many people.

Writing activity

Using information from the texts you have read in this chapter, write a pamphlet about women's rights to give to your classmates.

Brainstorming

In pairs:

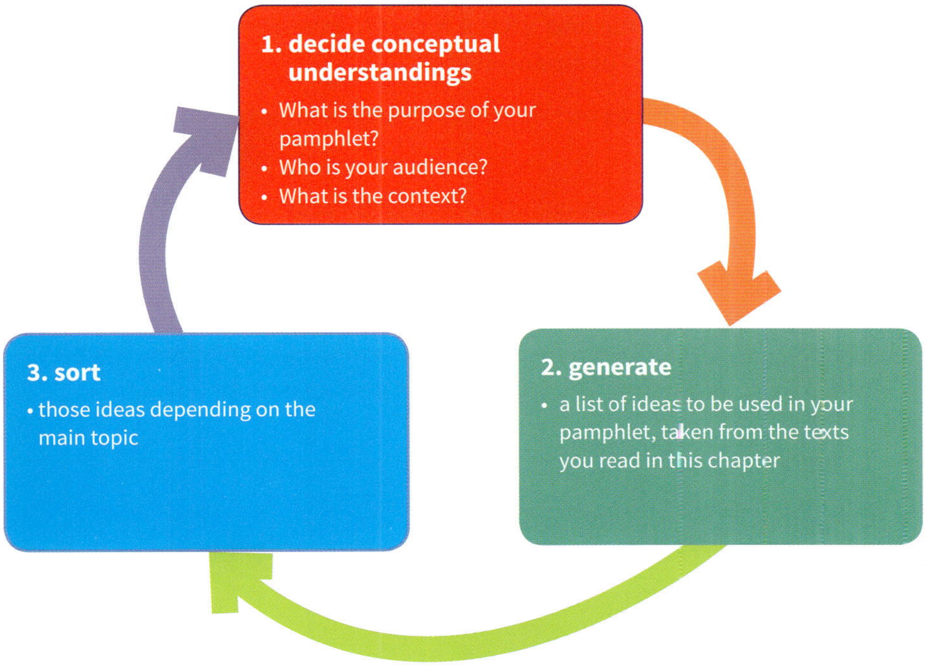

Planning

In pairs:

- decide how you will grab your audience's attention. What should appear in your introduction? What is your conclusion? Connect these to the conceptual understandings you have identified.
- decide how you are going to order your subtopics. Which should go first? Which should appear last? What should appear in the middle? Does your chosen order ensure that your ideas will be coherent and your writing will flow smoothly?
- decide the language you will use in your pamphlet. Will it be emotive? Emotive and persuasive? Connect choice of language and register to the conceptual understandings of context, purpose and audience that you have identified.

Drafting

Individually, write a draft of the body of your pamphlet. When you are done, revise this draft. Does it make sense?

Add your introduction and your conclusion to the body. Re-read what you have written. Do the transitions make sense? Are your paragraphs well connected? Have you avoided repetition of ideas? How interesting is your pamphlet?

Write an eye-catching title and do not forget to ensure that you have included all the features of a pamphlet.

Re-read the new draft of your opinion column one last time. Make any final changes.

Listening comprehension

Click the icon to practice the listening section of Paper 2. After you have listened to an audio track you will complete a set of accompanying activities.

Paper 1 (HL/SL) practice

Task 1: Your local council runs many projects to ease the financial suffering of poor people. You have decided to take part in informing the public about those projects, and invite them to donate to ensure the continuity and expansion of those projects by writing one of the texts below:

Opinion column | Pamphlet | Speech

Task 2: Instruct people how to use the public transport system in your town. Choose your audience. Choose your context. Choose a text type that will help you to achieve the aim. Write a rationale explaining what you are going to do and why. Carry out the task, then submit both the rationale and the task to your teacher for feedback.

Conclusions to research question C

How can we go beyond the narrow categorizations of gender roles?

1. Now that you have completed this section what are your thoughts and reactions to the question above?
2. What justifications would you give for your answers?
3. What more would you need to know before you can come to a definitive conclusion about the statement?

Conclusion to the chapter

Having completed the chapter, reflect on its research question:

What ethical issues arise from living in the modern world and how do we resolve them?

In groups of four, discuss the following two questions:

- What have you learned so far?
- What do you still want to know?

Revisit the newspaper headlines you wrote at the beginning of the chapter. How would you change them to reflect your deeper understanding of the general research question?

Beyond the text

In this chapter, we examined some topics that affect our understanding of the rights we should enjoy as human beings. However, this chapter is just the tip of the iceberg, for you may also wish to consider the following:

1. Do human rights standards apply to all contexts? Consider Cicero's "In times of war, the law falls silent."
2. Should euthanasia be considered a human right? Look up the plot details of Brian Clark's play Whose Life is it Anyway? Consider the perspective of its wheelchair-bound protagonist, Ken.
3. What effect does power have on human rights? Consider "All animals are equal but some animals are more equal than others" (Orwell, *Animal Farm*).

A TOK moment

TOK

Mrs, Ms or Miss: why do forms require women reveal their marital status?

Myf Warhurst

In my quest to find a doctor I like, in a new city, I've visited a few of late. Each initial visit begins with filling out the patient form. And with each I am required to reveal information of a personal nature that has nothing to do with my medical condition.

If you do identify as female, on all forms (whether it be at the doctor's, the bank, pretty much any place requiring you fill out a form to sign up) you must state if you are a Mrs, Ms or Miss. The same is not asked of our gentlemen friends. They get a plain and simple one-size-fits-all Mr. No form requires them to state if they are young, unmarried, old unmarried, or simply married.

I earn my own money, pay my own rent and have supported myself my entire adult life – whether I have a man about the house or not (and I do, though we're not married) isn't relevant. Male counterparts don't ever have to explain whether a lovely lady hangs around the house on any forms. Let's not even start on how annoying this must be for gay women and trans folk.

And don't tell me Ms is an option for those women who don't want to reveal their status. We all know that Ms is for older women who aren't married. Being forced to choose it due to lack of a better option, is yet another statement by default.

Should such questions about relationships pertain to a diagnosis at the doctor's, they could easily be asked in a consultation. If not, let's make the blokes state the same when they fill in forms. Give them some options too. Perhaps Mr, Mstr, Missr, Lad and Old Mate.

Is it time for a one-size-fits-all title? The Swedes recently introduced a gender neutral title, but they're evolved like that. Perhaps there's room for discussion about such a thing within the English language?

Read the opinion column and reflect on your reaction to the stance the writer has taken.

Do you agree with the writer's viewpoint? Why? What words and phrases will you use to express agreement or lack of? Why have you chosen those words or phrases?

In groups of four, discuss the following questions:

- What is your definition of political correctness?
- Is gender-laden language biased?
- How can we neutralize language and use inclusive expressions to promote women's rights?
- Have we taken political correctness a little too far? What is your opinion?

Beyond the classroom

CAS

Experience 1

For your CAS project, you are thinking of ways in which you can ensure that human rights standards are adhered to at your school and in your community. As part of this project, you want to address your principal/ mayor/ town council president to convince him/ her to support the project. Write your letter.

Reflect on the letter you have written: which of the CAS outcomes has writing the letter helped you achieve? How?

Experience 2

Design a poster that clarifies your opinion on trafficking in persons. This poster is to be displayed at major shopping centres in your town or city.

Reflect on the process of creating your poster: which of the CAS outcomes has designing the poster helped you achieve? How?

Experience 3

As part of your CAS project, you want to raise awareness about women's rights. Write a manifesto to be given to government officials regarding women's rights violations in your town or city.

Reflect on the process of creating your manifesto: which of the CAS outcomes has writing the manifesto helped you achieve? How?

CAS – learning outcomes

- LO1: Identify own strengths and develop areas for growth
- LO3: Demonstrate how to initiate and plan a CAS experience
- LO2: Demonstrate that challenges have been undertaken, developing new skills in the process
- LO4: Show commitment to and perseverance in CAS experiences
- LO5: Demonstrate the skills and recognize the benefits of working collaboratively
- LO6: Demonstrate engagement with issues of global significance
- LO7: Recognize and consider the ethics of choices and actions

Suggested reading list

Uncle Tom's Cabin by Harriet Beecher Stowe

A Vindication of the Rights of Woman by Mary Wollstonecraft

The Color Purple by Alice Walker

To Kill a Mockingbird by Harper Lee

The Help by Kathryn Stockett

Happy to Be Nappy by Bell Hooks

Suggested films

Twelve Years a Slave
Siddharth
The Supreme Price
Mandela: Long Walk to Freedom
Human
E-Team

The extended essay in English B

Introduction

The extended essay in English B is suitable for students who want to gain a deeper understanding of a topic related to the English language or English literature, or an aspect of culture in English-speaking societies. To write a successful 4,000-word essay you will need to carry out extensive research on the topic you have chosen.

What is the purpose of the extended essay?

This task introduces you to the type of independent study required at university. The extended essay is a research paper, not a descriptive essay, therefore, it should be seen as an exercise in using research, communication and self-management skills.

Possible research topics in English B

In group 2, extended essays must fall into one of the following three categories:

- **Category 1: Language**. This could be an analysis of some aspect of the English language, for example, Anglophone national language policies, the nature of bilingualism in an Anglophone culture, or the way the English language is formed to convey meaning.
- **Category 2: Culture and society**. This requires an analysis of some aspect of social nature within an English-speaking society. This category is divided into two subcategories:
  - **A: essays of a sociocultural nature with an impact on the language**
    If you are attempting this type of essay, the focus should be on how a cultural or social issue affects the use of the English language. For example, you could explore how immigration policies in the United States affect the use of English, or how internet jargon has seeped into Standard English.
  - **B: essays of a general cultural nature based on specific cultural artifacts**
    If you are attempting this type of essay, you have to base your analysis on a specific artifact like a film, a newspaper article, some photographs or a certain work of art. For example, you could investigate how pop music portrays a certain social issue like parent/child relationships, or how a film represents cultural minorities in an Anglophone country.
- **Category 3: Literature**. This type of essay focuses on the literary analysis of one or more literary texts originally written in English.

Successful extended essay titles in group 2

Here are some examples of successful extended essay titles:

- How are political correctness and rhetoric deployed in opinion columns in *The New Yorker* and the *Daily Mail*.
- What have been the consequences of forced adoptions within the Australian Aboriginal community?
- How does the Singlish legal lexicon differ from that of Standard English?
- To what extent are the female protagonists in *The Woman Warrior* by Maxine Hong Kingston and *Wild Meat and the Bully Burgers* by Lois-Ann Yamanaka able to find a balance between the differing Asian and American cultures and, thus, ascertain their identities?
- How does a character analysis assist an understanding of Kazuo Ishiguro's novels *A Pale View of Hills and The Remains of the Day*?
- What effects are achieved by the language used in editorials from *The Washington Post* and *The Nation* on the events in the United States on 11 September 2001?

Note

You have to be very careful when choosing your English B extended essay topic; English is a global language and you may be tempted to discuss this globalization without focusing on an English-speaking society. For example, the topic "Will the spread of English cause death to the mother tongue in Senegal?" is interesting, but it is not a suitable English B essay since the focus of the essay is on Senegal, which is not an English-speaking country.

The process of writing an extended essay in English B

Choosing a topic for the extended essay

Before writing the essay, you will undertake several hours of research and planning. Here are some general comments on how to proceed.

1. Start by reading the general section of the *Extended essay guide*. This will give you an understanding of the requirements of the essay and how you should go about completing it. Make sure you also read the assessment criteria.
2. It is essential that you find a topic that interests you. Once you have found a general area of research and a question that you would like to answer, discuss them with your supervisor to see if the general topic is suitable for an English B extended essay.
3. Find source material and skim read it. If you find the subject does not interest you or you cannot find enough source material to work with, it is a good idea to start again.

4 If you are making good progress, find a focus or specific idea that you want to investigate within the topic and formulate a research question; look again at the examples above.

Note

It is an excellent idea to develop a **Researcher's reflection space (RRS)** as a planning tool. In your RRS, write your reflections and add material that you find useful for your essay. This could include notes on topics related to your extended essay that were discussed in other classes, a newspaper article that could be used as a secondary resource, questions that you want to ask your supervisor, or mind maps that will help you focus your topic. Anything you write in your RRS may be used in the mandatory reflection sessions with your supervisor.

Reflection

Now may be a good time to hold the **first reflection session** with your supervisor. During this session, you might want to check that you have fully understood the English B extended essay requirements and assessment criteria, ask questions about the approaches you pondered, the suitability of the sources you identified, the initial research question you drafted, and so on. In addition, discuss next steps with your supervisor and make sure you record what you need to do before the interim reflection session takes place.

It is of utmost importance to complete the first "student comment" section of the Reflections on planning and progress form (RPPF) and submit it to your supervisor after the session. Refer to the section "Protocols for completing and submitting the Reflections on planning and progress form" in the *Extended essay guide* to make sure you are meeting the requirements of the RPPF.

Reading and researching

Once you have chosen your topic, formulate an essay plan including the scope, shape and direction of the essay. For example, if you had decided to investigate rap songs and whether they address human rights issues in an Anglophone culture, you would need to focus your ideas in your essay by determining:

- scope—which country, which rap songs, which human rights issues
- shape—will it be an analysis of language used in the chosen lyrics? Or discussion of whether the ideas in the lyrics reflect practices in that society? Which data should be used under which main headings?
- direction—will the essay try to prove a causal relationship? How will a conclusion be reached?

After you narrow down your research question, try to outline the major areas for discussion. Write down the research question, the broad areas you wish to cover in your Extended essay and any ideas about possible conclusions. This outline will become your first draft essay plan. Remember to look at your research question and check whether your essay plan enables you to answer your research question.

At this point, you have to read through the sources you identified earlier and try to find more specific ones. As you begin to read, it is a good idea to identify and note the sections worth re-reading and that will be useful for core information. Here are some useful questions to guide you:

- Does the information I am reading seem useful?
- If so, why is it useful? How does the information relate to my essay plan?
- How does the new information relate to what I already know?
- Does the new information confirm or contradict the information I already have?

It is also important to differentiate between **primary** sources and **secondary** sources at this stage. Primary sources are the literary work itself if you have chosen a category 3 essay or actual research which you carried out on your topic for category 1 and category 2 essays. Secondary sources are ones which discuss a literary work or research carried out by others. Try to focus on primary sources, and avoid merely summarizing secondary sources in your essay. Once you have read a section of a text, such as a chapter of a novel, summarize the information you have read in your own words. Look at your research question and categorize what you have written. Some students find it extremely useful to create visuals such as concept maps. You can use diagrams or charts of your outline essay structure, mind maps, or anything else that helps you to understand both the topic and your response to it. It is a good idea to go back to the main headings of your essay. **Do remember to make an exact list of all useful sources.** This will help you later when you source your quotes and when you compile your bibliography.

Exploratory writing: writing to think and plan

The purpose of exploratory writing is to help you know what you think. At this point, you are not yet writing the version of the extended essay that will be submitted for assessment. However, an initial draft will help you to sketch out your ideas and come to some general conclusions about your research question. It does not have to be written in full sentences; note form is perfectly adequate for the task. The initial draft will also help you to know if you have mastered your material or if there is information which is still missing.

You should sketch out all your paragraphs, including the introduction, with headings and then you can add detail to each. Draw an essay plan: research question and section headings. It may be that you still do not have a clear conclusion. Do not worry too much about this. Your conclusion may only come once you have finished thinking through your ideas. Plan the individual paragraphs with supporting details

(PEE: Point, Example, Explanation). At the end of the process, write up your thoughts and conclusions. Ask yourself whether your ideas make sense and whether they follow in a logical order. Now is a good time to see your supervisor again to make sure that your conclusion relates clearly to your research question and that your essay structure is clear and logical. Once you have clarified your ideas, you may be in a position to write a first draft for your supervisor.

Writing a thesis statement

A thesis statement states what you intend to prove. A good thesis statement can make all the difference between a sound extended essay and a simple listing of facts and opinions. Therefore, it is worth spending time making sure that you get your thesis statement just right. If, for example, your research question was "Will the spread of English cause death to the mother tongue in Mauritius?" your thesis statement should declare quite clearly whether you **think** the answer is: "yes", "no" or "to some extent". If you need to modify your research question and your thesis, now is the time to do both. A general rule for the extended essay is that the narrower and more specific the research question is, the easier it is to formulate and prove the thesis statement.

Reflection

Now may be a good time to hold the **interim reflection session** with your supervisor. Remember to use the notes in your RRS to ask any puzzling questions about the clarity of your line of argument, the appropriateness of a certain secondary source, whether your sources are varied or your approach is sound. In addition, discuss next steps with your supervisor and make sure you record what you need to do before the final reflection session takes place.

It is of utmost importance to complete the interim reflection "student comment" section of the RPPF and submit it to your supervisor after the session. Refer to the section "Protocols for completing and submitting the Reflections on planning and progress form" in the *Extended essay guide* to make sure you are meeting the requirements of the RPPF.

Note

Remember that you have to cite any ideas which are not originally yours, whether they are direct quotes or paraphrases. What is more, you have to be consistent when using a certain documentation style.

The following are examples of acceptable documentation styles:

- American Political Science Association (APSA)
- American Psychological Association (APA)
- Chicago/Turabian

- Council of Biology Editors (CBE)
- Harvard citation and referencing
- Modern Language Association (MLA)
- Numbered references

Here are a few links to online citation guides which will help you understand how to cite and reference your sources:

- http://www.wisc.edu/writing/Handbook/Documentation.html
- http://www.library.uq.edu.au/training/citation/harvard.html
- http://www.citationmachine.net/

Planning the first draft: writing to communicate

Draw up your revised essay plan. This should now consist of your research question, your thesis statement, section headings (if appropriate), paragraphs and conclusion. Plan the individual paragraphs with supporting details. Remember that you need to support your discussion with ideas from the sources you have read. Make sure that you have enough concrete detail and commentary in each paragraph. Ask yourself, "Have I got the big picture?" To reiterate, a clear essay will have a clear research question and a clear thesis statement. A very good extended essay will also have organized paragraphs that support the thesis statement and a structure that supports the way your argument is leading. This means each paragraph should have a clear topic sentence that relates to your thesis statement. Your paragraph structure and the use of sentences to link one paragraph to the next will help your supervisor understand the logic of your arguments.

Now you are ready to write your draft. Proofread what you have written This draft will be read by your supervisor and so you should make sure you have communicated your ideas clearly and accurately.

Have you read your work carefully?

- One trick is to read your paper aloud. As you go along check for spelling, vocabulary, grammar, punctuation and overall logic. A word of warning: a spell check will not catch everything and grammar checks are sometimes wrong!
- Double check all sources and references. What about referencing and documentation? Have you credited all sources? Have you used a formal, recognized referencing system?

Once you are completely satisfied with this first draft, show it to your supervisor and discuss the strengths and weaknesses of your draft. Do not think that you have finished yet. Your draft will almost certainly need serious revision and your supervisor can help you to remodel your essay However, do remember to discuss everything with your supervisor; he/she will not read another complete draft before you officially submit your extended essay.

Writing a final draft

In your final draft you will almost certainly need to work on different parts of your essay. At this point, you can think about adding a title page, a contents page, bibliography and appendices.

Proofread again and double check for grammar, expression, sign-posting and logic. Check that you have included concrete details and commentary in each paragraph. Treble check all sources and references. Refine your research question, thesis statement and conclusion.

Make sure you know the criteria for marking the extended essay and that you have met the requirements per criterion.

Writing a conclusion

You could include a heading "Conclusion" and write "The following conclusions were reached: …".

Alternatively, you can elaborate on your thesis statement to explain in detail your ideas. However, **do not introduce new ideas into your conclusion**. Instead, in the concluding part of your essay you may want to include ideas for further research or investigation.

You may want to use the following checklist to make sure that you have not forgotten anything.

	Extended essay checklist	Yes	No
1	I have written a clear and focused research question.		
2	My research question is clearly stated in the introduction.		
3	My argument is coherent, organized and clearly presented.		
4	My conclusion is clear, relevant to my topic and lends itself to further research.		
5	Direct quotations appear inside quotations marks and are properly cited.		
6	I have properly and consistently cited paraphrased ideas.		
7	I have used formal, academic English.		
8	Pages are numbered.		
9	I have included a title page on which the title of my essay and its category are clearly stated.		
10	I have not identified myself by either writing my name, my session number, school number or session on the title page or page headers.		
11	I have included a table of contents at the beginning of the essay.		
12	I have used a 12-point, readable font and double spacing.		
13	Sections have headings and, where appropriate, subheadings.		
14	My conclusion is clearly marked.		
15	Appendices are attached (where necessary).		
16	References are appropriately listed.		
17	I have completed, signed and submitted the RPPF form.		

Reflection

Now is the time to hold the **final reflection session, the viva voce,** with your supervisor. You are required to bring extracts from your RRS that show how you have grown as a learner in the process of completing the extended essay. You should also be willing to discuss your experience and the skills/conceptual understandings acquired as a result of writing the extended essay.

Your supervisor will ask you specific questions about your essay, the difficulties you faced and how you addressed them, what you have learned from certain sources or how you arrived at your conclusion. Be prepared to answer those questions.

It is of utmost importance to complete the final reflection "student comment" section of the RPPF and submit it to your supervisor after the session. Refer to the section "Protocols for completing and submitting the reflections on planning and progress form" in the *Extended essay guide* to make sure you are meeting the requirements of the RPPF. If this form is not completed appropriately, you will lose marks under criterion E, engagement.

Resources

The websites listed below might help you in writing an extended essay:

http://owl.english.purdue.edu/workshops/hypertext/ResearchW/notes.html

http://managementhelp.org/businessresearch/planning.htm

http://writing.wisc.edu/Handbook/PlanResearchPaper.html

http://literacy.kent.edu/Oasis/Pubs/0200-08.htm

A few final pieces of advice

- Always keep a back-up copy! Even better, keep two back-up copies!
- Keep everything in perspective. An extended essay may be worth only one or two points, but passing it is integral to obtaining the diploma. Therefore, plan your time carefully and try to find some balance between working on your extended essay and meeting the requirements of your other subjects. You should only spend about 40 hours on this project in total. Do not spend hours worrying or going round in circles.
- When in doubt, see your supervisor.
- Do not rely on memory alone. Keep a notebook for ideas and brainwaves (the RRS is perfect for this). Log visits to your supervisor so you both know how much time you have spent on the project.
- Complete pertinent sections of the RPPF immediately after each reflection session with your supervisor.

Good luck!

INDEX

E

F

S

T

U

V

W

Acknowledgements

We are grateful to the authors and publishers for use of extracts from their titles and in particular for the following:

Fleur Adcock: *Poems 1960-2000.* (Bloodaxe Books, 2000). Reproduced by permission.

George Bernard Shaw: Extracts from *Pygmalion*, The Society of Authors, on behalf of the Bernard Shaw Estate. Reproduced by permission.

Sandra Cisneros: From *The House on Mango Street.* Copyright © 1984 by Sandra Cisneros. Published by Vintage Books, a division of Penguin Random House, Inc., and in hardcover by Alfred A. Knopf in 1994. By permission of Bloomsbury Publishing Plc, Susan Bergholz Literary Services, New York, NY and Lamy, NM. All rights reserved.

Colin Covert Star Tribune: 'Movie review: "Sing Street" is another charmer by the director of "Once"' (TNS) May 20, 2016. Reproduced by permission.

Maddie Crum: 'Here's What Kurt Vonnegut Can Teach You About Life', The Huffington Post, 11 November 2011 © 2011 Oath Inc. www.huffingtonpost.co.uk. All rights reserved. Used by permission and protected by the Copyright Laws of the United States. The printing, copying, redistribution, or retransmission of this Content without express written permission is prohibited.

Beau Donelly: 'Damning report on exploitation in Australian fashion industry', The Age, 16 April 2015. Reproduced by permission of the Copyright Agency.

Roddy Doyle: Excerpt(s) from *The Commitments*, copyright © 1987 by Roddy Doyle published by William Heinemann. Used by permission of Random House, an imprint and division of Penguin Random House LLC and The Random House Group Limited. All rights reserved.

Azad Essa: 'Zulaikha Patel: How We All Wish We Were You', 4 February 2017, https://www.thedailyvox.co.za. Reproduced by permission of the author.

Virginia Ewer Wolff: *This Full House* Copyright © 2009. Published by HarperCollins. Used by permission of Curtis Brown, Ltd and HarperCollins Publishers.

Zoe Flood: 'Africa calling: mobile phone revolution to transform democracies' 18 August 2016. www.theguardian.com. Copyright Guardian News & Media Ltd 2018. Reproduced by permission.

Richie Frieman: '7 Worst Role models for Teens' (blog), from www.huffingtonpost.com. Reproduced by permission of the author.

Ashley Gilliam: 'The Diary of a Slave' December 23, 2010 from http://www.teenink.com. Reproduced by permission of TeenInc DK, LLC.

William Golding: excerpt from *Lord of the Flies: (Penguin Great Books of the 20th Century)*, copyright 1954, renewed © 1982 by William Gerald Golding. Used by permission of G. P. Putnam's Sons, an imprint of Penguin Publishing Group, a division of Penguin Random House LLC and Faber & Faber Ltd. All rights reserved. Any third party use of this material, outside of this publication, is prohibited. Interested parties must apply directly to Penguin Random House LLC for permission.

Michael Gove (former UK Secretary of State for Education): quote. Contains public sector information licensed under the Open Government Licence v3.0.

Laurie Halse Anderson: Extract from *Speak* first published in the UK by Hodder Children's Books, an imprint of Hachette Children's Books, Carmelite House, 50 Victoria Embankment, London imprint, EC4Y 0DZ. © 1999 by Laurie Halse Anderson. Reprinted by permission of Hodder Children's Books and Farrar, Straus Girioux Books for Young Readers. All Rights Reserved.

Lawrence Hill: 'So what are you anyway?' Copyright © 2000 by Lawrence Hill. Reproduced by permission of Lawrence Hill.

Earl Hipp: Excerpted from *Fighting Invisible Tigers: Stress Management for Teens* © 2008. Used with permission of Free Spirit Publishing Inc., Minneapolis MN; 800-735-7323; www.freespirit.com. All rights reserved.

A Renee Hutcherson: 'The benefits and challenges of urbanization', Leaf Group, © 2011 Leaf Group, Ltd. U.S.A. All rights reserved. Reproduced by permission.

Lloyd Jones: Excerpt(s) from *Mister Pip*, copyright © 2007 by Lloyd Jones. Used by permission of The Dial Press, an imprint of Random House, a division of Penguin Random House LLC and John Murray Press, a division of Hodder and Stoughton Limited, Vintage Canada/Alfred A. Knopf Canada, a division of Penguin Random House Canada Limited and Penguin Random House New Zealand Limited. All rights reserved. Any third party use of this material, outside of this publication, is prohibited. Interested parties must apply directly to Penguin Random House LLC for permission.

Maxine Hong Kingston: Excerpt(s) from *The Woman Warrior: Memoirs of a Girlhood Among Ghosts*, copyright © 1975, 1976 by Maxine Hong Kingston. Used by permission of Alfred A. Knopf, an imprint of the Knopf Doubleday Publishing Group, a division of Penguin Random House LLC, the author and the Sandra Dijkstra Literary Agency. All rights reserved.

Daniel Keyes: *Flowers for Algernon*. Copyright © 1966, 1959 and renewed 1994, 1987 by Daniel Keyes. Reprinted by permission of Houghton Mifflin Harcourt Publishing Company and The Orion Publishing Group, London. All rights reserved.

Jordan Kleiman: 'Love Canal: A Brief History' from www.geneseo.edu. Reproduced by permission of the author.

M Paul Lewis: "TOK moment": Migration and Language. www.ethnologue.com. Used by permission, © SIL, Ethnologue.com, October 2015.

Martin Luther King: Extract from 'I have a dream' speech. Reprinted by arrangement with The Heirs to the Estate of Martin Luther King, Jr., c/o Writers House as agent for the proprietor New York, NY. Copyright Dr. Martin Luther King, Jr., 1963; Copyright renewed Loretta Scott King, 1991.

Ocean Malandra: 'Advantages and disadvantages of rural urban migration', Leaf Group, © 2014 Leaf Group, Ltd. U.S.A. All rights reserved. Reproduced by permission.

Greg Mitchell: Extract from *The Recorder* (Greenfield, Massachusetts, USA). Reproduced by permission.

Julie Orringer: Excerpt(s) from *How to Breathe Underwater: Stories*, copyright ©2003 by Julie Orringer. Used by permission of Alfred A. Knopf, an imprint of the Knopf Doubleday Publishing Group, a division of Penguin Random House LLC and Penguin Random House UK. All rights reserved.

Alun Palmer: 'Vision of the future: 10 hi-tech inventions we'll hopefully be using in 2030', http://www.mirror.co.uk/news/technology-science. Reproduced by permission of Mirrorpix.

David Perkins: *King Arthur's Round Table: How Collaborative Conversations Create Smart Organizations*. Copyright © 2003 by David Perkins. All Rights Reserved. John Wiley & Sons Inc. Reproduced with permission of John Wiley & Sons Ltd through PLSclear.

Colette Phair: 'Does Language Affect Our Culture and Personal Ethics?' Leaf Group © 2013 Leaf Group, Ltd. U.S.A. All rights reserved. Reproduced by permission.

Rachel Raczka: Interview with stars of Sing Street, 13 April 2016, www.metro.us. Reproduced by permission.

Mallika Ramdas: 'Volunteering overseas: To Gap Year or not to Gap Year?' Former Head of University Advising, UWCSEA Dover. Reproduced by permission of the author.

Jerry Spinelli: Excerpt(s) from *Stargirl*, copyright © 2000 by Jerry Spinelli. First published in the UK by Orchard Books, an imprint of Hachette Children's Group, Carmelite House, 50 Victoria Embankment, London, EC4Y 0DZ. Used by permission of Hachette Children's Group and Alfred A. Knopf, an imprint of Random House Children's Books, a division of Penguin Random House LLC. All rights reserved. Any third party use of this material, outside of this publication, is prohibited. Interested parties must apply directly to Penguin Random House LLC for permission.

Wal Reid: 'Sing Street Film Review', 1 July 2016 from http:// thefullscene.blogspot.co.uk. Reproduced by permission of the author.

Alexander Robertson: 'Schoolboys, 14, who were banned from wearing shorts to school on the hottest day of the year used a uniform loophole to wear SKIRTS instead', MailOnline, 22 July 2016. Reproduced by permission of Solo Syndication.

Bess Rowen: 'Lost and gained in translation', http://www.huffingtonpost.com/. Reproduced by permission of the author.

Anup Shah: list of facts from 'Causes of poverty' 28 September 2014 from www.globalissues.org. Reproduced by permission of the author.

Phillip Spires: *Strangers* from https://english-magazine.org/english-stories/. Reproduced by permission of the author.

Donald Strachan: 'The five best translation apps for travellers', 29 January 2015, © Telegraph Media Group Limited 2017, www.telegraph.co.uk. Reproduced by permission.

Jan Tritten: 'Birth is a Human Rights Issue' from *Midwifery Today*, Issue 92, Winter 2009/2010. Reproduced by permission.

Richard Vaughan: Extract from 'A quarter of kids say playing computer games is exercise, research shows', 23 June 2015, www.tes.com. Reproduced by permission.

Alice Walker: *The Color Purple*, Copyright © 1982 by Alice Walker. Reprinted by permission of The Joy Harris Literary Agency, Inc and Houghton Mifflin Harcourt Publishing Company. All rights reserved.

Ian Wallace: 'Can we control our dreams?' www.independent.co.uk. Reproduced by permission of the author.

Myf Warhurst: 'Mrs, Ms or Miss: why do forms require women reveal their marital status?' 7 April 2015, theguardian.com. Copyright Guardian News & Media Ltd 2017. Reproduced by permission.

Naomi Wolf: 'Gender Equality', New York Times, 30 November 2012. Reproduced by permission of the author.

Advert from http://www.giv.org/institutes/current-issues/. Reproduced by permission.

Growing up in Oakland from Asian Pacific America Heritage: Angel Island, Li Keng Wong's Story Teacher.scholastic.com. Copyright © Scholastic Inc. Used by permission.

'Being a teenager in Singapore: 19-year-old Kiwi Jake on what it's really like', 6 August 2014 from http://www.expatliving.sg. Reproduced by permission.

'8 biggest benefits of exercise for teenagers' adapted from http://www.webmd.boots.com/fitness-exercise/guide/benefits-of-exercise-teenagers. Reproduced by permission.

'The Best Travel Tips by Dave and Deb' from http://theplanetd.com/best-travel-tips/. Reproduced by permission.

'Dear Diary, the story of my teenage life' by littlemissmystery. Reproduced with permission of the author.

'Discover Leisure Education.' This copyrighted article is reproduced from the National Center on Health, Physical Activity and Disability at www.nchpad.org. It may be freely distributed in its entirety as long as it includes this notice but cannot be edited, modified, or otherwise altered without the express written permission of NCHPAD. Contact NCHPAD at 1-800-900-8086 for additional details.

Adapted from 'Human Rights in Jamaica report', Amnesty International, www.amnesty.org. Reproduced by permission.

Extracts from pp 19 & 21, *Language B guide*, IBO, 2018. This work has been developed in cooperation with the International Baccalaureate (IB). Reproduced by permission.

Extract from 'Parents must be role models and foster respect', 22 May 2016, 'Adeleide Now'. Reproduced by permission of the Copyright Agency.

Extract from 'The Times of Northwest Indiana' and nwi.com. Reproduced by permission.

'Key language ideas' from www.theoryofknowledge.net. Reproduced by permission of Michael Dunn.

'Recycling Tips Guidelines' from www.westerndisposal.com. Western Disposal are the authors of the text on this page and Oxford University Press has permission to reproduce it. Please note that this information is unique to Western Disposal's Colorado market and does not necessarily reflect the guidelines in other parts of the state or country. Also note this information is subject to changes and updates.

'13-year-old Zulaikha Patel is Taking a Stand against School Policies That Frown at Natural Black Hair' by Woman.Ng, 2 September 2016 from http://woman.ng. Reproduced by permission.

'What does it mean to be a 21st century learner?' 8 March 2017 from https://southafricatoday.net. Reproduced by permission.

We have made every effort to trace and contact all copyright holders before publication, but if notified of any errors or omissions, the publisher will be happy to rectify these at the earliest opportunity.